INSIDE MTV

Inside MTV

R. Serge Denisoff

Transaction Publishers
New Brunswick (U.S.A.) and London (U.K.)

Library of Congress Catalog Number: 87-13820
ISBN: 978-0-88738-864-4
Printed in the United States of America

Library of Congress Cataloging-in-Publication Data

Denisoff, R. Serge.
    Inside MTV.

    Bibliography: p.
    Includes index.
    1. MTV Networks. 2. Rock videos—United States. I. Title.

PN1992.8.M87D4   1987
384.55'47   87-13820

Contents

To John Lack—the "Father of MTV"

Great Discoveries so often result from a curious combination of ignorance and insight, persistence and pure luck.

—Professor Richard Skolnik

Seldom have (crystal balls) been more clouded and misleading than when they were used to predict what cable TV would be like. Name the forecast, and it was wrong.

—Al Knight, newspaper editor

When you think of music video, the first thing that comes into your mind is not "Friday Night Videos" or "Night Tracks," it's MTV. It's a generic name, and a unique success story in an industry that's been up and down the last three years.

—Anonymous advertising executive

Foreword

This work is a study in the production of culture. It is as much about media economics and politics as about the product itself. MTV is the third major breakthrough in music broadcasting, the first being when Todd Storz gave birth to "Top Forty" radio in 1955 and the second being the advent of "free form" or "progressive" rock at KMPX in San Francisco in 1967. The early broadcasting innovations molded the state of rock music exposure for nearly twenty years. Then came MTV. MTV began as the third of four Warner-Amex Satellite Entertainment Company (WASEC) channels. The channels were created by two of America's largest conglomerates—American Express and Warner Communications Inc.

When this book was conceived MTV found Madison Avenue and cable operators in a state of uncertainty. The relationship between television and rock music was weak, at best. As the story began to unfold this new partnership became a stroke of genius luck and discrimination. One's American Express card paid for most of the creation of MTV. MTV is a corporate innovation of major proportions and a psychodemographic success.

Few would dispute the significance of MTV in resurrecting the music industry from the throes of the "great depression" of 1979 or its impact on contemporary film, fashion, and radio. In a mere five years, MTV has become the most profitable twenty-four–hour cable outlet beamed from a satellite. It reaches 30.8 million households.

This book examines the world of cablecasting, the evolution of WASEC, MTV, VH-1, and some of their competitors. The strategies, personalities, promotions, and the content that placed MTV on the road to prominence are chronicled. The controversies surrounding the channel and MTVN are thoroughly detailed and an attempt is made to correct a good deal of disinformation on the subject.

Acknowledgements

This work is a spin-off from *Tarnished Gold*. In writing the chapter on music videos, the printed material frequently raised more questions than answers. Consequently, once the previous volume was completed the author's focus turned to the then neophyte channel. In short time it became overtly apparent that cablecasting was a brand new game. Roger Wise, then of Wood Cable, taught me a great deal about the machinations of the infant industry. He also provided ingress to the then WASEC world. Slowly I was able to penetrate the corporate world of MTV and other cablecasters.

A methodological note: Quotes in this book came from direct interviews unless otherwise noted. Some of the "on the record" interviewees included:

Robin Beman

Jo Bergman

Marshall Cohen

Bill Chapmen

Pam Fekett

Cynthia Friedman

Pat Gorman

James Gary

Nancy Henry

Robert Hilburn

Robert Johnson

Barry Kluger

John Lack

Doreen Lauer

Jennifer Lerner

Eric McLamb

Randy Owen

Dale Pon

Hilary Schacter

John Schneider

Ann Schartz

Fred Seibert

Carol Hibbs Stevenson

John Sykes

Roger Wise

Connie Wodlinger

Many "off the record" sources contributed equally. Publicity departments proved invaluable.

As always, the secretarial staff at Bowling Green State University's Sociology Department provided invaluable assistance. Mrs. Pat Kane, particularly, performed a herculean task in typing and retyping a massive manuscript. Mrs. Kathy Hill equally helped. Bill Schurk of the Audio Center at the BGSU Library was an essential resource for this effort. Unfortunately he didn't have time to contribute to the manuscript directly. Bill Romanowski's contribution to the manuscript is equally appreciated.

February 1987

1

"Heartbreak Hotel"

This kid is a guitar-playing Marlon Brando.

Jack Philbin, executive producer, "Stage Show"

A New York City weatherman staring at the teleprompter read, "Increasing cloudiness and not so cold tonight. Lowest temperature 25 with a high of 30 degrees. Gentle, variable winds from the northwesterly direction." The WNBC-TV weatherman went on to rattle off predictions for the remaining part of the weekend.

As with many elements of the Elvis legend, even the weather on the night of January 28, 1956 has been exaggerated. The liner notes to *Elvis,* written by an anonymous artist of puffery at the RCA publicity office, read:

> Presley was facing a majority of viewers as cold and unprepared as the citizens of Siberia.
>
> In New York very few had braved the storm. The theatre was sparsely filled with shivering servicemen and Saturday nighters, mostly eager for the refuge from the weather. Outside, groups of teenagers rushed past the marquee to a roller-skating rink nearby. Just before show time, a weary promoter returned to the box office with dozens of tickets, unable to even give them away on the streets of Times Square.

The historic night was not quite as climatically melodramatic as biographers and publicists insinuate. "Stage Show" aired at 8:00 P.M. (EST) with a temperature of 29 degrees, dropping one thermometer point an hour. However, a Siberian chill may have existed between Jackie Gleason and the CBS brass at the time. The day prior to the transformation of the "Hillbilly Cat" into "Elvis, the Pelvis," the comedian railed at Black Rock executives about the Dorsey Brothers' "Stage Show" time slot. Perry Como was beating this variety show lead-in to the "Honeymooners." Como enjoyed a comfortable 32 audience share to the meager 14.9 of "Stage Show."

Midway into the show, Elvis stood in the middle of the stage on the assigned chalk mark. Sporting an ill-fitting, off-white jacket with dark trousers, he spread his legs, shrugged the padded coat shoulders, and rotated the right knee: "Wellll . . . since mah baby left me, ah've found a new place to dwell. . . ." The audience not tuned to Como couldn't believe their undersized black-and-white screen. "Heartbreak Hotel" continued. Presley's well-rehearsed Howlin' Wolf bump and grind, now second nature, intensified. "As Scotty came in on guitar," recalled Jerry Hopkins, "Elvis' legs jerked and twisted. He thumped his own guitar on the afterbeat beat, using it as a prop and almost never playing it now. He bumped his hips. He moved his legs in something that seemed a cross between a fast shuffle and a Charleston step." The now familiar sneer at the left corner of his mouth appeared. The dark eyelids seductively began to close. Television met rock and roll and the man about to be crowned its monarch: "The King."

Phone lines resembled Christmas Day. Teens rushed to call their friends: "Turn on . . . you won't believe it!" For a fee of approximately $1,250 the faltering "Stage Show" outrated Perry Como for the first time. In a frequently cited quote Gleason merely said, "It was and is our opinion that Elvis would appeal to the majority of the people."[1]

Whatever the magic, it shocked and ignited those watching. Television executives, particularly at CBS, read the numbers. Gleason was pacified for a while. The media and public reactions were mixed. The handful of written accounts were negative; few critics had seen the controversial performance. Adolescents loved it, while their parents scowled. The middle-aged titans of the Golden Age of Television—Bill Paley, Frank Stanton, David Sarnoff—didn't understand the phenomenon, but could read the "overnights." The musical genie was out of the bottle.

Elvis and the band climbed into their ever-present Cadillac, followed by Red West and Scotty Moore, and they were *allegedly* greeted by unpredicted snow flurries. Symbolically the chill augured the history of a new irreverent presence on television. Some twenty-five years later, John Lack would introduce a new satellite-delivered Music Television (MTV) network uttering one sentence: "Ladies and Gentlemen! Rock and Roll!"

Note

1. Hopkins, 122, 124

2

"We Are Family"

The announcement of the merger did not surprise many financial insiders on Wall Street. The September 14, 1979 press conference only served to confirm the rumors. American Express announced its intention to purchase 50 percent of the Warner Cable Corporation (WCC) for $175 million. The choice of companies may have startled some, but in light of its unsuccessful bids for Walt Disney Productions, McGraw-Hill, and others over a two-year span, the cash-heavy traveler's-check and credit-card corporation finally was able to expand into the communications field.

The joint venture would be named Warner Amex Cable Communications (WACC). It was hoped that a $250 million credit line could be established for the new enterprise.

Cable television (CATV) since the mid-1970s and early 1980s was economically perceived as one of *the* growth industries—a megatrend. Warner Cable Corporation was a leader in this field. Even with competition from Group W, Cox, and American Television and Communications (ATC), the Warners subsidiary appeared filled with promise, especially the interactive QUBE hookup.

WCC surfaced in 1972 as the result of the merger of Continental, Television Communications, and the Cyprus operation. The newly formed cable chain began to expand with the acquisition local cable companies and new franchises. One of the first was a Columbus, Ohio, company that would in 1977 come to be known as the Warner QUBE two-way or "interactive system." It received a vast amount of attention because of its ability to actually involve viewers, who could respond to what was on the screen by squeezing a button. The technology enthralled people. A more important ingredient of the Ohio cable company was its ability to produce original programs, such as "Pinwheel," which would anchor the Nickelodeon Network.

The Star Channel, a pay-TV movie network introduced in February 1973, was part of the package. Star was different from other all-film networks in format, as it provided late-night films. Research indicated that blue-collar workers in industrial areas were very supportive of movies screened in the early hours of the morning. For decades people on the swing shift had been an ignored segment of the population when it came to television. VCRs were then in their high-priced infancy.

Originally confined to CATV operations under the WCC logo, Nickelodeon and Star were on RCAs "Cable Bird" (satellite) by April 1979—five months prior to the revelation of the proposed joint venture. WCC, at the time, had amassed some 140 MSO (Multiple Systems Operator) franchises with satellite access and production capabilities. Optimists predicted in the early 1980s that at least half of America would be "wired" by the end of the decade. Gustave M. Hauser, then chief executive officer of Warner Cable, noted: "Looking down ten years out, or five years out we see a tremendous opportunity and a great requirement for capital—as the industry goes on—to wire America."

The chairperson of American Express, James D. Robinson, III, viewed the cable industry as being "on the leading edge of a major communications revolution in the United States. . . . [It's] a compatible extension of our travel and entertainment-related services and gives us entry into the fast-growing, at home consumer and entertainment industry."

Steven J. Ross, the stormy head of Warner Communications Inc. (WCI), which owned the cable division, applauded the additional capital.

The venture needed and received the approval of the Federal Communications Commission (FCC). In a period of merger mania, few doubted the stated intentions of the collaborators. One analyst voiced reservations to *Business Week*. In light of WCI's status in the corporate community, the observer suggested that Warners was gaining "respectability." "Some fiduciaries wouldn't let their clients touch the company [WCI]. But now, it's partnered with American Express, and the link will open doors to institutions that were closed before."

Prior to this venture the business press had been unkind to Steven Ross and the Kinney Corporation, which merged with Seven Arts to become WCI in 1969. *Forbes, Fortune,* and others printed rumors of organized crime connections and "squirreling away $170,000 when it had a net income . . . of $51 million in 1973."

The Justice Department had charged that Sol Weiss had accepted $70,000 to sell stocks to Warners that contributed to the "slush fund." A Wall Street insider noted in defense: "At the time, everyone was setting up slush funds. I don't think there was anything done not in the interest of the stockholders." This may have been correct, but WCI had other ghosts to tend with.

Reprise Records, part of WCI, was cofounded by Frank Sinatra, a musical phenomenon who is frequently rumored to have "mob" connections.

Alleged scandals plagued the Kinney Corporation. Ross, the president, at one time controlled a number of parking lots in the Bronx that were Kinney holdings. Steve Chapple and Reebee Garofalo in a muckraking volume suggest: "Since the Mafia has been heavily involved in New York City parking lots . . . *Forbes* magazine and others have *speculated* that Kinney and through them Warner have also been involved with organized crime."

The frequently cited *Forbes* story of June 1970 supposedly implied organized crime connections; however, the business magazine actually stated: "Rumors have long circulated linking Kinney with the Mafia. *Forbes* has been *unable* to find a shred of solid evidence to support them. . . ." Caesar P. Kimmel, executive vice president of Kinney Corporation, whose family ties fueled the rumor, noted: "I've lived with this over the years—the charge that we are run by the Mafia. It just isn't true. We don't wear shoulder holsters. We've never been under the influence of any underworld group."

On Wall Street, as elsewhere, the perception frequently *is* the reality. This joint enterprise of WCI and American Express put most of the innuendos to rest. Several years after the coupling, Lee Isgur of Paine Webber would tell *Newsweek* that WCI was "beginning to emerge as one of the major companies in America, bar none."

Programs, "Teenvideo," and Satellites

J. Dalton Knievel started a cable operation in Columbus, Ohio. Five hundred households originally signed up for the service in December 1971. Warner Cable then brought the system. Unlike the standard twelve-channel CATVs developed to import clear television pictures into suburban and rural regions, the Warner operation produced some of its own local pay programming. American Express' James Robinson pointed to the QUBE system as a consideration for the joint venture: "We looked at cable for a long time and decided that a company that could generate its own programming had definite advantages over others." Columbus, at that time, was Madison Avenue's demographic all-American test market. The innovative cable system was touted as the wave of the future, even by PBS's "Nova" series. This became a major selling point for WCC.

In 1976 Dr. Vivian Horner, formerly of PBS' "Electric Company," and producer Sandy Kavanaugh embarked on a project with a shoestring budget for the Columbus Warner cable system aimed at preschoolers. Sandy Kavanaugh said, "We had a theory but we didn't know how we'd pull the concept together. Then we had an adrenaline day, and created 'Pinwheel.' " On December 1, 1977 a new cable offering, C-3, began airing from 7:00 A.M. to 7:00 P.M., seven days a week. "Pinwheel House" was, according to producer Kavanaugh, "the only complete television channel in the world geared to the diverse interests of the very young child . . . entertainment, learning, and fantasy." "Pinwheel" included educational fare, animated films provided by the Canadian Film Board, and features from all over the globe.

"Pinwheel House" appeared to be in the "Sesame Street" genre, featuring puppets and adults focusing their activities around a mobile vegetable cart. Bradford Cody Williams, once with "Kukla, Fran, and Ollie," created the puppets. Like its PBS counterpart, the program included music, art, and mime. The "Sesame Street" comparison was difficult to shake. "Although we've always carried entertainment," Geraldine Laybourne, vice president of programming, told the *New York Times,* "when we first came on we were heavily oriented toward educational shows. Our initial success was with preschoolers, where the adults control the dial."

QUBE's two-way or interactive operation went into effect the same time as "Pinwheel" debuted, with 20,000 households connected to the cable. The *Columbus Dispatch* heralded the new concept of "participatory programming" as changing the face of cable and "all of television." Pollsters and merchandisers were excited as subscribers could merely press a button to register a social or political opinion, and in the future subscribers would be able to make bank transfers and directly order goods advertised on the television screen. The media coverage and plaudits were appreciated, but the operation was costing Warner Cable some $20 million in red ink.

"Pinwheel" was doing quite well in other WCC markets and became part of Nickelodeon when it expanded into a "satellite network for young people, preschoolers to early teens." Nickelodeon went into orbit March 26, 1979. Warner Cable would continue as the "major production facility for the network," said then general manager Columbus Nyhl Henson, supplying 20 percent of the programming.

Nickelodeon featured five programs: "Pinwheel," "Video Comic Book," "Nickel Flicks," "By the Way," and "Bananaz," a live talk show later renamed "Livewire." Several weeks after the initial airing, United Cable became the first non-Warners company to buy the satellite-fed service.

Vivian Horner became Warner Cable's vice president for educational programming and Sandy Kavanaugh was named director of programming for the channel. Their new boss was John A. Lack, who had just come from CBS.

At the time of his departure Lack was slated to run WCBS-TV in New York. Several friends of Gus Hauser recommended him as a "bright young" marketing executive. WCC made him a very lucrative offer. Lack saw this as an opportunity "that was a lot bigger than I could have had at CBS at the time."

John A. Lack joined Warner Cable on January 10, 1979 as executive vice president of programming and marketing. He would be responsible for the QUBE operation, the satellite services, Nickelodeon, Star Channel, and supervision of WCC's 140 systems nationally.

Lack's academic broadcasting and sales credentials are impressive. The then thirty-four-year-old native New Yorker had graduated from Boston University and earned a masters degree in broadcast journalism at Northwestern University. He studied for a doctorate at the prestigious Department of Communications at the University of Pennsylvania, but did not complete it. He became a producer-director at Westinghouse Broadcasting's KYW-TV in Philadelphia, working with the temperamental Tom Snyder on the evening "Eyewitness News" and other projects. Group W involved Lack in the cable activities as well. Leaving Philadelphia, he assumed the position of program director of the Reeves Telecom Communications radio stations in Baltimore.

From August 28, 1970 to January 5, 1979, he was employed by CBS in various capacities, ranging from account executive (particularly radio spot sales) to vice president and general manager of WCBS (New York), an all-news station. The New York station was the most profitable of the fourteen CBS-owned radio stations. When announcing the appointment Gustave M. Hauser told *Variety* that one of Lack's prime responsibilities would be to develop new directions for QUBE, Star Channel, and Nickelodeon. Jim Gray, president of Warner Amex Cable, said, "What they did was stress development." In light of his experience, Lack was to observe, evaluate, and formulate blueprints for the future. Sales and programming were his strongest attributes. Lack, according to one former executive at 75 Rockefeller Plaza, was a conceptualizer—a man most comfortable behind a desk or in a board room. Another recalled that "he knew what he wanted, but usually got someone else to do it."

The formal ELF biography in the media marketplace does not indicate his true interest. Fred Seibert notes: "John Lack loves music. He learned to love rock and roll growing up around the streets of New

York." Lack was part of a growing legion of white kids turned on to rhythm and blues before Presley, Domino, and Haley came to dominate the charts. Seeing Louis Lymon and the Teen Chords perform "Too Young" and "I Found Out Why" was impressive. Lack remembers: "I used to play games when I was a kid, you heard the first two seconds of a song, you had to guess the artists, the writer, the flip side, the company and the color." Alan Freed's four-hour "Rock 'n' Roll Party" on WINS, later WABC, was must listening. He attended the Newark, Brooklyn, and Broadway record hops sponsored by Freed and friends. To this day Lack can describe the four color changes on the obscure Fire Records label. Lack was, and is, a music aficionado. This affinity for music would shortly surface at WCC.

Lack's original task was to try to stem the flow of WCC's river of red ink. The Nickelodeon Channel was attracting considerable attention, in Jim Gray's words, as "something that's different." Star Channel's film fare and scheduling were competitive in some markets with HBO, Showtime, and others. The market share, however, was a mere 170,000 hookups. The key was to expand the audience and the households serviced. Sat Com I's transponders made Nickelodeon and the Star Channel available to a much broader market transcending the WCC affiliates. Lack commuted to Columbus three times weekly. The operation became more innovative. Jim Cazazzini was brought in as vice president of programming. Pay-per-view first-run movies and championship fights were one ploy. Boxing could be scored by the viewers by round and the results flashed on the screen. WCC also tried interactive high school football with the subscribers calling the plays. However, the armchair coaches did poorly, garnering national media coverage. The outcome of a locally produced Warner's soap opera was to be decided by the viewers.

Nickelodeon in its "Pinwheel" phase served preschoolers. Lack extended the programming to appeal to people in their early teens. The formula worked. An older teen base could be reached, he thought. Up to this point, only "Saturday Night Live" had succeeded in attracting this audience. Network executives generally dismissed adolescents as "low users." This view was a self-fulfilling prophecy. Only on the weekends, after the 11:00 P.M. news, was any attempt made to attract young people. "The kids who watch shows," said Burt Sugarman, producer of "The Midnight Special," "come home around 12:30 or 1:30, so we pick them up."

Lack, with "Saturday Night Live's" vertical demographics in mind, attempted to broaden Nickelodeon's audience. Visual rock would be the vehicle. WCC commissioned "Pop Clips" from ex-Monkee Mike

Nesmith's production company. Pacific Arts Corp., based in the scenic ocean-side Carmel area, was to produce fifty or more half-hour shows. "I think we delivered something like 52 programs," said Ann Schwartz, Pacific's general manager. The half-hour programs went into production in the summer of 1979. Mike Nesmith, the pioneer American video clip maker, told *Billboard:*

> To me it's the single most important event in the history of the rock and roll music industry—bigger than the Sun Recordings of Elvis Presley. And there is only one segment of the entertainment business that will understand what a video record is, the record business. The record business understands retail sales and that's where all this is going.

Nesmith, like Lack, viewed video clips as promotional tools. His now classic "Rio" was made as a marketing vehicle for the European market in 1977. Lack secured most of the clips. Jo Bergman of Warner Records recalls that "John Lack got together with Michael Nesmith, and they did the show, the "Pop Clips" show." This was months before Lack hired Robert Pittman to head the pay-TV division. Bergman, a part of the WCI team, supplied Nickelodeon with the clips.

> Lack was really the one who asked us if there were enough clips to make something work. Since we were probably the first group of people to actually put a catalog together of what we had, we were pretty sure there was enough material, and that if someone was going to show them then chances were good that we'd make more.

By October Lack had Nickelodeon in over one million cable-wired homes, but the highly acclaimed "kidvid" network still was not making money. Nickelodeon was being used as a "loss leader" to stimulate cable operators to take the Star Channel. MSOs were offered the children's signal free with the tiered or the pay-movie channel. Otherwise, Nickelodeon was in the "basic service" or lower tier reserved for advertiser-supported satellite networks, such as Turner's all-news Cable News Network (CNN) or ESPN, the sports outlet. The Warner's cable charge was ten cents per subscriber per month as a "basic," fifty cents if shown on the more costly "pay tier." Richard P. Simon, a media and cable analyst at Goldman, Sachs & Co., was a lone voice to suggest that Warner-Amex "are on the road to becoming a full-fledged network."

That fall Lack received an invitation to participate in *Billboard*'s first International Video Music Conference to be held at the Sheraton-Universal Hotel in Los Angeles. He would be one of three speakers at the opening session, which would be chaired by the trade publication's respected publisher Lee Zhito. The other tentative participants were to be Andrew Kohut of the Gallup Organization and MCA's president Sidney Sheinberg. The initial session was titled "Video Music—Tomorrow is Here Today." The title, alone, was seductive.

WCC would soon split into two entities, or divisions. Warner Cable Communications would continue as a distributor—or the "hardware" division, as Gray calls it. Warner-Amex Satellite Entertainment Company (WASEC) would be the "program development" arm of the parent corporation. The November 9, 1979 hiring of John A. (Jack) Schneider was a signal. Warner-Amex was to do more than merely wire America, especially in the climate of franchise disputes and ever-escalating costs.

Schneider, the subsidiary president and chief operating officer, had little experience in the conflict-ridden world of cable hardware. His reputation was as the abrasive former president of CBS-TV who had lost in one of Black Rock's recurrent power struggles. His philosophy was aggressive. He told reporter Robert Metz:

> Your hands got just as bloody if you were last as they did if you came in first. . . . If you are going to come to work every day, be involved in things, that is a seven-day effort. It is better to work at coming in first—to win.

This world view got Schneider into a considerable amount of trouble throughout his broadcasting career.[2] Ironically, Schneider learned this philosophy in yacht racing, as did Ted Turner, who would in time become a noisy but temporary player in the music video network game.

Born in the Chicago area, Schneider attended one of the more prestigious universities close to home, Notre Dame. Here his views were reinforced. His media career was launched at WGN-TV (Chicago) as a time seller.

CBS employed him in 1950 in the Chicago area. A brief stint in New York followed. In 1958 CBS appointed him vice president and general manager of WCAU-TV in Philadelphia. Within a year he was vice president of the entire CBS-TV affiliates division. He was confident and the strategy was working.

In 1964 he took control of WCBS-TV in New York, the nation's largest market. From the flagship station, he made the leap to Black Rock, displacing James Aubrey as the president of the CBS Television Network. Schneider's ascendancy in the CBS network, due primarily to attitude and self-motivation, would quickly put him in the power maze of Bill Paley, Frank Stanton, and Clive Davis. In 1969, he was raised to executive vice-president of the entire CBS Group, including the music division.

Two years later, the anticipated successor to Bill Paley had lost favor in the upper echelons of Black Rock. Charles T. Ireland from ITT was brought in to usurp the man who claimed he "could" fire Walter Cronkite.[3]

Schneider faced many conflicts in the corporate boardrooms. One chief adversary was Clive Davis, head of the music division.

According to Davis, Schneider felt that "television had carried records for *many* years." Then there was the matter of money. Davis was offered a position at WCI. This was to become a bargaining clip with Schneider. Davis was offered an additional $25,000 and an option of 10,000 shares of corporate stock. He stayed. He recalled, "I liked it there. I really didn't want to leave." Schneider, at the time of Davis' firing in 1974, was earning nearly $300,000 with the normal corporate perks. Davis seemed resentful. His treatment at Black Rock during the "drugola" investigations only made matters worse.

Davis' firing amidst the heat of CBS News' treatment of Watergate and the Jack Anderson columns has never been sufficiently explained. It was rumored that Davis spent $94,000 of CBS's funds for "personal use." Most industry observers concurred with a Warner Records' executive that "a company like CBS is idiotic to bust a president of one of the major profit-making divisions for a mere hundred Gs. They're affecting their stock and the entire record business." Davis' autobiography never fully dealt with the dismissal nor did subsequent interviews.

Schneider's remark that "I used to be a worker bee, but now I reign" was becoming hot air at CBS. In 1977, he was "kicked upstairs." He resigned six months later.

He was a firm believer in the delegation of responsibility while reserving the ultimate power. The technique worked, for a time, at Black Rock with its myriad targeted and specialized programs and audiences.

Extrapolating his CBS experience into the world of cable had its shortcomings. He maintained his status with creative underlinings. Never giving individual credit, he championed the group decision. He was the ideal organization man, but insisted on a leadership role. As Peter Drucker has noted, being a team player and a leader in corporate life is almost an impossible role. A WASEC executive noted:

Jack was not, at least in the eyes of the younger people, the most understanding of today's management, but he served a role. He played grandfather for a while, and gave credibility to a flegling organization that needed that reputation.

Schneider is not quite the ogre portrayed by Metz. While the corporate executive side of Schneider may appear remote and sometimes arrogant, on a personal level he has few detractors.

If you're going to be up front with a lot of things, frequently which you don't always enjoy, there are a lot of people that want to take stabs at you, and sometimes you have to make hard decisions. . . . I've always tried to say "please" and "thank you." I've always tried to explain to people why we're doing things and I've always tried to attain a high level of respect of individuals. I've never shredded someone of his or her dignity because that's really all we have. I think the clerks, secretaries, and middle boys always thought I was good for them. They always had my respect and I think I've got theirs.

After several years of consulting work, mostly for WCI, he moved to the presidency of the newly formed WASEC. In quick order with Schneider at the helm, the *Wall Street Journal* announced Star Channel would become a twenty-four-hour motion picture outlet to be called The Movie Channel (TMC). The wheels were slowly turning as WASEC had more transponders thousands of miles in the sky. "We are the only company [with a leased satellite]," he mused. "And you can only be credible if you have transponders to back up your claim."

Todd Rundgren, an American video music maven, had plans for a music network emanating from the singer's Bearsville, New York, studio. Manager Eric Gardner acknowledged defeat on the transponder issue. He noted: "We own a transponder on Sat Com III, which will be launched later this year [1981]. We had one on Sat Com II, but that's the one that disappeared. We *were* going to be the first twenty-four-hour video music channel, but since the satellite got lost Warner-Amex will beat us to it." The Rundgren plan never got beyond the production stage.

Schneider inherited more than just scarce transponders. Lack had ideas and plans. In October Lack hired Robert Warren Pittman, one of the most highly acclaimed operationalizers in broadcasting. Pittman became director of Warner-Amex's pay-TV division. This move surprised the rock radio community, as the twenty-six-year-old "psychographic boy wonder" was assured a successful career in broadcasting. His knack for market research and "number crunching" research was legendary. Lack's explanation was that "I wanted Bob to program movies the way he did records."

Robert Pittman is a product of Brookhaven, Mississippi, population 10,000. Born several days after Christmas in 1953, he began his broadcasting career while in his teens, not uncommon practice in rural areas of America. Country music star Waylon Jennings, media consultant Kent Burkhart, and many others began their rise in the same manner. At fifteen, Bob wanted to take flying lessons. He went to Jack's Shop, a local haberdashery, and applied for a job. Pittman was refused. He walked several stores down the block to WCHJ-FM. They hired him. Now he could pay for the aviation instructions. By the age of seventeen he was employed by WJDX-FM as a deejay in Jackson, Mississippi. While working at the station he attended Millsaps College, majoring in sociology. He remained at the station until moving northward to Milwaukee as the research director at WRIT. After a brief stint at the Wisconsin outlet, Pittman migrated to Detroit's WDRQ as program director. He continued his formal education at Oakland University in northern Michigan. In a year he moved to WPEZ in Pittsburgh and attended the University of Pittsburgh. In 1974 he ended his academic endeavors without a diploma. His broadcasting career became paramount. He joined the NBC radio system in Chicago, programming the network-owned and operated AM and FM stations in Chicago, where he established himself as a media wizard. The format of WKQX-FM was changed from all news to the top-rated album-oriented rock (AOR) station in the Windy City. At WMAX-AM Pittman fashioned the number one country station in the United States.[4] These feats did not go unnoticed by NBC executives. Success in one of America's major markets usually guarantees a crack at the largest—New York City. After three years in Chicago Pittman became program director at WNBC-AM in New York, the most competitive radio environment in the country.

Charlie Warner, WNBC-AM (New York) general manager, recruited Pittman to the network flagship station in August 1977. Warner had worked with Bob in the Pittsburgh and Chicago markets. As the new program director, he shook up the station. The studio was remodeled. Star personalities such as Cousin Bruce Morrow and Don Imus were let go. Imus' firing was controversial. His chemical dependency was unknown to the public. "I was pretty irresponsible," he admitted to *US*. "They couldn't have done anything else." An entirely new staff of people outside of New York were hired. Pittman announced a total format change as of September. One WNBC staffer said, "He literally gutted the station."

Like the top-rated WABC, the NBC station would be straight-ahead rock. Pittman considered three "different programming slants: AOR, urban contemporary, and Rick Sklar's proven approach at ABC.

The format decision would be based on psychographic call-out research. The sample would go beyond the usual "heavy users." Pittman told *Billboard* he was "surveying the total audience rather than just the 5 percent who buy records." "We researched the universe," he reiterated. One thousand records were tested via the call-out method. The responses were fed into a computer, which Pittman described as "an indicator" of audience preferences and a tool to build the "image" of the station. The sample would determine the format. The original verdict was album-oriented rock. This structure lasted exactly six weeks.

In late October 1977, Pittman refined his programming strategy. WNBC would fragment into "the best of AOR, the best of black music, and the best of Top Forty," he said. Pittman made no secret of the fact that he was "stealing" from his competitors. "The market is so fractionalized that we hope to pick up a certain portion of each of these listening groups and maintain them." The target audience was in the eighteen to forty-nine age group. Forty percent of it was black. Pittman stated:

> My rotation is not like the old-fashioned male singer followed by female singer followed by group formula. It's a unique balance derived from listeners' likes and dislikes. We track their tolerance.

The approach seemed to be working, as *Radio Index* and *Media Trends* reported a rapid 50 percent increase in listeners. "We play a song often enough to please people who want to hear it all the time, but not enough to annoy those of you who don't want to hear it at all," he would tell the WNBC audience.

Promotions were an important aspect of the Pittman game plan. Besides the usual free album giveaways and concert tickets, a $50,000 "we'll-call-you" cash prize was an effective audience-building gimmick. Even with this fairly traditional marketing technique, used very successfully at WABC, there was a motive. The "free" concert tickets were for acts featured on competitive AOR stations. This was a ploy to garner defections, especially from WPLJ-FM.

Pittman denied confronting WABC or any other station. He said, "I'm not underestimating them at all and I'm not attacking anyone, just trying to improve our own position in the market." He did. In 1978 he received *Hall Radio Reports'* Program Director of the Year Award.

While at the radio operation, he became executive producer of "Album Tracks," an NBC-TV offering to its local affiliates. Pittman's research orientation would be one of the key aspects of the MTV operation. His television experience would be equally useful.

A year later WABC was knocked out of its usual number-one ARB (Arbitron rating) position by WKTV, a disco-oriented FM station created by Kent Burkhart, an Atlanta consultant. WABC dropped nearly two share points.

At the same time Fred Silverman, the flamboyant head of NBC, began major changes in the parent radio division. Jack Thayer, president of the section, was moved to executive vice president in charge of "special projects." Robert Mounty took over NBC's AM operations, while Walt Sabo, Jr. was placed at the helm of the FM network. Pittman was not immediately affected by the shakeup, as he continued his various roles in AM and its New York counterpart WYNY-FM.

In January 1979 Silverman issued a directive stressing personality radio as a means of broadening the audience for NBC's eight radio stations. Mounty was put in charge of the "expansion" program.

Mounty, an executive vice president, especially expressed dissatisfaction with WNBC. He told Doug Hall: "Of course it's not successful. It's been changed too often. It doesn't have any identity. In the past seven or eight years it's been talk, MOR personality, and no personality." He further complained about the flagship's ratings. Silverman and Mounty's comments were merely "suggestions." Charlie Warner headed the WNBC management team. Bob Pittman was equally independent. A former vice president of the NBC radio network indicates that "at no point did Fred Silverman, and never did Bob Mounty, run that management team." He maintained: "I don't think they saw anything, always the same way. . . . But in terms of respect, being able to get along, they certainly did. They respected each other." At WNBC-AM there existed a considerable amount of command autonomy with accountability. Bob Pittman was entrusted with an enormous amount of responsibility and freedom because of the trust management had in him. Reportedly Pittman was the "highest paid program director in America."

The January Arbitron ratings were very discouraging for WNBC-AM management and staff, showing the New York market share at a lowly 2.6. The all-important drive-time period was in a mess. The prior year Lee Masters entertained the commuter audience. He enjoyed a somewhat respectable 3.5 number. Scotty Brink succeeded Masters in August 1978, joined by Richard Belzer as cohost. They would not survive the autumn of 1979.

General Manager Charlie Warner, Pittman's mentor, was removed on the basis of the ARBs. Bob Sherman replaced Warner in July. He and Pittman worked well together. "They were the team that brought Imus back from Cleveland," says Dom Giofre of WNBC. "They actually flew to Cleveland and literally sat in a motel room. He was doing afternoons on a Cleveland station [WHK-AM]. . . . They listened to him and thought he'd really gotten his act together, and decided they'd bring him back."

Dale Pon was appointed manager of advertising and promotion. He joined Pittman and Sherman on the management team at WNBC. Don Imus would resume his morning on-air antics as of September 3. Pittman's other NBC projects were going fairly well. He was, however, officially the program director of WNBC—a precarious position. A month after Imus' reappearance, Pittman was at Warner Cable with an untarnished reputation. "He left of his own volition," recalled Giofre. The reason for the departure allegedly was the insistent New York music market ratings wars.[5]

He had revived the AM station with a contemporary AOR format. With his input, the number of listeners to WYNY-FM had increased.

Pittman, sans long hair and handlebar mustache, joined Warner-Amex as director of pay-TV for the Warner Cable Corporation. One month later the "Wamex" (*Variety*'s jargon) venture was officially proposed. Pittman's move came as a total surprise in light of his phenomenal broadcasting career. "I never thought it would happen," said an associate. "I remember him and in those days he didn't seem to be the type." Jim L. Gray emphasized:

> From the very beginning, when he came in he had very much to do with the way the movies on The Movie Channel [then called Star] were scheduled . . . so whatever they saw in him, they [Lack and Hauser] were right.

According to one insider in the pay-TV division, Pittman was employed for his programming and research abilities, as demonstrated in Chicago and New York. She noted that John Lack was already thinking about "doing music," and Pittman fit perfectly into the scheme of things. He would be, by December, a founding member of the executive team at WASEC in charge of programming the twenty-four-hour movie channel.

On November 15, Lack found himself a voice crying in the wilderness of some 400 people assembled for the first International Video Music Conference. Most of the attendees were concerned with the merchandising and licensing of a visual "product."

Lack's early morning session, while well attended, was unproductive. Andrew Kohut stressed the viability of video cassettes and disks. He did add a caveat that Gallup's data showed a potential market comprised of the affluent and well educated. In Lack's mind that finding easily fit cable demographics.

As a number of record company executives were present, Lack asserted that an exposure vehicle for video music would be needed. He compared cable television to radio. "We want to promote software. We want to be your radio stations," he exhorted.

The Warner Cable vice president then announced plans for a twenty-four-hour video music network. The Nickelodeon service would increasingly be using music-oriented programming. "Pop Clips," he knew, was scheduled for a late March premiere. The problem, Lack told the audience, was the *availability* of video clips to be aired.

Sidney Sheinberg, engrossed in the Sony VCR home-taping suit, immediately retorted, "If we give it away free, who will buy it?" Lee Zhito, a veteran industry observer, must have felt a sense of déjà vu. An identical charge had been hurled at broadcasters prior to World War II. Lack was in the position of restating the arguments of some half a century ago. Several record company observers were quite aware of this comparison. One privately thought, "What does a film mogul know about marketing music?" The overseer of Universal Pictures went on to suggest that video software sales drop when cable is available—another not-so-subtle reference to the *Universal* v. *Sony* case. After the session Lack called New York and said, "I just got beaten up so bad I'm bleeding."

As the Video Music Conference progressed the producers of music videos became increasingly agitated with record companies. An exchange occurred between Seth Willenson of RCA's VideoDisc division and Todd Rundgren. Willenson took a highly pragmatic approach, stating: "What determines what sells is the taste of the American public." Rundgren disagreed: "No artist, given the flexibility of the medium, is going to consider first the amount of compromise necessary." The recording artist/producer went on to characterize most videos as merely "promotional devices." Todd had other plans.

Michael Nesmith, at another session, commented: "As a trusty scout, I bring back news. What's beyond the mountains? More mountains." These remarks from the president of Pacific Arts confused some in the audience. Was he referring to the Monkees' experience, marketing *Elephant Parts,* or producing "Pop Clips?" Nesmith's main concern was with *Elephant Parts.*

Lack returned to New York convinced that record companies were natural allies. The confused film makers were another matter. The fundamental goal of record companies was to sell records and prerecorded cassettes. Video clips were, as Rundgren suggested, "promotional devices." Video software manufacturers were primarily concerned with the potential aesthetics and profits of video clips. Many of their aims at this time were in the "blue sky" stage.

Record companies had other problems. The disco disaster of 1979 was beginning to take shape. While the official Record Industry Association of America (RIAA) figures would not appear until the next spring, many insiders felt a sharp sales drop was in the offing. Record executives would soon have a reason to look at alternative means of exposure, especially for new artists.

The *Billboard* conference taught Warner-Amex Cable an important lesson: Let the record companies act as the video brokers. Lack had impressed some of the power brokers. "John Lack was really the executive in charge of all this," says Warner Records' Jo Bergman. The video director also added that Lack was in control of an operational transponder that beamed Nickelodeon into over a million households, thereby exposing them to this music.

Jack Schneider, a television man, invested most of WASEC's original energies on The Movie Channel. Lack and four other executives formed a committee to select an advertising agency that would enhance the visibility of their satellite feeds, especially TMC.

Eight agencies were chosen to compete for the account. Presentations and interviews were planned for all, followed by a primary selection of three finalists. A winner would emerge from the three. Kenneth Roman, president of Ogilvy and Mather (O&M), reportedly halted the process prematurely, however, with an impressive display of understanding WASEC's specific goals and problems. O&M received the $3 million 1980 allotment for advertising. John Lack predicted the amount would grow to $5 million the following year. He also mentioned the possibility of the parent company's coming on board.

The selection committee was especially impressed with two aspects of O&M: their work for other clients, such as Mattel; and the agency's direct response program. Lack told the *New York Times* that "direct marketing is 30 to 40 percent of our business."

Lack denied that the selection was based on American Express' use of the Madison Avenue firm. The discarded bidders were skeptical—a reaction that in time would hurt WASEC's campaign to attract time buyers for the music channel.

Inside WASEC the general reaction was that "they had become the agency over the objections of almost everyone who was there."

Furthermore, the American Express connection *was* a major consideration.[6] In 1985, Lack still denies the accusation:

> It had nothing to do with that. We hired Ogilvy and Mather because we believe they could do a good job with all of our services. They were pretty good with developing distribution accounts. They were great with TWA. They could do lots of things locally in all these cities, which we needed because of the cable business. Unfortunately they were a disappointment creatively. And we didn't get the first team at Ogilvy and Mather. The secret of the advertising business is getting the great creative directors and the great account people.

Jack Schneider stressed that O&M's top priority would be promoting the twenty-four-hour film network. The advertising assault was scheduled to begin in May at the Dallas convention of the National Cable Television Association (NCTA). TMC had only 240,000 households, as contrasted to Nickelodeon's 2.3 million. The name change and the expansion to an all-night service raised the number of subscribers by only 60,000 to 70,000 viewers, much to WASEC's displeasure.

Pacific Arts delivered "Pop Clips" to the Nickelodeon Network in March. The format was a half-hour Top Forty show with animations, video clips, and comedians serving as the veejays. The program would be a "wraparound," aired two or three times a day. Nesmith described the project as a "visual record—it was the same thing that had happened on radio, a Top Forty TV show." The show had a mad cap quality reminiscent of the Monkees series. Howie Mandel, a Los Angeles stand-up comedian, was employed as the announcer. "We had Howie acting maniacal," director Bill Dear told an interviewer. "We wanted the veejay segments to be as crazy as the clips we were showing." Nesmith commented: "They tend to be more exciting."

Nesmith justified the concept to *Billboard* as a counter to the disco disaster:

> The sales slump is due to the change in the perceived value of an audio record. The public no longer perceives the value of an audio record because of TV. The visual dynamic of TV has impressed itself on the psychology of the American public to such a degree that sound without pictures is no longer acceptable.

> We're going to see a very quick dissemination of the notion of programmable TV sets, and it's probably a good bet to assume that the early programming will be movies. But programming will ultimately fall into the lap of what we now know as the record business.

> The record companies must address themselves to providing programming material for television sets. And that programming material must

be available at the retail level. The record business is the only arm of the entertainment business that knows retail sales. It knows merchandising and distribution. The television industry can't do it.

The role of "Pop Clips" in the evolution of MTV is a highly controversial one. Nesmith, no stranger to media polemics, claimed that the half-hour vehicle sired the music channel: "Without sounding too arrogant, I created MTV when I did 'Pop Clips.' " Director Bill Dear told Mike Shore:

> *"Pop Clips"* was basically MTV before there was an MTV." "Anyway," he continued, Warner Cable wanted to buy the name and idea of the show from us and develop it into what has now become MTV. When Mike Nesmith and I heard what they wanted to do with it, we nearly had heart attacks. . . . So they just watered down the idea and came up with MTV. Still, in a way, I'm glad they did it, because MTV certainly has validated the form.

WASEC spokespersons totally dispute this interpretation. Nickelodeon publicity manager Jennifer Lerner dismisses the short-lived show as affecting the MTV concept. John Sykes, MTV promotion director, stated: " 'Pop Clips' was something that we ran on Nickelodeon, and didn't last that long, I forget how many episodes. . . . It didn't have any real connection with MTV at that time. But it wasn't something that came as a result of MTV." Fred Seibert, an MTV executive, is even more emphatic:

> Mike Nesmith can go and jump in a lake. . . . I think Nesmith was a huge influence on everything I had ever done, but he had absolutely *nothing* to do with MTV. He can tell you about meetings he had with John Lack up the nose, but . . . the idea for MTV really came about at Warner-Amex in 1980 as it was being developed, and I'm sure a lot of people would like to take credit for the idea.

Lack's version of "Pop Clips" is a mix: "Michael had sent me a program concept which I reworked and that's what 'Pop Clips' became." Lack commissioned the standard thirteen episodes for the QUBE system, and these were repeated at least fifty-five times in six months on Nickelodeon. There were problems. Nesmith agreed to a twenty-four-hour format, but Lack did not like the use of the comedic announcer: "He took away from the music too much."

There were more significant difficulties. Pacific Arts wanted to use their own studios, and Bob Pittman didn't like Nesmith. Lack concurred. The result was that after "Pop Clips" had its run, "We didn't go back to Michael anymore," reminisces Lack. "We parted company, not terribly amicably, but he has a lot to do with being the father of the [American] music video. . . . The bottom line was, of course, we didn't need Michael anymore. . . . Bob did it without Michael."

In a historical perspective, Nesmith was a pioneer of American video clips. The original idea for an MTV-type network was Lack's. "Pop Clips" was used as a pilot for a concept, but rejected, as Lack, Pittman, and others had different ideas. Jack Schneider's observation is quite valid in this case: "There's a great deal of revisionary history going on right now."

In April 1980 WASEC purchased the rights to a Com-Star D-2 transponder from Total Communication Systems in Pittsburgh, bringing its total to four. Nickelodeon, The Movie Channel, and "superstation" KTVU (Oakland-San Francisco) were already on RCA's Sat Com I transponders. Schneider "indicated" that he had no plans to actually use the new acquisition. The Bay Area superstation was not in his future plans. He was quite cool to the channel as it negatively resembled Ted Turner's Atlanta outlet. He told *Advertising Age* that "one or two of them may make it," but he thought Turner would win the "shakeout." He openly admitted that a commitment to Satellite Communications Systems, a common carrier, kept it in the Warner's offerings to cable operators.

Industry watchers suggested that even the costly service fee for access to the unused Com-Star D-2, which would begin in June, was worth the investment by WASEC. It guaranteed a transponder on RCA's Sat Com III and promised to be operational by November 1981.

KTVU's days were numbered in the Warner-Amex structure, leaving the organization with two transponders to develop new programming. "I didn't think there was a future in that, and they were using up a transponder. . . . the retransmission of another television station is not what the company responded to, was not going to be all about," recollects Schneider.

Under the auspices of TMC, Lack and Pittman began assembling a staff of essentially record and radio people. Most were originally hired to work for TMC in various capacities. One of the first was Fred Seibert, largely credited with the development of the animated MTV logo. Seibert's experience was illustrative of some of the machinations taking place in the employment sector. "I made a choice to go into cable television," he candidly states, *"not* because I had any interest at all in television, but because I wanted to work with Bob Pittman."

Seibert was employed at WHN (New York) as director of promotion and creative services. His chief was Dale Pon, a friend of Pittman's.

Prior to that Seibert had been a professional musician and an independent jazz producer. Pon left WHN for WNBC. In April 1980, Pittman was looking for somebody to work on air promotion for TMC. Pon recommended Seibert. He went to work for TMC in May explaining, "Pittman had as little TV experience as I did, so I'm sure it felt comfortable for both of us to be not knowing what we were doing together."

One Movie Channel executive said that Lack reintroduced the concept at the National Cable Television Association meetings held in Dallas. The NCTA meetings, which lasted May 18-21, were overshadowed, however, by the Getty Oil Company's proposed Premier all-movie network. This was strongly opposed by all the possible competitors. TMC—in the midst of waging an industry blitz with full-page trade ads, various promotions, and a direct-mail campaign orchestrated by Ogilvy and Mather advertising agency—was especially opposed.

The Premier Network failed before it started. Several governmental regulatory commissions stepped in and spoiled Getty's plans.

Lack's original mandate from WCC chairman Hauser to develop new programming and broaden the market share led eventually to the concept of an all-music network designed to appeal to a twelve and older audience. His experience with Nickelodeon proved that youngsters would watch television. He saw a big demographic hole. "There's a real place for us," he asserted. "The networks are still programming for people who have never seen TV before. That worked in 1955, but it doesn't work today." WASEC had two entertainment vehicles—one seen as "kidvid" and the other as the all-day, all-night Movie Channel with an adult demographic. The "seam" was in the teen and young adult aggregate.

Lack's rationale for a music channel was based on three fundamental assumptions, most of which would be employed to eventually promote the concept of MTV. He explained: "MTV was founded for a couple of reasons, not just because it was a gleam in my eye, and because it was something that I wanted to do. It made good economic sense." He had witnessed the use of video clips while living in Europe.

Lack recognized that the record industry was in the throes of the Great Depression of 1979. New music and artists were not being exposed on radio.

Advertisers, the lifeblood of broadcasting, were not reaching the "under 34" demographic on television. "So if you were Beech Nut Chewing Gum, or selling pimple cream, or Coca Cola and you wanted to reach twelve to thirty-four year olds, television was not an efficient buy."

Finally, the cable market in the early 1980s was stagnant, dominated by all-news, sports, and "super" stations mired in old films and syndicated commercial network shows. In Lack's mind, the opportunity was there.

Lack took his idea to John Schneider. Reportedly, the WASEC chief operating officer agreed there was a neglected "window" out there in the narrowcast world of cablevision. "We were looking for opportunities, windows, blank spots on the spectrum. We had other things in mind, including a shopping service and a games channel," Schneider told Bob Hilburn. "But MTV was the easiest to do because it was the cheapest [using promotional video clips] and we could get it going quicker."

According to Lack, convincing Schneider was no simple task.

> Well, he was a fifty-five-year-old man in the rock-and-roll world. His biggest problem was how will people watch things. . . . So the music, the program was regenerative. . . . That's a nice way of saying inexpensive, but you realize the product was going to be inexpensive from a network standpoint because we weren't going to have to make it. . . . Jack had no idea, and until this thing was on the air for six months, hated every minute."

Responding to Lack's comments, the ex-WASEC president critically replied, "Oh, it isn't important whether one likes it or not . . . I was engaged in commerce, I was not engaged in high art form." Schneider indicated that his role was to program, not appreciate the product.

A telephone survey was authorized. Marshall Cohen, the original head of research for MTV but at this time with the Opinion Research Council (ORC), supervised the initial survey. The results supported Lack's thesis, and the findings were dramatic. This was the highest rated concept project undertaken by the ORC, outstripping the VCR study. "So we knew right then and there that we were on the right track," said Lack. "If we delivered on the promotional concept, of course that's the key, then we had a winner on our hands conceptually. And that gave us some security that we were on the right track. It wasn't just a great idea, but when it was explained to people it made a lot of sense."

Pittman continued to build the "visual FM" infrastructure. He met with John L. Sykes. Sykes, a graduate of the S. I. Newhouse School of Public Communications at Syracuse University, was the promotion director at CBS Records in Chicago. A half-hour interview was arranged by mutual friends in the Chicago market. Sykes recalls the original encounter.

> I had the bug to get involved in video music, anything, whether it was working for some of these new video music software divisions opening up as corporations, CBS had opened up a video music division. . . . I just wanted to get my feet into the business early, and I had heard from some friends of Bob in Chicago that he developed this concept for Warner-Amex, along with John Lack, and one of his friends mentioned to Bob that he and I should meet each other. So I flew in one day [to New York], met with Bob, and talked to him for about half an hour, and at that point we immediately hit it off. He gave me the job [promotion director], and I went home to Chicago, resigned from CBS, and three weeks later I was in New York.

He was on the payroll as of December 1, 1980. Pittman then flew to Universal City, where he participated in the second *Billboard* Video Music Conference. Speaking on the "Broadcast Video Music: A Cable/Pay-TV/Satellite Overview" panel, he argued that "radio stations' objectives are not the same as record companies' objectives." Given his broadcasting background, few were willing to dissent. He went on to blame broadcaster conservatism for the decline in record industry profits and contended that narrowcast, targeted cable satellite programming would be a much more effective marketing tool for the music business.[7] Not all the panelists concurred. Andrew Wald of ON-TV, a pay service, cautioned: "What's successful on video disk may not be what's successful on pay-TV." He maintained that "networks will not give up and they have unlimited development budgets." His point was only partially correct, as the three main commercial networks had soured on all-rock music shows. PBS continued to air "Soundtrack." Having rock stars on "Saturday Night Live" was one thing, but in the wake of the low rated "In Concert" and the "Midnight Special," they were not terribly interested.

Pittman's argument was lost in the glare of Stan Cornyn's keynote speech. Cornyn, the intellectual guru of the record industry, was highly critical of the trends in video.

> I don't yet understand what to say when a punk rock band comes up to me and exclaims, "Whee! Let's make a video disk!" . . . when I know they can't tell the difference between a video disk and a television special. When I know what they mean by video art is high school expressionism . . . all of this gives the phrase "state-of-the-art" a rather poor connotation.

While Cornyn's remarks were basically aimed at RCA's monovisual disks, he did paint a dark picture for music videos.

The MTV Productions hospitality suite at the Universal-Sheraton had partially filled seats, people watching a giant television screen featuring video clips, many of which came from Warner Records, in full stereo. Among those present were Lack and Schneider. Lack, called the "Father of MTV," was the major "imagineer" or intellectual architect of "visual radio." He coined the acronym "MTV" for music television. Jack Schneider had approved the concept and would attempt to convince others of the viability of the idea. Sipping his double-strength Twinings tea and puffing on an expensive cigar, he told the *Los Angeles Times:* "There were videos available in a body of work that had never been exploited. We had to do something different to reach an untapped audience."

"Although the target audience will be the twelve to thirty-four age group . . . the bulk of that audience—those twelve to twenty-four—aren't being served well by either radio or television," he repeatedly told interviewers. "Young record buyers have no place to sample their music. You don't reach young America with print ads. A generation raised by the glowing home screen and rock music would watch a combination of the two." WASEC conveniently owned a vacant transponder after disposing of the Cox-owned Bay Area "superstation." Once the collective decision had been made, they were faced with the formidable task of obtaining the funding.

In early January 1981, a directional meeting was held. The bottom line was funding the project. The participants included the command structure of WCI, American Express, and WASEC. Steve Ross, David Horowitz, Stan Cornyn, and Norman Senica comprised the WCI team. American Express was represented by James Robinson III, Sanda Meyer, Louis Gursner, and several others. The WASEC team included Schneider, Lack, Pittman, and Robert McGroarty. Several music videos were displayed. The most memorable was Dire Straits' "Stake Away." The British group, coincidentally, was signed to the Warner's label. "We want to do this twenty-four hours a day in stereo," said Schneider.

Robinson watched and listened to the presentation with his leg perched on the executive conference room table. It was in a white cast due to a skiing accident.

The American Express executives raised the opening demographic and cost effectiveness questions. Robinson queried the WASEC president, "Would he spend that amount of his own money?" The answer was an affirmative "Yeah." As to audience size and capability, Pittman predicted a "potential to reach 20 percent of the homes every week." European promotional clips were already available, the questioners were told. At that point the answer was overly optimistic. Robinson, in obvious physical discomfort, said, "Okay, you have my vote, you got the American Express vote." "We thought," said Lack, "well the worst is over." Steven Ross, weighed down by a myriad of economic difficulties, proved otherwise.

Ross' skepticism surprised the presenters. The WCI president battered them with his concerns. The WASEC brass was somewhat mystified, as WCI's record divisions were suffering from the recession plaguing the music industry. A participant characterized the flavor of the exchange thusly: "It was not an easy sale to make." Ross said, "I'm not sure, I don't know if there's a life in these video clips, I don't know whether people will watch them regularly, I don't know if there are enough clips, I don't know if you will be able to get them free. . . ." Several WASEC people wondered if Ross knew what his record people were doing. They were drilled for nearly thirty minutes. Then, according to one account, "Steve told a story about how the night before or a couple of nights before . . . he had a conversation with his daughter. . . . He was convinced by her that this is clearly the thing to do." His stepchildren and friends thought "video radio" was the wave of the future. Another observer sarcastically compared Ross' approval to the 1980 Jimmy Carter statement, during a presidential debate, about his daughter's fears of nuclear war.

According to the *Los Angeles Times,* Schneider was the key in the multimillion dollar startup. He was not some wild-eyed visionary raised on rock and roll. "There were a lot of people in the room who were over fifty," recalled Schneider, "and they looked at me like I was insane, but fortunately I was over fifty, too. They asked if I really understood the appeal of the channel and I said 'Yeah I do.' " After two and a half hours the new channel and the required $20 million were approved. The "Wamex" committee had decided to finance the music channel that Lack called MTV.

Lack, Pittman, engineer Andy Setos, and Sykes were assigned the task of operationalizing the project "as quickly as possible." "We had a half of a floor," remembers John Sykes, "or two halves of two floors [no window and a couple of phones] up at 1211 Avenue of the Americas, the Ceylonese Building, and that was MTV." Schneider would later tell journalist Bob Hilburn, "It's an easier story to write if you have a human interest peg—one brilliant person put his career on the line and sacrificed his second house in the Hamptons and mortgaged the farm to make this whole thing happen. But it didn't happen that way." While, officially, the corporate structure was a foursome, one person became quite visible. "Bob Pittman really was the one who mobilized everything and really put it together and made it work," commented Jo Bergman. "There's no doubt about that, but in terms of the kickoff, Lack was certainly instrumental in all of that."

The first step was to establish, with data and media arguments, that the concept would work. They would then have to convince the record companies to provide the video clips—free. Having accomplished this, easier said then done, they would then have to get cabie operators to take the signal. Finally the advertisers would come along. It was a simple game plan, but a very difficult task to execute.

Getting the "Building Blocks"

Lack turned to WACC to obtain some persuasive data. The QUBE system in Columbus, with its "hands-on program, was to be the demographic market. It would be quite different from the short-lived "Pop Clips." QUBE, being interactive, could provide the statistical profiles so respected on Madison Avenue and in some media circles.

Kevin Albin, whom Lack employed in August 1979 at the cable division, had suggested a music show on his second day on the job. Lack approved the idea. One episode was made and reportedly was "enthusiastically received." *Claiming* a dearth of video clips, the project was shelved. In January 1981 it was back on the table. Although WASEC was the programming arm of the corporation, QUBE still had "major production facility" in Columbus.

Within days of WASEC's approval of a twenty-four-hour music channel, Albin revived the "Sight on Sound" project and scheduled it to be aired on the QUBE system. One of the primary reasons for the restoration appears to have been "compiling some invaluable research . . . for the development and programming folk at WASEC." "Lack was well informed of it and he was helpful in our initial acquisitions of video clips," said Carol Hibbs-Stevenson. "Sight on Sound" (SOS) was "officially" independent of the proposed music channel in Manhattan.

"We produced a series here [Columbus] locally called "Sight on Sound,' " says Stevenson. "This was in many ways the precursor of MTV. It was a local effort . . . but the interest was already there on the part of WASEC in New York." Jo Bergman concurs: "Things were also being worked out with some of the people in Columbus, because they had that whole thing [QUBE] going."

"Sight on Sound" was to be produced minus veejays. This ninety-minute show would begin at 4:30 P.M. and would air to appeal to a 15 to 24 demographic—the "after-school" crowd.

Following board approval, Pittman juggled his duties as TMC's chief programmer with that of promoting the music channel. At the National Association of Recording Merchandisers (NARM) convention in Hollywood, Florida, he pushed the concept as a vehicle to sell records and other hardware. Addressing the prestigious Academy of Television Arts and Sciences' luncheon at the Copacabana, Pittman, speaking hurriedly, told the executives: "The only people who are going to watch this channel will be very interested in music and will be record buyers." MTV was characterized as "more like radio than TV: It catches their ear and they can come in and out of the room to watch." He called MTV a "special source." With this argument he approached record companies. His initial experience was discouraging. The reception was unlike that of a successful radio program director from New York or Chicago. "I went out asking all these companies for the use of the videos," he said, "and I tell you, a lot of them said this is the stupidest idea I've ever heard . . . that there's no chance it's going to work."

Even Jo Bergman of Warner Records, a video clip advocate, was cautious. "Record companies are still unconvinced about a visual medium, period." She added that "there's no way to prove that TV or video actually sells records, or what great a part it plays in the sales of records." Later she would add, "It wasn't so much that I was skeptical. . . . I've been doing videos for so many years, I wouldn't continue to do it if I didn't think it made sense. But in terms of the sales and promotion people at that time. . . ."

In 1970, Van Dyke Parks became the director of audiovisual services for the label. His plan was to produce ten-minute promotional films. These would be distributed to movie houses and shown on late-night television internationally. In less than a year the project was scrapped by company president Mo Ostin due to excessive costs—$500,000—and few available exposure outlets. In 1981 Ostin was still the head man at the Burbank operation.

A few people were willing to bank on Pittman's prior successes:

> There were people at the companies I'd had a relationship with for a while and I said, "Will you do me a favor and trust me?" I was asking for a commitment that they would supply clips if we could show that they were selling records.

Pittman was "poor mouthed" repeatedly. One executive said, "It's not a bad idea, but we can't afford it . . . not with record sales as they are now." Pacific Arts' Dick Broder, the production company that supplied Nickelodeon with material for the "Pop Clips" series, agreed with Lack: "Record companies are aware of the video revolution but still reeling from the problems in their own business. They haven't seen the revenue possibilities. But their involvement is something that's inevitable." WASEC was counting on it. Without the "building-block" commitments, the entire project was in deep trouble. "It's not who you are, but where you are" is an old media adage. Pittman and company were selling an idea to an industry impressed with units shipped and sold. At this historical juncture the proposed channel did not even have a broadcast studio or a distinctive game plan.

Success has a way of restructuring history. "Of course now it's a different story," said one publicist. John Sykes, who accompanied Pittman on several trips to promote MTV, is more upbeat but adds, "There will always be the nonbelievers at the start of anything. . . . I'm not saying it was easy to go out there because it took a lot of road work. A lot of personal meetings and a lot of personal presentations to properly sell the concept, but there were some tough times getting total support, still for the most part it was there." If the trade publications from the early 1980s are any indication, the nonbelievers easily outnumbered the converted.

Timing in the music industry, as in politics, is an imperative. To Lack, Pittman, and Sykes, 1980 appeared to be just the proper moment. In a *Los Angeles Times* interview, Pittman stressed:

> We think we are starting at an ideal time because a lot of the public's fascination with FM stereo has worn off. Stations are becoming more conservative in their programming and people are beginning to look for something fresh. We'll play the hit artists, but we'll also play the new music.

Most record labels, unless they already possessed a video clip library, took a wait-and-see approach. A few were openly opposed. The cynicism on the part of many record executives was due to a number of fears. Their experience with television had been unproductive since the heyday of "American Bandstand" in the late 1950s. Earlier attempts with cable outlets had not demonstrated a sales upswing. Promotion people were tied to radio despite the cries of AOR conservativism and worse.

Superstar formats irritated the industry, but the practice that really started a furor was the airing of entire albums without interruption. An Elektra/Asylum executive told *Billboard* that "radio stations are telling their listeners to gear up their tape machines. It's getting serious."

Groups like Led Zeppelin and Fleetwood Mac, sure-fire sellers, found volume sales drastically dropping. The RIAA issued a statement reading, in part: "This overt action to foster home taping saps the lifeblood of the recording industry. . . ."

Home taping was regarded by much of the industry, especially Stan Gortikov and Joe Smith, as the prime culprit in the decline in profits. An experimental cable music channel would do little to curb the main villains—the home "dupers." One executive summed up the ideological situation: "At that time MTV was 'blue sky,' nothing more, because it did not address the *key* problems, and nobody was about to abandon radio for something that had never worked." Off the record, another "bizzer" indicated that "a lot of people were just plain scared. People were being pink-slipped everywhere, and not just the office help. Endorsing a new project which would cost money was like jumping off the Capitol Tower." The *Wall Street Journal* estimated that more than 2,000 record company employees had been fired during the two opening years of the 1980s.

The resistance encountered by Pittman led Schneider and Lack to increasingly make their case in the print medium, particularly trade publications read by record company decision makers. In a February interview with *Billboard*—"the bible of the industry"—Lack told reporter George Kopp:

> The record companies got more successful because of the job radio did. If we can do the same job for them it will increase their presence in the video marketplace. The record companies will be one of the sources for our programming.
>
> Contemporary music has a demographic that isn't well serviced by TV. Imagine a radio station visually—that's the idea behind our twenty-four-hour channel. It will be both promotional and entertainment for its own sake, with clips, personalities, and commercials.

He promised more specifics in "the next month or so." It would be a matter of weeks.

Notes

1. The "Midnight Special" was cancelled due to poor ratings. However, the tradition of Friday and Saturday night rock videos on the commercial and cable networks is an established practice, as are cartoons or "kidvid" on Saturday mornings.
2. Some of Schneider's experiences at Black Rock are found in Metz's *CBS: Reflections in a Bloodshot Eye*. Schneider describes his interview with Metz as being "quite bizarre."

3. Schneider does not "recollect" this 1985 quote.
4. Film critic Gene Siskel, an MTV opponent, praised Pittman's country programming: "He's a very smart guy—used to work in Chicago on a country music radio station, and I think he was doing better work then."
5. Mounty's suggestion to rediscover personality radio in the meantime was successful. Pon's hiring was highly beneficial. However, by 1981 Don Imus' morning drive-time show dropped two points in market share. WNBC-AM bought a helicopter to report traffic conditions in hopes of increasing their "numbers." Another major shakeup followed. Imus survived this quasi-purge. Bob Sherman was promoted to executive vice president of the entire NBC radio chain. Robert Mounty was kicked upstairs as vice president of marketing, which was primarily concerned with television. Dom Fioravanti became general manager of the New York AM flagship. He would later migrate to MTV. Pon left in the fall of 1981 to participate in the formation of an ad agency.
6. David Ogilvy's legendary firm would prove totally insufficient for MTV after it aired. Several insider's suggested that "they just didn't understand the concept."
7. This theme would be repeated for several years to any group or journalist willing to listen by everyone associated with MTV.

3

Ladies and Gentlemen! Rock and Roll

On Tuesday, March 3, 1981 WASEC announced its plans to launch a twenty-four-hour video music network, which would begin transmission on August 1. John Schneider repeated to the *Wall Street Journal* that "there is a body of young people who are being ignored." This not-so-subtle appeal to record companies was restated in *Variety*. Jack Loftus wrote that the WASEC president "expects the companies and artists to provide MTV with materials free of charge in return for air play—much the same way radio stations operate."

This frequently quoted statement that video clips were "free" was only partially correct. Each clip cost MTV approximately $1,000 to clean up the audio and transfer the material to one-inch tape. The duplication involved running a tape through a picture transformer with color correction. In addition, there was a .14¢ air play licensing (mechanical) royalty to be paid ASCAP or BMI. Consequently, the clips were *not* totally gratis, but MTV's cost paled in comparison to the production expenses.

In a telephone interview with the *Los Angeles Times*, John Lack echoed the availability theme that "there's no paucity of product at this point." He pointed to the promotional clips produced by record companies for use in the United Kingdom, Europe, and Australia—an estimated fifteen to twenty per month. Having spent time in Europe during the 1960s and 1970s, Lack reasoned that a similar promotional strategy for records was applicable in the United States. "I noticed there isn't any radio in Europe with any consequence. There is a TV channel in every country, there's BBC-1 and 2; in France there's National One Radio. So music in Europe could not be prompted on radio the way it is in this country." Therefore, print and television were the alternative exposure vehicles.

> Records were sold in Europe through video shows. "Top of the Pops" in England is a very famous one. Germany has one, France has one. When an artist came to Europe to sell records, they made a little video clip, and these video clips appeared on television, and that's how records are sold abroad. And I was sitting with Bob Erring one day, and he said to me "there are thousands of them over there, there's all kinds of them." We

had to have new clips created to sell new music. We wanted to show these record companies that we wanted to sell.

These were viewed as an inexpensive source of programming. "We thought if we could get the videos," recalled Schneider, "and package them skillfully, there would be an appetite for them."

Bob Pittman, the so-called *Wunderkind* of radio, did the obligatory *Billboard* interview. WASEC could not have asked for a better front page subbanner: "Cable Channel Seen Helping Record Sales." Pittman told the influential trade magazine:

> It will be as important as radio, but more importantly, we are targetting to the record buyer. And we will be putting more of an emphasis on new music than radio does. We will take extra pains, in fact, to sell new music. We will also explain who the new artists is.
>
> Radio is going through a big problem now because nobody wants to take a shot with new music. But they are all complaining that there is no new good music out there, just the same old artists, and the excitement of music is dying down. What we will do is expose a whole new genre of artists and we will give them familiarity and break them. Radio will then have new artists to draw from. A music radio station will benefit from having this service in their market. The end result also is that record labels will now have two very strong promotional weapons for product.

In interviews and a press release a highly amorphous blueprint for the network was unveiled. Music Television featured stereo transmission. Subscribers would see and hear artists performing visual interpretations of their music, twenty-four hours a day, seven days a week. There would be special programs, such as concerts, movies, and interview shows hosted by video jocks or veejays.

MTV would be an advertiser-supported cable service targeted at the youth demographic—a group considered "light television viewers."

The music satellite network down-linked free to cable companies with eight minutes of advertising: six nationally and two for local MSO operators.

Schneider, finally, announced plans to hire seventy people. Already on the payroll were a number of young record people "who really know the business." This included Lack, Pittman, Seibert, and Sykes. Larry Divney, former station manager at Chicago's WSL-FM, was hired as sales vice president. Carolyn Baker moved from Warner Records to direct acquisitions and talent. Sue Steinberg followed in Lack's footsteps from Nickelodeon. At the time of the release most had been with the company for some time. One of the group speculated: "They probably didn't want to announce anything until the concept was approved by the board, at which point they started getting the press stuff out." Another employee indicated that the formal announcement was merely a ploy to create a sense of momentum.

John Lack sweetened the format by suggesting that clips should be three to four minutes in short form, taken from an established playlist. This would cut creeping production costs for record labels.

Pittman added the information that 80 percent of the programming would be video clips, with a veejay interrupting the music with two or three spots on the hour for rock "news" and tour dates. At the time MTV didn't have enough clips to fill dayplay yet alone a twenty-four-hour service.

Some record companies were beginning to have second thoughts about MTV. An A&M executive said, "My gut feeling is this would be a good idea." Al Bergamo at MCA noted that its a "positive step, people now have another source to go to sell their music to video." He also liked the idea of short clips due to the lower production costs. His corporate superiors disapproved. An unspoken truth was the bottom-line reality that the industry was spinning its wheels as sales continued to drop and company employees received pink slips, even in the executive suites. FM rock radio, once the savior of the industry in the 1960s, was stagnating. Les Garland, then at Atlanta Records, recalled: "How many times can you hear 'Layla' or 'Stairway to Heaven'? In my travels that's what I found on every station. I thought 'Gee, there ought to be something that radio is going to wake up and do.' MTV seemed like just what was needed." He was in a distinct minority at the time. Convincing the record labels to provide clips was a top priority. Then came the task of selling the concept to cable operators and advertisers.

Meanwhile on Madison Avenue and in Cable Country

"You'll never look at music the same way again" was the original slogan for MTV. Ex-senior vice president Bob McGroarty recalled the task to convince Madison Avenue: "At first, advertisers thought we were crazy, a bunch of guys working out of a phone booth." In the beginning he was right. Analyst Ira Tumpowski remembered: "We never saw them. It was a matter of getting them on the phone and getting them here to talk to us." MSOers described the MTV sales people as "impertinent, arrogant, punks, or worse." "Visual radio" or music television was perceived more as a negative concept than a "hands-on experience."

Madison Avenue as portrayed in books of fiction and film can resemble a Darwinian jungle. The battle for accounts can be brutal. Clients are wooed with charts, graphs, the results of tests, and presentations. For executives a new account can be lucrative, providing more status and usually a bonus. The loss of a client leads to less desirable consequences. There is a strong conservative streak in the corridors of ad agencies, but on occasion a company may take a risk. If it works, others will follow in lemming-like fashion.

Cable in the early 1980s was a "brand new game." The waters were uncharted. Advertising clients were very reserved. Arnie Semsky, media director of Baiten, Barton, Durstine, & Osborne, Inc., was cautious about a proposed all-music channel, telling the *Wall Street Journal* that "the execution will determine how well it is received." BBD&O was quite familiar with music on television, having supplied the "Your Hit Parade" charts for a number of years.

Larry Blasius of the same agency recalled that MTV had a "conceptual sales problem with clients who still have a problem with rock and roll, similar to the way they felt about rock radio when it first emerged. They'd rather not get involved."

Lack's Columbus-connection "Sight on Sound" premiered, some six weeks behind schedule, on Friday, April 3, 1981 at the prescribed time, 4:30 P.M. Producer Robin Brown promised, "We'll be offering viewers a bunch of menu selections. Each song will be chosen by the viewer. We might offer a choice of The Pretenders' 'Brass in Pocket' or Queen's 'Another One Bites the Dust' or AC/DC's 'Back in Black.' Viewers will vote [through their interactive QUBE console] for their favorite and the biggest vote getter will be played."

A library of 200 clips had been obtained. Brown did concede that the show's artist selection was uneven. "Some groups I have mucho tape on," he told the *Dispatch,* "and others just one clip." He might have elaborated that promotional clips were made available by a handful of major labels—primarily for the European market.

"SOS" included a Battle of the Bands weekly, pitting one group against another. The winner would get a new match the following week to heighten viewer interest. Eventually a "finalist" would be selected by the interactive viewers. This was a partial precursor for "Basement Tapes."

Trivia questions were posed to the audience. Each correct answer was worth a number of points. The first QUBE subscriber to reach one hundred points was to receive a prize from the sponsor, Golden Circle Stores, a dominant local record merchandiser.

The host of the ninety-minute show was radio personality Tim

Smith, the music director of WLVQ. The program was rerun four times weekly.

WASEC executives highlighted their case in the press. Most of the media blitz was in the trade papers, such as *Variety, Billboard, Advertising Age,* and *Cablevision*—the papers read religiously by potential contributors of clips, cable operators, and advertisers. Their participation was essential if MTV was to make it.

Publicist Margaret Wade, who joined Warner-Amex a year earlier after leaving HBO, orchestrated the press campaign. Her task was a difficult one. The mass media, print and electronic, ignored the planned music channel.[1] Nonindustry video and music publications bypassed the project.

The National Cable Television Association was scheduled to hold its annual convention in Los Angeles the closing days of May 1981. A week prior to the cable operators' meeting Bob Pittman provided *Variety* with a lengthy interview. He filled out the format and made another pitch to the record industry. Significantly, the writer was from the trades' music section rather than the usual video slot.

Pittman overcalculated and estimated that MTV would have a 400-clip library by the opening date.[2]

Some of the record labels were slowly beginning to cooperate. Some concessions were made in the interim. Pittman promised to "guarantee air play to *all* new acts." He might have qualified the statement with "if they fit the format." However, he was desperate for more building blocks, as clips were called. Another concession was the superimposition of the name of the artist, song, album, and label at the opening and close of each clip to be aired.

Perry Cooper, an Atlantic Records (part of WCI) executive, was still hesitant but planned an increase of video clips for MTV, which at the time was guaranteeing exposure. Dave Edmunds' "Almost Saturday Night," plus clips by Phil Collins, ABBA, and other concert excerpts were promised. The clips would be promotional, in keeping with MTV's strategy. "We're in the business of getting artists exposed. It wouldn't help to charge for the clips. This is a new format that's got to be given six months to a year to work out—just like a new radio station." Cooper tossed in a qualifier: "It's rare that an artist can break through video." One can only surmise Col. Tom Parker's reaction to that comment. Others were still pessimistic.

At Chrysalis, Linda Carhart was willing to experiment with MTV, stating, "We want to test it first." However, she added a sour note: "At some point we might want to start charging for the use of these clips." This ran counter to Pittman's game plan. "We don't want to get involved with producing. We've developed a mutually beneficial relationship with the labels. It's going to be much easier for them to get something on here than on radio." This was quite correct as there were only an estimated 800 clips in existence—one-third of the number of albums being released annually.

The format was beginning to flesh out. MTV would be AOR, similar to the format introduced at WNBC-AM in 1977. There was one major difference. The music channel would be "narrowcast"—a dirty word in the vocabulary of record makers disgusted with radio "fragmentation." "We're not playing all kinds of music," Pittman said. A fairly standard AOR rotation was planned: "power current," "current," "power oldie," and "oldie." These would later be renamed. Depending on the weight category, the visual product would be cyclically rotated in three-, six-, and eight-hour spans determined by call-outs.

Promotions also played a significant role in the format. "We are going to run a lot of contests," Pittman said, "but they are going to be on a big scale. We might rent a jet and fly four contest winners to Japan for a concert."[3]

John Lack carried the message to the NCTA convention. More than 15,000 people mulled around the display booths and exchanged information, mostly gossip, at the massive Convention Center. Despite the numbers there were few musically oriented exhibits or promotions.

Lack was the chief conference spokesperson for WASEC. He stressed the demographic and psychographic aspects of the planned network. He repeated the argument that the window or market MTV was aiming for had not yet been "narrowcast" on a satellite signal.

Convincing cable operators of the viability of MTV's product appeal was difficult. Many rural and suburban MSO systems had their traditional twelve channels filled. Adding another network meant bumping a familiar existing service. Lack's reply was, "We assured them it would give them lift—that is, new subscribers."

FCC regulations required that stations within a thirty-five-mile radius be broadcast even if duplication takes place. The "must carry" edict frequently forced operators to broadcast duplicate feeds strictly on the basis of geography. The three commercial networks could be multiply represented with a few independents, depending on location. The competition for slots on these limited cable systems was fierce, and watched with keen interest by Madison Avenue. The new franchises being granted in major markets were scrutinized. Cable operators were the ultimate gatekeepers for the satellite networks, as advertisers kept close tabs on the number and size of households an outlet was servicing. Numbers and household characteristics were preeminent. Number crunching was something they understood. Lack's ammunition consisted of surveys undertaken by WASEC's Marshall Cohen and the stereo requirement of the music network. While at WNBC Bob Pittman stated his belief that positive research findings should be used in a station's advertising campaign. In Los Angeles, the WASEC team was doing just that.

QUBE data showed that the ideal viewer for the "SOS" program was a teenage male from a middle- or upper-status level household. There is little doubt that these statistical findings "were used as part of the research that built the plans for MTV," acknowledged an insider. The Battle of the Bands especially provided invaluable information to WASEC as to the demographic profiles and musical preferences of the viewers. Carol Stevenson noted: "For example, we did one interactive music survey in which we asked viewers their opinions of various types of music." The show ran for ten weeks. The data traveled to New York. The "SOS" findings were overshadowed by the material commissioned by TMC's vice president of programming, Marshall Cohen.

Cohen was one of the "whiz kids" employed at the Movie Channel in 1980. The then twenty-nine-year-old native of Erie, Pennsylvania, graduated from Pennsylvania State University with a B.A. in communications. He also earned a masters degree at the University of Florida and was an A.B.D. (all but dissertation) in research and communications. In 1979, he was employed as a researcher at Hamilton and Staff, a Washington-based political consulting firm. Shortly afterward Cohen joined the Lou Harris and Associates polling firm in the same capacity. "I was senior research associate there," he recalls," which is really a research analyst." There Cohen worked on a number of marketing projects involving ABC Television, the Teleprompter Corp., and the Gannett newspaper chain. Cohen and others left the famous firm to form Dresner, Morris, and Tortorello (DMT). One of their clients was WASEC. "I was doing a study for the Movie Channel . . . presenting results, and having a lot of meetings with the executives, and then finally Bob Pittman hired me to come to work for him." In July 1980, he officially joined TMC. Cohen hired the Opinion Research Corporation (ORC) to conduct the first "concept test" of Lack's formulation.

The concept or feasibility test involved a random telephone sample in which participants were read a ten-sentence paragraph. The first question was, "How interested would you be in receiving an all-music channel?" Cohen commented further in the survey:

> This is a channel that you would not only hear some of the current rock music, but you would also see the performers performing the song. I remember saying it would have commercials . . . it would have announcers to tell you a little bit about the music and to give you some

information about the artists, up-coming tours, and album releases. The channel wasn't developed at that point, so we were talking about a vision that we had.

This data was used at the January meeting to decide the fate of MTV. After the approval, the second major music study was undertaken in April 1981.

This was the "market segmentation study." A sample was taken of 600 to 750 individuals in the targeted age bracket of twenty to forty. The respondents were asked the usual social demographic questions regarding gender, age, race, education, income, marital status, and other fundamental SES (socio-economic-status) items and musical preferences. Cohen described the second study:

> We were testing a big list of musical performers, and then we used the interest or likings scores of the performers to segment the groups. We actually had about six or seven different segments, all of which had slightly different demographic compositions that would play a different interest in the concept. And included in that research was asking people what they thought the veejays should look like, what they should wear, how they should act a little bit, what we should cover in the news, a little bit about their life style, and a little bit about some of their beliefs.

Cohen's version of psychographics and music "came from Bob Pittman's radio experience." The profile that emerged was "what we were looking for, and what we were trying to look at, was a way of building coalitions within playing a kind of music on this channel, but to not try to break over, and try to get everybody . . . some of the profile was dictated by the fact [that] we were delivering on cable. The twenty-three-, twenty-four-year-old educated, affluent, suburban viewer—that was essentially the profile of MTV and still is to a large extent."

"Psychographics," wrote radio analyst Rob Balon, "is quite simply, our way of categorizing people by stated attitudes, observable social behavior or lifestyle, and psychological traits." Once that has been determined, according to Arnold Mitchell of Stanford Research Institute (SRI), a media format or ad campaign can be devised by applying the values and life style information to the targeted group. "Choice is based on values . . . over more capability."[4]

Pittman was a confirmed believer in psychographics. He had used the methodology quite successfully in Chicago and New York. He told the *New York Times:*

> I'm concerned not only with how people use a product, but what is going on in their lives, . . . When you're dealing with a music culture—say

people aged twelve to thirty—music serves as something beyond entertainment. It's really a peg they use to identify themselves. It's representative of their values and their culture. You're dealing with a culture of
TV babies. They can watch, do their homework, and listen to music at
the same time.

The life styles of viewers were especially employed to explain the
twenty-four-hour format. "Some people get confused because your
highest viewing level is prime time. But 70 percent of viewing is done
outside of these hours. Anyway," said Pittman, "we're dealing with an
age group not on a traditional viewing schedule. They don't work a
nine-to-five day, so they have more flexibility." This all-day feature
suggested by the Movie Channel's acceptance separated MTV from all
its competitors, who segregated nearly all the rock shows on weekends
after the 11:00 news.

Using psychographic terminology and Cohen's data, Lack told the
media and assembled cable operators that MTV would deliver the "up-
scale adult" and teens: "Our concept is to reach out for target
audiences that are not traditional, high-profile TV viewers. Teenagers
are the demographic group least interested in TV." He also mildly
indicated that MTV might reach an older viewship. "It's exciting to us,
because we can sell more effectively," he claimed. "Saturday Night
Live," in its heyday, had fully 40 percent of its audience over thirty-
five years of age, beyond the prime demographic we're looking at."
The prime demographic was "the television babies who grew up on TV
and rock and roll."

This was a strong selling point as the postwar baby boomers,
depending on how they are defined, comprised an increasingly sought-
after segment of the population. This highly desirable but elusive
psychographic unit was regularly underrepresented in Nielson surveys
of television usage.

The April WASEC study found that a surprisingly high 85 percent of
their sample would watch music video. They equally expressed a
desire for stereocasts, as 94 percent owned the two-track systems.
Sixty percent of the respondents kept their equipment in the same
room as the TV set. Consequently, continued Lack: "Bob Pittman,
who's programming the station, insisted that every cable firm taping it
have a stereo audio capability and he convinced us he was right."[5]

He agreed with Becky Sue Epstein, of the "Radio Picture Show,"
that "it is only fair to mention . . . that television is not known for its
quality sound reproduction." To solve this problem, operators were
required to purchase a "stereo transmission processor" from "a company recommended by MTV," said one operator, Roger Wise. "It was

about two grand." The actual cost was $1,400. The processor developed by Dolby Laboratories featured two components that pick up the satellite signal and then transfer it to the operators' FM band. To allay operators' complaints, pollster Roth noted that "stereo came out as a very important factor in our research into the consumer." "What's more," added Lack, "it let them sell stereo capability at an average of $1.50 extra a month." In many communities stereo became a pay or tiered option. Subscribers got the programming in mono, and had to pay extra for the enhanced audio set-up. Some operators merely purchased the processor, but did not have an FM capability or just ignored it.

In the wake of the convention WASEC issued a press release claiming that 2.1 million households would be receiving MTV on August 1. This was some 400,000 hookups ahead of their original projections.

With computer printouts and other data sources, Pittman began putting the actual format and setting together. The market segmentation study of 150 artists was designed to discover the musical preferences of those sampled. Many of the higher scoring performers, however, did not have video clips or their record companies were being uncooperative. In some instances, as with "SOS," Pittman had to take what he could get in the way of "promo" videos. Candidly Sykes admits "Granted we were missing a lot of artists at the beginning because video hadn't really done anything until MTV launched." "Most of what we had was from new-wave British groups," recalls Ronald L. "Buzz" Brindle, formerly of MTV, "who were already very conscious of video's power. They had already cultivated a 'look' and the British directors had cultivated a style, one that still dominates. . . . Back then the British videos just looked better—they were instantly recognizable against the American ones." A sizable number were of bands virtually unknown across the Atlantic Ocean. This would prove a blessing in disguise as desperation would later become innovation.

The psychographically determined format created problems even prior to the launch date. Carolyn Baker, then the director of talent and acquisitions, recalls: "I voiced my opinion to Bob—we all talked about it. Bob comes from radio. . . . He knew what they wanted was an AOR channel. 'The AOR audience is not conducive to black music. Cable's in the suburbs.' " Radio in the early 1980s was segregated. Urban contemporary was for blacks. Lack concurred that it was "everything that was not AOR."

Pittman used the research data to support MTV's definition of rock and roll. "We chose rock because the audience was larger," he noted. "The mostly white rock audience was more excited about rock than the largely black audience was about rhythm and blues." One insider present at the time said, "He understands how to use words toward an end, but he's the kind of person who will only use 'the numbers' to tell you anything he wants at any given moment." Pittman's personal reasoning was fairly simply. Cable, nationally, was in predominantly white suburbs and rural communities. Many urban centers were not wired for cable or the channels were inaccessible. Veejay Mark Goodman would report this view: "We have to play music we think an entire country is going to like, and certainly we're a rock and roll station." Suburban, white youths were more affluent than their black, urban counterparts—a fact time buyers readily accepted. Black music did not fit the MTV narrowcast model; nor did oldies, as most of the video clips in the library were from the post-1977 era. Despite future charges of racism, Pittman and most associates were more pragmatists wedded to their perception of "who was out there."

At the NCTA convention MTV indicated that search for five "video jocks" was moving toward a final selection. The process was a long and arduous one. Cohen's research had provided a general model. Veejays should be clean shaven. Casual clothing styles were measured. The targeted audience did not object to a black video jock. Still, the recruitment team, led by Sue Steinberg, was not altogether sure what they desired. "Nobody knew what a veejay was and what they did—no one on earth," according to Fred Seibert. "No matter what anybody says, nobody knew." A massive search was launched to find the "right" people who fit the amorphous model. Pittman was vague as to what he was looking for. "Good guides who could sublimate their egos, be human faces you could relate to," said the ex-program director. This description easily could have come from his original WNBC-AM format. John Sykes had an inkling:

> There were no specifics except that we wanted to create a human status for MTV. We wanted those individuals who would get up and wouldn't try to become stars, that wouldn't try to become entertainers, but those people would come up and let the music be the star. That could move the music along, deliver the information, incredible information I might add regarding what music was coming out, anything special about the music that was already on the channel, and what MTV programming was coming up down the line. We basically put the jocks there to move the music. For that reason we didn't look for celebrities, we looked for those people who wouldn't be overbearing or overpowering, or overpower the audience, but someone who would be there to, in a casual way move the music along, that is exactly what we were looking for [in] the veejays.

Ads were placed in the trades announcing the openings at MTV. The response was more than expected. From all corners of the nation photos, resumes, air checks, and even video clips arrived. The applicants were predominantly media people, but many amateurs swelled the ranks. More than 1,500 potentials were auditioned. The overflow of applicants was narrowed down to 150 for taped interviews in New York, Chicago, and Los Angeles.

Jim Feldman, a journalist, described his unsuccessful attempt at video stardom. At his initial interview with MTV he was peppered with questions:

> "Why do you want to be a veejay?" "Why do you want to be on TV?" "Are you willing to give up a tremendous amount of your privacy?" "How much do you know about music?" "How would you handle interviews with rock stars?" "How well do you take direction?" "Could you start right away?" "Are you contractually obligated elsewhere?"

The interviewer attempted to impress Feldman with the difficulties of the role of veejay. The producer said, "It's almost a seven-day-a-week job . . . Veejays have to do lots of research . . . read biographies . . . listen to albums . . . watch all the clips . . . go to concerts, clubs, parties. . . . Veejays participate in writing scripts . . . shoot five days a week . . . personal appearances. . . ." The job description was more a scare tactic, Feldman believed.

Veejays would work nine-to-five and do promotional appearances on the weekends. Seven days of programming segments had to be taped in five. Wardrobe changes would interrupt the filming. One of the chosen would later remark, "When we say music all day and all night we mean it. I've never worked so hard at *anything*."

The morning of Feldman's audition he worried: "What to wear?" He experienced the usual "cattle call" jitters.

> When I arrived at the studio where the tape auditions were being held, I was handed over twenty pages of copy to study before my big chance. Short announcements, fully scripted news stories about Keith Richards, the Beatles, etc., copy for an MTV T-shirt pitch spot, short items about Ian Hunter, Glenn Frey, "Tainted Love," and Bill Wyman, and other short spots. Boy did I study hard."
>
> Finally, it was my turn. I twitched too much, but in general I think I handled the scripted news stories well. The short news items, some of which I had to improvise, were okay, too. And the T-shirt spot was fine; I made up a little story about going out dancing in my MTV T-shirt. But oh, did I blow it when it came time for my spontaneous video resume. And, if possible, things only got worse after that.

Feldman joined the legion of 144 that didn't make it. One of the judges said, "There were six who were chosen to begin with . . . after looking at the 1,500 people you would have picked those six . . . these were the people that made the most sense. There was nothing much more than that . . . who makes sense, who comes across."

The original choices were actress Nina Blackwood, Alan Hunter, Meg Griffin, and broadcasters Mark Goodman and J.J. Jackson. Martha Quinn was hastily employed after Griffin departed the proposed channel.

Official press releases announcing the employment of veejays stressed their role would be "maintaining the continuity of the channel." Martha Quinn provided one view: "The veejays are the human factor. The audience can identify with us. . . . They can certainly identify with me more than they can with Pat Benatar, I'm one of them." Image appears to have been a major consideration rather than musical sophistication or media experience.

Alan Hunter was an actor by profession. He has been described by Martha Quinn as "just the boy next door" or, in the words of a TV critic, as "a sophomore on his way to class." Hunter, while working as a bartender, met Bob Pittman at the yearly "Way Up North in Mississippi" picnic in Central Park. A month later, in mid-July, two weeks prior to take-off, he was invited to audition. He admits, "I was pretty horrible. I was confused about what the show was, so I didn't know what to do. As it turned out, that was okay because nobody knew exactly what it was. Every time I was called back, I got another explanation." A graduate of Millsaps College from Jackson, Pittman's old school and hometown, he was hired as the fifth veejay. Hunter kept his bartending position for several months after the launch, being totally convinced that MTV would fail. He was also dissatisfied with his salary. After the debut of MTV, the veejay selection process was called into question. One insider privately grumbled, "that was one roll of the dice that didn't quite work out."

There were other components of the "mood" to be put into place. Clips and veejays were only part of the visual package.

The Gumby Logo

Fred Seibert's major assignment from Pittman was to orchestrate the graphics for the emerging format. He immediately turned to a then "unknown" company, Manhattan Design. Pat Gorman admits:

> We were a fledgling company at that time, I guess we were only a year and a half old, or something like that. Anyway, he came to us, and I remember we had this tiny little office, one room with one window and the three of us . . . Patty Rogoff and Frank Olinsky . . . cramped in there

. . . in the Village . . . we had only one room. And he [Seibert] came and he sat down. He had to sit down on a wooden stool because there were no extra chairs, then said that he would like us to design a logo for a music channel. At the time they weren't even sure what the music content was going to be. They knew that it would have rock and roll, but they said that it might be mixed music. They were still formulating the content of the station, and they did not have a name. So everybody sat around trying to think up names of the station, and then come up with a logo.

Seibert's choice of the company was based on a lifelong friendship with Frank Olinsky. They had grown up together in Huntington, Long Island. They were boyhood friends. "Frank and I had listened to all manner of rock and roll records from our early childhood on, and when the whole assignment for MTV came my way he was really the first, and virtually the only person I wanted to consider working on it because I knew that not only did he have the proper design skill, but he had the right attitude," said Seibert.

The design firm had been chosen, but there was no specific sense of direction. The MTV blueprint was evolving. "It was like jello that hadn't set yet," says Gorman, "and you didn't know what shape we were going to be." There were several considerations. A twenty-four-hour music video channel in America was a totally new concept. Previous attempts had failed. Indeed, television and rock, except for the early days of "American Bandstand," had rarely mixed. Even Seibert was a bit leery. He told the *Village Voice*, "I was honestly skeptical about the concept. I had learned everything I knew about music from TV when I was a kid, when there was 'Clay Cole's Discotech.' Television and music had made sense, but it had never work." Later, he would state: "The fact of the matter is that they have never gone together comfortably. There are a lot of very good people who had tried to make it go together, but it just didn't work all that well." As the music channel concept began to formalize, Gorman, Rogoff, and Olinsky had some notion of what Seibert wanted design-wise. Seibert told them he wanted something as "distinctive as the famous CBS eye, he didn't give us any direction," said Gorman. "It could be letters . . . could be an image . . . it could be anything, but it should be as memorable as the CBS eye." MTV wanted something unique, but nobody had a specific model. The only stipulation was that MTV be included on the bottom of the logo. Various graphics were submitted. Seibert commented:

We were trying to work from various standard rules of how you do these things, like logos. One of the standard rules is that the logo is always the same. In any kind of marketing which is usually based in advertising you want to come up with a very stationary, a trademark that presents itself in somebody's eyes. Its the same always, so that no matter where you see that trademark, whether its on television, or in a magazine, or more importantly on the store shelf, you can identify the product rapidly, and therefore make a purchase of it. We knew that those basic rules were really correct. You needed something that would be memorable, that took care of all the marketing and business things. But we also knew that a twenty-four-hour a day network was radically different than any of the other networks that had really been presented on television. When the NBC Peacock moved in all of it was fine, but it was more or less cute. It didn't necessarily make you pay any more attention to NBC, because you were really more interested in if the program was something you liked. We knew that we were going to have an environment that was very competitive, and not only that, but at the time our material was not going to be explicit to us. You were going to be able to see video clips all sorts of other places. We knew that we had to make a constant impression on our audience as to how we were different than everybody else. Manhattan Design put together a plethora of sketches. Their notion was an "internative" or an animated logo. The reaction, originally, was "it was attractive, but it's too crazy."

Pat Gorman of Manhattan Design, lost in the accolades for the innovative logo, recalls:

We designed the M and the T and V, which was a little story into itself. Patty broke off, my partner did the M. She made the M big and blocky. She spent eight hours doing it. Frank wasn't in the office at the time, she and I were there. And she kept coming back and forth to me, because we're very interactive in our studio. And somebody would come up with this, and I would say, "Well you know I think the perspective should be from this direction, don't show it for one pop, show it straight on." And she came over to me and said, "It needs a TV, what would you do?" So I made a TV on the side. . . . And I made it very shifty, kind of pointed. Frank came back to the office at that point and said, "This is really ugly, and if we're going to submit this the TV needs to be different." So he took the TV, my idea for the TV, basically an idea I came up with, and he went out in the hallway and spray painted it. It should be more like a graffiti, it should be more like a safe rather than decorated. And we all liked that idea, the de-facing. You know, there are various spirits of rock and roll, how do you actually put the spirit of rock and roll where you don't draw musical notes, you know what I mean. You want something that's the personality of it. One of the personalities of it is that the big M to us was almost like Superman, literally. You know, that child-like da da da da, you know like big and important. And the TV is like a defacement of that. The rock and roll has both aspects. So that was the concept behind it.

For the trio the burning question was, "Would the designs fly?" It was revolutionary. A total departure from television and advertising norms. The reaction at "Wamex" was mixed. Seibert and consultant

Alan Goodman championed the design and concept. "We fought like hell to keep it that way," according to one. Opponents said, "You mean it itsn't going to look like *Star Wars?*" The space film was *the* movie, for teens, at the time. Reaction at Manhattan Design was defensive: "People actually came up . . . and said they didn't like it, and they thought it was terrible." "No, it's going to look like Gumby" was the twosome's standard reply.

After a great deal of haggling, the mobile concept was accepted. However, the opponents temporarily prevailed. Gorman recalled:

> Then they said no, go out and hire the best designers, the most famous design persons, and have them all submit. Because we won't go with the totally unknown, and some really wild ideas. So they went to all these other groups, and the other groups didn't really submit anything that was rock and roll. I don't think they were interested in the concept the same way Manhattan Design was. Then they decided MTV would go with it, and from there determined to commission different ad agencies to work with our ideas."

Ogilvy and Mather did not fare well in this dispute. They were "too traditional." "The fact of the matter," recalls Seibert, "is that the work that they did for MTV just wasn't very good." MTV executives were taking a critical look at the prestigious ad agency.

The slow growth of the pay Movie Channel was also creating dissension. Outside some specific markets, TMC was running a distant third to HBO and Showtime.

Privately a number of unfair "we told you so's" were being aimed at John Lack. Lack was the media front man, appearing in the *New York Times,* in on the hiring of the advertising firm, but he was only one member of the selection committee. Despite denials, the American Express factor was considered dominant in the account award. Somebody had to take the blame. The manner in which Ogilvy and Mather was chosen remained a sore point. MTV executives had friendships with other agency persons that would be manifest in the near future.

The entertainment world is almost an isolated planet. Personnel contacts are more important than credentials. A close examination of MTV, as with nearly all the media, reveals a web of personal ties that suggest employment and accounts are not totally based on objectivity. This can operate positively and negatively. One former MTV employee confessed: "I lucked out. . . . I rolled the dice and it worked." Others are not so fortunate and chief operating officers find their heads on the chopping blocks.

While the agency debate continued the "Gumby" logos began to emerge. The logos in final form ran the gamut from a jungle elephant to french fries and ketchup to shaving cream—all transformed into the big M little TV symbol. The most familiar is the moon landing scenario, which was the first to be aired on MTV. A white rocket with black trim breaks away from its launch site mooring. A blood red background, reminiscent of Antonioni's *Red Desert,* dramatizes the opening scene. A moon landing follows, with two astronauts implanting an MTV flag. The massive M overshadows, as planned, the TV. The M changes colors, with yellows, then stripes like Joseph's fabled multicolored coat. Segue to the studio controlling the broadcast content with video screens repeating the ever-dynamic color configurations. Back to the moon segment in a ten-second bite (segment). A voice-over announces, "This is MTV, music television. We're here all day, all night." Manhattan Design had prevailed.

The last week of July MTV sponsored the obligatory preview press party at the West Massachusetts Studio. Two somewhat conflicting reactions to the visual product emerged. *Cablevision*'s reviewer Robert MiDatteo wrote: "The preview I saw was impressive, including videotapes constructed around songs by The Pretenders and Dire Straits. Promotional video for recording artists has produced some amazingly wild and free-spirited tapes. By drawing upon these tapes, MTV should have some of the loosest imagery on television." Michael Shore saw it quite differently. A music video reviewer for numerous publications, he perceived the fare as "an endless avalanche of essentially the same corporate pomp rock acts that AOR radio had always been playing (and which rock video was supposed to supplant), like REO Speedwagon and Rush, and nary a Devo or Bowie in sight; loads of eyecatching MTV in-house promos; and sandwiched in between, the MTV VJs, the ones who'd had that magic . . . each appeared to have marched, made-to-order, out of a demographic test tube; together, they seemed to cover nearly all of the possible audience bases." This was exactly what the format was designed to do. Shore would be one of many to challenge the "magic" because it did not fit his aesthetic.

On July 31 a caravan of hired buses, taxis, and limos embarking from WASEC's Manhattan headquarters across the George Washington Bridge to Fort Lee, New Jersey, population 32,000.

Sandy and Bob Pittman went in a limo. Fred Seibert was accompanied by Alan Goodman and friends. Approximately 150 employees and friends traveled to the downstairs banquet room of The Loft, an average, two-level restaurant and bar that had been rented for the launching of MTV at 12:01 A.M.

Schneider absented himself from the liftoff. He explains:

I don't want to go there. I want to send the kid to work on Nickelodeon to [get the credit] for them, ok? Because then the people, they get the psychic impound. They're the big deal on the creative community and children's programming. I don't want people calling me, that's not what I do. I'll give you an example at CBS. I didn't fight with Norman Lear and the Smothers Brothers. I had the president of the network do it. Why did the president of the network do it? So that when these people had a beef they called him. And if I ever interceded or went and did all these things and took public bows, then I would have emasculated the president of the network, and whenever these guys had a beef they would have called me and gone over his head. So what you do is, you set up an organization, so that within the discipline of children's programming, movies, rock and roll music, you have a front person who has a title, and he or she does all that stuff, the good and the bad. I go home at 5:00 every night because I'm the president. I give support and I hire the right people, and I compensate them, and I discipline them, and show good example, and bail them out when they're in trouble, and teach them and train them, and develop this body of young executives. But I don't have to be out front myself.

Six television sets were strategically placed around the room. Robert Hilburn described the scene as resembling "a winning candidate's headquarters on election night. . . . They cheered wildly when anything came on the screen: the music, the commercials, the station logos." MTV T-shirts were in ample supply. The first words uttered on MTV were John Lack's "Ladies and gentlemen, rock and roll." Seibert's rocket ship logo followed.

The opening video clip was the Buggles' 1979 English hit "Video Killed the Radio Star," directed by Russell Mulcahy. Visions of television sets exploding and destroying vintage radios were accompanied by lyrics such as "pictures came and broke your heart. . . . video killed the radio star." It was nearly a chant. Pat Benatar followed the Buggles and in rapid succession came Rod Stewart, Ph.D., the Who, Cliff Richard, the Pretenders, and Todd Rundgren. Veejay Mark Goodman introduced the artists in a style reminiscent of FM radio.

For John Lack, midnight August 1 was the bewitching hour. His concept had become a hands-on reality. He told the *Los Angeles Times* (the only major daily to cover the event):

> This marks a new step in broadcasting. Most of the national cable channels are just giving you more of what you get on commercial TV: movies, sports, news. We're combining the best of radio—music and stereo sound—and the best of TV—the pictures—to give viewers something they can't get anywhere else.
>
> We want our programming to reflect that difference. We told our production staff to throw out the rules. We want to develop our own spirit and personality so we will relate to our target . . . group.

Seeing his idea come on the air was exciting, but Lack was tiring of the repetitive clichés involving "music and video" and the target audience. Hilburn recalls that "Lack just passed through the crowd most of the evening." Pam Lewis, then publicity chief Margaret Wade's secretary, has another version. She told Lack, "John, I'll never forget looking at you that night, it was like you had given birth to a child." Lack's personal thoughts were: "All of my dreams at that age in my life had been reached. I had a dream. I got someone to fund it. I hired the people to do it and it happened. I mean it was as great a thrill as one could have." Fred Seibert was jubilant:

> I have to say that when the rocket ship went up the first time I really never felt more a part of something on a creative level than I had felt at that moment. The reason is, that it was . . . a thoroughly collaborative project, and absolutely everybody who had had anything to do with any piece of it really had contributed substantially to its success. I just felt very good that I had had the opportunity to bring all of these folks together from Frank Olinsky, who I had known since I was four years old, to a friend from Colossal Pictures who I had met three weeks before. To me that was the exciting thing on a creative level to be involved in such an intensely collaborative effort that worked.

"It was probably one of the high points that anyone can have in life," was John Sykes' initial reaction. "You've seen something that you've put the time and effort into finally go on the air, go on the satellite. . . . It was the beginning of something we all believed in. There was a tremendous amount of excitement, the morale was up and it was just a chance to really do something that hadn't been done before, to really break music on television and create a network."

The uproarious festivities at the Loft did not alter some harsh realities. "We knew there were no more than a million homes watching and even able to receive the signal. Who knows how many people actually have their sets tuned into MTV" said one participant. There would be no overnight Nielson's to consult. Fort Lee's Vision Cable did provide MTV to subscribers. Manhattan and Los Angeles operators were noncommittal. The absence of the new network in the main media centers outraged executives, as it significantly created a major selling roadblock.

The reactions of the record companies and advertisers were more important. The official thirty-second advertising rate was $1,200. The spots were actually selling for $350 and $650. Only 30 percent of the commercial time had been sold to a meager thirteen or fourteen sponsors. "We finally persuaded thirteen hardy souls to come with us. We offered to do their commercials for them, which pissed off the ad agencies." McGroarty noted, "We offered to do special research and promotions. We offered anything and everything to get them to give us a try." Executives at Pepsico accepted the research option, but still harbored doubts. The most active of the time buyers were the film studios. Movie successes were determined by the repeat "youth market." Avco-Embassy, Filmways, United Artists, Universal Pictures, and Warner Brothers purchased advertising space. The Gap Stores, Dolby Laboratories, Pepsico, 7-Up, and the United States Navy joined Warner-Lambert and Jovan as original time buyers.

According to Sykes, most record labels did comply and supplied Australian and European video clips.

> Luckily most of the artists who were fairly well known in the United States were also doing fairly well in the foreign territories where they had to have videos. So it was really no cost to them to take a dab of that video and ship it back to the states and we'd air it. Grantedly we were missing a lot of artists at the beginning because video hadn't really done anything until MTV launched. But we felt that that kind of was an opportunity to play a lot of new bands because we did have some hits, but we also had the opportunity to play a lot of up new artists."

Only Polygram and MCA held back. Some MTV staffers in sour grapes fashion said, "They don't have any significant acts anyway!" Sardonically, John Lack mused to a reporter: "One thing's for sure, when you start out in the basement in Fort Lee, N.J., you can only go up."

Smaller affairs were held in some of WASEC's marketing regions. *Cablevision*'s Michael McCready was flown to Tulsa for the southwestern debut party. He was surprised by the fare on the screen. The montage of animated space walks was a revelation, of sorts. "After the intro," he said, "they broke into the first song, a new-wave number called 'Video Killed the Radio Star.' I was convinced that Warners had commissioned that song, but the Warner people in Tulsa told me otherwise. In any case it was a fitting part."

The Tulsa affair did not go smoothly. Ray Klinge, the local cable operator, had a roomful of potential and signed ad buyers. The network was late in airing commercials. "One of them at least was wondering into what black hole his ad might have disappeared," McCready noted. "There were some nervous moments then." Fifteen minutes later the Majestic Industries spot for school binders aired. "There was an audible sigh" of relief from the WASEC people.

The musical psychographic experiment had begun with "sales on the sluggish side." WCI and American Express were providing a cushion, but as Lack stoically indicated, "I'll be more excited by what we put on a few weeks from now."

Notes

1. The treatment of MTV by the mass media even after its appearance on August 1, 1981 is an interesting tale of what is newsworthy. Most of the major markets, including the media centers, were not receiving the channel. Therefore, it lacked "local interest," except in Los Angeles, an industry city. Most cable systems were either in the suburbs or in rural areas where media music writers are in short supply. *Rolling Stone* finally printed a piece on music video on "Night Flight" and MTV in December, some three months after the network debuted.
2. The actual number of clips in the original MTV library is based on each individual's memory. Estimates vary from 100 to 125.
3. MTV did just that with the "Asia in Asia" promotional contest where five grand prize winners and their guests were flown first-class to Tokyo, Japan, for a five-day stay and they attended Asia's Budokan Arena concert telecast on MTV.
4. Arnold Mitchell's *The Nine American Lifestyles* is one of the most cited handbook's in dealing with media use and buying habits.
5. Stereo was excluded from the original concept test in 1980.

4

"Taking Care of Business"

The gray dawn brought the cold chill of reality. MTV missed the desired mood. MTVers departed The Loft after watching the concept finally on a cable system. Emotions were mixed. It was finally on air, but John Lack, John Sykes, and Bob Pittman didn't like what they saw. Schneider, who did not attend, seemed more upset with MTV's cable exclusion from Manhattan, the nation's media center.

The programming was too slick. It looked like ordinary television. Sykes commented:

> MTV is a mood, not a show. Originally, we had a certain structure and plan. We scripted our veejays. Our set was perfect. But that didn't work. We looked at it and said, "Wait a minute, we wanted to make this irreverent. It's still not irreverent enough, let's mess up the set a little bit, let's dim the lights, and if we make a mistake let's just stumble on our words and keep going, let's not do regular television, that's not what we had set out to do." In order to be successful in creating the environment for this kind of music we had to reflect that in our outer look, which meant give it a rough edge because that's what rock and roll music is, it isn't perfect classical music, it's loud, distorted, irreverent music.

Pittman had stressed that "we don't want any TV show." He bristled at suggested comparisons to other rock music programs such as "American Bandstand." Saturday morning at The Loft he perceived two problems: the set and formal, stiff veejays reading copy and looking mesmerized by the camera. He thought the studio set was like many others on television. As Sue Steinberg would tell *Rolling Stone,* the environment should have an "anything could happen here" structure. John Sykes saw it as the fantasy rec-room of the young. He commented:

> We wanted to put a great stereo in there, lots of records, a couple of off-the-wall things found in old antique shops, and just kind of create an ideal setting, an ideal rock and roll basement, or an ideal rock and roll garage or room whatever, and keep it going, keep it changing as the music changed, and that's why the posters changed daily, the furniture changed once in a while, stereo was updated, things were thrown on and

off the set, to half a Cadillac to half a barber chair, whatever particular thing we could stumble upon.

MTV was not intended to be the "In Concert." There would be changes. Pittman's "gutting" of WNBC's studio was legendary. History was about to be repeated. MTV had to be "much rougher, real and more credible than TV—with plenty of room for spontaneity." This was the mood and the fantasy to be created.

Surgical alterations were to follow. The "idiot" cards had to go. The standard studio lights were dimmed or replaced. Elaborate set changes were made at the Lincoln Scene studio on the west side of Manhattan. Kathy Ankers and Roger Mooney arranged the proper "mood." The end result was "a well-designed studio that looked like something casually thrown together, scripted patter that sounded like it was made up on the spot, an ironclad format that proceeded like a random chain of events, well-trained actors who came on like folks you'd meet at a campus mixer, and a generally perfectionist attitude in bringing about a what-the-hell, let's-boogie mood," according to *Rolling Stone*. As one music critic noted, "Everything was tossed into its proper place." The "mood" was the format. The format created the perimeters for the content of the network.

Doctoring the set design was one problem that was relatively easily fixed; the veejays were another matter. On the takeoff show Mark Goodman appeared to be suffering from stage fright. He had no television experience. His reason for auditioning for MTV was, "I wanted to be a veejay to meet my idols." As Alan Hunter indicated, the veejays did not know what their role was to be. Martha Quinn told *People,* "At first I thought a veejay sat on camera and played records." Her female counterpart Nina Blackwood noted, "I love adventure and this was certainly going to be an adventure—all new and totally *unknown*." In the mind of MTV executives, structured chaos was fine, but that was not what was coming across on the screen.

Seibert admits, "I'll tell you honestly the hardest thing to solve for a very long time was what happened with the veejays, and what do you do with them. . . . In terms of veejay segments they rolled the dice, some it worked some of it didn't." On August 1 the roll came up "snake eyes." Jack Lack elaborated:

> It was very difficult for them to understand, because it was the first time that veejays had ever been created, what their role was to be. They were torn between being television personalities and being radio disk jockeys. It took time to realize what that role was, and how you play it. The first

night it was still in its embryo stage. The child wasn't what it should have been. It's a lot better today.

A *Rolling Stone* writer months later objected that the veejays had a terrible case of "continuing camera fright (severe in a couple of cases) and the apparent belief that they are speaking to an audience composed entirely of twelve-year-olds."

The "golden gut" selection of veejays did create problems. "Triple J" Jackson was the only one of the five with any television experience, dealing with music, having worked for ABC-TV's "Eyewitness News" in Los Angeles. On-camera nonchalantness had to be learned. Nina Blackwood said, "In this job I don't have to play a part. My role is to *play* myself." That is probably the best job description of a veejay, a term MTV introduced into America's lexicon. "I think we've all been learning to be ourselves on TV," Martha Quinn stated to Herb Swartz. Veejays were to ad-lib after doing their "homework." The veejays preview the video clips and follow the learned script. "It's part of our homework," says Alan Hunter. "When I'm looking at my show script to see what I'm going to be talking about and what I'll be 'playing,' if there's a video I need to refresh my memory on, I'll play it back and come up with an observation, maybe even write down a little tidbit to get my brain going right before they call, '5-4-3-2-1.' "

Mistakes are permissible. A goof now and then just added to the "informality." Jackson's ad-libs, like "This is brown Jackson here with news of Jackson Browne," did get people in the control booth uptight.

The casualness is role playing. The veejays come well prepared to the studio at 9:30 A.M. to film their forty-five minutes of filler between videos, commercials, and network IDs. These "live" spots, filmed days in advance, are to cover five hours of air time. After the "rah rah" five finish and break for a meal and wardrobe changes, another day of "intros" and outros" are recorded. The veejays do their spontaneous filming fourteen hours per day, five days a week. One veejay was quoted in *People* as saying, "When we say music all day and all night, we mean it. I've never worked so hard at *anything*." On weekends veejays did promotional work, such as personal appearances. The veejays are popular with fans, frequently mobbed by autograph hounds, but media critics have not been kind. Nina Blackwood, especially, has been mimicked, at times brutally, on "Saturday Night Live." Many music video industry people felt the satires of MTV on "Saturday Night Live" were inspired by Dick Ebersol, who also produces NBC's "Friday Night Videos," a direct competitor for the weekend youth market with MTV. Nina does have her defenders, however. Fred Seibert is one: "Poor Nina for four years has taken alot of abuse . . . even in the company. When I first saw her original audition tape, she comes alive on the television screen. Even if she is stumbling over the words that she says. And to this day she still continues to come alive. She doesn't come that alive in person . . . or in photographs, but you see her on that video screen and it's magic." Nina asked Columbus QUBE viewers how much they wanted to see her versus the other veejays. The response was "As much or more."

According to John Lack, "Martha Quinn is very good when she doesn't get too full of herself. They're all good, and they were chosen obviously for different reasons . . . different appeals, different audiences." The veejays were in a new genre. Sociologists term this "unclear roles" because formal guidelines have to be improvised. Another point that deserves consideration is that the veejays obtained the jobs due to potential "peer group" identification rather than media expertise.

An *Adweek* writer termed the veejays "Clearasil commercial graduates." Michael Fremer in the *Music Connection* described two of the veejays as suffering from "radio face" wherein the muscles of the face—being unnecessary on radio—atrophy, resulting in a smiling, stiff, expressionless face, as in the case of Jackson, or a smug stiff, expressionless face, as in the case of Goodman. The controversy even in 1986 appears to continue; the veejays are either idolized or ridiculed.

The launch reviews were cautiously positive. Bob Hilburn wrote: "MTV's campaign won't be known for weeks, maybe months (*L.A. Times,* August 4, 1981). *Billboard*'s Laura Foti's piece and Roman Kozak provided descriptions of the intentions of the music network (August 15 and 22, 1981). *Advertising Age* lead with "MTV Sells 30%" (August 24, 1981). *Cablevision,* a major CATV trade, was generally enthusiastic. Publisher Robert Titsch wrote: "We welcome MTV to cable's fold and wish it every success" (August 17, 1981). Reviewer Robert DiMatteo stated: "The channel is a bold example of the cable industry's move toward specialized audience programming" (August 24, 1981). In the next issue *Cablevision* proclaimed, "MTV gets the newcomer-of-the year award hands down." Outside of the trades and the *L.A. Times,* however, MTV received little media coverage.

The presence of *L.A. Times* "Calendar" section reporter Robert Hilburn at the Fort Lee celebration was the only bright spot in an otherwise objectively bleak mass media situation. Hilburn, a veteran music critic, was widely respected and read by record company executives. His positive response would help with MTV's campaign to gain respectability and clips.

The agenda-setting *New York Times* was absent from the happenings at The Loft. The significance of the *Times* is tremendous, as most media gatekeepers use that metropolitan daily as a weather vein. When the *Times* exposes a trend or breaks a story the networks, news magazines, and others generally follow. The "most powerful newspaper in the world" chose to ignore the advent of MTV.

The obvious explanation for this omission is that MTV in August 1981 had little metropolitan or national interest. Breaking into their home-base market became a highly sensitive and volatile issue. There was a growing bitterness toward Manhattan's two cable companies. The feeling transcended corporate goals and was rapidly becoming very personalized. Jack Schneider candidly expressed his sentiments: "We were stunned, hurt and angry. . . . I wanted to shake them and say 'Pay attention, we're doing something here that is significant.' But their reaction was 'yawn.' "

Data obtained in test markets such as Tulsa, Des Moines, Syracuse, and Wichita prompted testimonial ads that appeared in the trade magazines. MTV purchased a full page in the October 10 issue of *Billboard* citing a Tulsa survey with "results underlining the enthusiasm for MTV's unique format." Testimonials by merchandisers, a radio program director, and the local cable company were prominently featured.

Internally executives were concerned. One former top executive outlined the dilemma:

> What was happening is that cable operators were taking the position that they don't care what the programmers were doing because it's their cable system. And programmers were taking the position like, if you don't take our stuff you're going to fail. In fact most people found that they were dependent on each other, and that they better be friends. At the time though, there weren't a lot of friendships going on between cable operators and programmers. . . . But essentially what the reality of the situation was is that we had two things that we needed to do, not only did we have to convince the cable operators that consumers in their area wanted an MTV, but we had a very, very low advertising budget.

Disenchantment with Ogilvy and Mather was rising from in-house grumbling to almost open rebellion. One insider commented that O&M was "an old-line traditional ad agency" that did not understand the concept. Jack Schneider is more philosophical about the situation.

It may have been a mistake in retrospect. Perhaps we didn't handle our relationship with them well. Perhaps they didn't handle their relationship with us well. But you see, when you're starting a beginning business there are all matter of false starts and relationships that are embraced and turned over, but to say it was a mistake is a false statement. There are employees that we have who were right for a business of x-size but who were not right for a business of y-size.

David Ogilvy's legendary firm was not impressing many WASEC executives. The chance of renewing O&M's contract diminished daily. Despite Fred Seibert's expression that his heroes were Ogilvy and singer Ray Charles, the bottom line was grim for the advertising agency. Some of the radio-based promotional ploys planned at MTV didn't fit the more staid campaigns of O&M. Harper White's column in *Ad Age* aptly summarized the feelings at MTV: "These people were giants in the burgeoning industry in the 1950s, '60s and into the '70s. But time passes and so do the creative reigns of these [O&M] and other successful agencies."

Among the complaints was the second-line team O&M was using on the WASEC account. Their original presentation may have been brilliant, but the operationalization needed insight. An agency review was initiated. Reviews of advertising programs are quite common. Some large clients do this on an annual basis. Others engage in the practice when dissatisfaction sets in. One aspect of agency or account review entails other Madison Avenue firms being given the opportunity to compete for the account. At least twelve were anxious to have the lucrative Warner-Amex business.

On the surface John Lack was predicting a doubling of subscribers by the year's end. As of the last day of September, MTV was distributed by 252 cable systems servicing 2.1 million households. He suggested that MTV would break into the Los Angeles area by early 1982. This proved to be wishful thinking.

Advertisers remained on the sidelines. Bob McGroarty noted: "They still seem to be a little doubtful since they haven't quite got a handle yet on how to measure the effectiveness of advertising on cable."

Tom Freston repeated the value of MTV as a promotional outlet to *Billboard*. "But I understand if record companies are still a little unsure about the impact of MTV on LP sales, we think it will become much more evident in the future."

MTV could not penetrate the two major industry windows. Sales reports from other markets serviced by MTV did garner some attention, however. New acts, with MTV exposure, were selling in territories without radio play. A Des Moines merchandiser noted, "At first I couldn't figure out what was happening. Kids were coming in asking for artists I had discontinued. When I asked about their interest they told me about MTV."

MTV would be getting their free promo clips. Pittman's attitude toward Polygram and MCA was being vindicated. "When album rock came along in the 1960s there were record companies such as Buddah and Kama Sutra who did not want to participate . . . with FM radio. We understand where these labels are today. We can't expect every record company to have the vision. Polygram doesn't really have any acts that we want, and as for MCA, we have Tom Petty through his manager."

On a more conciliatory note, Pittman added: "The doors are still open. We will give them opportunities to get on board. But if they don't want to, God bless them. If we play a hit 500 times a year, on our rate card that is $1.5 million worth of free advertising." As the influence of MTV increased the two holdouts did "get on board." However, at the time there was resistance. "It's one thing to have field reports," Jo Bergman commented, "and selling Buggles records in Phoenix, now, that's nice but it's not the kind of thing that decisions get made in sales and promotion for them to actually expect this kind of reaction would take place. It was very early for this, so from our point of view, it was at that time not possible to tell what the relationship was to a video being shown and a record being sold."

Pittman promised "big-scale contests." The on-air promotions soon began in earnest.[1] Two weeks after the August debut, the channel introduced a "One Night Stand" contest. For the price of a stamped postcard, the winner and three friends would be flown by Lear jet to either New York or Los Angeles to see Journey. The dream trip would begin with a limousine ride to the local airport. Boarding the private plane they would find tour jackets for the concert, a Sony Walkman, and Journey's prerecorded tapes. Food and soft drinks would be offered plus a telephone connection to the group.

Eighteen-year-old Margaret Doebler won the first "One Night Stand." She was flown from Stevens Point, Wisconsin, to New York. Another limo greeted her at the airport. A gourmet meal followed, topped off with a concert at the Nassau Coliseum and a backstage meeting with the group. Within nineteen hours Margaret was back in Stevens Point. "It's a fantasy thing for anyone," said John Sykes, the promotions head.

Rumors abounded that Journey's record company, CBS, or the act was actually paying for the well-publicized junket in return for cable exposure. Officially, the Journey promotion was the joint undertaking of MTV and Nightmare, the group's management company. A seasoned broadcaster mused, "Promos of that kind, involving a big name artist or act, are usually paid for by someone besides the station. On that scale it was probably the management group or the label." "It's always a barter situation," says Florida broadcaster Billy Mitchell. "They rarely pick up the entire tab. There's usually some kind of assistance in there somewhere." The usual arrangement is a big-name promotion in exchange for air time for less established acts. MTV needed Journey, however, they didn't have leverage at the time.

A similar one-nighter was scheduled for the Rolling Stones' December appearance at the New Orleans Superdome. Writer Roman Kozak openly wondered "whether Keith or Mick will deign to speak to the winner." Tom Freston aptly summed up the purpose of jetsetting concert promos: "Wherever there's a winner or a destination there is *newsworthiness*." Contest winners did make their local papers and a few of the trades, but MTV was still ignored by the major media, especially in the localities that most mattered. However, the promotions did foster a grass-roots consciousness in the eyes of MTVers. "Through any excitement that they generated it did get our face on the map," says John Sykes forthrightly. "They reflected the image of the programming we had put together. They said something about the attitude of the channel and the way we were going to do things. I think we were almost going to have some fun with television versus a slick serious medium. The promotions always for us have been [sic] a chance to really sweat, like a rough-cutting attitude that we want the channel to possess, to give off the viewers. For that reason the promotions had to be irreverent enough to turn some heads."

Once MTV was actually telecasting, industry critics began popping out of the woodwork. One of the salvos occurred at *Billboard*'s International Talent Forum held at the Sheraton Center Hotel in New York. Not surprisingly, the conference spent a good deal of time on radio bashing. John Sykes on the "Exploring Other Areas" panel took his turn: "AM radio has been forced to add artists to playlists, by the exposure on MTV. In Tulsa, Squeeze is selling for the first time. Where radio stations are afraid to break new acts, because of competition, we're breaking them. We are even giving exposure to unsigned acts, along with the major stars. Balance is the key." This view was one of John Lack's major rationales for the development of music television, which he would call MTV.

Jim Daniels, Rush's manager, felt MTV might hurt concert attendance. "Three years from now," he said, "I don't want somebody to see a video I did today and think "That's Rush.' " John Scher, the moderator, suggested that music videos merely "whet the appetite." Sykes attempted to soothe the talent sellers and buyers with an offer of cooperation. "On a local level we have giveaways, and we advertise and promote up-coming concerts. Right *now,* video and live appearances can coexist," he concluded.

By 1985 Sykes was proved correct. "It's interesting today that we have those concert clips on the air. I think once again at that time because this was a new media form, and one that was not understood by everyone, there were preconceived notions. All at the time anyone had to do was look at the radio model. The fact that old records were played on radio, that helped to sell catalogs and in no way affected what someone thought of the artists today because they were inexperienced."

Sykes' argument may have cooled the panelists, but in reality one of MTV's strongest selling points to record companies continued to be the demographic distribution of its audience. With approximately two million households on line MTV could reach a much larger number of record buyers than a national tour and for less money. The interests of concert promoters and record companies, while similar, did not always coincide. In the midst of the music recession of 1981 subsidized touring was rapidly becoming an expensive luxury that record companies shied away from. Promoters wanted "name" artists in their markets at the lowest cost possible. MTV was an alternative. ON-TV in Los Angeles aired a live "Rod Stewart: Tonight He's Yours—Worth Staying Home For!" from the Forum. Stewart, at the peak of his career, still sold out the Forum. Promoters were clearly uncomfortable with the possibilities, as were managers and artists who made a living off the road. The issue was far from resolved. The day after the Stewart show, the "Rolling Stones Rock and Roll Video Party" was shown on pay-TV.

The polemic was heightened when fourteen to twenty cable markets offered a pay-per-view (PPV) Rolling Stones concert. Some 200,000 households paid $10.00 to watch the Stones and their opening act guitarist George Thorogood. FM simulcasts were included in the package. ON-TV aired the special in the Los Angeles market. Economically the program was labelled a success. ON-TV general manager Richard Whitman acknowledged, "We will be doing more live pay-per-view simulcasts in Los Angeles." Compounding concert promoters' fears, he added: "It has to be considered as a practical alternative to touring." This was a year *prior* to MTV's entry into the L.A. market.

From its inception, MTV was narrowcast as an AOR, adult contemporary, and hits radio network—a formula Pittman used at WNBC-AM. The mix was a blend of sounds designed to appeal to the under-thirty-four set *with* cable potential. Bob Pittman once described it as "a coalition like a politician. We couldn't be too broad, trying to appeal to everyone and no one." As a radio person he was quite comfortable with targeted programming. Narrowcasting, as the father of AOR Mike Harrison suggests, is defined "as much by what they are *not* as by what they are." MTV was rock and roll, not country or urban contemporary *unless* the material had crossover or universal appeal.

With the so-called "outlaw" phenomenon a historical footnote: few country performers viewed rock outlets as a viable vehicle of expo-sure. Alabama's Randy Owen had mixed emotions about MTV. "I think it was great when Michael Jackson . . . made them play his videos. . . . A lot of people that come to our shows really don't know anything about country music, but they know who Alabama is. . . . They're [MTV] not going to be Number One very long, because there are a lot of video programs that are getting a lot of play and exposure that are just as good if not better because of the reportoire content that they ["Night Tracks"] feature." Alabama's exclusion was a curious one as their roots are strongly influenced by the country-rockers of the 1960s.

As of 1985 three country artists have appeared in the MTV rotation: with "She Loves . . .," Ronnie Milsap with "Loves My Car," and Eddie Rabbit and Hank Williams Jr. with "All My Rowdy Friends Are Coming Over Tonight," which contained cameos by Waylon Jennings, Willie Nelson, Kris Kristofferson, plus Cheech and Chong.[2]

Urban contemporary or black soul and rhythm and blues (R&B) performers were seen as much closer to the rock scene. Some were definite crossover artists, such as Stevie Wonder. However, the bound-ary between R&B or soul and rock was an arbitrary line. The ten-person network acquisitions committee made judgments on this highly quixotic demarcation line. Their decisions spurred the beginnings of a prairie fire.

At the Fort Lee debut, David Bramson, president of Backstreet Records, applauded the potential of the new network but warned, "I only hope they don't end up with a bland, homogenized approach that duplicates what has happened to so much radio. I hope, for instance, they show us some of the best of black and country music as well as rock." Bramson's "hopes" clashed with the "format."

The first sparks flew at *Billboard*'s Video Music Conference staged some two months after MTV aired. A panel addressing the role of record companies in the video music business quickly focused on the absence of black artists on MTV.

Jeff Ayeroff of A&M sarcastically stated: "God forbid people should be exposed to blacks on cable." The audience seemed to agree. Motown's Nancy Leviska-Wild added, "I was told that MTV has an AOR base, but I don't understand why MTV is not accepting [Rick] James' promo." James was the hottest black artist in 1981.[3] Other label participants chimed in. John Sykes was bombarded with charges of racism. He was attending a session on video music, but this uproar came as a surprise. "Why wasn't Rick James on the music channel?" The question was asked repeatedly by friend and foe alike. Sykes, finally, replied without much apparent success. Sykes no doubt was wondering about *Billboard* conferences in general. His previous experience involved defending the channel from the assaults of talent buyers and sellers.

The topic of controversy was Rick James, a Motown artist. Although a highly successful urban contemporary performer, rock was not considered James' forte. *Los Angeles Times* music critic Dennis Hunt noted, "Playing blistering funk tunes is more his style." Motown press releases labeled him the "King of Punk Funk." His smash "Super Freak," while a bestseller, was played by only a handful of urban AOR stations in 1981.

"We don't sit in a room and say, 'They're black, we won't use them,' " he said. "We are going after a rock audience. We play Bob Marley and Peter Tosh. We do play music that goes beyond the AOR radio station." He added: "James probably is only popular with 2 percent of the rock audience." Jeff Ayeroff answered, "Just try playing the James video and see what happens. Then, come back next year and tell us how it worked." MTV ignored the suggestion.

Sykes candidly recalls the unpleasant exchange:

> They had no foundation except for saying, "Hey man, music is music and let's put it on" and on that point I treat a lot of music. I don't see the country music association here picketing the convention, I don't see the classical music lobby in America in here. It was only at that time a question of format, we were album-oriented rock at that time, we were a family focus, and that's what we chose, that was the segment of the audience we chose to go after the same way that Marshall Fields or Bloomingdales or Macys chooses certain departments to focus into its certain audience. That's basically a very clear-cut decision, something that radio had done for a long time, and we decided to go into at that time in our AOR-type channel. And if we wouldn't be playing Journey into Rolling Stones . . . we'd be playing Rick James, Smokey Robinson, and a

lot of real strong hit-oriented R&B, but it was our decision at that time to focus in on that kind of music, and it was purely a mutual decision. Unfortunately that [sic] is a very sensitive issue when you bring race into anything. So what we felt was a very grounded programming statement people took completely the wrong way, and they took it out of context and it blew up.

The "black artists" controversy did not end at the Los Angeles conference. MTV's response—"it's the format"—was unconvincing, especially to labels with potential black crossover acts.

The panel moved on to key issues such as money. Len Epand, speaking for Polygram, repeated: "We would like pay for play from MTV. We're not just making advertisements for records. We're making video art." Later Epand would divorce himself from the statement, claiming he was merely presenting the label's position. The economically troubled record label was factually on thin ice. Ayeroff, the panel's "devil's advocate," questioned: "Why is it promotion in Europe and art in America?"

MTV did find some support. Most of the panelists, especially Warners' Jo Bergman, were aware of MTV's shaky financial status. Moreover, as several participants thought, "What about radio station service?" Getting exposure for new acts on AOR and contemporary hits radio (CHR) was difficult enough without asking broadcasters to pay for the product. Some promotion people in secondary markets were already subsidizing the salaries of program and music directors in order to get on playlists.

Rolling Stone finally published an article in December 1981 on cable and rock music. Marc Kirkeby was assigned the task. The journalist focused on "Night Flight" and MTV. He interviewed Jeff Franklin and Robert Pittman. "Night Flight" was still in its film phase and Pittman repeated the usual "narrowcasting" alternative medium arguments the trades had been carrying for nearly a year. The three-page piece ended on a fairly sour note, indicating that both men were "gambling on the repetitive value of their programs." The piece was generally even-handed. The litany of potential and real obstacles was fair. Kirkeby's treatment of MTV would be one of the first and last somewhat objectively cast stories to appear in the mass circulation rock press. One reason may be that in late November few writers took the phenomenon seriously.

Stephen Holden's "Year in Music" wrap-up in *Rolling Stone* totally ignored the advent of music video, but did devote considerable space to criticizing radio formats.

The external controversies, while an irritant, had little effect on the majority of the top executives at MTV. Pittman was adament about maintaining the format. Lack concurred: "It was everything that was not AOR. So it wasn't a segregationist black/white thing." In light of his adolescent years, he was anxious to do an urban contemporary version of MTV. However, the command structure was very conscious of the predominantly white male demographic structure of its middle-class audience. Had his plan been adopted, the infamous "Rick James controversy" might have been avoided.

The more pressing issue was the advertising agency review process now in full swing. WASEC wanted an agency familiar with the machinations of the cable industry. "We went and interviewed a dozen agencies," recalls Fred Seibert. Some of the firms making presentations were O&M, Bozell and Jacobs, Wells Rich Green, Scali, McCabe Green (a subsidiary of O&M), and Lois Pitts Gershon (LPG). Dale Pon was president of LPG's entertainment division. One member of the review committee said, "Most of them never understood what WASEC wanted, especially MTV."

LPG's inclusion surprised many on Madison Avenue as the entertainment branch had emerged only on October 1, 1981. Pon confesses that "the only agency that I did not recognize by name and reputation was my own," which is a slight exaggeration as Lois Pitts Gershon were seasoned advertising and media executives.

George Lois, who began his career as an art director in 1957, has been described as "the industry's most celebrated art director and creative innovator." Three years later he started his own agency, Papert, Koenig, Lois, where he conducted successful campaigns for Xerox, National Airlines, Quaker Oats, and others. In 1967 he founded Lois Holland Callaway. His clients included many of the *Fortune* 500. During this time he cowrote *The Art of Advertising,* a popular text in mass communications. Lois Pitts Gershon emerged in 1968, the same year he was installed in the Art Directors Hall of Fame. Later he was inducted into the Creative Hall of Fame. The *New York Times* proclaimed him "a genius of mass communications as he acclaims himself to be. . . ."

Bill Pitts, a Harvard graduate, was no lightweight. He was a thirty-year veteran in marketing with experience in promotions, merchandising, and demographics. He coauthored *George Be Careful* with Lois.

Dick Gershon was media director for Benton & Bowles at the age of thirty-one. He did media drives for *U.S. News, Redbook, McCalls,* and other media advertisers. Like Pitts, he had a Harvard sheepskin, an MBA.

Dale Pon, at age thirty-five, was chosen by Lois and colleagues for his expertise in "the emerging world of cable television." His credentials were impressive, having worked for three top ad agencies—Young & Rubicam, Compton Advertising, and three years with O&M. He also enjoyed broadcast experience, having been with all three commercial networks. Careerwise his stint with the NBC radio network was perhaps the most important. He was, under Fred Silverman, vice president assigned to audience development. In this capacity he was involved with WNBC-AM. At the New York station Pon was impressive. Accolades such as "wonderful," "imaginative," or "I would work with Dale in a New York minute" abounded. Dom Giofre of WNBC observed, "He was magic at the station." Bob Pittman, who briefly worked with him, had a positive perception. He joined LPG in October 1981. As his official biography indicates, "He was one of the first to recognize the potential of MTV, which became *his* first client" (emphasis added). Pon's reputation got the firm into the bidding game. He explained: "I think what I got from the friendships, associations, and the knowledge these men had of me was how I got to compete for the business. But, I will tell you that there was no fix that was in."

Scali, McCabe Green received the Movie Channel and Nickelodeon accounts and LPG landed MTV—further fueling the insider charges. This was a definite case of sour grapes. Wells Rich would have gotten the account had they "done better work on the presentation," said one insider. MTV's marketing people, Bob Pittman and Fred Seibert, explained the choice: "The thing is that Dale Pon and George Lois were the creative people in charge. They were people that we knew from past life radio and advertising. We knew that they would understand how to go about doing the job." Pon recalls it this way:

> We offered MTV exactly what MTV was looking for. We had the power of a full-service, well-established, medium-size advertising agency. And we had the energy of a brand new entertainment advertising agency in LPG/Pon. So I think that we won the business based on our thinking . . . and all our credentials. . . . They both made up a combination that's impossible for any other agency to beat. But we competed for the business. It was not like Fred and Bob thought, "Dale's a helluva a guy, let's give him the business." It wasn't that way at all."

Pon's "Imus in the Morning" campaign at WNBC impressed the industry. Working as the station's entertainment marketing manager, he came up with the concept of employing sets of twins to do commercials for the morning radio show. After screening 2,000 candidates the number was pared to forty. At the Deflippo Studio the finalists practiced with the zany Imus. The result was four-and-a-half hours of film.

Animated material produced in London came from the Harold Friedman Consortium. These were sequenced into the live studio material.
Part of the commercial included Imus in a WNBC T-shirt. The end
result was fifteen possible usable spots. The campaign worked, as Imus
became the top-rated morning man in the market.

Following the holiday season, Pon and LPG were officially commissioned to convince cable operators in New York and ten other major
markets to broadcast MTV. Cable was MTV's main problem. No
public announcement of the agency changeover would be forthcoming
until much later. The reason given was that "when one discontinues
using an ad agency like Ogilvy, you do it in a sensitive way." Pon, of
course, had formerly been employed by the company and Seibert was
a great admirer of the legendary founder, as is the entire industry. No
mention of the changeover appeared in the *New York Times,* unlike the
initial coverage of the hiring of O&M by WASEC in March 1981. *Ad
Age Yearbook* was equally silent on the subject.

Fortune brightened the holiday season for MTV staffers. The financial magazine chose the network as one of "The Products of the Year."
The criterion for the award, as set forth by Andrew C. Brown, was:
"new noteworthy products—and services—assembled by *Fortune* for
this year-end album epitomize the continuing technological develop-
ments, economic exigencies, and real (or hoped for) consumer needs
that shaped the American marketplace, circa 1981." The musical
channel was praised for "its ability to serve up specific audiences for
advertisers, much as specialized magazines do." Other new develop-
ments cited were "The Nightly Business News," RCA's Electa-Vision
Video Disc Player, and John DeLorean's "Live the Dream" metallic
sports car.

In the last week of December 1981, United Press International, one
of the two major U.S. wire services, featured MTV and Bob Pittman in
a futuristic piece suggesting music video "will make the phonograph
record obsolete by 1990." Pittman, of course, rejected this thesis:
"We're not going to replace radio or records. FM didn't kill AM. It
reached parity with AM."

On the down side, no data appeared to support Lack's optimistic
contention that MTV would have 4.5 to 5 million households by the
end of the holidays.[4]

Planning for the New Year's Rock and Roll Ball at the Hotel
Diplomat was in full swing. A four-hour telecast, covering all the time
zones, would hail in 1982, and hopefully bring more attention to the
network. The ringing in of the New Year on satellite started at 11:30
P.M. EST and lasted until 3:30 A.M. The actual partying began at 10:00

P.M. (EST). Produced by Jim Wittee, the telecast highlighted ex-New York Doll David Johansen, Karla deVito, and Malcolm McLaren's 1979 find, Bow Wow Wow—all "needed major commercial exposure." BWW—the "Sex Pistol's of the '80s"—stole the show visually and musically. The Pistols' former manager had set the aura with sixteen-year-old Annabella Lwin posing nude on the *See Jungle* LP, arousing the ire of her mother. Several members of the group, including the female vocalist, sported Mohawk punk haircuts. Sykes' notion of "irreverent" was being more than realized. *Video* described the festivities:

> At exactly midnight Central Time, amid a champagne-guzzling, confetti-covered crowd, Bow Wow Wow's Mohawk-headed guitarist, a bass player in a Wehrmacht helmet wrapped in the British Union Jack, a drummer, and two young nubile scantily-clad black singer/dancers take the stage. They are followed by the star of the show, five-foot-two lead singer Annabella.
>
> Annabella is dressed in a tiny yellow dress to offset her light-chocolate skin. Cinching the dress is a thick leather belt in the current pirate style. . . . As the hand starts a heavily percussive jungle beat, the young dancers move in hot, sultry undulations and Annabella, who's just turned sweet sixteen, starts to bump and grind and howl.

The veejays interviewed celebrities in the crowd of more than 1,000 people. One participant described the veejays as "prejournalism majors." Bob Pittman commented that "120 percent of the people we invited showed up." The late John Belushi, Bob Welch, Rick Derringer, and ex-Monkee Peter Tork attended.

Video went on to observe: "Not everything on MTV is as adventurous as this, but it does show what is possible. Like it or not, the music world is *changing,* and cable TV is helping it change."[5]

The contrived relaxed "mood" of MTV—"where anything can happen"—is based entirely on computer printouts and repeated weekly callouts. The post-Fort Lee changes were closely studied. In January 1982 Warner-Amex and Pepsico released the findings of a joint survey conducted by Dresner, Morris, and Tortorello, Inc.

The results from MTV markets showed that 60 percent of the targeted audience had seen the channel. Eighty percent were conscious of MTV's existence. Of the 932 respondents, 77 percent rated the programming as "good" or "excellent." Pepsi was now convinced of the wisdom of its time buy. MTV would be on 600 CATVs and MSOs with some four million households by May 1982; subscribers viewed the network an average of 4.6 days a week, averaging one hour during the week. The viewing time was a bit less than Lack had predicted.

On Tuesdays ten people gathered at Rockefeller Plaza to decide the week's rotation. This was the Acquisitions Committee, which reviews submitted video clips. A high percentage of new clips will be aired if they pass the "standards" of MTV, which excludes "gratuitous sex or violence," smoking, gambling, hard liquor, and drug paraphernalia. The network's code states it will "rightfully accept, decline or revise the advertising of any product or service." These guidelines are mailed to time buyers and video providers. Duran Duran's "Girls on Film" and David Bowie's "China Girl," which contained a nude beach scene a la *From Here to Eternity,* were among the 10 percent that had to be edited to make the playlist. Publicist Dorene Lauer, who participated in the meetings, states: "We make our best collective judgment to decide if a clip belongs on MTV. If we can't reach a consensus it goes to Warner-Amex for creative review."

Concerning this gray area an MTV source told *Rock Video* that "this place is incredibly political." Culture Club's original clip of "Do You Really Want To Hurt Me?" was turned down in late 1982 because it contained a courtroom scene with a jury made up of black-faced minstrels. It was rejected because of the "racism" issue. The clip used on "Tops of The Pops" from the BBC—minus the judicial scene—was accepted. The Rolling Stones' "Neighbors"—a four-minute version of Hitchock's *Rear Window,* complete with a dismembered body in a suitcase—was aired until callouts found significant viewer resistance. Mick Jagger, as always, refused to edit the clip. It was dropped. The respondents considered the material "gratuitous violence." Rob Baker of the *New York Daily News* got the answer in general: Superstars despite the quality of the music or the video would be played because, according to Les Garland, "What we ultimately do is program what the people who watch MTV want to see." The Stones were in that category until data proved the contrary. *Rock Video* magazine since its appearance in April 1984 has run a series of "What You Can't See On MTV" articles with glossy color photos. Although the publication exhibits a strong heavy-metal slant, it does bring into question the decision-making process as to "acceptable" content. The status of the artist or act appears to be a factor in which selections are chosen without editing or subject to absolute rejection.

Once a clip is accepted it becomes an "add-on." The rotation is determined by the Acquisitions Committee. The clip is then transported to Smithtown, Long Island, to be remastered in stereo and rematched to the video portion. Andy Setos then adds in the veejay intros from material stored in a Rolodex, thus finishing a "live" television segment of five hours. "People say, 'Well, MTV isn't really live,' " he told Bob Hilburn, "and they're right in the sense that it doesn't go straight from the studio to your set. But what happens at operations center is live." *Rolling Stone* mused that Setos was the "only live presence" on MTV. The vice president of engineering and operations sees his role as supervising an "up-light facility" and feels that "the way you use your TV set changes when the music becomes a primary part of the programming."

A selection is aired for several weeks before the scrutinization process is unleashed. A survey of 150 retailers is undertaken and results compiled. Then the fifteen-minute callouts or phone interviews begin. Sample size can range from 1,500 to an average of 3,000 during a seven-day period. These data determine the fate of the clip.

Callouts, if properly conducted, are a valuable research tool. They are immediate. MTV employed a staff of five to eight phone interviewers, who randomly contacted the targeted twelve- to thirty-four-year-old audience. Having established that the person was an MTV viewer, the interviewers would pepper the person with questions regarding specific clips and artists. If the respondent had not heard the song, a bit from the piece would be played. The response was then rated on a scale of 1 to 10. A 1 was "can't stand"; a 10 was "can't get enough of it."

Callouts are laden with methodological problems, as Pittman realized. They must be complemented with other data sources if most of the inherent problems of the phone technique are to be overcome.

Pittman also consulted *Billboard*'s singles charts and the popularity of video clips at nightclubs like the RockAmerica service. Indeed, the growing number of video clubs provided a ready-made test market for MTV. Based on the data, clips were originally placed into four rotations. *Heavy* indicated a video would air four times per day, *medium* signified it would air three times daily, and *light* meant it was shown once in a twenty-four-hour segment. Add-ons were mercurial and strongly influenced by callouts. However, Tom Freston did indicate that an inferior clip by a "name" act would be "put on" the rotation. After all, he reasoned, "the videos that aren't of the highest quality do very well."

In the wake of the *Billboard* video gathering, the race issue kept creeping up. Labels with black artists were loudly complaining of a lack of exposure. Pittman responded:

> We are the art gallery and not the artist. We are as broad as we can be and yet have the same audience. Fortunately, when you're doing . . . [our] . . . audience, that's easy. Country has very little appeal. Disco has some; interesting enough, it's strongest from ages twenty-five to thirty-

nine and mostly female. But 85 percent of the target audience likes rock, and they were in direct polarization to those who liked disco. In our initial samplings we found that everything they liked about rock, they hated about disco.

In Pittman's view, urban contemporary artists and dance music did not fit the format. The data seemed to support Pittman's narrowcasting view.

The narrowcasting issue was a relatively minor problem in comparison to some of the others bedeviling MTV. The major difficulty was selling the station to cable operators. MTV could not build an audience sufficient to attract badly needed advertising dollars with the MSOs and CATVs currently airing the network. "We knew that there was one roadblock to the success of MTV at the time," said one former MTVer. "That was the cable operators, the people who were outside of the MTV demographic, and they weren't going to quite understand why they should do this thing."

Margaret Wade and the marketing people, in late 1981 again, went to the trade publications with full-page ads in some instances full of testimonials. These were geared toward cable operators, advertisers, and record companies. Obtaining clips was still a problem.

Les Garland, destined to become a major executive and spokesperson, joined MTV in February 1982 as vice president of programming. Garland, a fifteen-year veteran in radio broadcasting with a two-year stint as general manager of promotion for Atlantic Records in Los Angeles, was ideal for the position. He had spent three years as program director for KFRC-AM (San Francisco), a Top Forty station, prior to joining Atlantic in June 1980. Prior to working in the Bay Area he was program director for WRKO in Boston, CKLW in Detroit, and KIQQ in Los Angeles.

His new duties involved programming concepts, coordinating music industry relations, and acting as spokesperson for the network, along with Sykes.

His view of MTV was that it was "a radio station you can see." This perspective fit precisely with the Pittman philosophy. He was a rock trivia buff. He and John Lack reportedly had music history contests that became legendary at WASEC. He quickly made his presence felt with trade paper interviews and programming concepts. "We're streamlining in on the way we're presented and promoted. . . . We definitely plan to stick with shorts, especially since there are more and more available."

John Sykes, then director of promotion, provided playlists to merchandisers and record companies. The playlist originally released in

March 1982 found eight titles in the "heavy" category (appearing four times a day). These included the Police's "Spirits in the Material World," J. Geils' "Centerfold," Blue Oyster Cult's "Burnin' for You," and "Harden My Heart" by Quarterflash. The "medium" rotation had forty-three clips, featuring Squeeze, Billy Squier, Rod Stewart, Styx, Tom Petty, Pat Benatar, and the seemingly always present The Pretenders. Eighty-nine other artists comprised the "light" list (one to two plays during a twenty-four-hour period).

Garland's contacts helped in obtaining additional clips. His associations would be significant in Jack Schneider's game plan to capture the Manhattan cable market. The print campaign did find one New York cable system offering three hours of air time per day. The offer infuriated the WASEC president, Bob Pittman: "Manhattan Cable is saving a couple of its channels, as is Teleprompter. Saving them for what?" This question evoked a plethora of responses. The most common was "channel incapacity." "That's when MTV went to war," said Schneider.

Schneider's army consisted of MTV's publicity department and LPG plus Dale Pon. Their assignment was to remedy the situation. At times it seemed like an episode from *Mission Impossible*. Pon describes the situation:

> MTV had many problems, to tell you the truth, because anything that is radically new is going to be misunderstood, its potential cannot be understood. Here is a brand new idea, spanking new idea called MTV. One of the groups that misunderstood MTV was the cable television community—the cable television operators whom MTV was reliant on, [sic] to establish its distribution. MTV could not be seen in homes on cable television sets if the operator—whether it's Manhattan Cable or an operator in Arizona, or an operator in Los Angeles . . . pick a place, it's the cable television operator who has the franchise with the municipality—doesn't agree to accept MTV and put MTV on the cable offering. Then the point in fact is that MTV can't distribute its product. So, we felt that MTV had a very big distribution problem. . . . The men and women who run cable television franchises, operate cable television systems for municipalities, are not Bob Pittman's age. They are not people who necessarily love and want rock music.

MTV was in the same position that the recording industry found itself several decades earlier in dealing with middle-aged rack jobbers or merchandisers who totally disdained rock music. As Jack Holzman, then president of Elektra, observed: "Rack merchandisers . . . are not aware of the music on esthetic and social levels." During the 1960s Stan Cornyn at NARM (National Association of Recording Merchandisers) implored the delegates to "listen to the new music." His pleas fell on deaf ears. Record executives privately called rack jobbers "cherry pickers" most comfortable with the *Sound of Music* or crooners such as Dean Martin or Frank Sinatra. The generation gap was equally prevalent in the cable business.

There was an added twist in the CATV industry. "Cable incapacity" was a buzz word for MTV and other satellite networks. It served as a rationale for rejecting new programming. In some localities the argument was more than a mere cop-out. A majority of rural and suburban CATVs frequently did have only twelve outlets. Seventy percent of the cable systems exhibited the traditional dozen channels. Expansion, according to World Entertainment's Wayne Baruch, involved "discretionary income for these extra services [that] just isn't there."

A new addition, despite costs, involved bumping an established channel. Kicking a familiar station off the air for a rock music service was not greeted with enthusiasm in many communities, especially in rural areas.

Wood TV in Northwest Ohio added MTV. The first of the melees started when Wood executive Roger Wise decided "there isn't any channel really that serves our music needs as we would like them served and MTV was going across the country in great shape. Four hundred people directly accosted me about why wasn't it on our cable system in light of the fact that we had several what they termed repeat network offerings. Why didn't we have one that was entirely music oriented and that was the favorite that they suggested."

Wise, after some study, including a report by Marketing/Media Research Associates, decided to program the music channel. The question became which of the twelve channels, at that time, was to be eliminated.

The first candidate was Cleveland's Channel 8, the CBS feed. Some asked, "Why not Toledo's CBS affiliate, WTOL?" The FCC would prohibit it because of the "must carry" edict. As some of the letters to the local paper and Wood TV appeared, a storm of outrage occurred when rumors of a rock station replacing Channel 8 surfaced. The idea was dropped. Instead NBC affiliate WLIO-35 left the cable system. Again the complaints came storming in.

One upset writer said, "I would like to have Channel 35 in Lima back on Cable 10 instead of MTV." Other writers were not as kind. A viewer wrote on the back of the bill: "Whose hair-brained idea was it to include MTV?" Wood TV was down to only two NBC-TV affiliates.

"A lot of people said don't drop Channel 35. But our reasoning was 35 was not going to carry the Cincinnati Reds anyway."

The underlying cause of the first part of the dispute was outlined in a study in Bowling Green conducted by Marketing/Media Research Associates under the direction of professors Jerry Wicks and Richard Zeller of Bowling Green State University. They concluded: "Subscribers expressed a preference for a greater variety of channel selection in their cable TV service; and cost is neither a problem for the subscribers nor an objection of nonsubscribers." In an earlier part of their report they state, "Popular music programming was especially desired by the young."

The generation gap and channel incapacity were the major obstacles facing Dale Pon, George Lois, and their associates.

"I Want My MTV!"

In the spring of 1982 everyone involved agreed MTV's main roadblock was distribution. Most previous ploys had not worked. Trade ads, convention demonstrations, and even the promotions were generally ineffectual. "Hawaiian Holiday" with Devo or the "House Party" got some local press coverage for winners and perhaps a rare mention in a rock magazine, but cable operators were oblivious to these attention-getting events. One observer noted, "If they entered a contest the odds are they already lived in an area served by MTV."

LPG/Pon developed a strategy that could easily have been taken from the pages of John Naisbitt's best-selling book *Megatrends,* which stressed the significance of grassroots participation.

The agency "recognized that the cable operator, the head executives at a cable franchise operating a system, that man or woman," says Pon, "might not be the person who most appreciated rock music." The advertising game plan would be to "create a campaign that would demonstrate the ground swell of the popularity that MTV enjoyed, and what is more persuasive for them than if they hear from their constituents? So we created a campaign where the popularity of MTV could be demonstrated to, among other people, the cable operator. That was our thinking. It's guided the work that we've done during these first few years for MTV," concluded the ad executive. MTVers signed on. John Sykes noted: "We were hoping to motivate the audience to get up, and if they really wanted it to call up and order cable television." According to Seibert, "We knew that our success would lie in going directly to the viewer, the potential viewer, and letting them know that it was there."

The concept appealed to MTV management, as most had migrated from media and the record industry. One of the MTV command notes:

LPG developed a strategy which was probably the single biggest stroke in MTV consumer success. The marketing success was the idea of surrounding cable operators—which was not just a cable strategy, it's a media strategy. We were going to get the biggest bang for our buck immediately. The way we decided to do it was by ganging up where we had the most subscribers, and the most subscribers to gain against how much our media cost in each of those markets. Essentially what happened was, it looked like we were spending five times more than we were.

Tactically LPG's blueprint was close to a standard radio promotional technique. What Pon was advocating in part was a "spread." The term refers to surrounding a target. In the music business records are pitched in smaller cities around a major market in hopes of creating enough listener interest that the desired metropolitan stations will add the song to their playlist. Occasionally the method has worked, but it is far from infallible.

Blueprints are only points of departure—a road map. The more arduous task is operationalizing the game plan. Many an excellent advertising or record company plan has fallen flat because of the manner in which it was implemented.

Schneider liked the concept. "There's a lot of ways you can get something done," he recalled. "You can go around the keeper of the gate, if you will. We went around the gate, we went to the public, we went over his head. So the public called him and said 'We Want Our MTV.' "

Slogans are the lifeblood of Madison Avenue. George Lois and Dale Pon brainstormed a number of mottos. Mottos can make or break any campaign. Pon and Lois had to come up with something as creative as the MTV logo. "You'll never look at music the same way again," the original slogan, didn't have the necessary "hook." Dale Pon wrote a line reading, "Cable brats, rock and roll wasn't enough for them, now they want MTV." George Lois looked at the cumbersome motto and proposed "Wouldn't it be better as 'Cable brats, rock and roll wasn't enough for them, now they want their MTV,' " adding "I want my MTV." This version, according to LPG, was run in several trade publications.

Bob Pittman disapproved. His reasoning was that telling a rock audience they were "cable brats" appeared presumptuous, especially to the older end of the demographic spectrum. The opening clause had to go, in Pittman's view. "Bob asked us to ash can 'cable brats,' " observes Pon. What remained was, "I Want My MTV" Lois' closing phrase became the battle cry.

Motto in hand, the campaign was designed to have thirty-second television commercials and one-minute spots for radio. It was suggested that recognizable rock stars do the spots. Members of the MTV management team knew a number of the visible names in the rock world. Using their previous associations, MTVers approached rock's elite. A number of stars agreed to do the spots at their convenience. John Sykes recalls:

> We found that there were artists behind what we were doing, so we wanted to harness them, to help us march the concept because it wasn't easy to convince every cable operator in America to put MTV right on the ship because it was not your average television network. . . . Bands like the Stones or Peter Townshend of the Who, they all got behind it because to them it was an opportunity to push something that was going to help them sell their music and expose their art, too. It not only is a vehicle to sell records, but it is a vehicle to express themselves on a whole new network. So they were behind us. No one was paid any money, it was all just done, helping each other out.

The clips showed rock personalities stating: "I want my MTV . . . Pick up your phone, call your local cable operator and demand your MTV." In Peter Townshend's words, "Call your cable operator now. Call him and say 'I want my MTV!' " The volunteers included Adam Ant, John Cougar Mellencamp, Pat Benatar, Stevie Nicks, Hall and Oates, David Bowie, Peter Wolf, Sting, Rick Ocasek of Cars, Joe Elliot with Def Lepperd, and others.

Pon, Sykes, Sparrow, and Les Garland scattered throughout the United States and across the Atlantic with camera crews to film the half-minute television spots. Pon and Garland flew to Paris to do Mick Jagger. After taping the Stones' flamboyant lead singer, their next stop was London and the Who's Peter Townshend. Then on to Switzerland to record David Bowie. Sparrow, an ex-Epic Records promotion person, traveled to the West Coast for Pat Benatar and Fleetwood Mac's Stevie Nicks. John Cougar Mellencamp's bit was filmed at Indiana University. Pon orchestrated the entire logistically complicated venture.

The nontestimonial portions of the spots were animations. One had a stereo tuner leaping, a pair of speakers dancing, a cable decoder climbing a television, and, according to George Lois, a video screen "smoking in an attempt to approximate the multi-media impact of the music channel."[6]

Few protests to the campaign were publically aired. Two anonymous Philadelphia cable operators objected to the *Inquirer* that WASEC was using strong-arm tactics. Generally the spots obtained the desired effect. "We saw that in a given neighborhood, the kid with MTV was perceived as cooler; everybody came to his or her house to watch," noted Les Garland.

Jack Schneider was winning the war. He bragged to the *Los Angeles Times:* "The New York operators were swamped with calls. They finally said 'Call off your dogs.' They couldn't get any in-coming calls, service calls, or orders for new homes. All they had were young people calling asking for MTV."

The WASEC president's comments were a bit strong. "We pitched [them] very hard," says Dorene Lauer, "because it's an important market for us." The publicity person went on to label any statements of coercion as "absurd" and "ridiculous."

Denise Bozi, the 1985 promotion manager at Manhattan Cable, owned by American Television and Communications (ATC), acknowledged that the "I Want My MTV" campaign was nothing short of "brilliant." It illustrated that the music network was "very viable." Manhattan Cable would later add the service because of consumer interest. Some schedule "rearranging" was required, but they did have, as Pittman indicated, an open channel. Bozi concurred with Lauer that the so-called "Call off your dogs" white-flag surrender was an excessive statement. Other cable operators agreed. They did receive numerous cards, letters, and telephone calls in targeted markets, however, as in Los Angeles the decision to add MTV had little to do with the switchboard's being gridlocked. The "I Want My MTV" project did create a ground swell of interest that was conveyed to the MSOs, but it was hardly as intimidating as Schneider's interview would imply. Most MTVers in retrospect back away from the former WASEC chief's comment, dismissing it as a sign of the network's frustration with cable operators in the early years. There is little value in opening old wounds.[7]

Schneider, no longer with MTV, is not contrite. "In business you conduct war," he said. "When I was with CBS we were at war with ABC, CBN, and NBC all the time. As individuals we all endured each other." So it was with the cable operators.

In the meantime Margaret Wade continued to establish a better inner-industry impact. Her job was to "present the thinking and the feelings of the top executives at MTV," recalled one of the members of the management team.

On May 12, 1982 Bob Pittman appeared before the prestigious National Academy for Television, Arts, and Sciences at the posh Copacabana restaurant. He was still officially the program director for the Movie Channel (TMC). Pittman, reading rapidly, advocated the potential of cable to the visual media audience. Using a prepared text, Pittman predicted: "There will be about 20 million pay subscribers by the end of this year, and we project that by 1985 there will be 45 million pay subscribers . . . benefits will be dramatic." While the statement was addressed more to servicing TMC, it also applied to MTV. Fundamentally Pittman was "nurturing pay-TV," or cable.

In July, Polygram, one of the two holdouts, reversed its position. "Our perception has really changed with our putting clips on cable," Len Epand, Polygram vice president, told *Billboard*. "Our promotion and marketing people see it as an equivalent of getting a record played on a radio station. We are finding sales off video play. We can't expect to win the battle of being paid for use of our clips, we were giving it a shot as record promotion."

MCA remained unmoved. The label did not have a video department, unlike its major competitors. Joan Bullard, vice president for press and artist development, said: "We have videos available, but they're from the artists themselves." She added, "We're just not convinced that video sells records."

Other record companies were coming around, although Jo Bergman's main concern continued to be that "MTV's not being shown in Los Angeles and New York. . . . this and a lot of other factors make it difficult to predict where video will take us." She added that "it's a suburban phenomenon" outside of major markets. She did admit that where MTV was available, "it's a factor in sales."

Some label executives were more enthusiastic. Arista saw video clips as "an increasingly important sales tool." RCA's Jack Chudnoff flatly stated that "MTV does sell records." Despite MTV's growing credibility with the labels, the payment issue kept surfacing. "Bohemian Rhapsody" was produced by Bruce Gowers for a mere $4,000. Most 1982 costs were five to ten times that figure. Realizing MTV's economic status, most companies reluctantly provided the clips gratis, but a majority echoed A&M artist development director Bert Miller's view that "MTV's statistics show viewers buy albums based on what they've seen on the channel, and we know that's true, but no way does it make up for our costs. We're just not selling enough records to offset all the costs."[8]

On August 1, 1982 MTV celebrated its first birthday with several promotions. Parties were held in Peoria, Hartford, and other localities coming on line. The New Year's broadcast was repeated. Les Garland reminisced over the past year. Given his short tenure with the network, Garland was not the best choice. "We haven't experienced any rotation problems. We have more than 500 [clips] in our library. About 30 percent to 40 percent of the music we play is not on the typical AOR radio station, so we're an important place for record companies to break new acts." He repeated the usual pitch to the labels: "We're a promotional source for music. We have proved we sell records. . . ." Welcome to 1982. The vice president for programming promised anniversary specials, such as interviews with fleetwood Mac, Mick Jagger, and Robert Plant. A special Go Go's concert was also planned. Rumors had it that Rick Carroll, Lee Abrams, and Sebastian Casey were "searching" for a sixth veejay.

The same month the Museum of Modern Art underscored the aesthetic value of video clips by selecting a few for their archives. Two of Captain Beefheart's endeavors, the promo for his *Lick My Decals Off* album and "Ice Cream for Crow," were chosen. Laurie Anderson's "O Superman" was also added to the museum's archives, along with the Talking Heads' "Once in a Life." None of these clips had appeared on MTV—a point critics immediately noted. The only museum selection that had been rotated on the music network was Toni Basil's "Mickey." When asked about the excluded tunes Pittman snapped, "Musically, those songs do not fit into MTV's format. They're too avant-garde." Some executives thought Pittman entirely too rigid. John Lack recalls, "I would have handled it a little differently." Others concurred. Lack had future plans, but they would never come to fruition.

MTV did win several awards at the International Film and TV Festival ceremony. For On-air Promotion Spots they received a gold medal, and "Draw Winky," and a silver for "MTV to Go."

More importantly, beginning September 1982 Manhattan Cable became the 825th CATV to broadcast MTV. The network now had 6.75 million hookups. This was a symbolic victory, but a partial one as the northern part of the island was served by a competitor, Group W. This Westinghouse subsidiary also controlled the Los Angeles market.

The September 11 issue of *Billboard* was most gratifying for the video executives at 75 Rockefeller Plaza. The headline read: "Survey Finds MTV Strongly Affecting Record Sales."[9] In a national survey of retailers in smaller cities the publication found that MTV was generating sales by providing exposure for new acts. The survey results read as if the copy had been written by Dale Pon or Margaret Wade. Merchandisers throughout the country pointed to growth in sales. Some reported requests for albums that they weren't aware existed. The article read like the October 10, 1981 ad MTV placed in industry publications. It contained a sampling of quotes from retailers:

"These innovative groups are up 15% to 20% because of MTV."
"Our business is up for the summer by about 20% over last year."

"It seems to spur sales of obscure groups, and it helps because *radio stations won't play new artists*" (emphasis added).

"It's giving older groups new life and new groups a way to promote their albums."

Finally, the tour de force: "Radio is a skeleton. MTV is the greatest thing that ever happened. Our customers had to go 150 miles each way to Seattle to see touring acts until MTV," said Bob Goldstone of Budget Records in Yakima, Washington. Groups mentioned as benefiting from video exposure included Adam and the Ants, Flock of Seagulls, the Human League, Judas Priest, Bow Wow Wow, and Men at Work. While *Billboard* survey's of retailers have a tendency to lean toward the positive, no one at WASEC was complaining. Les Garland totally concurred with the merchandisers. "We broke Men at Work." He was referring to the heavy rotation of "Who Can It Be Now" on the music network.

> Nobody knew them, but we liked the video and gave it light to medium rotation. Four weeks later Columbia called and said we had a hit. They'd done a test in Dallas. In those parts of the city wired by cable Men At Work albums were selling like mad. It didn't sell elsewhere because the radio stations weren't playing it.

Business as Usual made the top of *Billboard*'s album chart in November 1982. Al Teller, then a CBS vice president, objected to the credit MTV was receiving for Men at Work's success. He told *TV Guide:* "MTV doesn't break an act, but MTV was certainly a contributing factor in bringing the record to the public's attention." Ironically, when faced with the release of the group's second album, *Cargo,* he complained, "No one knows who they are from the first record *aside from what they've seen on MTV.* And, frankly, that's not enough to carry them very far. They need a visual identity, a recognizable face. Otherwise, we got a problem."[10]

Teller's argument would be challenged by *Billboard*'s end of the year "Talent in Action" issue. Quarterflash, Human League, and Flock of Seagulls ranked in the top ten of "New Pop Artists," based on combined charted albums and singles. Men at Work placed at fourteen. All these acts were heavily rotated on the music channel.

Fred Silverman, Pittman's former CEO, contended to a NCTA meeting in Los Angeles that while the state of cable programming was "abysmal," the music channel was a visual breakthrough. He scolded the gathered crowd: "By and large, what's being broadcast is the eighty-second rerun of "Gilligan's Island" on the superstations. Warners has introduced the most innovative programming in television in two decades: MTV. The music channel is the most revolutionary idea to come along in a while." Pittman must have savored the statement. He and Lack would later pitch MTV to the assembled cable operators.

At that Los Angeles conference, MTV received the ACE award— cable television's version of the Grammys.

MTV's appearance in the New York market and the ACE award piqued *Time* magazine's interest.[11] In a bland article unimaginatively titled "Cable's Rock Round the Clock," a *Time* staffer commented: "The simulated performance clips tend to be dull and repetitive: lip-synch clips. But the best videos enhance the mood of a song and expand TV's generally unadventurous visual vocabulary." The writer was lukewarm to the veejays, but indicated they were basically inoffensive. Overall, *Time* was descriptive in its approach.

And the Contests Keep Coming

To further enhance the mood or "fantasy" aspect of MTV, the contests never ceased. A "Hawaiian Holiday with Devo" followed the 1982 New Year's party by a matter of weeks. J.J. Jackson and Martha Quinn dug deep into an enormous wooden crate to pick Dolli Markovich from—ironically—Akron, Ohio, where Devo started. *Billboard* ran a photo some three weeks later. A "House Party" contest followed. The veejays repeated:

> Party 'til you drop! Win the MTV house party contest, and we'll come to your house with videos, veejays, food, Pepsi. Stay tuned for details. . . . Your chance to win! Sony widescreen TV, Akai audio system, a year's supply of Pepsi, and a night you'll never forget. Stay tuned for details.

In mid-April a fifteen-year-old boy in Michigan was informed he had won the contest. One fifty-seven-year-old matron sent in 1,300 cards to have the "House Party" at this residence. *Cablevision*'s video critic went to the affair. He reported:

> What struck me as I followed the MTV House Party was how many bases were being covered, and how well MTV was covering them. The House Party, to which Rob Kettenburgh was allowed to invite 200 friends (and to which passes were being scalped for $20 a piece), turned out to be a threefold success—at once a perfect piece of pop Americana (from a journalist's viewpoint), a skillful commercial stratagem (from MTV's viewpoint), and a 15-year-old media freak's dream come true. Commerce may have been the bottom line, but there was definitely something irresistibly larky (and down-right surreal) about the House Party—and even something warming about it.[12]

The backyard event cost an additional $300 to clean the rugs the morning after.

Then came the Pac-Man contest. WCI's Atari division supplied 100 computers and the arcade cartridges. For more than a month MTV viewers heard:

> MTV goes Pac-Man wocka! And you wocka way a contest winner! You think Pac-Man has it easy? Well, it didn't happen overnight. He came from Anytown, U.S.A. But he wasn't like the other kids. So he left home to find himself. You know what that's like . . . Day jobs. Bit parts in board games. Meaningless encounters. Then he discovered video! A real woman! An empire in the arcade! The hearts and homes of America! Now video game meets video channel in a legendary contest! MTV wants you to win! 100 first prizes from Atari: the famous video computer system with the world's only Pac-Man cartridge.

For the Pac Man drawing a chimpanzee named Zippy was brought in to choose from the thousands of cards submitted. The monkey proceeded to hit Alan Hunter. "He didn't get bit but something funny happened." *The Wall* accomplished more than merely getting the network's "face on the map;" it was an omen of things to come. This promotional effort was followed by contests used to plug the network, a movie, products and a video cassette. Other games during the year involved Fleetwood Mac, The Who's farewell tour (which drew some half-million entries), and several other house parties and equipment giveaways. Although these events were "irreverent," a certain pattern was slowly beginning to emerge.

The cosmopolitanly oriented *New York* magazine did a three-page story by Bernice Kanner titled "Can't Stop the Movie Channel," which was one of the best early histories of MTV published.[13] However, Ms. Kanner concluded the piece with "Good-bye, perhaps, to video games and "Charlie's Angels." But not for me. I'm moving uptown to Group W Cable territory, where MTV just isn't." Little did she know that MTV would follow her to the north side by New Year's day.

The publicity department continued to count cable companies. Utilizing their state-of-the-art data bank, the MTV staff capitalized on the generalization conflict it was creating. John Lack told *New York* magazine: "Parents complain that they can't listen to this stuff downstairs so they order a cable for their kids." Household profiles indicating an average income of $30,000 per year and two or more television receivers made the argument very attractive. Cable operators appeared to appreciate MTV's empirical data. A network salesperson once mused, "Argue 'til [sic] you're blue in the face—nothing, but drop a printout and you've got a customer." Broadcasters live and die on the basis of the almightly "numbers" or ratings; in the case of cable, its hookups.

Critics have attacked MTV for its devotion to printouts, the most accepted form of promotion in the broadcasting industry. Strictly applying the "hot hand" approach of the rock world has little credibility with media gatekeepers and advertisers. Ray Klinge, who hosted one of MTV's opening parties, said, "MTV is rapidly becoming ACT's second most popular advertising channel . . . [and, that] definitely prompts second sets and FM hookups."

As predicted, MTV was mired in red ink at the year's end despite a reported 9,350,000 subscribers. The number promised to further increase as two Group W cable systems would begin airing the music network in the northern part of Manhattan (where most of the MTV execs live) and large sections of southern California (population 3 million in January 1983). National ad buyers had swelled in number to nearly one hundred, with prime-time thirty-second spots selling for $2,500. Still, as Chip Rachlin, director of acquisitions, cautioned, "They have not come to grips with how they [advertisers] want to allot their dollars because there's no rating system yet." A.C. Nielson would begin rating MTV's market share in March 1983.

The bottom line for 1982 was dismal. Their five-month-run in 1981 was a well-kept secret buried in the annual Warner's financial statement. The first year's revenue total was a paltry $515,000. Executives predicted a $14 million earnings figure in 1982. The final number was half of the anticipated amount. The operating losses were a staggering $10.8 million. Joe Smith of WCI estimated the net debit at $15 million. Stories on Wall Street, according to Bernice Kanner, abounded with the prospect of a third partner with money being added to the venture. The rumors, when applied to MTV, proved to be unfounded.

The Wall Street speculation was fueled primarily by the overall financial condition of Warner-Amex. Media analysts expected the new music network to lose money in 1982 and 1983. Of much greater concern was the Warner-Amex Cable Communications operation. High-level management changes and substantial losses were attention getters at brokerage houses and ad agencies.

In August Jame L. Gray was appointed president of WACC. He would preside over 124 cable systems with more than 750,000 subscribers. A seasoned cable man, having been with the Warner Cable Company since 1974 in Columbus, he viewed himself as "a chamber of commerce for cable." He would continue to operate out of Ohio's capital, assisted by Frank Nowaczek and the newly appointed head of customer operations, Ruth Finley. WACC would not be involved in the twenty-three metropolitan major cable markets that would remain under the jurisdiction of the parent company.

Changes make stockbrokers nervous and spawn rumors. A cable analyst with Drexel Burnham estimated to the *New York Times* that Warner-Amex lost in the vicinity of $10 million in 1981 and that losses could reach $30 million by the end of the year.

On November 23, 1982 the man who hired John Lack resigned as the chairman and CEO of WACC after almost a decade of service. Gus Hauser, a cable pioneer, announced:

> I've done my part, I think everyone would agree, over the past ten years. I built this company from a very small one to a very large business. Phenomenal growth. We've been through the most difficult growth period. We've been through everything. I want to change my own personal life style and goals. This is really a personal decision. Everybody has to decide how to lead his life. . . . I've been running organizations like this for almost twenty-three years. Now I'm going to say it's time to shift gears.

Hauser's decision shook up an embattled cable industry. The highly publicized interactive QUBE system was begun under his tutelege, as was the Nickelodeon Network. He commissioned Lack to expand the WCC hookups, the embryo of WASEC and later MTV. Despite statements of regret issued by James Robinson III of American Express, it was widely believed that the credit card company was dissatisfied with the massive costs of construction and franchise bidding wars. American Express executives, off the record, were candid. "No one likes losing a lot of money," said an insider. "The payout kept getting postponed into the future." Another executive partially blamed Hauser. He was "an innovative thinker, but he didn't know how to run a construction company." Hauser responded in *Business Week:* "All companies lose some money if they're going to wire America. You can't do it all and show a quarter-to-quarter profit. Those who care about that should not be in the cable business."

The profitability of wiring the nation was rapidly fading as the balance sheets clearly indicated. "Millions of dollars must be spent to fulfill promises made by competing MSOs," wrote James Roman in *Cablemania.* Warner-Amex was involved in almost sci-fi bidding wars in Pittsburgh, Houston, and Dallas.

The *New York Times* best summed the situation of Hauser's departure. He was leaving "at a time when an atmosphere of considerable gloom has enveloped the cable industry and when it faces the monumental financial task of wiring big cities. Since his name has become synonymous with Warner-Amex, his departure raises the question of what impact there will be on the business."[14]

There was a fly in the corporate ointment: the sins of the fathers. WCI and American Express were having massive economic cash-flow problems. Both reported losses in the millions for 1982. A retrenchment was definitely in the wind, as a plethora of articles in the influential financial press was suggesting.

The troubles at Warner-Amex, according to Jack Schneider, had little direct impact on WASEC or MTV. It was the cable division that was mired in a sea of red ink. WASEC, however, could not totally divorce itself from the parent company's problems. The disposal of The Movie Channel would have a direct bearing on WASEC. Schneider opposed the sale, but he said, "They own the store." Now retired, the former WASEC president can be philosophical about Warner-Amex, but the reality of the situation was that the fortunes of American Express and WCI affected both divisions not just WACC.

While the troubles at Warner-Amex were being dissected in the financial press and by stock analysts, MTV was again attacked on its racial policies. Richard Gold wrote a story on the paucity of black videos. His angle was that Motown and other labels were not producing videos costing $10,000 due to a lack of nationwide exposure. The translation was obvious: MTV wasn't airing black video clips. Alvin Hartley, with New York's Pro-Vision Production Company, commented: "The problem is, the record labels feel there's no immediate market." Motown was very cautious. Only name artists such as Smokey Robinson, Stevie Wonder, and Rick James were receiving video support, but only the crossover artists such as the British reggae group Music Youth ("Pass the Dutchie"), Prince (1999), and the Los Angeles black rockers the Bus Boys were rotated on MTV.

The Bus Boys, one of the premier visual acts, ironically were ideal for MTV for all the wrong reasons. Urban contemporary stations dismissed them, as they were in the tradition of the West Coast Motels and Missing Persons. AOR avoided them on the basis of color. "The Boys Are Back" made the MTV playlist as the Bus Boys were defined as "straight ahead" rock.

Bob Pittman pointed to these acts and said, "It's not a color barrier—it's a music barrier." Rick James was on the wrong side of Pittman's "borderline." Pittman did mention to Gold that WASEC was interested in urban contemporary. "I'd like to see a black music channel," he noted. "It's been discussed here, but we can only do one thing at a time." John Lack, who grew up on New York "doo-wop" and WINS, was the major proponent of the concept for MTV. There was a great deal of resistance to the idea. Had Lack prevailed many of the problems of 1983 may be have been muted or avoided. Len Epand of Polygram Records seemed to have a reasonable solution: "There are a lot of outlets—you don't have to live and die by one." Robert Johnson promised that his Black Entertainment Television (BET) "Video Soul" show would be expanded "to accommodate as much black video music as the labels will supply." This would occur in September 1983.

There was the traditional international market for black artists. Motown's Leiviska-Wild explained the rationale for the label's "chosen few" by noting that these videos were targeted "for international exposure." Another executive indicated that black videos are "more geared to sales overseas." Perry Cooper, who gave up on MTV for some of Atlantic's artists, said, "Internationally, video is more out front in breaking an act." His U.S. philosophy of "radio is number one" was ineffective when employed in the United Kingdom or other crossoceanic markets. State-controlled radio, internationally, was the bane of the music industry. AOR's and MTV's rigid formats paled in contrast to the BBC in the United Kingdom. "The British people, that's all they get rammed down their throats every day," said Peter Frampton. BBC-1 was a prototype in that it was a heavily rotated singles-oriented Top Thirty station. British musicians underlined the significance of television and the print media in the Commonwealth. On tour in America they generally marveled at the diversity of the broadcast media in the United States.

Ironically, it was just this diversity that most record executives misunderstood. Except for Turner's Atlanta-based "Super Station 17" the most successful cable offerings were narrowcast. CNN, ESPN, Nickelodeon, and MTV are all directed to a demographically defined audience, primarily in the suburbs and rural regions of America. Record companies do not think in narrowcast or specialty market perimeters. Promotion and publicity have traditionally been aimed at the twenty-five major population markets. Secondary markets follow. The rest are considered tertiary or satellite markets. It was precisely in these smaller areas that the cable systems predominated.

As the year ended, two of MTV's goals had been satisfied. Video clips were coming into the studio at unprecedented rates. Cable operators' resistance was eroding. The next hurdle would be the advertising community. If MTV was to return a profit, the time buyers of Madison Avenue had to be sold on the music channel.

Notes

1. Even *Washington Post* television critic Tom Shales, who has attacked MTV frequently, admits that "the network's clever animated logos and promos are probably the best in the business" (August 25, 1985).
2. In retrospect Milsap was ideal for MTV. The blind singer said, "Country music is down to a 6 percent share of the record business and only five years ago we had a 24 percent share. I'm a believer in the traditional side, but I'm also a believer that you have to perpetuate that broad-based appeal."
3. *"Solid Gold,"* the syndicated TV show, excluded James' "Give It to Me Baby" from the program, indicating that the lyrics were too explicit. James merely responded: "It bothered me a bit. They would rather I do another song. I don't think I'm being blatant." *Billboard,* June 13, 1981, p. 35.
4. Official MTV estimates for 1981 are 2.1 million subscribers.
5. *Video,* April 1982.
6. *New York Post,* August 5, 1982.
7. Off the record one insider explained: "At the time that he gave the interview . . . there was a lot of dissension between cable operators and programmers."
8. July 31, 1982, p. 26.
9. Roman Kozak in the same issue titled his "Rock 'n' Rolling" column: "Caution: MTV May Be Hazardous to Your Mind." The story described the banning of MTV in a Hartford, Connecticut, mental hospital. The reason given by a spokesperson was that MTV was "too inciting." This did not bode well for the future, although few realized it at the time.
10. *TV Guide,* November 29, 1982, p. 97.
11. *Time,* November 29, 1982, p. 97.
12. *Cablevision,* June 21, 1982.
13. *New York,* October 11, 1982, pp. 18, 20–21.
14. *New York Times,* November 24, 1982.

5

"It's the Format!"

When MTV's 1983 New Year's Eve Rock and Roll Ball, featuring Duran Duran and Flock of Seagulls, was televised Group W Cable (New York) included MTV on its roster. All Manhattan would now have the service. This added 75,000 potential subscribers in the northern half of the borough. The "I Want My MTV" campaign had succeeded in the world's largest media center.

Advertisers could now view MTV before making a decision on a time buy. It worked. MTV sold more ad time in the first quarter of 1983 than all the previous year. Veejays would no longer have to explain their professions to friends and acquaintances. They were receiving 200 fan letters, individually, per week.

Three weeks later, Group W in Los Angeles—with 176,000 households—began airing MTV at 6:00 P.M. Saturday evening with "Video Killed the Radio Star." The Southern California cable operation serviced Santa Monica, West Los Angeles, Fullerton, Buena Park, Newport Beach, Ontario, and "The Valley."

Frank G. McGillis, a regional vice president, explained the acquisition: "When the CBS Cable Channel disappeared on December 11, we were wondering what we were going to replace them with. That was when we decided to go with MTV and the Satellite News Channel." Survey research showed, according to president Burt Staniar, that "the two areas which people wanted were music and news."

The Los Angeles market had been equally bombarded with the "I Want My MTV" blitz. Ads on radio and television did have an impact, although McGillis merely noted that the marketing drive had caused inquiries to Group W outlets.

In a rare moment of understatement, Bob Pittman said, "Los Angeles is a very important community for us. After all, the music industry is located here." Nearly a year and a half after Fort Lee, MTV had finally broken into the opinion-making capitals of America.

Jo Bergman cites January 1983 as the real launch of MTV: "It's one thing to have reports coming in from the field, it's another to go home at night and put it on in your bedroom." "There's the world before MTV hit New York and Los Angeles," she continues, "and the world after that. That's when rock video began to grow at an incredibly fast rate." "I think it's psychological" being in the media centers. MTV entered into its second incarnation in January 1983 by "hitting New York and Los Angeles markets." Being in the two media capitals of America legitimized MTV. No longer would most observers scoff at the network. Ann Lieberman, program acquisition manager for Twentieth Century Fox, summed up the situation at the Visual Music Alliance seminar: "Outside of MTV and sporadic projects, there's not a lot going on in visual music," (MTV's competitors will be discussed later.) MTV was becoming an important medium vehicle with all the advantages and problems it brings. John Sykes' view, which worked in the beginning, of "we strive to be irreverent" became much more difficult when media critics and special-interest groups began to scrutinize the channel.

Billboard—"the Bible of the music industry"—at the end of January began to publish MTV's video clip rotations. The influential trade announced the chart, describing the network as enjoying an "acknowledged success in exposing and helping to establish new and developing acts [and] has led to increased attention to the entire video music field from industryites at labels and in radio and retail, as well as artist managers and artists, venue operators, producers, and others." The new chart contained the original twenty-four-hour "clock" of heavy (three to four plays per day), medium (two to three), light rotations (one to two), and add-ons.

MTV had broken through a number of barriers. However, it was far from being out of the economic woods. The video clip service temporarily seemed solid, even though record labels and music publishers were still complaining about the exposure value. The cost issue was far from resolved.

Subscribers appeared fickle. In November 1982 MTV had 6 million; in December the number jumped to 9.6 million and then began to decline. The slide was cyclical, according to *Market & Media Decisions,* an advertising trade journal. Ad revenues grew as time buyers began to appreciate MTV demographics, but on the horizon was the resurrection of the Rick James race issue and internal conflicts at WASEC were surfacing.

The five men who constructed MTV were all strong, creative personalities. Inside observers, using almost the same terminology, described the founders as "not the easiest persons to get along with" or "work with."

There was an internal cohesion supplied by the goal of overcoming seemingly insurmountable barriers. As these barriers began to fade some of these dominant, innovative egos, which pioneered the network, would surface. False rumors were rampant involving a "business' dispute between Schneider and Lack. Lack blames the Movie Channel and Showtime Viacom venture as the principal reason for his departure.

> It wasn't such a conflict with Schneider as it was that the company [WCI] . . . wasn't going to grow anymore. There was not going to be any more development. There was not going to be any game on this channel. There was not going to be any shopping channel, which were in development at Warner at the time. . . . They were much more exciting even than MTV. Then I decided hey, it was time for me to get out of here and do my own deal.

A friend counseled, "When are you going to be smart and start playing with your own chips?" Lack's major rationale for leaving was the state of WCI.[1] Warners was having problems with its cable and record divisions and Atari. Lack also had unrealized vision of an urban contemporary format in the mold of MTV.

After the holidays, he went globe hopping. Following a recuperative period he returned to the broadcasting industry. He is currently coowner and chief executive offer of ELF Communications, which operates eight radio stations in Nashville, Knoxville, and sections of the southwest. Many of MTV's middle management founding team was already gone. Others were seriously considering the option. Of the original eight names cited by Jack Schneider as "people who really know the business" only two remained by mid-1983. Many others not on the *Variety* list were absent.

Sue Steinberg, who played a major role in the selection of the veejays, left shortly after MTV went on air. Robert Morton, the creative director, departed around the same time. Both withdrew on "amiable" terms. Carolyn Baker, director of talent and acquisitions, exited. She would later criticize some of MTV's "sexist" content and rigid programming.

Another defector was Fred Seibert, who cofounded Fred/Alan Inc. with Alan Goodman, a consultant on the development of the MTV logo. Goodman was a former advertising copy chief at CBS Records. He explained the move to the *Village Voice:* "There were opportunities for us at Warner-Amex, but the opportunities we saw ahead of us on our own seemed more exciting and dangerous."[2] The twosome opened an office on the top floor of the Sheraton Hotel. The first client was the Playboy Channel, with an abortive project called "Hot Rocks." The program aired once on Hugh Heffner's network on July

29th. Seibert's present goal is to make jazz "visually exciting." "I think it can be done, I don't know what the solution is." He is still on excellent terms with many of the top executives at MTV. Trade paper items on these departures were notably absent. Fred/Alan Inc. would later supervise the animated logos on VH–1.

One personnel change at Warner-Amex did garner media attention. Drew Lewis was hired as chairman of the board of the parent corporation. His reputation, having stubbornly fired the striking air traffic controllers at the behest of the Reagan administration, preceded him. The former secretary of transportation was viewed as a "hatchet man." It was widely believed his appointment was to dismantle Warner-Amex. Tied to the rumors that The Movie Channel was being sold to Viacom International, Lewis' appearance created a stir. "Had Hauser and Lack known something that other executives had missed?" was a common question. One insider recalled: "He created an air of uncertainty. We had all heard the rumors. Everyone was losing money. The question was, "What was to be chopped—and who?" Lewis did cast a menacing shadow, but WASEC vice-presidents had more pressing problems to contend with.

Rick James, Michael Jackson Versus Narrowcasting

Music publishers at the California Copyright Conference held in January 1983 repeated the controversies of the first *Billboard* Music Video gathering. The major issues were payment for clips and black music. Ben Begun, Warner-Amex's legal affairs vice president, portrayed MTV as a "promotional service" not a "program," therefore they should have a fee waiver. David Cohen of CBS partially supported the MTV position with the contention that labels subsidize expensive promotional clips and therefore should have control of their usage without any mechanic or copyright payments, as the promos were advertising devices. Begun happily concurred saying, "The record company which produces the clip, is the actual rights user." Music publishers in the audience and on the panel disagreed. Jay Lowy of Motown's Jobette division told the audience, "It seems to me that it's like freebies all around. Other music shows on television are paying hefty synchronization rights. These shows star the music, and the writers and publishers are receiving due compensation as a result." MTV's definition of being a mere "service" to expose and sell records did not impress the assembly. The royalty payment situation would escalate as music video broadcasting increased.

Begun was bombarded with questions concerning black music,

especially by Lowy and publishers with minority artists in their portfolios. Begun's reading of a short list of urban contemporary acts rotated on the music channel only heightened the tension. The audience was unpersuaded. The heat was building on the MTV "corporate philosophy" and narrowcasting.

The MTV racism controversy that arose in the early months of 1983 was a case of economic interests wrapped in the mantle of civil rights. The rhetoric did not always point to the underlying monetary motivations pulling in some very well-intentioned persons, such as David Bowie, Bob Seger, and *New York Times* television writer John O'Conner.

A&M's Jeff Ayeroff had told Sykes at the 1981 *Billboard* Video Music Conference, "Just try playing the James video and see what happens," and MTV ignored the suggestion. Bob Pittman stuck to his format philosophy: "You can't go too far into black music or country music or easy listening or you'll alienate your target audience, which is interested in rock." The demographically and geographically defined cable viewers of the network were white males in the suburbs and rural areas. Pat Wadsley of *Video* magazine revived the question for Pittman. The response was predictable, in light of radio's fragmentation and cable's narrowcasting structures. "Rick James is great. So is Parliament-Funkadelic," he told the writer, "but we turned down Rick James because the consumer didn't define him as rock." He cited the statistic that 85 percent of the targeted audience prefers rock adding, "But we do play black artists—Joan Armatrading, Gary U.S. Bonds, Jimi Hendrix—because they fit within rock and roll. So it has to do not with race, but with sound."[3] He could have added the Bus Boys, and Phil Lynott, then a hard rocker from Ireland (he died in 1986). *Variety* got the same reply with one caveat: "We hope to find more black musicians doing rock and roll and new music."

After MTV turned down the "Super Freak" video, "Slick" Rick James finally got into the fray. He told the *Los Angeles Times* that MTV was "racist." His main objection was clear: "I figure if they played my video I could probably sell hundreds of thousands more records than I do now." Slick Rick had a point. Black Entertainment TV in 1982 had about 2 million subscribers—20 percent of that of MTV. Worse yet the RIAA estimated that the urban contemporary market accounted for about 2 percent of record and cassette purchases.

At a Los Angeles television studio James would expand views. "I'm hoping my speaking out in public about MTV's discriminatory policy will make other acts go on record about it." "I'm just tired of the bullshit," he later told *Rolling Stone*. "I have sold over 10 million records in a four-year period . . . and I can't get on the channel. I watch all these fluffed-up groups who don't even sell four records on a program that I'm being excluded from. Me and every one of my peers—Earth, Wind, and Fire, Stevie Wonder, the Gap Band, Marvin Gaye, Smokey Robinson—have great videos. Why doesn't MTV show them? It's like taking black people back 400 years."[4]

Rick James was a gadfly. Pittman cordially complained to a *New York Times* writer, "Why doesn't anyone talk about all the music barriers we have broken down, like the areas between punk and new wave and mainstream rock?" The rhetorical query really didn't address the charges, but was a defense of the format.

Schneider was silent on the issue. Some MTVers claimed it was aloofness. In retrospect he claims: "I think we got a bad rap, but I've been in that sort of arena before. I just thought that the first thing you do is hunker down and don't make any stupid statements." The WASEC president's argument makes some sense in light of his CBS experiences.

At the same time A.C. Nielsen brightened the MTV picture. The television polling firm found that MTV viewers spent an average of 4.6 hours per week watching the channel. The October 1982 survey also found that 85 percent of the target audience watched the network. Record-buying decisions were found to be equally affected, as 63 percent of the 2,000 respondents answered that they did purchase an album after seeing an act on MTV. Eighty-one percent indicated that their first exposure to some acts was via the music channel. The most significant finding was that 68 percent of the sample rated MTV as important or very important, surpassing radio's 62 percent.

A demographic profile from the same study showed that the typical viewer was around twenty-three years old with an average household income of $30,000. More than 50 percent of those over eighteen in the viewership were college educated. These were the kind of numbers record companies and advertisers notice. The findings released in February underlined the import of MTV exposure—a fact that further fueled the black music polemic.

Veejay Mark Goodman, after conducting one of his usual fluff interviews with David Bowie, found the roles reversed. Bowie peppered the puzzled veejay with questions. "Why," asked the superstar, "are there practically no blacks on the network?" Goodman, who merely introduced the clips and announced concert dates, explained: "We seem to be doing music that fits into what we want to play on MTV. The company is thinking in terms of narrowcasting." Bowie pressed on. "There seem to be a lot of black artists making very good videos that I'm surprised aren't being used on MTV." Goodman, placed in the highly uncomfortable position of defending a format totally beyond his control, echoed the company's demographic policy: "We have to try and do what we think not only New York and Los Angeles will appreciate, but also Poughkeepsie or the Midwest. Pick some town in the Midwest which would be scared to death by . . . a string of other black faces, or black music." He went on, "We have to play music we think an entire country is going to like, and certainly we're a rock and roll station." The exchange got hotter. Bowie asked: "Don't you think it's a frightening predicament to be in?" The intimidated veejay resorted to the radio analogy, "Yeah, but no less so here than in radio." The British singer pounced on the reply: "Don't say, 'Well, it's not me, it's them.' Is it not possible it should be a conviction of the station and of the radio stations to be fair . . . to make the media more integrated?" Leaving Bowie's hotel suite Goodman may have had second thoughts about "meeting his idols." In all fairness, Goodman was in a very difficult position. Had he agreed with Bowie it would become a matter of disloyalty. Statuswise he was no match for the international superstar. Offending David Bowie was not the thing to do. Reportedly "Entertainment Tonight" was planning a segment on the inflammatory debate.

Looking back on the James charges, John Sykes, almost with resignation, says: "Once the racial issue steps in everyone forgets everything else; it becomes a show of prejudice versus liberalism. Then everyone read into it who is being held back."

James' allegations would create one of the biggest unsolved mysteries in the development of MTV.[5] This is in an industry where any significant move hits the "street" before actually occurring.

Epic Records, a subsidiary in the CBS Group, geared up to equal the success of their *Off the Wall*. Produced by Quincy Jones over a prolonged period of time with some of Los Angeles' top session people, the nine-cut *Thriller* album contained a duet with Paul McCartney ("The Girl's Mine"), Eddie Van Halen picking high-powered guitar solos ("Beat It"), and a Vincent Price narrative in the title song. Several Jackson biographers estimate that studio costs surpassed $500,000. CBS had a hefty commitment to the effort, going in.

Off the Wall had been an 8 million, multiplatinum crossover album of the year in 1980. To obtain this sales status a wide appeal to those beyond the urban contemporary market had to be established. If *Thriller* was to parallel or transcend this, the first Epic release had to reach the AOR and MTV audience. Neither were airing artists with Michael Jackson's sound. Although it was widely believed that the network practiced a quota for black artists (an unproven allegation), MTV appeared an easier vehicle to promote than tackling the resistance of the myraid of nationally scattered AOR stations. There was also the question of the good will of music directors.

Michael Jackson's *Thriller,* his second solo effort, bulleted up the *Billboard* chart to the number one slot by the last week of February. "Billy Jean," the single from the LP, reached the same position on the "Hot One Hundred" a week later on March 5, 1983. Both had been on the trade charts for at least seven weeks. A video clip of "Billy Jean" was commissioned to support the single and the album. Steve Barron of Limelight Productions directed the visual. The "concept" video cost considerably more than the average, which at that time was in the $8,000 to $20,000 range. Estimates are that the label spent $60,000 to $75,000 on it.

The five-minute video was a response to the plethora of paternity accusations against the singer. The lyrics intone: "Billie Jean is not my lover . . . the kid is not my son." This is the essential storyboard, complicated by a plot of an unpleasant private detective dogging Jackson. In surrealistic fashion attempts to photograph the hero bare only blank film. When touched by Jackson, objects, sidewalks, and even a bum's ragged suit take on a bright glow. The investigator, unlike TV private investigators, is ultimately arrested as a "Peeping Tom." Jackson then conveniently disappears.

CBS Records' aggressive promotion vice-president Frank Dileo took the clip to MTV, "the music video" network. He recalls, "In the beginning they did not know what would be acceptable to their audience," which was an understatement at best. MTV's response was generally negative. Bob Pittman: "We chose rock because the audience was larger. The mostly white rock audience was more excited about rock than the largely black audience about contemporary rhythm and blues." Les Garland echoes his superior's view: "You cannot be all things to all people. You cannot play jazz and country music and funk. You lose your focus." Privately, Pittman was labelling his critics as being "ignorant" of the format.

CBS was adament. Dileo went back to MTV on several occasions to restate the label's case. MTV continued to repeat: "It's the format" and the decision had nothing to do with race.

Pittman's argument was consistent with past pronouncements. Originally he shunned "golden oldies" even if the clips were available, saying: "I don't think our audience is very interested in the past." The same applied to futuristic videos: "Musically, those songs do not fit into MTV's format. They're too avant-garde."

While enjoying some support within the broadcast community, MTV was rapidly being pushed into a public relations corner. The perception was becoming, for some people, the reality. CBS Records, as many have discovered, is a company that is willing to exert its clout. Epic did have an argument. "Billie Jean," with its chart position, was an obvious crossover hit appealing to both races. *Thriller*'s success only reaffirmed the contention. This view did not seem to originally persuade most of the MTV brass.

The March 2 MTV playlist had "Billie Jean" as an add-on. This 180 degree shift led to considerable speculation. None of the individuals reportedly involved will directly discuss the about-face.

In late February an informal meeting had been arranged at Black Rock, where some top executives met to consider their options with MTV. Persuasion was not working. One executive suggested having Michael Jackson appear on "The CBS Morning News" and repeat James' charges of racism. Several participants indicated that the ploy had little effect in the Slick Rick situation. Several other strategies were discussed and dismissed. Finally, the ultimate weapon was introduced: curtail MTV's supply of free videos—especially of name acts, such as Billy Joel.⁶ This was a step Motown never dreamed about, as their roster and market share were limited. "What could [Berry] Gordy do, threaten to pull the Dazz Band video?" noted *Rock & Roll Confidential* (RRC). The CBS Group, with almost 25 percent of the recording market, could withhold Journey, Pink Floyd, Billy Joel, and many other artists aired on MTV. Allegedly, Walter Yetnikoff played this card and won. One CBS company employee cautiously noted, "All I can tell you is that *if* that story is in fact true it was a helluva gamble. Chuzpah!! MTV could have held firm. Then what?"

In light of the record companies' experience with radio and the home taping issue, the outcome could have been quite different. Many broadcasters refused to go along with labels' "friendly persuasion" to halt playing entire albums without interruption. Record label executives at that time conceded that withholding product service would be counterproductive. Pulling the plug on MTV, at the time, could have similar consequences. One CBS artist stated, "I was on MTV at that time. It was definitely helping record and concert sales." The implication was that he would not have been overjoyed with an MTV boycott, especially with the state of AOR in early 1983. "Walter [Yetnikoff] and I never had a discussion about 'Billie Jean,' " says Pittman. Dileo was negotiating the matter with MTV executives representing Pittman's views. Deniability is a practice common in organizations outside the confines of the intelligence gathering community. It is doubtful Pittman or Yetnikoff would have been *directly* involved. Still, given the stakes even corporate vice-presidents were not individually empowered to make the kind of hard decisions that situation invoked.

MTV put the best face on the turn-around possible. "By the time we put that video into rotation," John Sykes told a writer, "there was really no way for us to ignore 'Billie Jean.' It had moved beyond being a 'black music' hit; it was an across-the-board smash, pop, black, dance charts, you name it. It was a rock song, a pop song . . . it fit our format." Veejay J.J. Jackson said, "I think we all wanted to see 'Billie Jean' on the channel." Garland would later deny any coercion: "No, that's absolutely untrue."

The addition of the clip has been cited by many as *the* racial "breakthrough." The debate raged on. Radio broadcasters, privately and in trades, had misgivings. Formats by their very nature had borders. One program director observed, "Jackson's a universal, maybe Prince, but what happens if one of the biggies decides an urban contemporary artist should be on AOR?" Off the record another retorted, "I didn't realize affirmative action applied to playlists."

Jeffery Kelly, operations manager of WDMT (Cleveland), went public on the controversy. He wrote in *Billboard* that artists "have expressed their view that MTV should play 'all' contemporary music that is hot and on video. But isn't it true that, like radio formats, this type of television programming is segmented. MTV doesn't air Rick James' video; it doesn't air Neil Diamond's video, either. MTV is a *rock* format . . . [it doesn't] play black or soft rock or country music, because it doesn't appeal to their segment of the audience." Kelly went on to suggest that in the future an urban contemporary network would appear "appealing to that active, black, music-loving public." Dave Marsh in his monthly newsletter, without referring to Kelly, condemned MTV and the AOR radio fragmentation. "MTV's racism is more dizzying in its complexity and dimensions simply because the channel is nation wide." The cause for the writer was radio. "MTV's prgrammers—Bob Pittman, Les Garland, and Lee Abrams—all learned their tricks at AOR, a true school for scandal." Marsh's newsletter piece would later be reprinted in the mass circulation *Record* magazine.

In the Basement

On Monday, March 14, 1983 MTV introduced "Basement Tapes," a monthly half-hour competition with local bar bands willing to send in a three-quarter-inch video cassette. Six clips were being aired each month. At 11:00 P.M. viewers were invited to call a 900 number to select the winner. One show had 81,000 voters. The six-month contest would involve a play-off system with the winner being awarded a contract for an EMI mini-disk or EP and the production of a video clip. On the debut show groups from Detroit, Chicago, Cincinnati, Los Angeles, New York, and Washington, D.C. would vie for the next round. One of the regular veejays would host the show. A selection panel of music industry folk would chose from the clips submitted but the call-ins would determine the winner. The six first-round winners would fight it out in September for the grand prizes.

The Slickee Boys from Ocean City, Maryland, appeared on the first show with their most requested original song, "When I Go to the Beach." This was their big break. "This could be it," sparkled Kim Kane, the rhythm guitarist. "If it is, we're prepared to quit our day jobs. It's our biggest opportunity." Kane described the video as, "Real wacky. . . . It has some animation, dancing hot dogs, Pac-Man chasing us around, surfboards, chicks dancing in bikinis, a fake motorcycle fight, the police chasing us down the beach, the boardwalk, the whole beach scene."

Mark Noone, the lead vocalist, described the song, itself, as a Venture's arrangement featuring "nothing but fun." The video was financed by Vox-Cam Associates of Silver Spring, Maryland.

The appearance could be a watermark in the act's career. Noone acknowledged, "All the record people watch MTV. They don't listen to radio, so it's nice that they're doing this for [unknown] bands. It takes something like this to open people's eyes." It is a "great platform for new groups," according to superstar Lindsey Buckingham. "Radio over the past two years has become more and more constrictive in terms of what they will play . . . this opens up a whole new venue for new bands. I think it's the healthiest thing in the world." Kim Kane partially supported the rock star, but wasn't quite as generous in his assessment: "It's kinda gross that radio and music doesn't speak for itself anymore. . . . Not everybody can afford to do videos." The Slickee Boys did not make it to the September finals. Seattle's Rail won the first EMI prize.

Some characterized the program as a mix blend of CBS' old "Talent Scouts," "The Gong Show," or rock and roll home movies. For MTV this was a good promotional move. It added a "local interest" aspect to the network. "Basement Tapes" had several problems familiar to sports fans marking a ballot for baseball's All-Star Game. The Slickee Boys, for example, played in an area much of which lacked cable. What Is This, from Los Angeles, with a much greater cable penetration could literally "stuff" the ballot box. Despite the flaws, the concept worked for MTV, raising ratings where they counted; the artists, as Noone indicated, got exposure. The finalists also picked up new sound equipment and instruments.

Racism Charges Resurface

The race issue hung on. The "is" versus "ought" dialogue continued. Eddy Grant's "Electric Avenue" appeared on MTV. Grant, an iconoclastic funk-fusion artist, originally dropped by Epic in 1980 only to be resigned for the *Killer* album on Portrait, was sanguine about the MTV issue. He informed *Record*'s Anthony DeCurtis: "I've never bowed to format or whatever it is, because, I don't *understand* it. I understand only one thing: how to make music. And I make the music, and if people like it at the radio, or the TV, or wherever, fine. If they don't, well that's fine too. Because I'm used to it both ways." Some of Grant's urban contemporary's were not so laid-back over the issue. He was on MTV, and they were not.

Prince's "Little Red Corvette" continued to complement "Billie Jean" on the cable network. On April 23, Garland Jefferys had two songs, "What Does It Take" and "El Salvador" on the light rotation; "Beat It," from *Thriller,* directed by Bob Giraldi and costing nearly $150,000, started in the "heavy" or most repeated category.

"Beat It" was perceived as the "Stairway to Heaven" of music videos. Bob Giraldi, the director, had reservations concerning Jackson's ability to perform the role. The singer, perceived by many as "sissified," had "never been in a gang war; Michael Jackson's probably never been out of that house. I think the world knows he's been watched and protected all his life." But Jackson wanted to do "something street."

The director arranged with the Los Angeles police department to provide authentic extras. "The police warned us to be very careful," he told *Record*. "We were, and I've never had a more wonderful experience in my life as a director than watching these tough gangs. They were taking my direction, but they were dubious, skeptical. . . . They found another kind of macho from that piece. From that point on, we were home free." The basic plot has Michael Jackson transposing himself into a peace maker who descends into a ghetto garage and prevents a gang war fight by turning the assembled warriors into a communal dance scene easily reminiscent of the Broadway production *West Side Story.*

"I think violence stinks," recalled Giraldi. "The whole beauty of

'Beat It' is how it shows that the macho trip is a joke. I had peace come through this magical creature named Michael Jackson. Obviously, if anybody ever analyzes it properly, they will see that it's anti-violence, not pro-violence." Michael approved the finished product. He told Giraldi: "Okay, this is my anti-violence statement through music; this is your anti-macho vision as a director. Peace through dance." Video watchdog Dr. Thomas Radecki of the National Coalition on Television Violence labelled "Beat It" as having "probably educational impact." His annual report stated, "Gang violence with chains, clubs and switchblades. Jackson gets gang to stop fighting and dance with him. Suggestion that gang violence is wrong."[7] *Thriller,* prior to MTV, had sold some 3 million units. With video exposure it was in the 800,000 per month category.

Prior to James' comments in the *Los Angeles Times*, the "racism" debate remained in the trade magazines and specialty publications such as *Video*. This was "inside baseball" material, as its termed in journalistic circles. A locally sponsored music video six-hour symposium in Atlanta, April 16, found Les Garland denying "racism" charges and rattling off the black artists on MTV. Consultant Dwight Douglas prematurely objected, "I'm sick of the press jumping on MTV about this 'racism' business, it's not true. You have to remember that MTV has a very expensive format to protect. If they broke their narrowcasting pattern, somebody could come along and blow them out of the water." Douglas, president of Burkhart and Abrams, was hardly an objective observer.

Manny Sanchez, the marketing director for Franklin Music, retorted: "Forget this black/white thing. The issue is 'green.' We need to get on with the business of selling records. That's what we're here for." In May the nonexistent "press coverage" would surface. Ed Levine in the *New York Times Magazine* would write a lengthy piece on MTV published May 8; five days later ABC-TV's "Nightline" addressed the same subject, music video. Casey Kasem and Rick Dobbis, of Arista Records, were joined by Rick James. James, it appears, was apparently incensed by the inclusion of other black artists. According to several insiders James felt even more personal discrimination because of the addition of Jackson and Prince to the MTV playlist. He would again exclaim his displeasure. The show opened with generally high praise from industry executives and even Ted Koppel, not known for his verbal generosity, commented, "It has done wonders for the sagging record industry. It has made overnight stars out of rock groups whose records had been gathering dust." James dissented. The Motown artist complained that MTV "has refused to play five of my

Table 5.1
BLACK ARTISTS ON MTV AFTER APPEARANCE OF "BILLIE JEAN"
(1983 ON)[1]

Date	Artist	Rotation
March 2, 1983	Michael Jackson	Addition
March 30, 1983	Michael Jackson	Heavy
April 2, 1983	Michael Jackson	Medium
	Prince	Medium
	Eddy Grant	Light
April 16, 1983	Garland Jefferys	Addition
	Michael Jackson	Heavy
	Eddy Grant	Light
April 23, 1983	Michael Jackson	Heavy
	("Billie Jean" and "Beat It")	
June 4, 1983	Michael Jackson (two songs)	Heavy
	Eddy Grant	Medium
July 9, 1983	Donna Sommer	Light
	Eddy Grant	Light
September 3, 1983	Herbie Hancock	Addition
November 26, 1983	Paul McCartney and Michael Jackson	Heavy
December 12, 1986	Ashford and Simpson	Addition
	Herbie Hancock	Addition
	Paul McCartney and Michael Jackson	Heavy
December 17, 1983	Paul McCartney and Michael Jackson	Heavy
December 24, 1983	Lionel Richie	Addition

[1]MTV's rotation did not appear in print until January 1983. Previous playlists have either been lost or are unavailable from the network.

videos." After some elaboration Koppel asked, "What's wrong—I mean we tried to get a representative of MTV to come on the show; they wouldn't. But they're saying in effect, 'Hey, Bloomingdale's has its market, "Nightline" has its market . . .' Why not?" James responded, "Well, then they shouldn't call themselves Music Television." The discussion continued:

KOPPEL: That's their privilege, isn't it?
JAMES: Yeah, but why call yourself "Music Television" then? I mean, why not then call yourself "We Play Sometimes Black Music Television," or "Let's call ourselves White Television or something." See, number one, you have a lot of black people out there and white people—they all buy records, they mix it up. You've got urban contemporary music happening, which is a form—the basis of it is a black music form. That's where it comes from. The beat, the tribal beat, as they say, or whatever, you know, all that crap. . . . This show has a very strong impact on the market. What about all the white kids out there who have a Rick James and a Michael Jackson or—excluding

Michael, who's on the show. They didn't put him on the show until he went number one. And then I also heard that Columbia almost threatened to take off every video on MTV until Michael was put on that show. When you get a record company threatening a cable show, telling them that if you don't play this act, we're going to pull our videos—that means something. It means something for us to get our music to people, and it means something for us to get our visual concepts to people.

In retrospect, Pittman and associates mishandled the "Nightline" show. Addressing the guests Koppel concluded, "You've reached a few people tonight who may never have heard anything about this before." The ABC host was right. The Jackson episode went unanswered. Rick James' fiery rhetoric went unchallenged. Les Garland's belated denial was unconvincing as it came at a time when the CBS "video boycott" story had become conventional wisdom in the industry. John Sykes, who could have appeared on the program, might have diplomatically treated the topic as in the past.

Black Entertainment Television (BET) president Robert Johnson's introductory comments unfortunately got lost in the passion of the telecast:

MTV is not racist. MTV may have made a mistake in just selecting a narrow focus on music . . . they formated rock music as their video concept. They decided that the audience they wanted to reach was a young, white audience that didn't have any interest in R&B or soul or urban contemporary, whatever you want to call it. I think they may have made a mistake on that score, but they have the right to provide specialized programming. That's simply what cable television is all about.

Recalling the ABC interview and the controversy, BET's head says:

I think narrow in terms of their particular music preference. I think at the time MTV was doing nothing but what they call rock and roll, and I thought that in terms of the amount of music that was out there . . . they could have reached a broader audience with a broader selection of a music format. MTV got a bad rap for what they were doing. Obviously they had a format. My point with MTV was, that if I was doing MTV I would have done a broader format from the beginning.

Johnson's knowledge on the issue was impeccable. He had been with the Corporation for Public Broadcasting and later served as vice president of government relations for the NCTA. He was a firm believer in targeted broadcasting, as he would later tell the *New York Times:* "Unless you are part of a mass audience your needs aren't being served. . . . If you like sports you watch ESPN, and if you want black programming you watch BET."[8] He once commented: "Our network is not a radical departure for TV. . . . We have not reinvented the wheel, only painted it black." In keeping with this philosophy, BET expanded "Video Soul" in the fall of 1983 to showcase black artists for an urban contemporary audience.

Unfortunately, many artists, managers, and labels knew little if anything about the mechanics of the cable industry. CBS's disastrous foray into the medium was a case in point. Reportedly, it turned into a $75,000,000 course in cable misprogramming due to its traditional mass appeal format.

Blacks increasingly were added to the MTV playlist, such as Donna Summer's "She Works Hard for the Money." The clip did not satisfy everyone. Speaking at the American Film Institute, scriptwriter Keith Williams charged he was instructed to use a white family in the clip. He, equally, revealed the way "the girls are dancing at the end of the clip [is] anti-women."

Detroit's hard rocker Bob Seger complained to *Musician,* "The thing I hate about it is that there's no black music or R&B on it unless it's syrupy stuff." Seger found an ally in John J. O'Connor, venerated television columnist of the *New York Times.* After describing the network as an important presence in programming and record sales, the journalist entered the debate. He wrote that MTV appeared to be "bent on returning the black musician to the status of 'invisible man.' . . . Critics have wondered if this 'oversight' is intentional, a demographic ploy for making MTV more palatable to the suburbs of middle-class white America. MTV executives, for their part, have insisted, not a little arrogantly, that their product is focused on rock-and-roll, an area of music that supposed is not frequented by black performers. Roll over, Chuck Berry." O'Connor outlined the broad scope of rock music prior to returning to the race issue. He suggested that Michael Jackson, Donna Summer, Musical Youth, and Prince were merely "promotional spots for MTV" or are being "used prominently in commercials for the format."[9]

The racism controversy was fueled by idealism, self-interest, and stubbornness. John Sykes' original statement concerning "left out" artists had merit. Maurice White of Earth, Wind, and Fire, a fusion act, complained on ABC-TV's *"20/20"* that "I have trouble getting to play on it [MTV]. Even though our music has broken all barriers they consider our music R&B, so they say that they're only playing rock music, which I don't believe."

The loudest voices of protest came from artists excluded from MTV, such as James and White. Bowie and Seger's position was one of conviction. Michael Greene of Atlanta's Video Music Channel concurred with BET's Johnson. "I take exception to claims that MTV is "racist," he told Laura Foti. "Their format excludes some wonderful black artists, but that's the way they choose to format the channel, similar to radio."

The MTV high echelon, especially Bob Pittman, was (or at least appeared) intransigent. Rick James was considered by most people in and outside of the industry as urban contemporary. Michael Jackson was an entirely different matter. He had clearly demonstrated a pluralistic market appeal. Pittman played directly into the hands of his critics by the original rejection of "Billie Jean" with the "it's the format" rationale. The widely held belief that CBS forced the video clip on MTV only made matters worse. MTV's arguments for the expansion of the playlist for more minorities because they were moving *into* rock music had a hollow ring to it. Rick James' tactic failed. He admitted, "It hasn't gotten any better for me. . . . Michael Jackson was forced on MTV . . . [he's] sold millions of albums. . . . I still don't like MTV."

None of Slick Rick's albums repeated the success of *Street Songs,* which reportedly sold three million units. After getting his act together[10] he acknowledged, "It doesn't make me feel bad. It just makes me feel sometimes that I *need to be more in tune with what the kids want"* (emphasis added).

Belatedly the Rolling Stones' Keith Richards joined in the fray. The "first thing I said after I watched a bit of MTV, you're lucky to see one black act every two hours, if that. Michael Jackson gets played; I heard MTV was playing the Bus Boys a few months ago, but it's real tokenism. When you consider the contribution black people have made to American music, it's disgraceful . . . it's a little bit one-sided."[11] MTV would remember these observations.

One year after the "Billie Jean" affair, Pittman would tell *Variety*'s Richard Gold, "Of the new artists being exposed on the service, some 25 percent are from the black music field." Later senior research vice-president Marshall Cohen would explain a ratings downturn with "we really got a huge benefit from playing the [title] clip from Michael Jackson's *Thriller* at the height of Michaelmania." He added that the ratings dropped "due to no *Thriller.*" Pittman concurs with Cohen's assessment, but prior to the so-called "lull" he used *Thriller*'s title song for other purposes. At a roundtable discussion at *Cablevision*'s offices chaired by Victor Livingston he observed:

The record was out fifty-three weeks before MTV played *Thriller.* Radio had the opportunity to make *Thriller* a single, but chose not to. CBS had the chance to push *Thriller,* but chose not to. Sales dropped about 250,000 a week from summertime levels of 1 million, 1.2 million. The first week MTV played it, sales jumped from 250,000 to 657,000 copies, next week to a million, and the third week in excess of a million.

You've got to figure that if they sold an extra 3 million albums at $2 an album, they make $6 million. Spending even 1 million on a video was a damned good investment, even if they didn't get a penny of it back by selling the video.

By mid-1986, Rick James remained absent from MTV's playlist, but the tempest he had instigated smoldered.

In the fall of 1983, Robert Pittman was sick of the sniping at his format and the demands being made on MTV. The Acquisitions Committee had added Michael Jackson, Eddy Grant, Prince, Musical Youth, and other black performers. This silenced some concerned citizens, but others persisted. David Marsh's *Rock & Roll Confidential,* beginning with its first issue in May, urged: "If you're as sick of this bullshit as we are, why not write MTV. . . . And call your local cable outlet." The same issue accused MTV of "deceptive advertising." The next issue accused MTV of a "significant market failure" and continued to attack: "We billed them for a subscription to *R&R,* sent them the first issue, and still haven't been paid." Next issue contained: "Number of black performers with MTV concerts or specials in the history of the channel is still zero. . . . MTV honchos like Bob Pittman aren't lying . . . when they claim that black and white music have 'always' been segregated." In the following issue David Bowie was urged to "withhold videos and interviews until the channel opens up." One of the few pro-MTV letters arriving at the magazine refuted the writer's view that "MTV is for entertainment; it does not make a statement. It needs the money, not cultural values." The writer, Marty Bell of Hamilton, received a reply. Letters condemning the channel as "Moron-TV" went unchallenged. Steven Levy, in a lengthy *Rolling Stone* article titled "AD Nauseum: How MTV Sold Out Rock & Roll," presented the following "simulated" exchange with Pittman:

SL: Some people might argue with your definition of rock & roll, Bob.

BP: Our definition is not speculation. There's a million dollars' worth of research there.

SL: But the power of MTV has made this a bread-and-butter issue for black artists.

BP: It's *our* bread and butter. If anyone says we should change, I'd like them to take our losses. I'd change our losses with theirs right now. They don't recognize that this is a business. Bloomingdale's wouldn't work if it carried every kind of clothing ever made. MTV is a phenomenon of the youth culture. Our point of view must be hitting home.

SL: Some say that's because while you may not be racist, you're catering to white suburban racism. And that you're in a position to change that, to expose people to great black artists as well as white ones.

BP: I don't know who the fxxk these people are to tell people what they should like. (Pittman fumes.) They sound like little Hitlers or people from Eastern-bloc communist countries. The good thing about America is that people rule. That's the essence of America!

But it was not "the people" who designed the format of MTV. It was Pittman and his assistants.[12]

Robert Christgau described the *Stone* piece as a "well reported but tendentiously conceived jeremiad . . . obvious and overstated." A friend of the MTV CEO explained that Pittman expected a "hatchet job," as he and *Rolling Stone* owner Jann Wenner were at odds. The result was a very uncharacteristically hostile interview.

Despite the inclusion of Lionel Richie's "All Night Long," Bob Giraldi portrayed MTV as "racist bastards." They "can say all they want," he noted, "about over the line, across the line—they are obviously racist and there's nothing else to say about it." Insiders speculated the charge stemmed from the network's rejection of the director's "Pieces of Ice" by adult contemporary singer Diana Ross. Ross was noncommittal on the turndown. Appearing on "Adam Smith's Money World," Giraldi changed his tune. He praised MTV and its contribution to the music industry. Nary a word about racism. In part he told the PBS audience, "I don't think they even realize . . . [it] would have such an impact. But it has."

As the management group seemed to be shaking the "racism" image, the Black Music Association (BMA) held its annual conference at the Sheraton Center in New York. Les Garland represented MTV Several members of the "Black Music Summit" panel revived the issue. Joe Tamburro of WDAS (Philadelphia) suggested a quota system for MTV based on the size of the black populace. The radio program director urged, "We should be getting our share of videos programmed on MTV. . . . I think the companies can get that for us." An obvious reference to the CBS "Billie Jean" episode. Producer James Mtume concurred: "The companies support the attitudes that allow MTV's racist programming policy to exist." The 250 people assembled in the audience, according to Nelson George, seemed to be in agreement. Several participants dissented. "Not everything on MTV," said CBS vice president Larkin Arnold, "as we can attest, sells. Our music will not necessarily sell more if programmed on MTV." Disbelief swept over the audience. His "Land of the Good Groove" had been rotated on MTV.

The "New Technologies" panel opened with a statement by publicist Ken Smikle: "We're not here to put Les [Garland] on the chopping block." Smikle deflected many hostile questions posed to Garland by saying, "The answers are available in the press kit." BET president Robert Johnson repeated his previous view on narrowcasting saying, "You wouldn't go to a classical station to get your rock product played, would you?" He went on to suggest that his network in time would provide the exposure most blacks wanted.

Some grumbled that BET was "struggling." BET's major problem was that urban markets such as Detroit, Cleveland, Baltimore, and Washington, D.C. were unwired. Twenty percent of the black population couldn't get BET. The network also experienced transponder problems as well as limited air time due to economic problems.

A handful of militants perceived Johnson's remarks as too conciliatory. Johnson's logic made a good deal of sense. He did not want black music being coopted. "Black music is an integral part of black life," he said. In an *Electronic Media* interview he made his position quite clear: "I think it'd be a slap in the face if an operator added MTV . . . or another music video channel and then said he's reaching out to the black community."[13]

Since the beginning of music broadcasting and record marketing segregation had been rampant. *Billboard* at one time labelled it "race music." In the early years of white rock and roll, black artists were "covered" by the likes of the Crewcuts, Pat Boone, and a host of crooners. The Penguins' "Earth Angel" stopped this practice when the original black version outsold the watered-down release by the Crewcuts. The late Muddy Waters was an embittered man when the Rolling Stones popularized his music. Only then did he receive the attention he richly deserved. MTV would broadcast an in-depth bio on "Liner Notes" upon his death.

Other major black artists—Chuck Berry, Ray Charles, Fats Domino, and others—were absorbed by a predominantly white radio market. History would repeat itself with the "Motown Sound" and later disco when the Supremes and Donna Summer moved directly out of urban contemporary. As Bill Speed, producer of "Video Soul," would acknowledge, "The software's there and the personalities are there." Johnson wanted to keep it that way. "First, music is a very important part of black entertainment and culture," he told *Billboard*. "Second, black artists wanted a broader outlet for their videos. So we made a heavy commitment, which was fine, because it's such good programming for us."[14] The soft-spoken president and founder would later explain: "It's different from BET. BET is not just a music channel, we are a vertical network in that we offer everything from sports to public affairs, to music, to gospel and religious. In that sense BET is different . . . you might say our music is targeted, and it is in the same way, to the same extent formatwise that MTV is chartered, but we're not just a single music channel."

The symphonic FM station and rock music made the fragmentation argument. However, there was another angle that some broadcast veterans may have picked up. In 1966 the FCC put into effect a ban on simulcasts in markets of 100,000 and above. The ruling was in response to symphonic music lovers' complaints that the FM band could be used for less profitable, more quality broadcasting. When the rock camel stuck its free-form nose under the FM tent and advertising dollars poured in, many speciality stations went progressive rock, leaving Bach, Beethoven, and Brahms behind.

The December 24, 1983 *Billboard* editorial seemed to put the "racism" issue to rest (except in *RRC*.) "Do our eyes and ears deceive us, or is the MTV playlist becoming a shade more liberal?" the unsigned statement rhetorically asked. The editorial went on to suggest that the playlist obviously had to fit the network demographics, but "It's good news that Les, John, and their colleagues now believe that acts such as Ashford and Simpson and Earth, Wind, and Fire are capable of that compatibility." The "compatibility" was based on the crossover potential demonstrated by artists such as Michael Jackson and Lionel Ritchie. Pittman and associates could not ignore the popularity of these performers with whites. *Thriller*'s sales exceeded the entire black population. Obviously many whites were buying the album and swelling MTV's subscribership. Les Garland noted at the Video Music Conference that black artists were beginning to adopt the "MTV sound." *Billboard* editorialized:

> This turn of events is not without irony. It was MTV's willingness, early on, to program new artists and music that brought many in radio (especially AOR programmers) to the recognition that their conservatism was not sufficiently in tune with the public mood. The switch of

many AOR stations to top 40 has intensified the public's appetite for hits—which, in turn, may be influencing MTV to tilt just a tad more "horizontal."

Billboard welcomes the development. Multi-format hits, the kind that trample underfoot every programming barrier, are good for the music business, in creative as well as commercial terms. They reach the broadest possible universe of consumers, and excite their taste buds for more.

Ironically the National Coalition on Television Violence (NCTV) criticized MTV for airing Michael Jackson's " 'Thriller' video, banned in Australia, [which] features a very appealing young hero having fun terrorizing his girlfriend with horror violence." Publicist Dorene Lauer rejoined, "We're not worried about Radecki and his group." The *Guardian*'s Eayne Rapping accused MTV of being "sexist" because of the 'Thriller' video, writing: "While no overt physical violence is shown, the stereotypical, scared, clinging girlfriend role is clearly that of a victim." Moreover, "All in all, 'Thriller' is one cheap thrill we could have done without." The left-of-center publication quoted Dr. Radecki of the NCTV as saying, "Rock stars are role models for kids, so it's not hard to imagine young views, after seeing 'Thriller,' say 'Gee, if Michael Jackson can terrorize his girlfriend, why can't I do it too'?" To further compound the situation the Rev. Jerry Falwell, founder of the Moral Majority, on "Crossfire" questioned Jackson's fitness as a male role model. Louis Farrakhan, a Black Muslim leader, vilified the singer as "female acting, sissified." A sociologist asked *Time*'s Jim Miller, "Is this the role model we want for our children?"[15]

Merchandising, Radio, and Mayhem

While attending the NARM convention in Miami, John Sykes cleverly arranged to have MTV piped into the Fountainbleau Hotel rooms, displacing the CBS station on a Sunday. This ploy worked until the highly rated "60 Minutes" aired. Due to numerous complaints the hotel management pulled MTV in favor of the investigative news program. MTV was back on the next day.

Speaking to the merchandisers Sykes unveiled a Nielson study of some 1,296 cable users in the South and West. NARM members heard that the music channel outstripped all other vehicles of exposure in record-buying decisions—leading radio by six percentiles. He rattled off various statistics to support the argument that MTV was *the* medium of major consumer influence.

Sykes backhanded potential music video competitors by suggesting that they did not share his network's concern for promoting records. As John Lack originally indicated, MTV's primary role was to act as a stage for the music industry and its product. "We have felt from the start that we could experience our strongest growth working together," Sykes observed. "We believe that if the music industry in general thrives, then so will its components." By "coincidence" *TV Guide* presented, for the first time, "MTV as a shrewdly devised nonstop promotional showcase for the record industry" the same week. This was exactly what NARM people wanted to hear, as the record-buying public was slowly beginning to stir after a three-year downturn.

In the aftermath of Sykes' presentation the day before, David Geffen in his keynote speech told NARM delegates:

> MTV is a very effective tool in exposing and breaking new artists. In turn, it's stimulating and encouraging recording artists to expand their creativity both visually and conceptually. Now the music industry can become the predominant art form through which the new generation seeks to express itself. We—music in video—can monopolize the imagination of a new generation.

Les Garland traveled to the International Music Industry Conference (IMIC) at the Algarve in strife-ridden Portugal. Like Sykes, he presented the gospel according to MTV. Record sales as usual were paramount. Viewers purchase nine albums per year. Four were attributed to network viewership. Again, the "partnership" with the music industry was stressed.

Few would dispute MTV's role in making "Beat It" and *Thriller* megasellers. AOR stations began airing the two after MTV exposed the songs. *Thriller* became CBS' best-selling album in history, surpassing Simon and Garfunkel's *Bridge Over Troubled Water* and finally entering the *Guinness Book of Records* by doubling the sales of *Saturday Night Fever*. By this time MTV's ability to expose acts was generally recognized. Duran Duran, Flock of Seagulls, and Stray Cats sold without airplay in markets serviced by MTV. Merchandisers were delighted.

Tulsa was MTV's southwestern psychographic test market. Tulsa Cable hosted the regional opener for the network. MTV's local penetration was 100,000 households. The Oklahoma city was used in a full-page *Billboard* ad, using testimonials on the channel's impact in October 1981. Leo Sacks returned to Tulsa for a follow-up, filing a report in the April 16, 1983 issue of *Billboard*.

Sacks interviewed Steve Mitchell, a buyer for The Sound Warehouse, a chain of three local stores, and programmer Jeremy

Whitworth of KMOD-FM (Tulsa). Mitchell, like many observers, saw MTV as the vehicle that motivated the record-buying teenager out of the video arcades and back into the record store. "It definitely stimulates product that we couldn't move ordinarily." Mitchell had nothing but good things to say about the music channel. "MTV has opened up our business to sell a more diverse group of artists" and recognizable older acts "can sell even more units. . . . It's amazing that within a few days, product which has been sitting on the shelf for as long as six months can start selling again. The effect is almost like the disk is a new release because the music has reached a new audience."

Sound Warehouse closely monitored MTV for selections and their rotation position and stocked product accordingly. For merchandisers, the music channel was rapidly becoming a major vehicle of exposure. This allegation was supported by the Nielsen studies. This fact only heightened the tension between radio and music video operations. Within record companies conflicts were also raging over video clip versus radio exposure.

Retailers, having lived through the "disco disaster" of 1979, were delighted to applaud any upturn from the doldrums of the past three years. AOR was given little if any credit for pulling retailers out of the tailspin. This was a bit unfair, as *Thriller*'s initial breakout was on the audio medium, although MTV's reluctant acceptance of "Billie Jean" and other clips from the album did revive the momentum for the record. *Thriller* was now selling 300,000 units per week.

Record executives were still uncomfortable with cable casting. A Capitol vice president indicated, "Good chart product appears to be selling better than a year ago, but I don't see any significant increase in catalog sales." The upturn was based on the volume of MTV-featured video acts such as Jackson, Men at Work, and the soundtrack from *Flashdance,* which went on to sell some 12 million units. MTV featured four videos from the album. Retailers were moving dormant product. Clearing the bins of albums they once would have returned if the labels had not altered the credit system for poor-selling albums. The so-called recovery was only affecting selected aspects of the entire merchandising sytem.

Billboard's Marcia Golden found in a national survey of merchandisers that MTV's sales impact was sporadic in light of "cable's limited penetration." In qualified statements, most of the retailers contacted, with reservations, praised the music channel. "I don't think they get the audience of radio," noted Bruce Bell of the Listening Booth in New Jersey, "but still, I'd have to say 'absolutely yes' that MTV has had a positive impact on our record sales." A Lantham, Maryland, merchandiser was more emphatic: "The impact has been spotty, mostly be-cause MTV is not available throughout our store areas, particularly in the Baltimore area. . . . Most of the major urban areas are not covered by MTV. Washington, D.C., for example, has no cable TV. So radio still has the greatest penetration." Another seller said, "Regardless of these shortcomings though, I think music video has helped record sales. It's like having another merchandising aid."

MTV Versus AOR

MTV's roster of cable customers was rapidly growing. Record company executives, however, were keenly aware of the limitations of cable. Polygram's Len Epand noted: "MTV is no longer the instant karma it was a year ago, which is not so much a critical comment as an observation on the maturation of the medium. We find what works best is a national/regional approach." Les Garland replied, "We stayed with [Stray Cats] . . . without much radio airplay at first. Their manager told me he even plotted their tour by the markets MTV serves, and they sold something like 200,000 records without any significant radio exposure. Once radio kicked in, they took it that much further. . . . With Quiet Riot we started seeing the effect weeks ago—before the record took off in such a big way." MCA's Leo Solters' countered with, "The service reaches only twelve million subscribers." His figure was incorrect, but the thrust of the argument was widely held. Epand admitted: "There are some accounts who order an additional 700 to 1,000 pieces of product simply on the basis of there being a video on MTV."

AOR broadcaster Jeremy Whitworth dismissed the assertion that MTV influenced the KMOD-FM playlist. Instead he contended that the music channel frequently highlighted radio's song selections. His response was not surprising. Mike Harrison, the programmer who coined the term "AOR," contends that radio people suffer from "screenis envy"—a deeply ingrained feeling of jealousy of the visual medium. "MTV becoming readily available to the public is making radio's tweeters turn green," he wrote.

Many broadcasters well remembered the original MTV campaign aimed at record companies. Much of it consisted of using AOR as a timid idiom afraid of new artists. This was a sentiment shared by merchandisers and record labels. Robert Christgau summed up this posture retrospectively writing, "MTV won't ever be as conservative a culture force as AOR." Christgau's long-time friend and colleague David Marsh, one of MTV's most ardent detractors, blamed most of

MTV's perceived shortcomings on the AOR backgrounds of many of network's top brass.

During the interview Whitworth partially lent credence to the conservative stereotype of AOR, saying Lynyrd Sknryrd, ZZ Top, and Led Zeppelin were still very popular. "But we're trying to experiment with new music at the station, and MTV helps to open the door for records we might otherwise not play."[16] He cited Adam Ant's "Goody Two Shoes" single. "Had we rolled the cut without video exposure," he observed, "it would *never* have had the success it experienced with our audience. We would have been afraid to play it. But the clip was good, and it affirmed our gamble." Whitworth had great difficulty in resolving the role of MTV vis-à-vis radio: "It's not like they're trailblazing, because most of the music we add reaches us before the clips reach them." He added a caveat: "But they are making our 'new music' transition easier."

Sacks pursued this "complimentary difference" argument with other broadcasters.[17] Video exposure he found did motivate some add-ons on AOR stations, but some of those interviewed saw MTV as a potential threat. Bob Hattrick, a consultant, expressed this view: "MTV has been very helpful, and rock radio will become fresher and more exciting because of it. But I don't discount their ability to pull quarter-hour shares of listeners from AOR." Others reinforced his perspective.

Sacks found broadcasters at both extremes. KSRR's (Houston) Andy Beaublien told the *Billboard* reporter: "They help break records, which makes them good for rock 'n' roll. And anything that's good for rock 'n' roll is good for AOR radio." In Atlanta, with some 100,000 cable households, Alan Sneed, programmer director for WLKS, rejoined that MTV was a direct competitor. "MTV is blatantly robbing AOR radio of its audience," he maintained, "and programmers who don't recognize this are just naive." WLKS banned commercials from MTV and Atlanta's Video Music Channel from its sponsors list.

Lee Abrams, consulting for some eighty AOR outlets *and* MTV, was much more conciliatory. He was caught in a highly precarious position. He dismissed the view that MTV was in open competition with AOR. "Some programmers regard MTV as 'the enemy,' " he noted, "but it's helped radio to open its eyes, it's like having a real aggressive station in town. More than ever, our stations are taking a hard look at what MTV is playing. We were almost a year late on Duran Duran, Billy Idol, and the Stray Cats, and I don't ever want that to happen again." As in the days before "American Bandstand," broadcasters were now monitoring MTV for add-ons. With considerable pride Dick Clark insisted that "everyone's talking about the influence video has on radio, and there are a lot of new acts who owe their livelihood to video. But thirty years ago, Top 40 stations had secretaries sit down and list all the songs that were played on 'Bandstand.' "[18]

Morning drive-time deejay Richard Blade, then one the highest rated Los Angeles music personalities, concurs with the significance of video: "Video had had the power to force new music on radio because suddenly the kids can visualize how cute the boys in the band are."

Eighteen of the top twenty singles on the "Hot One Hundred" in the fall of 1983 had a video clip. Forty-seven of the best-selling top fifty charted albums featured a cut accompanied by an MTV rotated video. Recording artists were increasingly telling their companies, "I Want My MTV Video Clip." "Videos got me quicker exposure than any other form of promotion," Pat Benatar told Vernon Scott, "and helped spread the word on my nine-month tour. Kids knew who I was and what I looked like in addition to how I sang."

"MTV is wonderful for people who can't get out to concerts or for rock fans in rural areas and smaller towns who don't have a chance to see their favorite performers," she added. Duran Duran's synthesizer man, Nick Rhodes agreed. "MTV was instrumental in breaking us in America."

Getting Back to Business

A.C. Nielsen's audience and market-share reports had legitimized MTV in the minds of advertisers. As a result ad revenues in 1983 rose by an impressive 252 percent over 1982. As of June 15 MTV enjoyed 13.5 million subscribers and 1,650 cable systems offering the music service.

[These verified Nielsens eroded much of Madison Avenue's resistance to the network.] In June MTV had 140 national time buyers placing some 240 sponsors on the channel. Jack Schneider divided the new-found advertisers into two categories: "There are those who use it as a traditional media buy, to fill in the gaps . . . the areas where network is under-represented, and that area is nailed by MTV." Bob Daubenspeck, vice-president of Foote, Cone, and Belding, praised the narrowcast: "That audience is hard to reach through normal broadcast channels. There aren't many shows devoted to that audience segment." FCB brought time for Embassy Films and Levi-Strauss. "It's a new opportunity for a lot of people," said Arnie Semsky, an early MTV supporter, "particularly the fourteen to thirty-four age group, which has found some programming made just for them. He expressed pleasure with the use of MTV to advertize soft drinks and chewing gum. One of his clients was Pepsico. (Through the use of MTV, Pepsi would engage in the Great Cola War of 1985—more to follow.) A colleague noted that the client "barrier" against rock videos "was beginning to crumble." Young and Rubicam, looking at the demographics, placed ads for Suzuki, CBS Records, and Cadbury. "It's difficult to reach teens on network TV, although there are some fine vehicles . . . MTV is an incredibly good environment for gums and mints," observed Larry Grossberg of J. Walter Thompson.

Schneider's other category was for sponsors fitting MTV's mood and approach: "There may be products invented just to appeal to the MTV audience," such as films and fashions. Paramount Pictures, he insisted, "gives MTV credit for the success of *Flashdance*." The producers of *Ghostbusters* and several other teen-oriented movies could echo the same sentiment. A cynic retorted, "The clips and commercials frequently are better than the films themselves." Segments of the fashion industry plugged into the MTV mood, following the blue denim jean companies as sponsors (more to follow).

During the summer McKinsey and Co., a highly respected consulting firm, was commissioned to conduct an efficiency study of WASEC, including MTV. An outside analyst told *Billboard:* "The results are likely to teach them different disciplines. It will cut down on waste, create a better product, and distinguish the creative from the business side of their operation." Paul Green felt MTV needed more focused leadership and a sense of direction. Much of MTV's success was based on the perception suggested by Sue Steinberg: "Anything could happen here." Even the sacred narrowcasting format, despite denials, did bend when necessary. The last thing MTV wanted was an efficiency probe. The old nemesis of the entertainment industry was rearing its head: creativity versus profitability.

"Freedom's just another word for nothin' left to lose" wrote Kris Kristofferson in "Me and Bobby McGee." This line could easily be applied to MTV. As its promotional power grew, ad revenues rose, it became an institution. It became almost a brand name for music videos, just as Coke and Kleenex are for cola and tissue paper. "When you ask for a tissue you don't ask for a Vanity Fair, you ask for a Kleenex," says "Night Flight" producer Cynthia Friedland. "And when you talk about music television you talk MTV."

Irreverence, to use John Sykes' term, is difficult when the network was becoming an institution. Many of the early innovations were not planned by the "most researched" network in cable or even overground television broadcasting. Many of the innovations were pure serendipity or chance. As a member of Duran Duran would note, the group may never have gotten on the American cable system if a video clip of "Stairway to Heaven" had been available. MTV's award-winning logo was a total gamble chanced by Fred Seibert. Candidly, he felt that rock television would probably fail. History supported his view. Many artists originally exposed by MTV were chosen on the basis of clip availability and the need to fill twenty-four hours of air time. The mutually beneficial relationship between Michael Jackson and MTV during the height of the Michael-mania probably would not have occurred except for the pressure exerted by the CBS Group. MTV, partially, was akin to the "Columbus Syndrome"—the navigator landed on the American continent in search of the China passage.

Pittman's increasing snappishness and irritability with the press was growing, as was evident in several of the few interviews he would grant. The "format" issue was misunderstood, he felt, and a distraction from more important internal demands. The central problem was the company deficit. Operating costs were outstripping growing revenues from advertisers and new CATV downlinks were charged ten to thirty-five cents per hookup.[19] Some costs were being recouped from existing on-line cable systems. Still, "MTV will not make money in 1983," Jack Schneider confessed to the *Los Angeles Times*. "There is no question in my mind that it was a prudent business investment, but the start-up and development costs were enormous."

Rumors had MTV $30 million in the hole as of 1983. The actual figure would be higher. The sum total of losses from 1981 through 1983 added up to $33.9 million. According to some the spin-off shows, although clustered on weekend nights, could cut into MTV's steadily growing advertising earnings. One industry observer said: "Their market is substantial, but it can only be fragmented up to a point since they're all going for the same sponsors." (As will be seen MTV's competitors would become more aggressive in 1984.)

"Madison Avenue is a show-me kind of situation, and we're just coming out of the show-me stage. There's good word of mouth, good PR, and most important, good ratings. The Nielson figures . . . validated everything that our sales people had been saying for maybe a year," said Dom Fioravanti, ex-WNBC-AM general manager then with MTV.

Despite the rosy appraisals, Warner-AMEX was becoming increasingly nervous over the financial status of the cable operation. According to Schneider, "There were enormous money problems with the cable side, there were not money problems on our side. . . . We were building a business and it wasn't going, the industry wasn't going the way Warner Communications thought it should or was going to do or they wanted it to go." Schneider is not totally consistent in his argument. The Movie Channel, as noted, was a division of WASEC. Warner-Amex, in economic difficulties, decided to dispose of it. Schneider commented: "Well, I didn't want to, but it doesn't matter how I felt about it. There's no use getting emotional about these things, you've got an owner, they want to sell the company, they sell the company."

One Warner executive characterized Gus Hauser as a "real visionary . . . but the industry has changed." John Lack was cut from the same cloth. They had built ideas into communication realities. By 1983 both perceived the writing on the wall and fled Warner-Amex. Neither envisioned any future growth potential. WACC had won more major market franchises than any of their competitors. MTV was becoming a full-blown cable network. Both were in the red. Referring to the machinations of the parent companies and politics within MTV, Lack once prophetically snapped: "I didn't like what was going on there."

The crux of the problem was the excessive expectations of corporate giants for the cable industry. Al Knight, managing editor of the *Rocky Mountain News,* aptly summed up the situation: "Seldom have [crystal balls] been more clouded and misleading than when they were used to predict what cable TV would be like." Warner-Amex, including its hard and software divisions, had banked on an incorrect forecast.

American Express, which invested some $175 million in 1979, found their shareholders growing restless. The goal of wiring America was costing considerably more than anticipated. By late 1982 Warner-Amex had paid out $300 million. The management of American Express wanted a faster return on their outlay. Rumors abounded that the card company wanted out or at least was in search of a "white knight" to pick up some of the debt.

WCI was experiencing its own problems with their Atari games and home computers. Teens were losing interest in Pac-Man cassettes and Knickerbocker dolls. Atari, which carried WCI during the record recession, was reporting accumulated losses of over $536 million during the first three quarters of 1983. Ironically, one factor advanced for the losses was the teen defection to MTV and the record stores. Warners did not greatly benefit from the transfer of allegiances. WACC had overcommitted to Dallas, Pittsburgh, Houston, Cincinnati, and Milwaukee, as well as outlying urban suburbs. By the close of 1983 34.1 million subscribers had basic cable. Less than one-third of television households had a cable capability. The wiring of America lost much of its promising glitter. WASEC retreated on drawing-board projects and cut back on personnel.

By cable standards MTV's 17.6 million subscribers was respectable and appealing to advertisers. Few disputed the music channel's impact in areas it was transmitted. Going into 1984 MTV had sixteen companies manufacturing jeans and twenty-seven different types of apparel firms buying time. By the end of 1983 advertising sales were a healthy $24.8 million. MTV's loss for the year was $12 million.

By the end of 1983, to paraphrase Bob Dylan, "the times they were a-changing." Robert Alter, president of Cabletelevision Advertising, cautioned: "There's no question that the expectations that people had about cable were unreal." Wiring large urban areas presented economic and political problems. "Virtually every city that granted a franchise in the last five years has had a lot of trouble," Cynthia Pols of the National League of Cities told *Newsweek*. Interactive systems such as QUBE proved cost ineffective. This failure affected Warner-Amex, the pioneer in the technology.

In 1983 VCR sales jumped 50 percent in one year to over four million units. Their appeal in part was explained by a merchandiser: "The first time they come in, they say, 'I can't stand TV any more and cable is not enough.' "

In light of these trends Warner-Amex was no longer satisfied with the *eventual* profitability of Nickelodeon and MTV. They wanted results. Nickelodeon had accepted a few ads during the fall and caught considerable flak from the watchdog Action for Children's Television group.

MTV had increasing competition from other music video shows nationally and at the local level. Growing rumors of a second all-music network abounded. In 1984 the speculations would be vindicated. Few observers believed cable could carry two similar youth-oriented networks.

The moment of truth was definitely on the horizon.

Notes

1. Rumors persist that a falling out had occurred between Lack and Pittman. As with Hauser, innovators become expendable.
2. *Village Voice*, October 4, 1983, p. 88.
3. *Video*, April 1983, p. 113.
4. *Rolling Stone*, April 24, 1983.
5. The *Thriller* affair is one that most participants will not comment on either off the record or even on background. Consequently what follows is a circumstantial account of the events and the players, taken from various sources in print and interviews with journalists and others.
6. CBS can play hardball, as various print medium outlets have discovered. In April 1986 Yetnikoff pulled his advertising from *Rolling Stone. The Los*

Angeles Times was boycotted in July 1985 at the very time Michael Jackson's *Victory* album was released, much to the displeasure of merchandisers.

7. November 1983, 36–37.
8. *New York Times*, January 24, 1984 and *Broadcasting*, October 4, 1982.
9. *New York Times*, July 24, 1983.
10. See *Record*, October 1985, p. 10 for details.
11. *Record*, October 1985, p. 32.
12. *Rolling Stone*, December 8, 1983, p. 37.
13. *Electronic Media*, September 27, 1984.
14. *Billboard*, March 30, 1985, p. 30.
15. Jackson was honored by President Reagan in May 1984 for lending "Beat It" to an anti–drunk-driving commercial targetted at teenagers.
16. *Billboard*, April 16, 1983, p. 63.
17. *Billboard*, May 28, 1983, p. 66.
18. *Los Angeles Times*, August 21, 1983, p. 33.
19. The cost differential was based on the "basic" versus "pay" tier. This charge to operators would generally not affect most CATVs until 1984, as most free service contracts were still in effect.

6

The Rule of One

*Anyone who gets involved is crazy . . .
a second service doesn't work. MTV's
sophistication as a channel is so deep
that it wouldn't behoove anyone else
to get involved.*

Bob Roganti, MTV vice president for
national accounts

On December 31, 1983 seventeen to twenty million viewers tuned in
MTV at 11:30 P.M. (EST) to usher in 1984 with the most elaborate New
Year's Eve Rock and Roll Ball in the network's history. It was a far cry
from the first. Appearing for half-hour sets were Cyndi Lauper, the
Stray Cats, Thompson Twins, and from Wembley, England, via satellite The Police and the reunited Animals. Billy Idol opened the four-
hour bash with "Ready, Steady, Go." "Host" Pee Wee Herman failed
at being comedic (Herman aptly illustrated the reason for the demise of
slapstick vaudeville).

Free champagne in cheap plastic cups flowed steadily. The veejays
acted like political reporters covering a national presidential convention. Various name rockers were questioned as to their new albums and
tours. Triple "J" manned the backstage. The entertainment seemed to
escape numerous guests. Many rockers and others in the crowd were
there primarily to be seen. The music appeared incidental. Somehow,
despite the performers, the event was a political gathering of sorts,
which was appropriate.

Executive plans for the in-coming year were already in motion. Bob
Pittman and his aides saw the danger signals and time, like sand in an
hour glass, was running out. Pittman counted 265 "imitators." He
dismissed most saying, "None of the other services are major factors
in the youth culture. They don't generate the mass hysteria that MTV
does." Pittman had not read Pat Goldstein's description of a cluster of
high school girls gathered around a television set watching MTV. In the
Los Angeles Times he wrote, "After a few hours even these pop
fanatics grew bored with the constant procession of video, with the

conversation turning to boys, the beach, take-out pizza and, inevitably, more talk about boys."[1]

Michelle Peacock estimated the existence of some 300 broadcast and cable network music video programs. Most were local, posing little threat to MTV. However, the nationals competed for the same advertising dollars MTV sought, as well as world premiere videos. The "pay-for-play" issue was heating up again. Video costs were climbing at unprecedented levels. The end of "freebies" was definitely on the horizon. Gossip about Warner-Amex's intentions for the music network abounded on Wall Street and Madison Avenue, creating an air of uncertainty. "We're always reevaluating our financial state," said Pittman. The corporate machinations at 75 Rockefeller Plaza would prove considerably more fascinating than the New Year's gala. Schneider, Pittman, Garland, Sykes, and other executives were set on cementing the "Rule of One." In cable industry jargon "the rule" refers to the dominance of a single network, as CATV capacity plus the limited number of subscribers precludes two similar "basic" formats in news, sports, or music.

The MTV braintrust was faced with a strange contradictory dilemma. As the *Billboard* testimonial insert of August 6, 1983 indicated, MTV was an acknowledged exposure power in the record industry. Weekly some twenty or more clips arrived at the headquarters for the Acquisitions Committee to review. Artists were demanding clips from the companies. Clip costs were escalating, however. Directors Bob Giraldi, Steve Barron, Russ Mulcahy, and others were asking and getting six figures for videos. Some top-name Hollywood directors, such as John Landis and Brian De Palma, could be lured for the "right" price. The competition to get on MTV was becoming fierce.

Skyrocketing production costs and the uncertainty of MTV exposure for the labels were increasing problems. Accounting and promotion departments were complaining. Costs and the added problem of program directors asking "Does this record have video support?" were plaguing the companies. The previous largess of "free videos" was fading. "You don't need a weatherman to see the way the wind blows," goes a Dylan line appropriate for MTV's situation. Payment for clips and royalties were in the offing. Based on this assumption MTV wanted something in return to maintain its dominant position. The building blocks, as they were originally called, had to transcend the fare on the competing rock programs. This would guarantee growing advertising dollars and higher fees to the cable operators.

Despite its power position, MTV did not have the economic resources to produce a twenty-four-hour operation. Some strategy had to emerge to overcome real and imagined barriers to eventual profitability.

The answer lay in the realm of the unthinkable: Pay for play. For a radio person like Pittman, this tactic was heretical. Still, it had merit. The other side of the coin was paying for the rights to clips. WACC was an albatross. WASEC, while close to profitability, with Nickelodeon and MTV, still was in the loss column. The game plan had to consider an alternative. A stock offering was the option chosen. Selling the stock was no simple feat, even with MTV's status and visibility.

Exclusive debuts in the music industry are fraught with difficulties. Providing product to one station or network at the expense of competitors can easily backfire because this gives the receiver a distinct advantage over the competition. The MTV hierarchy reasoned that if they debuted them, "Night Flight," "Night Tracks," and others would object. Record labels had the "cop out" of citing the rising costs of clips" or better yet they had to establish a precedent for payment.

A game plan was put into effecct in the fall of 1983. A thin veil of secrecy was dropped over the enterprise. But in many aspects the music industry is akin to a small town. It is nearly impossible to keep a secret. Rumor mongering, correct or incorrect, keeps Watts lines busy and gossip columnists employed.

The "Other" Purveyors of Music Video

"The days of MTV being the only outlet are over," Capitol's outspoken Michelle Peacock informed the listeners at the Cervia Video Clips Festival in Italy. In a description of the television medium, NBC's chairman of the board, Grant Tinker, concurred: "One of the things wrong with programming. . . . there's too much copycatism. We tend to go the safe way because television is so incredibly expensive. This has produced a menu that is less varied." In the quest for advertising and world premiere product MTV's major rivals were USA's "Night Flight," WTBS' "Night Tracks," BET's "Video Soul," all satellite signals, and NBC-TV's "Friday Night Videos."

"Night Flight" first aired June 5, 1981 at 11:00 P.M. (EDT)—two months prior to MTV—as a four-hour wraparound shown twice on Fridays and Saturdays. The program was the result of an agreement between the USA Cable Network and American Talent International (ATI), one of the six most important booking agencies in the music industry. The launch date was chosen to take advantage of a writer's strike that had immobilized "Saturday Night Live."

USA was a network in search of an identity. Originally created as the

Madison Square Garden Sports Network (MSG Sports), it succumbed to ESPN to become USA in a joint venture with United Artists–Columbia Pictures on April 9, 1980. The newly formed network debuted in September. Howard Polskin of *TV Guide* wrote: "USA Network dabbled in many programming genres. Its identity foundered in the early 80's. . . . Three guys in a windowless office in New Jersey dubbed the 'bunker' called cable-system managers and tried to persuade them to offer their service . . . It wasn't fancy but it worked."[2] In June 1981 the network claimed 7.5 million subscribers.

Jeff Franklin, the head of ATI, frequently clad in jeans, a pull-over sweater, and western boots, took the concept of "Night Flight" to USA vice-president J.B. Lawrence in February. "We thought it was worth the risk," said USA president Kay Koplovitz. Four months later it began airing on a thirteen-week renewal basis. The original notion was to showcase ATI clients.

While Franklin, as executive producer, was initially the most visible, Cynthia Friedland and Stuart Shapiro actually operationalized "Night Flight." Ms. Friedland, a graduate of New York University, had managed Lainie Kazan and worked on "Scenes '70," a syndicated rock music show, before joining ATI.

Shapiro was a cult film distributor (*Cocaine Cowboy* and *Tunnelvision*) prior to approaching Franklin for access to pay-TV. His movie experience nicely fit the "Night Flight" blueprint.

Coproducer Cynthia Friedland commented: "We had that programming, and we were selling the programming, which was one of the reasons we were able to get on the air, but the other side of it was there was this gap, and because that was the programming I had available it was the most natural programming to go on the air. Of course, after we played what we had from the agency, we went after other groups as well." "We will give unrecorded acts their first real chance at being seen," added Franklin, discussing the targeted fourteen-through thirty-five-year-old audience.

The format was to present feature "rockumentaries," cult motion pictures, high-camp television serials such as "Space Cadets" and "New Wave Theatre," a Los Angeles based half-hour of new—punk—music talent.

This iconoclastic David Jove creation created a stir even at "Night Flight." "New Wave Threatre" scheduled The Sickettes doing "Chop Up Your Mother." Stuart Shapiro liked the song as pure satire. Friedland had other ideas. "That's where I drew the line, for the mothers out there." Later Shapiro told the *Daily News* that she wanted "good taste—no violence, no chain saws, no songs with titles like 'Chop Up Your Mother.' "

The title of the show stirred debate. Some people believed it emanated from Antoine de Saint Exupery's French literary classic. Not so, "We felt that we were taking people out of their living room and then on some kind of trip," says Friedland.

USA's vice-president of programming liked the notion. Prior to "Night Flight," Dave Kenin recalled: "The audience interested in alternative programming had been neglected with the cancellation of such network shows as 'Midnight Special' and 'In Concert.' 'Night Flight' filled the void and spawned many imitators. In fact, MTV . . . did not premiere until a few months after 'Night Flight's' critical acceptance." The on-air chronology is correct. WASEC, however, was doing music videos prior to the Franklin proposal. Neil Young's *Rust Never Sleeps,* a box office flop, opened the debut show followed by Shapiro's *Tunnelvision* with former "Saturday Night Live" stars Chevy Chase and Lorraine Newman, then "New Wave Theatre." Films scheduled included *Reggae Sunsplash, Jimi Plays Berkeley, Volunteer Jam, Alice Cooper Special,* and *Lenny Bruce Without Tears.* On New Year's Eve the classic *TAMI Show,* described as "the greatest gathering of rock performers ever assembled for one film," would be shown. The 1965 film featured Chuck Berry, Marvin Gaye, the Rolling Stones, and many more.

"Night Flight" allowed ten minutes of commercial time per two hours on the USA Network and two minutes for local operators. The rate card was $1,600 per minute. Pepsi, Wrangler Jeans, and Miller Beer comprised some of the original sponsors.

Following the emergence of MTV, Franklin altered some of the demographic tactics. "We've focused on a 16–40 age range," he informed writer/publicist Toby Goldstein. "When you run *Jimi Plays Berkeley* and *Lenny Without Tears* as a double feature, you're getting fathers and sons."[3]

> It was really to cross the generation gap, and to put together a program that would appeal to both parents and their children, and to provide the kind of programming that would make for communication between the generation, which is why we played stuff like Jimi Hendrix, coupled with Lenny Bruce. And that was the idea, was family programming, and don't forget the families we were talking about were the sixties kids who were grown up and becoming parents.

"Take Off," then a lead fifteen-minute minimagazine, was added to the format as support for "New Wave Theatre." Unlike MTV, the quarter-hour offering focused on a specific theme, ranging from punk rock to rock choreography by dance impressario Toni Basil. A *Rolling Stone* review compared Franklin's program to MTV and concluded: "

'Night Flight' seems the surer bet primarily because it is a much simpler idea, with no VJs, no host, almost no trimmings at all."

Franklin attempted to avoid comparisons: "I have a lot of respect for Bob Pittman . . . and I'm not about to knock something he's just started." He told *SOHO:* "We're more willing to go out on a limb for something that isn't strictly mass-market stuff, whereas MTV is basically a computerized AOR thing." Others at "Night Flight" were a bit more combative.

In a *Billboard* interview Stuart Shapiro backhanded WASEC. He told Laura Foti that lip-synched clips were "harmful.." "They're overblown. If you take a blend between what you can do with video and add in live performance, it's much more creative." He, also objected to the costs of videos. "They'd be better if they were cheaper."

Cynthia Friedland explained that "until all the commercial time is sold, my budget for program purchasing won't expand." She joined Shapiro in zapping MTV. "They're trying to be a radio station. I'm in television. My show is for people who have the capacity to concentrate. We give more than a superficial glance at an artist by presenting in-depth programs. . . . Pacing is important to the show. The people who are awake at 2:00, 3:00, 4:00 A.M. have a different mentality than the people watching at 8:00 P.M. We're programming a creative explosion, trying to put together an aesthetic puzzle to create something pleasing to all the senses."[4] This contradicted Pittman's emphasis on the Joycean stream of consciousness: "The strongest appeal you can make is emotional. If you can get their emotions going forget their logic you've got 'em.' " Pittman has been accused by some of having a very brief attention span. "That's why he likes printouts so much," noted an observer. Others describe him as a "quick study."

In the early months "Night Flight" enjoyed a numerical superiority over MTV. ATI was a recognized power in the music industry. USA appeared in *the* media markets. The conceptual Achilles heel, however, was the availability of full-length feature films. Marc Kirkeby's observation, "How many times will viewers watch *Rust Never Sleeps,"* had merit.

Shapiro, as of April 1982, stuck to the format. "We like to use concert films such as *Rust Never Sleeps,"* he said, "because they're a full set. The entire industry never gives a set, and this is destructive to the power of the artist."

The July 9 issue of *TV Guide* proclaimed the offering the "Best Pop-Music Magazine show on cable." *USA Today* would later honor the program as "the most creative use of music and video on television today" (December 2, 1982). Still, as USA's marketing vice president Andy Besch said in resignation, "MTV came along and it got all this terrific publicity, and we got lost in the noise." "When you talk about music television," says Cynthia Friedland, "you talk MTV, which doesn't mean you're talking about the twenty-four-hour channel, but you're talking about music video on television. . . . When people talk about music television, or music videos they mention MTV."

"Night Flight," while critically acclaimed, was virtually invisible. Part of the problem was the publicity department, which operated on a shoestring budget. There were objections to the "hodgepodge" format. Terry Atkinson wrote: "Its something-for-everybody format will just have a lot of viewers flipping away when something uninteresting is on. An even bigger minus: *too many reruns*" (emphasis added).

"Night Flight" executives objected to this characterization. "We don't mind if you walk away from it," says Franklin, "as long as you don't change channels. Go get a beer or make popcorn. When you get back, chances are something totally different will be happening." Friedland is more definitive:

> I think what "Night Flight" means is something for everybody, whether you're an intellectual into video art, and the more avante-guard type films that come out of the kitchen in New York, or you're into new bands, and a new kind of music, which was exemplified by "New Wave Theatre," which has certainly become a classic in its own right. . . . So I don't know what Terry Atkinson meant when he said it was too broad. I think we still do fill that gap of "Night Flight" being the show where you can see what you won't see anywhere else.

"Night Flight's" reliance upon feature films would prove transitory. As a basic service the music "magazine" was receiving crumbs off the pay-tiered movie network's table. The film roster, while having adult appeal, consisted of cult rejects by HBO, Showtime, and TMC. The "pays" had a lock on most of the big-budget rock motion pictures, ranging from *The Girl Can't Help It* to The Band's San Francisco "farewell" concert *The Last Waltz*. Viewers were tiring of reruns. By the fall of 1983 this unpleasant reality impacted on USA producers. Hilary Schacter noted: "The major film makers obviously are going to go to the pay services, or to the [commercial] networks for the bigger dollars. There's no question about that."[5]

After denouncing lip-synched video clips, they appeared in great abundance on the USA Network. Movies disappeared. "Take Off" opened the show with fifty to fifty-three minutes of clips covering everything from politics, protest, sexism, to body language. The "Take

Off" in one episode was described as "a look at lyric censorship, includes footage of the Senate hearings." Friedland's rationale was that MTV changed the audience. "It was to meet the demand of our audience. We get a lot of fan mail, and we listen to what our fans want, and they said that they wanted to see the top ten videos, so we gave it to them. It was our top ten though. It was the top ten that we felt was appropriate, and we took that top ten from information that was gathered from *Album Network* and other publications. So that's why we did that. We also put together the 'Heavy Metal Heroes,' which was filing a demand from our audience." In time more format changes were in the offing.

The summer of 1983 found MTV clones springing up everywhere. Two were major networks. Ted Turner's Superstation WTBS (Atlanta) introduced "Night Tracks" and the overground NBC-TV network followed with "Friday Night Videos." These were giant media players.

"Night Tracks" debuted the first weekend of June. The six-hour video clip show counterpointed MTV. Described as a "Chinese menu" format, the midnight-to-dawn program featured country and western, urban contemporary, and softer rock artists. Heavy metal was barred. Former executive producer Scott Sassa explained that they were trying to reach "a broad cross-section" of viewers. The show's Nielsons, given the WTBS cable hookups, were on occasion three times that of MTV's.

Their Friday edition was repeated on Saturdays with a different rotation, carrying the previous day's clips. The "Superstation's" audience share presented the biggest threat to MTV, not the narrowcast versus Top Forty aspect of "Night Tracks." This approach created advertiser resistance. The days of Sassa's "broad format that appeals to a broad audience" were anathema to the cable market. While claiming to target the eighteen to forty demographic, the coupling of Prince followed by Barry Manilow didn't make much psychographic sense on Madison Avenue. One observer intimated, "If WTBS didn't have the 'numbers' nobody would take the show seriously." (Turner Broadcasting System's involvement with music video will be discussed in the next chapter.)

"We Want Our Own MTV": Video Soul

"R&B is one segment, other than rock music, that does hold potential," prognosticated Bob Pittman somewhat gratuitously. MTV's executive vice president allegedly opposed the concept when Lack suggested it in 1982. The data indicated that the core for an urban contemporary network resided in unwired major urban markets. Robert Johnson and his associates, based in the nation's capital, enthusiastically concurred on the "potential." Their motto being "BET on it."

Robert L. Johnson, the founder and president of Black Entertainment Television (BET), announced on August 8, 1979 the formation of the nation's first black cable network.

Johnson started to build the network with a $15,000 loan and help from Tele-Communications Inc. (TCI). TCI president John Malone explained the rationale: "Nielson studies show there's a black audience that wants to watch black programming. There are advertisers who want to reach the black-consumer market and there are black performers and artists who want to work. But there's no distribution system for them." Johnson's background made him the ideal candidate for creating such a system. A movie casting director could not have made a better choice.

A graduate of the University of Illinois, Johnson obtained a masters in public affairs from the Woodrow Wilson School of Public and International Affairs at Princeton University. His career goal was to become an ambassador. Working in the Washington area seemed the logical starting point. After interviewing with the powerful, Johnson became public affairs officer for the Public Broadcasting System (PBS).

He migrated to the position of press secretary for Congressman Walter Fauntroy, the lone representative of the District of Columbia in the House. He had reached the halls of power. In 1976, at a neighborhood party, Johnson spoke to an associate of National Cable Television Association's president Bob Schmidt. The topic intrigued Johnson. He joined NCTA as a vice president of government relations—a euphemism for "lobbyist"—representing some 1,500 cable operators' interests to Congress. The three-year experience proved invaluable, as he established contracts with some of the top cable executives from Viacom, Tele-Communications, HBO, and Teleprompter. "You make your friends before you need them," Schmidt advised. Later Johnson would say that NCTA "put me in the right place at the right time to develop television projects."

One of his original tasks at NCTA was coaching USA Network head Robert Rosencrans, who was about to give testimony before a congressional subcommittee. Rosencrans would later agree to provide Johnson with three hours of transponder time at 11:00 P.M. (EST), on the USA Network. "Night Flight" would later occupy this time slot.

TCI president John Malone, who Johnson encountered in Denver, would again prove to be an invaluable ally. TCI would buy 20 percent of BET for $180,000 when the company desperately needed funds.

TCI, in Johnson's terms, had "deep pockets." The pockets got deeper when TCI joined with Taft Broadcasting. Malone became more than a financial backer. "If I've got an idol," BET's president told Tom Granger, "it's him . . . I can pick up the phone to ask John any question about business and know that he's going to give me a straight answer."[6]

BET was launched on the basis of "potential" on January 25, 1980 to 3.8 million subscribers in 350 markets across the country. The neophyte network broadcast only on Friday nights from 11:00 P.M. for two hours. Into that short time span BET squeezed black collegiate sports and "specials." The charter advertizers consisted of two beer companies—Anheuser-Busch (the first time buyer) and Champale, Time Inc., Pepsi-Cola, Kellogg cereal, plus the merchandising giant Sears Roebuck.

The launch party was elegant, in sharp contrast to MTV's The Loft in Fort Lee, although the nation's capital lacked a cable capacity. Johnson entertained guests with "BET on it" buttons in the Gold Room of the Rayburn Building. *The Washington Post* covered the event. Legislators, advertisers, sports stars, and network executives attended, posing for the obligatory photo sessions. Walter Fauntory addressed the crowd. "Tomorrow morning I'm gonna eat some Kellogg's Corn Flakes, I'm gonna join the Pepsi Generation, and I'm gonna read *Time*." Johnson briefly touched on some of the obstacles facing the project adding, "I want to provide a showcase for black entertainers that would be attractive to blacks and whites."

The invited dignitaries moved from strategically placed TV sets. One flashed a station promotional clip. At the end of the room *A Visit to the Chief's Son,* planned for showing the first week, was previewed. Watching the film was Fritz Attaway, vice president of the Motion Picture Association. "I'm glad we could play a small role in all this," he said shaking Johnson's hand. Never one to miss an opportunity the BET head answered, "You still can. I need more film products."

The September *Cablevision* numbers found BET serving 5 million wired households in 499 markets in 47 states. As the figures prompted greater revenues the channel added two new half-hour programs—"The Bobby Jones Gospel Show" and "Black Showcase."

One year following the premiere BET had amassed fifteen major ad buyers. To expand the demographic "Video Soul" was inserted into the three-hour roster. This was some three weeks following the advent of "Night Flight."

On June 26, 1981 BET announced an eleven-week series of one-half hour music concert programs to be called "Video Soul." The thirty-minute show would air on Friday evenings following the Jones segment. Groups scheduled to appear included Earth, Wind, & Fire, Teddy Pendergrass, LTD, and jazz guitarist George Benson. According to Bob Johnson the taped material would be supplied through an arrangement with Video Music, an Indianapolis-based syndicated cable service. The producer of the program was BET's Virgil Hemphill. The BET president commented, " 'Video Soul' is another example of [the network's] continuing efforts. . . . We are sure this eleven-week concert series will be popular."

As "Video Soul" was being unveiled, Percy Sutton, former Manhattan borough president, announced plans for the Black Music Cable Television Network. It would air as of June 30, 1982 in forty cities, with a start-up cost of $4 million. The urban contemporary network would stress long-form, six-minute video clips delivered by AT&T land-lines. Optimistically, the ex-civil rights spokesman asserted, "Hypothetically, you can make me quite successful with only 5 percent of the market." He promised a strong promotional campaign with a one-hour demo. The screening was to occur at an August press conference. Asked by Leo Sacks about the use of a transponder, Sutton admitted: "The shortage up there for satellite space is really unbelievable."[7] With that comment Sutton nearly raised the white flag of surrender. The use of land lines for remote retransmission CATVs would be prohibitive. In 1981, the name of the game was access to the transponders 22,300 miles in space. He never was uplinked.

Johnson's main concern involved internal structural matters. BET repeatedly was greeted with CATVs' objections to a three hour per week service. In August 1982 this would change. Having received commitments from twenty of the nation's major cable operators, nineteen prime advertisers, and a promise of further participation by Taft Broadcasting, Johnson took a chance and left Sat Com I for Westar 5. The change of "birds" allowed an expansion of on-air time to seven days per week, six hours per day—8:00 P.M. to 2:00 A.M. (EST). The transfer meant a loss of 6 million viewers, but a gain in the prime-time window. In September 1981, BET had 742 systems signed with a total viewership of 8.1 million viewers. The satellite transfer found them with less cable access, sporting a mere 122 operators and 2 million households. It was a riverboat gamble, the stakes being the recoupling of the lost millions of subscribers and revenues.

"Video Soul" expanded to a ninety-minute format. The proposed Black Music Cable project never materialized. Johnson's gamble made him highly visible in the cable industry and the black community. In 1982, he deservedly accepted the NCTA's President's Award and the NAACP's Image Award.

The Rick James/Michael Jackson narrowcasting polemic found him on Ted Koppel's "Nightline." Johnson defended the practice on cable as normative, but threw in the caveat that MTV may have "made a mistake in selecting so narrow a musical format." In thirty seconds BET's president nationally established himself as the voice of reason in light of the succeeding comments (see Chapter 5).

With his background in the cable industry, Johnson accepted narrowcasting, but this was not the game plan for BET. He says:

> I don't think we consider ourselves narrowcasting in the sort of traditional definition of the word that we're going after the feminine audience. We're going after a very broad audience that happens to reflect the particular ethnic cultural viewpoint or interest. So the 26 million black Americans I think wouldn't constitute narrrowcasting. And we also assume that our video programming as much of our other program appeals to broader than a black audience, so in a sense I would say that we're more after an urban audience.

A pragmatist, Johnson found himself in the middle of two schools of broadcasting strategies. "Soul Train" producer Don Cornelius provacatively opposed "reverse crossovers" saying, "How can you give shots to someone who isn't going to visit your station, who won't even talk to you if he sees you on the street?"

In the wake of the MTV controversy, Robert Johnson announced at the mid-June Houston NCTA meetings the revivial of "Video Soul." The expanded program would reemerge. Veejays Shelia Banks and Donnie Simpson would host two-hour shows from 9:00 to 11:00 P.M. (EST) three days a week.

At a press conference Johnson did not mention the polemic, but said, "If a network chooses to target a particular audience that's fine. That's what cable is all about." Adding, "BET's decision to produce and televise six hours a week of video music is in response to a demand by black cable consumers who want to watch black and urban contemporary video music performances. We are also responding to demands by the record industry and particularly black recording artists who want access to a *national video outlet* that can serve as a primary vehicle to promote black music videos." Reporters attending the press conference rapidly noted the not so subtle MTV undercurrent. "The key ingredient to 'Video Soul' will be the fact that we will show video clips that encompass the broad spectrum of contemporary music entertainment," said Johnson. In September "Video Soul" became a reality.

As promised, "Video Soul" did "showcase any and all music clips from country to soul that we felt would appeal to a contemporary urban audience." The foundation was, obviously, urban contemporary, but, it was not as narrowcast as MTV. This cosmopolitan approach would, in time, give MTVers pause for thought and countermeasures.

The reincarnation of "Video Soul" focused on an MTV-like format. The programming surrounded the available clips. BET's policy was more liberal or open. "Blue-eyed" soul artists were included regardless of skin color. Hall and Oates, Boy George, and other white performers influenced by the Motown or Philadelphia sound were welcome. They fit the format of "Video Soul" and presented quality clips. One program nagging urban contemporary artists was the poor visual production of some clips offered to BET and other networks. A similar situation vexed the Nashville Network (TNN). Measuring audience size, labels generally shortchanged noncrossover black and country artists.

The two "Video Soul" veejays parroted those on MTV. Donnie Simpson, a media veteran, was an immediate sensation within BET's then 6 million window. Sheila Banks rapidly moved to host "This Week in Black Entertainment." "Video Soul" became Simpson's personal playground. Unlike the MTV jocks, he has been generally immune from journalistic and public bombasts.

Simpson's broadcasting credentials surpassed most of the veejay staff at MTV. He started his radio career as a teen reporter in Detroit at the age of fifteen. A year later he became a full-time announcer with Detroit's WJLB, where he stayed for seven years. Gaining the nickname "Love Bug," the deejay was voted the top radio personality in the urban contemporary market. When not introducing records, he earned a communications degree from the University of Detroit.

In 1977 he migrated to the nation's capital. Simpson was hired as the afternoon or dayplay man at WKYS, an NBC-FM affiliate. In time he moved to the more prestigious positions of morning drive-time and program director. During this tenure he joined "Video Soul" as BET's first identifiable veejay. "Being recognized on a national level was initially kind of . . . weird! When I went to visit relatives in Alabama, people came up to me on the streets and said, 'I know you man' . . . now I know how Michael and Prince feel—just kidding." Aesthetically, BET's music ventures were a success. "They've never really been tested," one competitor objected at the time.

"You begin to wonder why BET isn't doing better," observed Johnson. The biggest obstacle, as noted, was the unwired metropolitan population. There also existed the generally unspoken but covert problem of racism. Johnson has characterized cable operators as being insensitive, ignorant "programming slum lords." He told *Broadcasting:* "They don't see. It's there, but it isn't there. . . . It's just blatant out and out discrimination. I can see a cable operator saying, 'I'm in a lily-white community and I've got limited channels and I don't see BET being valuable in this market.' But I cannot accept cable operators telling me 'I've got a 20 percent, 30 percent, 40 percent, 50 percent, 60 percent black market and I've made all my programming selections and not one is a black programming service.' "[8] Johnson rejects the "cable incapacity" argument, pointing to the music video arena in San Diego, which, he claims, has "duplicate services." "I think it'd be a slap in the face if an operator added MTV or another music video channel and then said he's reaching out to the black community." Trade magazine writers and cable operators are sympathetic to Johnson's argument. *Broadcasting, Electronic Media,* and *Cable Television Business* have examined the issue. Group W made a commitment to BET to carry the network in markets with an 8 percent or greater black populace—a figure Johnson advocates. He is, however, concerned with "lunar rotations." Citing Manhattan Cable's time allocation, Johnson complains that "BET is programmed at night, so we get the ghetto time." Most of his criticism is voiced to insiders such as the National Association of Black Journalists or the Black Music Association.

A *TV Guide* article cited the major resistance to BET as its inferior production and the network's repetitiveness. Storer Communication's marketing vice-president Douglas Wenger noted: "I hope that he can go to more significant programming in the future." Bill Johnson (no relation), president of black-owned KBLE in Ohio, agrees. Once the economic difficulties are mitigated, Bill Johnson contends that BET "will be in deep trouble if he doesn't develop the programming." In Washington, the other Johnson counters that his viewship is too small to finance new productions. "We don't have deep pockets here. We can't go out and spend lots of money on programming."

If at First . . . Try Again

NBC-TV's entry into the music video competition overshadowed the cable systems'. Even WTBS was dwarfed by America's first national network. Through local affiliates "the home of the peacock" could reach more than 50 million potential viewers. Pittman, having programmed "Album Tracks" for WNBC (New York), was painfully aware of the network's population pool. But programming head Brandon Tartikoff had a "turkey" on the air. The Canadian-produced "SCTV," a spoof of television, was following in the lowly rated footsteps of "Midnight Special" in the Friday post-Carson rerun slot. At best it pulled a 3 percent Nielson rating with a 16 audience share. Syndicated adventure shows and old movies were destroying the once highly popular Canadian Broadcasting Company's comedy show, which is loosely based on "Saturday Night Live" news segments and other take-offs on the visual medium. NBC, then slowly climbing out of the Nielson numbers cellar, was losing nearly $2 million per season on "SCTV." The show couldn't attract the youth market.

Dick Ebersol was to assume leadership. He was cut from the Johnson, Lack, and Franklin mold. He left Yale University in his sophomore year to become a researcher for ABC Sports in 1967. He remained at ABC on a part-time basis while completing his last two years at Yale. He graduated in June 1970 with a B.A. degree in history. He was elevated to a production assistant for ABC Sports and produced the award-winning Olympic special, "The Ancient Games." He ended his association with ABC as director of program development and administrative assistant to the president of the sports division.

He moved to NBC-TV in August 1974 as director of weekend late-night programming. Several months later he was promoted to the newly created position of director of late-night programming. In that capacity Ebersol had overall administrative responsibility for the ill-fated "Midnight Special."

At the age of twenty-eight he was named vice president of late-night programming, the youngest in NBC's history. The promotion was based on "his guidance being largely responsible for the successful launching of NBC's "Saturday Night," said vice-president John McMahon. His role in "Saturday Night" provided Ebersol with considerable credibility with the then floundering NBC brass saddled with "The Silver Bullet." He survived the Fred Silverman era and the critical peaks and valleys of "Saturday Night." His reputation, as a concept developer, was unique at NBC. Ebersol's outline for a potential replacement of "SCTV" featuring music videos received attention. The memo fit Tartikoff's philosophy; "As a program director you try to *extract* the essence—the dynamic, if you will—of a given show's popularity, and then distract the viewing public from your deed by dressing up your new program with some fresh new elements."[9]

The network programmer liked the proposal, reasoning that MTV and music videos were hot and the "price for programming was right." The "dressing up" involved, as noted by Ebersol, "emphasis on 'conceptual' videos and the fact that 85 percent of viewers have read about MTV but have never seen it. MTV is a hostage to the fact that it's on cable." The format was troublesome for MTV.

In June, David Benjamin was appointed producer for the project. Prior to joining NBC-TV he was vice-president of business affairs for CBS Records. This position involved talent negotiations and the acquisitions of musical properties. Benjamin was a graduate of Hofstra University in Long Island with B.A. and J.D. degrees. In 1978, CBS hired him as a senior attorney in the music division. The next year he was transferred to the West Coast with the title of assistant general attorney. Within a year Benjamin returned to Black Rock to direct financial activities for the international branch of CBS.

The July 29 version of "Friday Night Videos" highlighted a "Video Vote" pitting David Bowie's "Let's Dance" against "Beat It." Viewers were invited to cast a telephone vote costing fifty cents each by calling a 900 number to express a preference. Styx's "Haven't We Been Here Before" and Elton John's "That's Why They Call It The Blues" were "world premiered" ("That's Why . . ." had actually originally aired on "Night Tracks"). The Elton John clip was billed as Russell Mulcahy's farewell venture, as the director had chosen to migrate into big-screen, long-form production. Other segments included a "Hall of Fame" that featured the Beatles, "Private Reels" with a Rick Springfield interview, and "Where Are They Now" profiling keyboardist Ray Manzarek, an ex-Door. Twelve videos were scheduled, three by black artists. Most had MTV exposure. Ebersol stated: "We have no quotas for black or white performers." Asked for a reaction, Bob Pittman told the *Los Angeles Times:* "I think if the shows are done well, they help video music because they expose it. In the case of Ebersol's show, it's like buying a 90-minute commercial on NBC in the sense that it whets people's appetite. . . . But ["Friday Night Videos"] only lasts for 90 minutes and it's only one day a week." The argument had considerable merit, assuming the viewer could get MTV on cable. NBC introduced another wrinkle antithetical to MTV: payment for world premiere clips, with an offer of $3,500. Pittman was silent on the payment offer.

The Nielsen "overnights" conducted in New York, Los Angeles, Chicago, and several other major markets showed a ratings leap over "SCTV." These were read with caution, as the original "In Concert" surpassed Dick Cavett's talk show numbers only to be cancelled after two years of low ratings. Following the first episodes, NBC-TV's press relations described the format as: "An array of dazzling conceptual

videos blended with strong sound into a distillation of the newest and
best music each week with across-the-board appeal. . . . A special
weekly feature is the "Private Reels" exclusive interview—a segment
coupled with performance and video clips of major recording artists."

Pittman, having spent a good portion of his adulthood with NBC,
respected Ebersol and realized the potential outreach of the network.
The disappointing Nielson numbers for "SCTV" would generate ec-
stasy for any satellite cable service. In the summer of 1983, the real
economic threat to MTV came from 30 Rockefeller Plaza.

If You've Got the Money . . .

"We have had discussions since day one with regard to paying for
video clips," commented a WASEC executive. Polygram originally
was wedded to the notion of "pay for play." At the 1981 *Billboard*
Video Music Conference a spokesman claimed the label was creating
"art" rather than promotional product. The listeners scoffed at the
proposition. Polygram's clips in Europe were categorized as "promos." Producer Ken Ehrlich noted that "video began as a promotional
film art, and has turned into consumer art." Recalling these statements
John Sykes stated: "We made it very clear to them that we couldn't
afford it, but more important we were a promotional vehicle." Jack
Schneider reiterated this position to label executives: "MTV stands
ready to promote for you." While record companies harbored doubts
about MTV's value as an exposure tool, they understood Sykes'
contention that the neophyte network couldn't afford to pay for clips.
One participant used the cliché "You can't get blood out of a stone"—
this was especially true for a stone mired with a $30 million debt.

Field reports legitimized MTV's value as an advertising medium for
albums. Polygram was mellowing, putting together twenty-three clips
on a ninety-minute video entitled "Magical Musical Video Show" for
merchandisers' use. The growing recognition of the sales value of the
short form video—three to five minutes—proliferated their numbers.
In July 1982 *Billboard* published an analysis of costs: "Video clips . . .
don't come cheaply: it costs between $20,000 and $40,000 to produce a
typical example." In the same article A&M's Bert Miller stated,
"We're just not selling enough records to offset all the costs. It does
bother me that MTV and other outlets don't pay for the clips. I'm
hoping things will change." CBS's vice president for business affairs
noted: "Eventually MTV and "Night Flight" . . . will make money and
you can change the way things are. Now it's a question of survival, and

we do want to help. But when they make money we'll start asking for some." That CBS vice president was David Benjamin soon to join the "other" side—NBC-TV.

Polygram surrendered. Clips returned to being "record promotion." Concert clips gave way to the more expensive and elaborate concept videos. Expenses soared. "Billie Jean," "Hungry Like the Wolf," and "Beat It," while critically acclaimed, inflated the production costs from five to six figures for hot artists. "We used to moan when we got 10,000 pounds [$15,000] for a video. Now we're getting 100,000 pounds [$150,000] and it's still not enough," said Scott Millaney, president of MGMM and partner with Brian Grant, David Mallet, and Russell Mulcahy. MGMM constituted *the* British video production unit with Duran Duran's "Hungry Like the Wolf," Kim Carnes' "Bette Davis Eyes," David Bowie's "Let's Dance" and "China Girl," Donna Summer's "She Works Hard for the Money," and a bevy of other hit videos.

MGMM productions are expensive. Mulcahy described his creations as "epic dramas." He and Mallet used exotic sites such as Sri-Lanka, Hong Kong, Singapore, or Sydney, Australia. "Wolf," "Save a Prayer," and "Lonely in Your Nightmare" were produced on the island previously called Ceylon. "Let's Dance," which earned David Bowie a platinum album—his first—was taped in Australia. Bob Giraldi, who produced "Beat It" and was accustomed to TV commercials in the $250,000 to $500,000 range, noted: "Madison Avenue just can't believe it. For $60,000 they [record labels] can get a piece of work for five minutes . . . it turns the world of promotion topsy-turvy." "Beat It" paralleled Madison Avenue advertising and sports in dollars spent. Giraldi, MGMM, Steve Barron, and a handful of other "name" producers could command six-figure sums. These were reserved for superstars like Bowie, Duran Duran, and Michael Jackson. Lionel Richie's "All Nite Long," with forty dancers, cost $100,000. The average outlay was $50,000 to $60,000. The budget was divided: $10,000 for the actual production, $10,000 for labor or crew salaries and perks, $20,000 for equipment and set, and $5,000 for editing. The producer/director, depending on his status, averaged $15,000.

"American Bandstand" veteran Dick Clark raised the obvious question: Who pays? NBC's Dick Ebersol, executive producer of "Friday Night Videos," offered to spend "somewhere between $1,000 to $3,000" per showing. The $3,000 figure was for a "video premiere" and exclusive use for two days. "If NBC pays, will MTV have to pay?" asked Clark. "Will I have to pay? You can't have one pay and not the other." MTV executives were furious. One insider, no longer with

MTV, recalled: "We were talking about it, but Ebersol made exclusives almost an imperative." The "video premiere" notion was the most vexing aspect of the proposal.

Warner Brothers Records selectively began charging $250 for video service. MTV was excluded. ABC's local "New York Hot Tracks" reacted. Brooke Bailey told Ed Levine, "We will not be airing any Warner videos, except clips produced by bands. We can't afford it."[10] Kevin Wendle, the show's producer, added, "If we pay Warner we have to pay everyone." Other nonnetwork music video shows echoed this sentiment. A few conspiracy-minded executives suggested that Warner Brothers was attempting to stifle competition with WASEC. The argument was weak, as many rock video shows were in urban markets that lacked a cable outlet.

The battle for the playlist intensified. A Los Angeles director said, "Many newer video producers and directors have sprung up. It's a little more competitive." Costs continued to skyrocket. Established film directors such as Brian de Palma were courted to direct short-form videos. Record companies looked at the Ebersol offer, Warner Brothers video fees, and MTV's predicted 1984 profitability. Pay for play was in the offing. It was merely a question of when.

Some labels wanted to maintain the status quo. One spokesperrson at MCA said, "We intend to continue this [promotional] policy as long as financially *feasible*." The qualifier was an important one. Without going public on the subject, executives worried that MTV would "pay" for superstars at the expense of new and marginal artists. An agreement between CBS and the music channel could provide premieres of Michael Jackson, Bruce Springsteen, Culture Club, Men at Work, Bonnie Tyler, Quiet Riot, Billie Joel, and others. Michelle Peacock characterized exclusives as a "big can of worms." If implemented, Capitol would reduce its music video production—unless included in the deal.

CBS maintained its earlier position. "I don't foresee any sweeping policy," said Debbie Newman, director of artist and video development. "We don't want to put people out of business who can't afford to pay. Policy will emerge as precedents are set." She failed to mention that Warners and NBC had already established precedents. Another executive at CBS accentuated, "It's possible we may ask for money in the future, especially for exclusives and the like, but *now* there's no set policy."

The National Cable Programming Conference took place for two days in December in Los Angeles. Cable network executives argued over the viability of music video programming. HBO's president Frank

Biondi labelled *Flashdance* a "fluke." Archrival Showtime countered with a promise of concerts by Stray Cats and Flock of Seagulls.

Robert Pittman chaired "The Video Beat" panel. Touting MTV, he stressed that the advent of music videos was "the first time a major new form of programming hasn't been offered by the networks first." Capitol's Jim Mazza, privately mulling an MTV offer for exclusives, observed, "Visual exposure of the artist is esentially for developing new talent." He went on to note that Capitol/EMI had spent $1 million on music videos and projected a seven-fold increase in 1984. Was Mazza covertly replying to Pittman's secret offer of December 1 for an exclusivity deal?

Robert Johnson, apparently unaware of the MTV proposal, waxed ecstatically about the inexpensive manner in which music video shows could be produced. "If you show one hour of programming comprised of eight videos costing an average of $40,000 each, that's a $250,000 (sic) show."

Without correcting Johnson's multiplication, Pittman asked him how he would respond to pay for play. The articulate BET president snapped back, "I'll call the NAACP!" After the laughter subsided he added, "The record companies giveth and the record companies taketh away."

"Ultimately, MTV will be paying 'X' dollars for 'X' number of years and obtain an 'X'-long period of exclusivity. That money would obviously help cover production costs, although that's not a stipulation of the agreement. MTV wouldn't own the videos; they would just have them exclusively for a certain period" an informed CBS source backgrounded to *Billboard*.[11] The notion of special world premieres had considerable appeal as a quid pro quo arrangement. Jerry Durkin, business affairs vice president for CBS, perceived MTV as the key to pay for play. "When MTV is paying, everyone should pay," he said. Durkin's statement had considerable appeal to MTV. An arrangement with CBS unquestionably would harm many of the nearly 200 music video shows appearing throughout the country. Sub rosa, labels were giving MTV premiere product, but usually on a one-shot basis. On weekends the video premiere exclusive was literally for a matter of hours before the competition aired the same clip.

RCA Records followed Warners' lead. Jose Menendez, executive vice president, announced in February plans to charge in certain music video markets for "dubbing" costs. MTV and "major" networks were exempt. Behind the scenes MTV and several labels were on the verge of an arrangement. Bob Pittman, while ducking direct questions, hinted to *Billboard* and *Cablevision* that deals were pending.

Anticipating a pay-for-play concord, producers demanded higher budgets. Sentiments were expressed at the Production East seminar staged at the New York Hilton. Ken Walz, producer of Cyndi Lauper's "Girls Just Want to Have Fun," Dr. Hook's "Baby Makes Her Blue Jeans Talk," and some fifty more music videos complained that budgets were "painfully inadequate." This was a complete reversal from his previous position ("Most labels end up throwing as much money away as they save by wanting the clips made so fast."[12] "I don't want to be in that $35,000 trap again unless its an extremely simple, easy to manage piece of work. . . . The budgets will get into the $100,000 range in the next year or two. That's a figure we can live with and be comfortable."

Needless to say, labels' responses varied. Those negotiating with MTV were a bit more positive than their counterparts. RCA's Chuck Mitchell commented, "The business is structured on very tight, low budgets. There's just no way you can get the kind of quality for the same dollar you got a year ago." He cautioned, "If I was a producer, I would regard the making of video clips as a high-visibility, low-income business." Elektra, not a party to the exclusivity talks at the time, found their vice president of creative services discounting six-figure productions until clips at least were economically self-sufficient. "I don't agree," said Randy Edwards, "with his [Walz's] numbers." Record companies and music video creators were already fighting for a slice of the pie before it was even cut. MTV, as Pittman would suggest, welcomed better quality clips. "That's between them," said one representative. The network was primarily concerned with maintaining its preeminent position in the cable music video world.

The MTV power structure saw the handwriting on the wall. Pay for play was inevitable. CBS's use of the term "exclusives" provided a gate of opportunity. It would legitimize some rather heavy-handed practices to insure world video premieres.

The slogan "I Want My MTV" was turned *camera obscura* as the campaign to drain the red ink intensified. The MTV brass overtly desired world premiere product. "Nice guys finish last" a fiesty baseball manager once retorted. This philosophy reportedly was rampant at MTV. With the amount of new video clips arriving weekly the motto was "No More Mister Nice Guy." The days of almost total dependency on the labels had passed. "It makes me wonder," Michelle Peacock asked, "if we released Duran Duran today, would [MTV] be as willing to make the commitment they did a year ago?"

MTV enjoyed a distinct advantage with day and prime-time airing seven days a week. The national rivals, prior to Ted Turner's abortive

Cable Music Channel, consisted of fragmented or divided weekend late-night programming. A.C. Nielsen estimated an average hourly viewership of 225,000 cable subscribers. MTV's overall Nielsens remained fairly respectable at 1.2 since the TV polling service included the network (Nielsen will rate when 15 percent of potential viewers are available). The demographics, compiled by Nielson, were impressive. The average income of MTV households was $31,000—some $2,000 higher than the average wired domicle and $10,000 above all homes with television. Despite these impressive numbers, MTV was still wrestling with its musical counterparts.

Bob Roganti, a newly appointed MTV senior vice president, told *Cablevision* that despite the numbers "we have to overcome objections to cable, low numbers, and questions of a commercial's compatibility with the format . . . [we still have] miles to go."[13]

Ira Tumpowsky of Young and Rubicam, while praising MTV as a good time buy, did not totally dismiss the competition. "Obviously they can't be as aggressive with one segment of the programming schedule as MTV can." NBC's "Friday Night Videos" aired at 12:00 A.M. for ninety minutes—minus commercials—once a week. Turner Broadcasting's "Night Tracks" was a 12:00 to 6:00 A.M. Friday and Saturday morning presentation on the East coast.

Madison Avenue did not ignore the weekenders when shopping for time buys. "It's a case where the genre is engendering the momentum. If somebody wanted to [be in] music videos they'd want to get in as much as possible," said Foote, Cone, and Belding's Greg Blaine. His company brought a million dollars of commercial space from MTV, but dealt with the antagonists.

Tumpowsky, referring to the other rock video shows, added: "I'd think about them when I weigh the alternatives." Jay James at Doyle, Dane, and Bernbach accented MTV's concerns by indicating that the contenders "take away the profit. . . . But they're not stopping them dead in their tracks. I really think MTV is the best outlet." "Take away" worried the executives at Rockefeller Plaza.

These anxieties manifested themselves in several ways. On March 15 a new show, "MTV Countdown," debuted. It was a ninety-minute Top Twenty show hosted by Mark Goodman, in the "Your Hit Parade" tradition. The selections were gleaned from four trades: *Billboard*, *Radio & Records*, Kal Rudman's *Friday Morning Quarterback*, and *Album Network*, an obscure music industry publication. "Night Flight" and several opposing programs already used a shorter but identical format.

The "anything could happen here" atmosphere was MTV's original goal. They did not take "kindly" to spreading their "mood." "When it [the video clip] comes out, you want it to be a major happening. If it's everywhere, it's a commodity," emphasized Bob Pittman. Les Garland was more adament, telling a writer: "We have difficulties when a group shows its loyalties are not with MTV. We have to have the chance to get it *first* [emphasis added]. We're doing the groups a favor by playing their videos." David Benjamin, producer of "Friday Night Videos," elaborated: "Artists come to me and say, 'We'd like to give you this video, but MTV says if they don't get it first, they'll never play any of our videos again.' I tell them, 'Don't risk your career, give it to them.' "

"This place is incredibly political," an MTVer anonymously stated to Jonathan Gross. *Rock Video* has chronicled in an on-going series the number of video clips MTV has either rejected or required changes on. Some clips are rejected on the basis of "standards," others on "political" grounds. "You know, it's strange," noted an observer, "Just how insecure those people are, reminds me of Watergate." Terms like "Buzzy's Basement" and "lunar rotation" entered the industry lexicon. These phrases connoted MTV's sanctions against the "deviants." The status of offenders was inconsequential. World premieres were the name of the game.[14]

The most widely circulated tale of "You don't spit on MTV's cape," to borrow from Jim Croce, involves "The World's Greatest Rock and Roll Band." The Rolling Stones submitted "She Was Hot" to the Acquisitions Committee. It was to air on MTV February 10, two and one-half hours prior to "Friday Night Videos." MTV insisted on some editing. Art Collins of the Stones organization had promised David Benjamin the clip. NBC accepted the clip and debuted the video as scheduled. MTV was upset. Several weeks passed. The Rolling Stones finally climbed on MTV's "light" rotation. The clip appeared once a day for three weeks. "I don't think we punished them," Garland insisted to *TV Guide*. "The album was going down the charts." Two months later "She Was Hot" surfaced on Buzz Brindle's "heavy" rotation. That followed a cocktail lounge confrontation where Collins warned executives that MTV "shouldn't play games" with superstars like the Rolling Stones.

Robert Hazard's "Change Reaction" contained a crowd scene with television news cameras. Producer Richard Carey added the NBC logo to the equipment for authenticity. The clip was rejected because of the network logo. Carey was furious, especially after viewing Billy Joel's

"Tell Her About It" which showed television crews operating equipment with the CBS eye prominently displayed. One former insider explained, "They didn't have a music show."

Billy Joel was equally vulnerable, however. NBC's early morning "Today Show" originally aired Billy Joel's "The Longest Time." Subsequently MTV ignored the star's clip for nearly a month. Joel's management company affirms that the song was boycotted during that period because of the NBC exposure prior to MTV.

Privately one trade journalist interpreted some of the machinations.

> There is no love lost between the two networks. MTV is a cable net as opposed to NBC's over-air capacity. That means "Friday Night Videos" and "Saturday Night Live" consistently outscore MTV, and there is nothing they can do about it. That was the reason, in part, for the exclusives. MTV is *the* big fish in the cable pond. NBC swims in the ocean.

Pittman views these comparisons as "ludicrous," claiming that "Friday Night Videos" "Clearly is not reaching that kind of numbers" (comparing MTV to NBC is akin to "apples and oranges").

MTV's informal sanctions were partially effective. Some marginal acts had little chance of breaking into a network with ninety-minute or two-hour programs. MTV's twenty-four-hour format provided considerably more flexibility. Estimates of the number of clips aired daily on the music channel ranged from 160 to 180. MTV could and did exert considerable influence on these artists. Pressuring superstars—the big draws—was a different story. A Rolling Stones or Mick Jagger world premiere did more for MTV than one by Lindsay Buckingham or The Enforcers. MTV had a unique stratagem up its corporate sleeve.

Exclusives

In light of the mild skirmishs with competitors, a huge accumulated debt, and other problems, MTV executives pondered a formal strategy to quell the dilution of the telecast music video environment. "We thought exclusivity was important," says Jack Schneider. In the electronic world of broadcasting the mere term bordered on profanity or blasphemy.

Exclusives, the service of "hot" new product first, to specified broadcasters, is a tradition that nonbeneficiaries dislike intensely. There was a time when KHJ (Los Angeles), WABC (New York), CKLW (Detroit), and several other stations received this preferential treatment due to their overall influence on the trades and the broadcasters. The fragmentation of the radio market in most areas diminished the practice. Cleveland's WMMS-FM was one of the few stations nationally to scoop their competitors with live broadcasts from the Agora, the location for Paul Simon's film *One Trick Pony,* and concert tapes provided by the artist's management in return for "breaking the act." Unofficially, appreciative record labels might ship a "few days early" to WMMS. WMMS's clout was undisputed and their lower-rated rivals moaned "Oh, well. . . ."

The 1980s was a different story. Most of the highly rated stations were knocked off their pedestal. Top arbitron stations usually succeeded by a point or more of the audience share. MTV, however, was different. Bob Pittman told participants at a *Billboard* radio conclave, "We're having a significant effect on music, and I suspect we're having a significant effect on radio." Despite grumblings in the audience, Pittman was correct. MTV did "break" a number of acts, one being Duran Duran.

MTV received an exclusive of Duran Duran's "Union of the Snake." The video clip was issued a week prior to radio service. The audio community was outraged. Even Dwight Douglas of Burhart/Abrams termed the action as "foolish" and "bad business." Programmers were more adamant. "I feel like Capitol slapped me in the face," objected WMMS's program director John Gorman. "Granted, most stations didn't play the group when they first came out. But, we did, and that should be worth some kind of exclusive. That's always a just reward when a station gets behind an act."[15] MTVers retorted, "the shoe's on the other foot" and "hurt egos are the name of the game."

Capitol was caught in the middle. Walter Lee, vice president of marketing, tried to put the best face on the issue. He told *Billboard:* "I won't sit behind someone else and pretend nothing happened. Something did happen. There was a screw-up and I won't deny it."[16]

Some of the aggrieved program directors refused to list the English act's single. *Billboard*'s Roman Kozak dissented to this action as the trade was dependent on broadcasters in compiling charts. He wrote: "No matter that MTV played Duran Duran for months before the brave trend-setters in commercial rock radio ever got near the band . . . this sort of thing appears to be business as usual in radio. We think it stinks."[17]

As the "Union of the Snake" controversy raged, Jim Mazza, president of Capitol Records (ironically Duran Duran's label), received a proposal from Robert Pittman dated December 1, 1983. The document, obtained by *Billboard* investigative reporters, offered Capitol/EMI a monetary payment of $1,250,000 over a three-year period and a guaranteed number of free advertising spots. The value of the spots, proposed, would begin at $1,600 per thirty seconds in 1984 and terminate at $4,500 per thirty seconds during 1986, the final year. In exchange for the exclusive use of 35 percent of the labels' clips for a thirty-day period, ten ad spots would be provided. The proposal stated that this would cover exclusivity over "all forms of television programming." In responding, Mazza told Leo Sacks, "We're studying the document and feasibility of payment."[18] He maintained that the offer had appeal because it would be a "new income source" and "there's no way you can make music without visual support and remain competitive."

As in the "Billie Jean" controversy, MTV refuses to discuss the details. Former president Jack Schneider summed it up by stating, "I really don't want to get into the exclusivity thing." The Securities and Exchange Commission did, however, force Warner-Amex into disclosing the arrangements when MTV went public with their stock offering. With the escalating costs of videos and production, the offer did have considerable appeal. It was estimated, at the time, that an entire artist/record package came in at $150,000 to $250,000.

The proverbial cat was out of the bag. Rumors had circulated since the summer of 1983 concerning some planned quid pro quo arrangement between MTV and some major labels. However, the music channel even off-the-record only would say: "We hope we never have to pay" for clips. A week prior to the leak an anonymous source admitted, "There have been discussions about the arrangements that might take place." The reaction to the proposal was swift. "It's an opportunistic move by MTV, but I can't believe the record companies are silly enough to cut off their other sources of promotion just to concentrate on one outlet," retorted producer Cynthia Friedland of "Night Flight" to the *Village Voice*. Previously Scott Sassa of "Night Tracks" made a similar statement: "The whole idea behind video originally was to promote new artists, and exclusivity detracts from promotion." *Rock & Roll Confidential* scolded, "If all the freshest eggs are placed in MTV's basket, who'll be able to compete?" The muckraking newsletter went on to insinuate that MTV was attempting to seize control of the music video television market, which was broadly their intent. In the narrowcast world of cable, with its limited audience, the fewer competitors the better. The demographic pie was too small to slice into many pieces.

"It made all the sense in the world," Joe Smith, then a consultant for WCI, told the *Los Angeles Times*. "The only problem MTV ever foresaw wasn't getting on more cable systems or the demographic and selling it, it was competition—that somebody could look exactly the way they did it, steal all the good things, cast out some other things that may not work, make a prototype, and put it ont the air."[19]

After her initial reaction, Friedland changed positions saying:

> I didn't really feel that it was going to harm us. And I think that I've been right in that regard. The exclusivity has not hurt us, particularly because of the kind of program "Night Flight" is. We build our shows according to what is, what we feel new and hot, and not necessary in the top ten, or the top twenty, or the top forty. So we haven't really been hurt by them, it doesn't bother me at all. I have much more programming to choose from than those shows do as well.

MTV did find one guardedly sympathetic voice at CBS. An executive observed that the channel had to do something to "protect their Madison Avenue investment."

Mazza's promise for a quick decision turned into silence. Nothing was officially heard about the MTV offer in the Capitol Tower. Allegedly, MTV's original terms were stiff. One industry executive told the *Los Angeles Times:* "The original deal they were asking for was ten times tougher, it was watered down a lot. For one thing, the original deal was that MTV would share in video royalties, which they didn't even come close to getting, in fact, we couldn't believe they even asked." The Capitol deal fell through.

Many record industry people were brainstorming the criticisms voiced after the initial leak in *Billboard.* Some contended that they should go for the cash, pointing to cost factors. Promotion executives did not appreciate the prospect of being at the mercy of a single cable network. Their reaction was philosophically predictable. "The idea of exclusives means you have to rethink the entire idea of promotion," one promo person informed *Billboard.* However, several labels, notably RCA Victor, were discussing an "arrangement" with MTV.

A writer for the Fordham University paper, *The Observer,* underscored MTV's power. Caryn Rose decried MTV's sponsorship of concert tours, a practice originated with The Police in 1983. Rose complained that the network controlled the advertisement of concert dates and ticket availability. This practice, it was intimated, excluded the "cableless." As only 25 percent of the population could get MTV at the time, this was viewed as discriminatory. *Rock & Roll Confidential* used this dissent as an illustration of what exclusivity argued.[20] The illustration was a bit spurious. (Rarely did *RRC* miss an opportunity to bash MTV.)

Bob Pittman, finally, at a *Cablevision* panel discussion, broke his silence on the controversial issue. Responding to Victor Livingston, he said:

> Basically, the terms we're asking record companies for are really no different from the terms we now have on an ad-hoc basis. MTV basically world premieres every video that's significant to us. . . . MTV is stabilizing the business by guaranteeing the record companies continued access to MTV. . . . We're formalizing what they give us now—the early windows on the videos we think are important to the MTV sound. We're putting money into the record companies to make sure that the quality of these promotional videos continues to improve, which benefits us, but all the other video music shows as well.

The *Cablevision* panel did not follow up on Pittman's statement. The moderator easily could have proposed that the concept was designed to give MTV a distinct edge over its competitors. The world premiere issue also needed further exploration. Instead, Pittman was asked about future plans. He avoided answering the query. The discussion then turned to Miles Copeland. The Police's manager partially dissented: "Record comanies don't really have the power to grant exclusivity without our approval. I certainly want a share of the money in, particularly if the full cost of making the video is coming out of my royalty." Aerosmith's management had similar objections. Tom Hamilton complained to Bill Knoedel-Seder, "They contain no solid provisions for the artists to get compensation. . . . It's just a new version of the old rock and roll film-flam where the artist gets exploited." These were important but tangential responses as artists had little, if any, say in music video finances. MTV was dealing with the labels, not the artists. Video production expenses were a matter decided by the company and the act. Payment for exclusives did heighten an already touchy subject: "Today, nobody looks at video as a luxury anymore, it's a necessity" said Randy Edwards.

In mid-1983 record companies began adding deduction clauses to contracts, particularly of new acts, to recoup video costs. Artists such as Krokus, Alex Call, and Robert Hazard had chargebacks on videos in their contracts. At the time this appeared as an extension of the production cost formula applied to studio time, producers, and many of the other expenses incurred in the making and marketing of a record. Video changed much of this. One executive noted: "Video is still a marketing expense unless a large amount of money is requested by the artists, and then they have to chip in. Labels have borne the brunt of video expenses until now. . . . It's a sensitive issue."

Artists' video demands were a problem. "Get me the guy who did

'Allen-town,' get me the guy who did 'Billie Jean,' " complained Len Epand. "They don't understand that Russell Mulcahy charges more than $85,000 and Steve Barron costs $65,000 and up." Another producer added, "They all want directors they have heard of—Giraldi, Barron, Mulcahy, Mallet—and these directors won't talk to you for less than $80,000 or more."

There promised to be continued heated discussions as to who pays for and owns royalty rights to clips supplied to television. One highly pertinent fact was revealed: MTV was negotiating "arrangements" with record companies.

In the meantime several competitors, especially Scott Sassa and Mike Green at Atlanta's local Video Music Channel, temporarily looked at antitrust legal actions.

On Thursday, June 14, MTV released a statement that the network had signed agreements with four labels for exclusive thirty-day rights to video clips. The labels involved originally were the worst-kept secret in the music business: RCA, MCA, Geffen Records, and most importantly the CBS Group. CBS releases nearly 30 percent of the product sold. The terms of the arrangements were fairly similar to the offer made to Capitol, although the duration of the agreements and cash plus ads involved varied. CBS Records, the supplier of approximately 200 video clips per year, was to acquire $8 million in a two-year span. In exchange, MTV would choose 20 percent of Black Rock's clips. The company could place another 10 percent on the MTV rotation in the medium or light slots. The only comment CBS would proffer was, "All along, we've said that at the appropriate time, we would be charging the users of videos for their use."

MCA and RCA reportedly garnered $2 million for three years of exclusives. Geffen Records obtained the same amount, according to insiders.[21] Officially the costs to MTV in 1984 were "approximately $4,575,000, offset by $925,000 of advertising time purchased or exchanged pursuant to the agreement."[22] The net effect of these concords was to guarantee MTV 35 percent of the available clips.

Mixed reactions to the exclusivity contracts surfaced. The most articulate critic proved to be David Benjamin, producer of NBC's "Friday Night Videos." He attacked the limitations of MTV, telling several publications: "MTV wants to end competition . . . [it] wants to own rock and roll. The viewer who doesn't get MTV will lose, because he can't see the videos. And the artists whose videos are only on MTV may lose, because their videos are not being seen anywhere else . . . people who buy records are not only white and middle class." Benjamin's comments, although overstated, were predictable from a commercial network executive. "NBC, CBS, and ABC pay for programming that is definitely exclusive," responded Les Garland. MTV's 1.2 Nielson share in the world of the "big three" networks was insignificant.

Narrowcasting was a cable and radio concept. Exclusives merely postponed blanket distribution to MTV's competitors. Most of the other video competitors originally were fairly tranquil about the situation. Scott Sassa told *Billboard,* "It's a pretty aggressive action, and we'll take whatever steps are needed to counteract it." John Popkowski, a vice president at WTBS, home of "Night Tracks," was basically unconcerned. He told *Cablevision,* "I don't see it impacting on our numbers because I don't see them releasing" (the premieres between midnight and 6:00 A.M. when "Night Tracks" is on). Talking to *Cablevision,* "Night Flight's" Jeff Franklin was nonchalant: "The real question is who will be programming MTV—MTV or the record companies?"

Andy Besch, USA's marketing vice-president, came up with a clever countermove. USA purchased time on forty cable systems to air on MTV. Local operators have two minutes of ad time on the music channel. In one thirty-second spot a teenager is shown viewing MTV. The set tells the boy, "Excuse me, but if you're watching this commercial you're missing USA's 'Night Flight,' the most creative video music show on television." Using Seibert-like animation, the set admonishes, " 'Night Flight' isn't on twenty-four hours a day. Why waste time? Turn now to the USA Network for 'Night Flight,' more than just music television." The commercials were placed when "Night Flight" was being broadcast.

A number of spokesperson's thought artists would be the greatest losers in the arrangement. Kevin Wendle, then of ABC's "Hot Tracks" said: "The only people hurt will be the artists. It will simply delay the time in which their sales can take off." "Why should the label get all the money," asked an insider, "when the artist is paying for half the video or more?" By July 1984 most standard recording contracts called for at least a 50 percent recoupment charge against royalties for video clip support.

Some of the print medium appears to have treated the exclusivity deals with greater credence than MTV's competitors. *Billboard* in a rare editorial suggested a debate in its "Commentary" column: "We encourage those on both sides to consider the pages of *Billboard* as a medium for that debate. . . ." The polemic lasted exactly one week, with a contribution from Telegenics' Stephanie Shephard. She asserted that "exclusive service will significnatly limit the number of viewers exposed to current video product."

RRC entered the discourse by charging MTV with monopolistic practices, but CBS caught the thrust of the polemic: "There's also a question of what happens to the money—millions per year in the case of CBS—paid by MTV. . . . However, most videos are at least paid for out of artist royalties." This was not entirely correct.

Rolling Stone's Michael Goldberg declared, "Rock-video fans who don't get their MTV . . . were at the losing end of a recent deal." Almost the same week Elektra/Asylum proclaimed it would sign a pact with MTV after originally refusing to join the "unknown" four. In June, Lou Maglia stressed, "Every record does not need a video . . . we want freedom and flexibility." Chairman Bob Krasnow, after "really agonizing over this," decided to "support MTV" by becoming the first mainline WCI label to announce its intentions formally. Given the corporate structure, MTV had been enjoying WCI's largess since its inception. (In May 1985 the deal was consumated with all the other Warners labels joining in).

The New Music Seminar was staged in New York in August. On one panel Les Garland defended the exclusives policy: "Where videos are seen is important" (meaning MTV was the "proper environment"). A spokesperson from "Night Tracks" dissented, saying: "Music is not a product, it's not meant to be heard by only a privileged class, but is created for as many people who want to listen." Her point had merit, but WTBS was also a basic cable service, as MTV. At the very last minute a panel was organized to treat the phenomenon. None of the MTV brass participated. David Benjamin used the forum to repeat his criticisms. "If NBC tried to sign deals like this, we'd be off the air in five minutes. But since cable isn't affected by FCC regulations, MTV can get away with it." He admonished that "the big stars call the shots on the marketing of their product and control their videos, while no one cares about the baby acts anyway . . . [or] the almost stars." Listed among the "almosts" were Quiet Riot and Cyndi Lauper. Mike Greene of VMC complained that the label representatives were telling him, "Now the rules have changed." He couldn't get clips. Greene pointed to the case of Elvis Costello. "He didn't have the show response or sell-through in Atlanta the way he would have" if clips were available.

Industry producers applauded pay for play. One said, "MTV is putting a big chunk of money in the labels' budgets for video production, and that is obviously a good thing for us." As the dialogue wore thin it was blantantly apparent that the networks and labels were acting in manifest self-interest.

In all the verbiage David Benjamin came the closest to what the exclusives arrangement was designed to accomplish. "What you have is a masterstroke intended to wipe out a number of problems," he informed *Rolling Stone*. "Massive debt—what do you do? You go public and raise money. In order to do that, you need a guaranteed supply of product. Bob Pittman needed long-term deals so he could tell his stockholders that MTV wasn't going to die on three days' notice."[23] The ex-CBS Records vice-president learned his lessons well at Black Rock. MTV was in the business of survival and the stock offering was the key to the world of solvency.

Buy a Piece of Irreverence: Wall Street and Rock and Roll

Warner-Amex's after-tax losses in 1983 came to a staggering $99 million. Various money-raising schemes circulated in financial circles. Wall street was abuzz with tales of "white knights"—a joint venture with possibly Viacom and a public stock offering of 20 percent of WASEC. Warner-Amex, it was contended, needed to bring in $40 million in such an offering. Officials snapped "no comment" to questions regarding their future plans.

According to analysts, the fate of MTV was the key to any WASEC stock offering. F. Eberstadt's Mark Riley stated: "In the long run, it depends on how much of a franchise Warner has in music videos. It's a fairly easy format to duplicate, and I don't think they'll be able to get much in the way of exclusivity—a week, maybe." So much for the sage prognostications of Wall street. He elaborated, noting: "Over time, the audience will start to fragment as cable reaches more homes and as more video clips are produced." This is precisely what MTV was desperately trying to prevent. Edward Atarino of Smith Barney perceived MTV as a growth company, but added: "The problem is in the product, though. Is there enough product to support two services, or has MTV locked in an invincible position?" Answering his own question, he said, "I can't see cable operators in a channel-capacity crunch turning to another service unless it's specifically aimed at another audience." Merrill Lynch was bearish, citing competition and payment for music videos. Prudential Bache Securities emphasized the bullish aspect of a stock issuance, telling *Cablevision:* "With the excitement that's being generated by MTV," said Barbara Russell, Warner-Amex executives "are probably saying, 'Why don't we capitalize on that?' . . . the time might be ripe to capitalize on MTV via its market value. . . . Many cable operators feel they cannot do without MTV. They've created a lot of loyalty."

The reservations of the stock firms proved incorrect. However, they did highlight the import of MTV to WASEC and Warner-Amex. MTV in any possible stock offering was the lure or bait—particularly after ultimately reaching profitability with an operating profit of $3.3 million in the first quarter of 1984. Nickelodeon also made money. Wall Street, like American Express, had written off most of the Warner-Amex cable division. Columbus, Ohio, and a few other community systems were making money. Pittsburgh, Dallas, and other major markets were a substantial cash drain. "I've never thought much of their cable operations," observed Harold Vogel of Merrill Lynch. "They're fundamentally in bad shape. They'll try to sell them, but who would be foolish enough to buy them?" "The rush into Cable TV Is Now Turning into a Retreat" headlined *Business Week*.

MTV Networks (MTVN) Inc. was incorporated on February 22, 1984—seemingly in the dead of night. No mention was made of the incorporation until the summer. The name was chosen to capitalize on the music channel. The acquisition of MTV and Nickelodeon from WASEC was finalized on July 17. MTVN borrowed $75 million from a consortium of banks, paid $67,718,000, and issued five million shares of common stock plus five million of convertible preferred stock to WASEC. The public offering of over-the-counter common shares was to net $70,386,000—more if Ted Turner had not upset the apple cart— to repay the bank loans. The offering became official August 10, 1984 after the second-quarter profits became known. MTV chalked up $4.8 million.

The original filing involved 5.125 million shares at an estimated price of $16.00 to $18.00. Warner-Amex would give up 36 percent of the financial control, but reserve 90 percent of the voting power. This was a problem. The control and price factors created scepticism. Norman Fosback, editor of a stock tip sheet, suggested that the asking price was too high.

The emergence of MTVN witnessed the firing of Jack Schneider. A spokesperson claimed Schneider "resigned" to pursue business opportunities. While not bitter, at least publically, Schneider's account contradicts the MTVN line:

> They didn't want me to stay, and they had their reasons. I had a contract to work for them, which I signed as a fully developed individual adult. They honored the contract to arrangement claims, and they wanted me to leave. . . . It has to be within American Express and WCI [Robinson, Horowitz, Ross]. . . . I don't ever want to be not wanted and if they didn't want me to stay I left. . . . It was the day that the company was to go public, and I thought the way it was done was very bad form, but life is poorly conducted . . . I felt a little used in the process.

He is retired, living in Greenwich, Connecticut, devoting time to various projects at his alma mater.

Margaret Wade, director of press relations, would exit a few weeks later. Smith Barney analyst Mara Miesnieks mildly objected to the timing of Schneider's dismissal, as did some record labels. Only Pittman, Sykes, Freston, and Cohen remained from the original team that assembled MTV. Jo Bergman's designation of January 1983 as the channel's second phase had ended. The emergence of MTVN marked the third, and it started on a sour note. The personnel changes seemed drastic. One journalist mused, "They're playing musical chairs. Call up and so-and-so is no longer there."

David Horowitz took over MTVN as chief exercutive officer and president, replacing Schneider. He immediately was faced with problems surrounding the stock offering. The fifty-six-year-old native New Yorker is a prototypical network executive. A graduate of Columbia University Law School in 1950, he clerked for Judge Stanley Fuld of the New York Court of Appeals. Having served his apprenticeship, Horowitz joined Screen Gems' Manhattan office as general counsel. Climbing the entertainment industry ladder he was appointed vice-president and general counsel of Columbia Pictures Industries. He transferred to WCI in 1973 as a senior vice president. Promoted to executive vice-president a year later, he became a member of the Office of the President in 1976. Horowitz's main task was the multitude of record divisions. One notable assignment was to negotiate an end to the conflict with the National Organization for Women (NOW) and the California-based Women Against Violence Against Women. The feminist groups were advocating a boycott of WCI because of the "violent and sexist" album covers. The vice-president was instrumental in the formation of WASEC, along with Jack Schneider. Horowitz participated in the famous meeting that agreed to fund MTV in January 1981. The same year he rose to co-chief operating officer. With Schneider's messy departure he became the president of MTVN with an annual salary of $250,000 plus the usual corporate perks. "Another lawyer" complained an employee. Worse yet, Horowitz is an opera maven, a member of the Metropolitan Opera Association. "That makes *two* MTV executives who don't like rock and roll," noted an anonymous source.

Brokers planned to float MTVN shares at $16.00 or more. The announcement of alternative all-music channels altered the price. "Ted Turner had a lot to do with the pricing," said a broker. "I'm not sure if Turner did it deliberately to sabotage the deal or not." Whatever the intentions, MTVN lost money. A number of articles appeared in the financial press supporting Porter Bibb's contention that "it would be a lousy investment for the public." *RRC* ran a lengthy piece suggesting that Warner-Amex had tried to divest and having failed, "Now they've turned to the public." Dave Marsh and associates had their facts straight. The offering was amended to $15.00 per share. Of the now anticipated $70 million, $30 million was earmarked to pay off MTV's start-up costs, the rest was to retire other bank indebtedness and help pay for the exclusives. Horowitz and Pittman did well with options to buy 100,000 shares at $9.00 until 1994. All five million shares sold in a trading week. Harold Vogel cautioned, however: "You have to wait two or three weeks or months to see how well the stock does."

MTVN's economic riddle was solved, but Warner-Amex remained in a financial hole. Still, they retained control over 66 percent of the MTVN equity with 91 percent of shareholders' votes. The strategy of using MTV to bait the economic trap proved successful for all concerned. The common stock's value would rise in a bullish market. A year after the bid MTVN closed at $27.00—nearly double the opening price.

Stock analysts can be sages on rare occasion. Predictions of other music networks proved correct. Minus the usual fanfare for such events, the Discovery Music Network (DMN) unveiled an intention to uplink a second twenty-four-hour music channel in December. DMM preceded Ted Turner's flamboyant entry and MTVN's stock issuance by nearly two weeks.

DMN was in the planning stage for nearly a year by Glen Taylor and Karen Tyler. The two had previously founded the successful Financial News Network (FNN). In a year's time the business service had jumped from 4 million households to 16 million. Their premise was that MTV fare was too teen narrowcast, making room for an alternative. Dain Eric, a former national program director for Walter/Weeks Broadcasting, was DMN's director of programming.

"We'll be slow to go on what we consider clips of questionable taste or violent content," Eric told *Billboard*. "Unless bands like Motley Crue or Twisted Sister have legitimate hit records with videos suitable for family viewing, I doubt we'll program them." A sigh of relief was heard from Manhattan. Eric's description created consternation in Atlanta, home of the Turner Broadcasting empire.

The few record company executives willing to "go public" were affirmative. "I would think all the labels would support a new music video network," said Arista's Peter Baron. He cited acts such as Barry Manilow and Air Supply. "It's going to help us with a lot of acts who don't get their videos played elsewhere." Epic Record's Harvey Leeds enthusiastically stated, "Competition will make everyone work harder, and the overall industry would wind up with a better product." These sentiments were echoed by Atlantic, A&M, and Capitol. None of these labels were involved in the exclusivity arrangements.

DMN dismissed the contentious pact, indicating MTV's fare was generally unsuited for their projected playlist. Besides, MTV could only premiere 35 percent of the available clips. Their attitude seemed unrealistically confident and optimistic.

Eric was asked about the dreaded "cable incapacity." He casually replied, "In markets where we won't initially be able to get into a cable system, we'll shoot for the UHFs." Eric seemed to have most of the answers.

Bob Alter, president of the Cable Advertising Bureau, raised one obstacle: the ingrained "Rule of One" in cable. The rule, he insisted, for "specialized programming holds." History upheld his view. CNN, ESPN, and MTV had demonstrated that in the limited world of telephone pole hookups, must-carry rules, twelve-channel limitations, and subscriber demographics two basic services doom one to failure. This was the Rule of One.

The self-assurance exhibited by Dain Eric eroded as the weeks passed. "I found out there were certain videos I needed that I couldn't get because of the deals," he would say. He told a reporter that "MTV is cutting us and all other music programs off from the superstars, and that makes it very hard to compete." He told the *Washington Post,* "We felt that MTV was trying to lock out any full-time competition. . . . MTV saw full-time competition coming and they wanted to prevent that. Seeing as how the average life expectancy of a hit video is two to four months, those videos don't do us any good after a year."[24]

DMN's indifference to the exclusives rapidly melted when facing the harsh reality that while MTV may only be obtaining 20 percent of the new video clips they took the hot acts and superstars. (These usually number less than twenty in any period.) CBS product development executive Arma Andon would later observe that the biggest difficulty with music videos was "unquestionably the tremendous increase in costs and expenditures in producing videos. Some of the factors that contribute to these spiraling costs include the 'can you-top-this attitude.' Video outlets only want to play these high-cost, high-quality videos, subsequently leaving the new artist out in the cold, because they cannot compete for funds. We therefore run the risk of programmers programming superstar videos only." MTV had a lock on most of them. Polygram Records joined the MTV arrangement roster in mid-September.

On September 19, 1984 Tyler and Taylor were in Los Angeles Central California U.S. District Court, represented by Joel R. Bennett, filing suit against MTV.[25] The action charged MTV with creating a monopoly violating the Sherman and Clayton Antitrust Acts, "effectively stifling competition in the distribution of music videos." Moreover, the arrangements "had the purpose and effect of improperly interfering with . . . [Discovery] and to eliminate plaintiff and others as competitors." The complaint further alleged, "Unless the exclusive dealing arrangements are enjoined by the Court, Discovery Music Network may be denied entry into the relevant market . . . [and is therefore] adversely impacted. . . . Profits and its going-concern value will be substantially diminished, reduced, and eliminated." Bennett requested a jury trial, damages, and an injunction to cease and desist.

Outside the courtroom a reporter was informed that the litigation was prompted by the scheduled appearance of VH-1 (MTV-2, as it was originally called), which would be in direct competition for the DMN window. Karen Tyler, DMN president, explained that MTV was "not a serious issue for us." But with MTV-2, "MTVN has intensified its efforts to gain exclusive contracts."

"Since we have not yet been served," an MTVN spokesperson fudged, "we can't make an official comment right now. We get the impression, however, that they are more interested in the publicity aspect than the legal one."

Later Eric told *Rolling Stone*, "If they're seeking exclusivity on the cream of the crop there, then we're really in big trouble. That locks us out completely." MTV's promotion vice-president Margaret Wade, in the process of cleaning out her desk, said: "We are currently viewing the complaint. However, we also believe their action is totally without merit. Exclusivity is a common feature of entertainment industry contracts." She implied that they were therefore exempt from antitrust laws. The U.S. Department of Justice had doubts. Disclaiming any connection to the Discovery suit, they claimed the probe was "preliminary." The description was significant as the law enforcement department indicated action would be taken if violations were found. MTV responded, "We are cooperating fully."

One additional aspect of the MTV agreement did surface. MTV, as noted, enjoyed a thirty-day exclusive, in some cases two months. The new information was that with a rival twenty-four-hour service the timeframe was extended to six months to a year. This easily explained DMN's consternation.

The latent hostility brewing since the exclusives arrangements became manifest at *Billboard*'s Sixth Annual Video Music Conference held in mid-November at the Sheraton Premier Hotel in Pasadena. The hotel is best known as the temporary home of Rose Bowl contenders.

It proved a fitting environment for the "Seen in the Right Places" panel. Participants represented the Cable Music Channel, Discovery Music Network, Black Entertainment Television, MTV, and California Music Channel. Spokespersons from "Friday Night Videos" and "New York Hot Tracks" were present. Epic's Harvey Leeds moderated—more precisely, refereed. Les Garland ignited the discussion by stating: "The current state of affairs is that there is too much music" (a somewhat strange statement in light of the planned VH-1). A Turner CMC vice president predictably asked, "Why did you start another twenty-four-hour service?" Garland found an unexpected ally from "Friday Night Videos." Bette Hisiger concurred with him, arguing that the proliferation of video shows contributes to overexposure and that her NBC program would be "in a lot of trouble." Ellen Davis of "Hot Tracks" quarreled, "The consumer has decided that they're not sick of it, they want more." Hisiger wasn't so sure. "By the time the consumer decides, you're off the air," she countered. The verbal brawl went on. Some of the polemicists would be unemployed after the Rose Parade in January, as the entities they represented folded.

The wheels of civil justice grind slowly. In early December the beleaguered Dain Eric announced that DMN was shifting to overground UHF broadcasting, as it is a major carrier. "We won't turn down a cable affiliate," he said. "But at the same time, the company recognizes the difficulty in finding a niche in cable." The Rule of One prevailed. "Back Porch," a production by high school students, and a series based on Anne Murray's *There's a Walrus in My Tub* album were mentioned as potential programs. During Christmas week DMN announced the delay of the New Year's Day launch, citing the need for more affiliates and the installation of a "new" holophonics sound system. They would be aiming for a February 1 premiere.

Andrew Setos, MTV's engineering and operations guru, voiced reservations. Holophonics had limitations. "It may be a system that is far superior to two-channel stereo, but will it be any practical advantage if listeners aren't in the perfect environment, which is less than 1 percent of the time?" He also questioned the feasibility of transferring original tracks to the experimental system, without distortion.

While still on the court docket, DMN's David was stymied by MTV's Goliath. Ted Turner, who refused to collaborate in the suit, was another matter. His track record was irrefutable. WTBS, Channel 17—the "Super Station"—was the number one cable network in the country with 32 million subscribers. Turner usually succeeded in his projects, especially in the world of satellites and cable oeprators. Even in failure, Turner was a formidable gadfly.

Notes

1. *Los Angeles Times,* August 23, 1983
2. *TV Guide,* September 22, 1984, pp. 41–44.
3. *Creem,* April 1982, p. 37.
4. *Billboard,* April 3, 1982, p. 67.
5. Schacter, now in USA's program development position, was a Movie Channel employee in 1979. He tells an interesting anecdotal tale. "Bob Pittman took me out to lunch just before the formation of MTV, sort of asking me what I wanted to do in this business. . . . When I was working in Washington [WDIV] I said to my program director, 'You know what I'd really love to do, I'd like to take rock music and put pictures to it, and make little stories of the songs.' And he said, 'Oh come on, that's crazy, it will be years before that happens.' So Pittman took me out to lunch. At that time, I didn't have the political sense to tell him what I really wanted. I didn't say, 'Bob, I'd love to do MTV, I think I'd be good at it.' I don't know whether I didn't have the nerve, whether I was too naive at the time, but for whatever reason I never said that, so it never came to be."
6. *Satellite Orbit,* June 1985.
7. *Billboard,* June 27, 1987, pp. 3, 75.
8. *Broadcasting,* February 18, 1985.
9. *T.V. Guide,* September 7, 1985, p. 3.
10. *New York Times,* August 21, 1983, p. F–3.
11. *Billboard,* February 11, 1984, p. 74.
12. Michael Shore, *The Rolling Stone Book of Rock Video* (New York: Quill Press, 1984), p. 74.
13. *Cablevision,* April 30, 1984, p. 24.
14. *Rock Video,* April 1984, p. 20.
15. The Agora in Cleveland and WMMS have teamed up to showcase unknown acts with a live broadcast and heavy radio promotion. Aerosmith and Bruce Springsteen are only a few of the artists who benefitted from this practice.
16. *Billboard,* December 3, 1983, p. 67.
17. *Billboard,* December 10, 1983, p. 39.
18. *Billboard,* December 18, 1984.
19. *Los Angeles Times,* August 26, 1984, p. 4.
20. *Rock & Roll Confidential,* April 1, 1984.
21. *Rolling Stone,* August 16, 1984.
22. *Prospectus,* August 10, 1984, p. 13.
23. *Rolling Stone,* August 12, 1984, p. 31.
24. *Washington Post,* October 10, 1984, C–4.
25. The original four labels were cited as coconspirators. Neither Polygram nor Elektra/Asylum were included.

7

Ted Turner's Crusade: Economics Versus Morals?

"Terrible Ted" Turner—the "Mouth of the South"—debuted the Cable Music Channel (CMC) on October 26, 1984 by telling the assembled guests: "We're going to play a wide range of music." He paused and added, "We're going to stay away from the excessive violence, violent or degrading clips to women that MTV is so fond of putting on."

The fifty assembled employees nodded in support. Some provided the expected applause. The few media people in attendance were skeptical. The sanitized version of MTV was considered a good selling point to cable operators weary of parental letters objecting to the content of the Warner-Amex music channel.

It was 9:00 A.M. in Hollywood. Media people, even with East Coast deadlines, were unaccustomed to the early hour. Most mass print and electronic media reporters were absent. The trades were present. The *Los Angeles Times,* with its large entertainment industry readership, assigned a reporter. The makeshift studio was decorated with green, yellow, red, and pink telegenic balloons. Twenty-five-inch, wall-mounted television screens were strategically placed around the converted Fox theatre, testing the CMC logo—a large dark blue star with the name in yellow gold lettering. A voluminous banner, with a star-shaped backdrop surrounded with a brown coloration and a red, white, and yellow border, dominated the makeshift stage. A large LP-shaped red button was to the right (The military significance did not escape all the participants). Waiters passed offering refreshments. At 9:04 A.M. (P.D.T) a physically drained Ted Turner pushed the album-sized button exclaiming, "Here we go! Take that MTV."

This statement was in keeping with Christian Williams' description in the *Washington Post* of the man as "a dizzying mixture of fierce pride, non-stop high-decibel speech making, philosophical gloom, night-marish evocations of a ruined earth populated by *homo sapiens* gone to seed." CNN's Hollywood reporter Sandy Kenyon and his crew dutifully recorded every monent for broadcast at Peachtree Street Studios in Atlanta, the home of Turner's twenty-four-hour daily all-news channel.

Randy Newman's video clip "I Love L.A." filled the monitor screens. Turner stood alone staring at the opening clip. "Olympia" by Sergio Mendes followed. Turner then accepted congratulations and answered reporters' questions. Kenyon, preparing a sixty-second bit on his employer's new venture, asked the obvious "why" question. Turner appeared bored but answered, "I am very concerned about the violence and the sadism [of MTV]. My wife used the description 'satanic.' So did *Fortune* magazine, so I figured we'd decided to clean it up. Something that would not be damaging for young people to watch." As the interview concluded a Doublemint chewing gum commercial aired. Stevie Wonder's "I Just Called to Say I Love You" and "A Hard Day's Night" by the Beatles continued the programming. Several of Bob Pittman's narrowcasting rules had already been violated.

Turner circulated in obligatory fashion. The flamboyance was subdued. This was not the charismatic personality who stunned the broadcast industry with a satellite "superstation" or swept the bases during the fifth inning at Atlanta Braves home games or pushed a baseball from first base to home plate with his nose or had players married in pregame ceremonies. On CMC's opening day Turner *appeared* as just another jet-lagged businesssman desiring to cash in on the megabucks of music video. Few believed Turner's statements that CMC was to be more than just a commercial alternative to MTV.

CMC president Robert Wussler guided Turner and a *Los Angeles Times* reporter to the rented car that would take Turner to the airport for the return flight to Atlanta. Turner would be glad to retreat to the security of his plantation in Marietta, Georgia. This was a project he was uncomfortable with.

Turner's business sense kept bumping into the symbolic crusade that the Cable Music Channel was becoming. Yet, he was tenacious (the name of his newest racing yacht).

As the car glided down the dreary Santa Monica Freeway to the airport, Turner apologized to David Crook, the *Times* writer, "I'm tired. I'm tired most of the time—physically tired." On this trip Turner was preoccupied. Reporters do not appreciate this superficiality, especially in Crock's case, since CMC would not even be broadcast in the major Los Angeles metropolitan area.[1]

On the flight eastward, Turner had a good deal on his mind. In his encounters with the news media no mention was made of the mecurial economic status of the venture. The project was definitely a "riverboat gamble," but his previous successful business enterprises were risky as well.

A TBS stock prospectus filed with the Securities and Exchange Commission noted: "The company anticipated that Cable Music Channel [previously MVN] will lose in the range of $5 to $10 million in its first year of operation and may continue at this level thereafter."

These facts were generally unknown outside of Turner's inner circle in Atlanta when he announced the establishment of the Music Video Network (MVN) in the first week of September 1984.

Warner Amex—still smarting over the $3.00 drop in the value of MTV network stock, an estimated $15 million paper revenue loss—countered by unveiling plans for a new network. Video Hits One (VH-1) was scheduled to air on New Years Day. Turner knew from his cable news experience that system operators and consumers would not support all the projected music video systems. He announced early in September an October 26 opening. "Night Flight's" Jeff Franklin would later comment, "I believe that this country cannot absorb more than one contemporary music network." Wall Street analysts appeared dubious, as were advertisers and most significantly cable operators.

The Turner Empire

Robert Edward Turner III had come a long way from his humble beginnings in Cincinnati, Ohio. At forty-six, his life had been a series of gambles.

"Terrible Ted"—a nickname he received while attending the McCallie School in Chattanooga, Tennessee, a college preparatory school "in a Christian context"—had problems with his father. Turner's first wife Judy Nye Halisey recalled: "He wanted Ted to be insecure, because he felt that insecurity breeds greatness. If Ted was insecure then he would be forced to compete." The disciplinary approach appears to have worked.

The military-oriented McCallie School primed young Ted to aspirations of attending the United States Military Academy. The senior Turner had other plans. Ted was sent to Brown University for a business degree.

Rebelling Ted originally majored in the classics. After a considerable amount of family conflict, Turner changed his focus to economics. At Brown Turner developed and pursued an interest in sailing. He finished first in nine regattas in college dinghy competitions. The Norton Yacht Club offered him a summer job and the opportunity to race. His father insisted he work in the family advertising business as an account executive.

After several drinking bouts that resulted in university incidents he was suspended. His father enlisted him in the Coast Guard for a six-month tour. Ted returned to Brown only to be expelled for having female visitors in his dorm room.

Ted returned to the family billboard advertising business. His father was in the process of purchasing the General Outdoor Advertising Company, the largest of its kind, in Atlanta. Financially overextended, Ed Turner committed suicide six months after the acquisition.

With an unbelievable zeal and energy Ted Turner rebuilt the fledgling family companies. By 1970,, they were on a sound economic footing. He purchased WTCG, channel 17, an independent Atlanta-based UHF station floating in red ink. Many considered the purchase foolhearty at best. The first year Turner lost $2 million on the venture. The losses were offset by the billboard revenues. Turner juggled the station's format with syndicated sit-coms, a steady diet of old movies, and local sports events. The formula worked as the station had an impressive 16 percent of the audience "cum" or share of market.

In 1972 Turner hired Kent Burkhart to consult for WGOW-AM in Chattanooga. This was a year prior to the founding of the Burkhart/Abrams consulting firm. Burkhart would be an important player in Turner's music video adventures. Turner's main interest, however, was television, especially the cable industry. Prior to the launching of Sat Com I in 1975, community antenna television was designed to bring signals into suburban and rural areas. These signals were transmitted by microwave to the antennas. The FCC monitored these transmissions. One regulation was to exclude independent stations from most cable markets outside of their immediate locality.

In 1975 RCA launched the first American communications satellite. Home Box Office (HBO), owned by Time, Inc., was quick to use the "bird" circling the earth some 22,300 miles above ground. Eight days before Christmas 1976 WTCG-TV joined HBO in outer space. In two years WTCG was received in two million households. The value of the station was estimated at $40 million.

Turner was able to attract national advertisers while other independents were tied to the caprices of local time buyers. The unaffiliated stations were basically mirror images of themselves, like Top Forty radio. They relied on old movies and syndications ranging from sit-coms to daytime talk shows with Dinah, Mike, Merv, and Phil.

Realizing the similarity, Turner bought the cellar-dwelling Atlanta Braves and the National Basketball Association's Atlanta Hawks. In purchasing the two professional sports teams, Turner was guaranteed a strong sports venue not enjoyed by competing independents.

Turner's management of the teams, especially the Braves, brought him national attention. He was accused of tampering with players from other clubs. His on-the-field antics also made news. Commissioner Bowie Kuhn suspended Turner from the sport for a year. In time, Turner would be instrumental in ousting Kuhn.

Amid the controversies Turner improved the Braves ("America's Team") and the "Superstation's" percentage of the cable market. He also managed to repeatedly win the prestigious America's Cup and was named Yachtsman of the Year a record three times.

The success of WTBS-TV, "the Super Station that serves the Nation," allowed Turner to introduce in June 1980 the Cable News Network (CNN), a twenty-four-hour commercial information enterprise.

Three years after predictions of its demise, the Cable News Network was in 26 million households, which translated into 71 percent of cable homes or 30 percent of households with television sets. CNN Headline News, syndicated to independent stations, had 10 million homes after buying out Satellite News Channel, owned by ABC and the Westinghouse Group. Turner told a reporter, "On a level playing field, ABC and Group W got their brains kicked out, and they had resources at least 100 times ours."

With its 1984 presidential campaign and convention coverage, CNN successfully challenged the Big Three networks. "It's the difference between reading a book from the beginning or from the middle," observed CNN's political news director Bob Furnad.

Walter Cronkite was quoted in *USA Today:* "I've been watching CNN during this convention, and to a political buff it's fascinating because you're getting all the issues, even the less important ones." Most of the major print media concurred. The *Los Angeles Times* wrote, "When it came to *real* news, ABC, CBS and NBC largely stiffed the public . . . and Cable News Network proved its value." *The New York Times, Washington Post,* and a host of other influential papers echoed this sentiment. Most applauded the gavel-to-gavel coverage, but questioned the use of ultraconservative commentators such as Robert Novack.

Turner's Music Ventures

In the wake of his news successes, Turner focused his attention on music video. Turner was no stranger to music broadcasting. His Turner Communications Group included several rock-oriented stations. Radio, of course, was not his main interest. He preferred the "rough and tumble" of the video world.

In June 1983 "Super Station" WTBS unveiled "Night Tracks," a six-hour program designated to highlight eighty video clips. Fifteen different music videos were scheduled to premiere each weekend. The music program was thrown into the Friday–Saturday night ghetto of video shows competing with "Night Flight," "Friday Night Videos," and the offerings of MTV. "Pity the poor guy who's just trying to find an old movie to watch," wrote a *Los Angeles Times* critic. Initially twenty-six shows were planned.

Tom Lynch, previously the producer of "Don Kirschner's Rock Concert," was hired to perform the same tasks for TBS. Scott Sassa was the executive producer. Both wished to avoid the MTV "narrow-cast" format.

No veejays would be used. Instead, "voiceovers" by Los Angeles radio personalities would be employed. Bob Coburn of KLOS and Joanne Erhart of KNX would introduce the clips and do the station identifications.

The maiden show aired on Friday night, June 3, with Men at Work, Hall and Oates, Billy Joel, and Lionel Richie. They were picked, according to Sassa, "for their audience familiarity" and appeal to the 18 to 40 demographic. Lynch added in a *Billboard* interview, "Any song that's in the top 40 has a built-in black and white core." This was a backhanded slap at MTV, which was frequently criticized for its lack of black performers.

Consultant Dwight Douglas, of Burkhart and Abrams, viewed the "Night Tracks" show as an extension of contemporary hits radio (CHR), a successful format in the mid-1980s. Included in his playlist were Sheena Easton, Eddie Rabbitt, Kenny Rogers, Michael Jackson, and Kool and the Gang.

"Night Tracks" received mixed reviews. Dick Ebersol of "Friday Night Videos" said, "Turner's ("Night Tracks) is the weakest. It has no rhyme or reason. They'll put on Willie Nelson right after Michael Jackson. Those are both fine artists, but with different audiences. If you did that on radio, you'd lose half your audience in a second." The NBC producer was unaware of Ted Turner's fourteen-year-old daughter "who just loves Willie Nelson." Terry Atkinson, a *Los Angeles Times* critic, described the show as being modeled after MTV with "a broader range of musical styles—including some country and R&B—and no veejays."

"After seeing 'Night Tracks,' " said a critic, "I sorta miss veejays." The discontinuous clips were grating on some nerves. Scott Sassa countered, "We don't see that as a big problem. We have a broad format that appeals to a broad audience. From the conception, we've had Burkhart-Abrams advising and programming and I think Lee Abrams knows a lot more about pop programming than Dick Ebersol."

The "pop top 40 light CHR image" as of December 1983 enjoyed a 1.0 rating in the households it serviced and, according to a WTBS spokesperson, was performing at a much higher ratings level than some of its competitors.

Sassa noted: "Say an advertiser wants a complete buy, both younger and older people. This show gives it to them. The market can stand competition." Sassa was the "out-front person," but "Night Tracks" was Turner's creation, as no six-figure project is broadcast on the "Super Station" without his wholehearted approval. Most observers saw "Night Tracks," strength as being on a station that had over 25 million households.

WTBS was a late starter in the music video field. With the households in the "Super Station" fold, "Night Tracks" could compete with most cable music offerings. When the program originally aired it was made very clear that WTBS was not attempting to compete with MTV.

The MTV "exclusivity" arrangements posed a direct threat to "Night Tracks." When rumors of pending litigation circulated in the Spring of 1984 Scott Sassa, producer of the WTBS music show, was consulting lawyers over possible antitrust violations. They vetoed any litigation.

When the MTV contracts became a reality in mid-June, Sassa was more combative. "It's a pretty aggressive action and we'll take whatever steps are needed to counteract it," he hold a trade paper.

Sassa was not happy. He informed *Billboard* that WTBS would be using the lower "30 to 60 range on the charts." The songs would be played on "a higher rotation earlier." MTV, in the producer's view, was definitely hurting the "Night Tracks" playlist.

Privately, MTV with its newly acquired power was a threat to Peachtree's music video broadcasting—especially during the highly aggressive ratings battles for the weekend late-night music viewer.

Since the departure of Sassa, "Night Tracks" exhibits a Janus-like convergence. Ex-CMC publicity director Eric McLamb says the "Chinese menu" approach has been down played. "Power Play" is based on trades such as *Cash Box, Billboard,* and other charted sources. He claims: "It would come closest probably to CHR because of the heavy (repeated) rotation of Top 40—play a golden oldies of the Beatles or something like that, but you have to look at those new artists arising and have a video out now that's just starting—if it's good we will play it. We also look at what the people want to see in terms of viewer requests." They actually do play requests. Another executive described the overall format as "top ten plus new music." The Chinese menu is still defended. McLamb noted, "I would rather have a variety of music than listen to heavy metal for twenty-four hours [note MTV]. With us, you won't have to watch 'Night Tracks' all day long to see videos that you like. Someone who likes James Brown wouldn't have to wait until the last hour on 'Night Tracks' to see him."

Turner Broadcasting executive adopt a curious posture to MTV. One executive says, "We are talking a lot about MTV doing this and what MTV does really doesn't matter as far as 'Night Tracks' is concerned because 'Night Tracks' has its own show, is separate, not twenty-four hours." However, any interview conducted with Turner staffers rarely is an opportunity missed to bash MTV, however subtly.

Turner's self-esteem may have been hurt by MTV's coup, but with his successful news and other video enterprises this was far from a major economic blow to the Atlanta cable empire—or so it seemed.

Turner, as usual, had bigger plans, especially after cornering the cable news market. This time profits plus power were minimal. Turner saw MTV as the platonic moral corrupter of youth. In an era of Ronald Reagan and Jerry Falwell, he could be the St. George slaying the MTV dragon of black leather and supposed violence.

During the summer of 1984, rumors of a Turner-sponsored twenty-four-hour music video network began to surface. Was the "Mouth of the South" serious?"

One cheerleader was Mike Greene of Atlanta's local Video Music Channel. He observed, "If he says he is going to do it, he'll do it, period. He's got the money—he's got hundreds of millions of dollars." It appeared that way at the time.

On August 7, 1984, 8,000 letters were sent to cable operators throughout the country (see Figure 7.1). They appeared to be trial balloons as to the feasibility of a new music video network. An anonymous TBS spokesperson said that the launching of the service depended on a positive response from the systems representing ten million cable households. Economically, the strategy seemed realistic. The five-year "free" service was timed to compete with MTV's contract renegotiations with some of its 2,470 affiliates and the stock offering. The response to Turner's two-page letter was at best cautious. Roger Wise of Wood Television Corporation in Ohio said, "MTV has better professionals than Turner . . . they have more creative people to draw on." A major cable operator told *Advertising Age* that he would have to review the Turner service to prove itself. In general cable operators were skeptical about the proposed venture. Two rock channels could prove unworkable. *Electronic Media,* a trade paper, retrospectively noted that CMC was "unwanted, unneeded."

Figure 7.1

August 7, 1984

Dear Cable Operator:

As you may know, Turner Broadcasting System is seriously considering launching a new 24-hour per day rock music video programming service for distribution to cable opertors free of charge. We have had substantial experience in producing rock music video programming since June 1983, when we began airing "NIGHT TRACKS" on WTBS. We now seek to broaden our commitment to this video music format by launching this new service. It is our current plan to launch this new service via SATCOM IIIR on December 5, 1984—the opening day of this year's Western Show.

I am sure you can appreciate that providing the cable industry with a quality video music service will require a considerable investment of money and corporate resources. Accordingly, before we can proceed with this project we must receive commitments to carry our music service from cable operators representing an aggregate minimum of ten million (10,000,000) subscribers. That is why I am writing to you.

To assure us of the subscriber base necessary to launch this service, we are prepared to offer our video music service free of charge for five (5) years (unless the service is terminated sooner) to all cable operators who commit before August 24, 1984 to supply us with any part of the first 10,000,000 subscribers. This offer shall be subject to the following conditions:

1. This offer shall apply only if TBS has commitments representing an aggregate minimum of 10,000,000 subscribers who will be actually receiving service within thirty (30) days of the launch of the service.
2. This offer must be accepted by you and returned to TBS no later than August 24, 1984.
3. This offer shall not be effective unless it is accepted by cable operators who commit an aggregate minimum of 10,000,000 subscribers to the service.
4. TBS reserves the right to proceed with a Video Music Service if it receives commitments for less than 10,000,000 subscribers.
5. TBS further reserves the right not to proceed with its plan to launch a video music service for any reason, regardless of the number of subscriber commitments it receives from cable operators.

We will not require any cable operator to subscribe to any of our programming services as a condition of this offer. I would like you to know, however, that we have no plans to offer a discount on Cable News Network or CNN Headline News subscriber rates to cable operators who subscribe to our video music service.

If you are willing to accept this offer and join with us to bring a new and exciting programming service to your subscribers, please indicate your acceptance by providing TBS with a specific number of basic or tiered subscribers that you will commit and sign this letter in the space provided below. Please return the executed original copy of this letter to Terry McGuirk at the above address prior to August 24, 1984.

We anticipate that we will reach a final decision on whether to proceed with this project on, or prior to, September 1, 1984. We will, of course, inform you of our decision as soon as possible.

We appreciate your support of our programming services over the years and look forward to a long and mutually beneficial relationship with your company.

> Very truly yours,
> R. E. "Ted" Turner
> President and Chairman

Turner did not receive his desired replies by the August 24 deadline. A launching decision was promised on September 1.

Business sense dictated that the cable operators' responses, lukewarm at best, should have terminated the project as the "numbers" were not there. Privately, Turner was aware of the financial institutions' guardedness of the project. Banks had limited Turner's credit to a $1.5 million loss in 1984, $7.5 million in 1985, and $5 million in 1986. This was far less than Warner-Amex's investment in MTV during its first three years of operation. MTV lost over $30 million during that period.

Statements emanating from the converted Fox theater in Los Angeles and Atlanta were vague and contradictory. The announcement of an October 26 start-up date created an industry stir.

Trade magazine reporters asked a number of questions on both coasts and found a "ball of confusion." A press release stated that MVN "expected" to have five million subscribers by the take-off date. However, vice president Arthur Sando said, "We don't get into that game," replying to a question posed regarding the number of cable companies committed to the enterprise.

In Hollywood, Sassa indicated that the decision was made to move forward despite "significantly lower numbers of subscribers." Almost apologetically Sassa added, "We hope the record companies will recognize the . . . risks. After we get in, we'll share in our benefits. But we don't need ankle-weights now." In less corporate language the TBS vice president was pleading poverty to the record titans in New York and Los Angeles.

Turner continued on, hiring Digital Productions in Los Angeles to devise a MVN logo and employing a California-based staff of disk jockeys to perform the "voiceovers" in the "Night Tracks" motif.

Several days after the MVN logo was commissioned, an abrupt name transformation took place. MVN became the Cable Music Channel (CMC) on September 5. Turner explained that the change was made for "a more descriptive name for a broad-based video music service." Again, this action was made in haste. CMC was already the logo of a California-based cable firm.

Victor Livingston, editor-in-chief of the influential *Cable Vision* trade magazine, asked "Why Turner wants *his* MTV?" Not surprisingly the editor supported Turner's move on the grounds that music video could "thrive in a variety of venues—following the segmented, demographic approach that has revitalized radio." He also stated that the projected 18 to 49 demographic Turner was targeting was a realizable goal. Then, Livingston got the crux of the Turner venture:

"Groups such as the National Coalition on Television Violence have sharply scolded MTV for running videos containing graphic mayhem. With some playlist restraint and daypart programming to put the more suggestive videos in nighttime rotation, Turner could score marketing points among operators under pressure from decency in programming types."

The FCC and the Supreme Court have ruled that cable television is exempt from local regulatory control over fees and most importantly content. MTVN's Nickelodeon featured a children's show called "You Can't Do That on Television." The program has garnered high marks from critics and educators, but the title is the important thing. Cable networks are self-regulated. There is a wide variety of programming available to subscribers in certain communities. This freedom, especially in the case of MTV, has created a mixed dilemma for local cable operators. MTV is popular with adolescents. Their parents in some cases are strongly opposed.

MTV has been attacked at the grass roots and by media watchdogs. Wood TV is a relatively small MSO located in a rural Northwest Ohio university community. MTV since its introduction has been a highly controversial issue. The main complaint against adding MTV to Wood TV's offerings was its impact on the youth of the community.

Roger Wise of Wood TV comments: "I've heard not only obscenity but . . . the use of instruments in certain fashions, and violent production techniques where it is back lighted and rear projected. Yes we've had some serious objections."

These objections come not only from concerned parents, but also school teachers and even some university people. A typical letter to the cable company was: "MTV is completely disgusting and a waste of our money. If people want to watch it they should pay extra. It is suggestive and offensive for young children." The same writer labeled the channel as basically a "negative influence."

Other letters and calls to Wood TV "have been a little more frank than that." Unfortunately, the more adamant notes and phone objections have been lost. Wise added, "We've had some really tough letters and phone calls."

Popular music, particular rock and roll, has always been a source of debate and "generational" battles. While rock has been labeled "the devil's diversion," and some zealots have encouraged teenagers burn their records, this conflict is nothing new; it is decades long. The jitterbuggers and bobbysoxers of the 1930s were equally condemned, as were the fans of "Elvis the Pelvis." Others viewed the Beatles as little more than a "communist plot to hypnotize American youth."

Rev. David Noebel made a career pushing this argument. The ghost of Plato, who wrote that music corrupts the young, still stalks the land.

Many songs of the late 1960s were supposed to contain drug-oriented messages that urged listeners to "turn on." Even the children's tune "Puff the Magic Dragon" by Peter, Paul, and Mary was viewed by a few as a proponent of marijuana.

Looking back on those days and arguments, much seems laughable. However some serious-minded people took it quite literally, including a vice president of the United States and the Federal Communications Commission.

Backward masking—putting hidden messages on records when played in reverse—and MTV are the culprits of the 1980s.

As Roger Wise points out, there is a clear-cut difference today from previous decades. With Benny Goodman's New York Paramount Theater concerts and Top 40 in the 1950s, adults had little control over the media. They protested, but "rock and roll was here to stay."

Cable is another matter. It is a subscription service. Wise defined the difference: "I have a one-to-one relationship more than we ever did in the broadcast business. It was never as pointed or as vicious as the attack on MTV."

Disgruntled parents can always cancel the service. This wasn't possible in the past. Few people blacklisted Benny Goodman or threw their radios into the garbage.

"Deviance," wrote sociologist Howard Becker, "is in the eye of the beholder." This seems to be the case with MTV. The major monitor of deviance on media is the National Coalition of Television Violence (NCTV). The group is headed by Dr. Thomas Radecki, a University of Illinois psychiatrist. On January 10, 1984 the NCTV issued a report that has been the foundation for attacks on the Pittman format. Liberals and political conservatives alike cite NCTV's findings to support their diverse social positions.

The organization claimed that "18.0 instances of violence" occurred every sixty minutes. Moreover, 35 percent of MTV violence was sexual in nature, and "over half of MTV videos featured violence or strongly suggested violence." Dr. Thomas Radecki cited Michael Jackson, the Rolling Stones, and Billy Idol as promoting "sadistic and sexually sadistic violence of a very intense nature." This motif, he charged, was "common on MTV." He concluded that MTV is "out to guarantee that the second television generation will be more violent than the first, which turned out to be the most violent . . . on record." Many social scientists in the field question these assertions.

The NCTV repeated its charges in a press release issued December

10, 1984. Their findings were that 17.9 instances of violence occurred on music video stations every sixty minutes. "This was virtually no change compared to one year ago when NCTV issued its first report." Ironically, Turner's WTBS was included in the sample along with MTV. While Turner's reaction to the study is impossible to tell, he did accept the general notion.

Turner, with his values, concurred that "the world was going to seed" and that MTV was a strong force in the moral decay. His view of Warner Communications as "sleazy" was deeply felt, as he expressed in an interview with *Rolling Stone*. Turner's comments for the founding of the Cable Music Channel and its purpose explain many of the contradictions in the emergence of the station.

The reason for establishing the network was moralistic: "I was really disturbed with some of the clips they were running. You can take a bunch of young people and you can turn them into Boy Scouts or into Hitler Youth, depending on what you teach them, and MTV's definitely a bad influence." He concluded his short interview with an apocalyptic statement reflecting his fundamentalist background: "I think in the final analysis good's going to win out over evil. If it doesn't, then at least we fought. We tried, and you can't fault us for that."

Bob Pittman would diplomatically reply, "I don't know if Ted felt that way or if that's just what Ted said. I think with MTV, we are representing change. There are certain people who are resistant to the change, just as people thought long hair on men would destroy the moral fiber of America." Later he added, "The only similarity between CMC and either of our music networks is that they both use videos somewhere in the mix. I think everything else was completely different."

Back in Atlanta, Turner's fatigue only underscored the fact that the Cable Music Channel was built on a house of cards. The media, surely the all-important trade magazines, would soon be looking into the financing of the venture. Saving the world from MTV had little persuasive power on Madison Avenue in the board rooms of major money lenders or Wall Street stock analysts. The feared reaction was not long in coming. Even CNN concluded its coverage of the opening with a negative quote from cable analyst David Cooks: "[MTV] is pretty hard to beat."

MTV Versus CMC

At WASEC Turner's letter was taken as a declaration of war. His reputation preceded him. The announcement of a new competing music video network was met with diverse reactions. "Terrible Ted" did his best to antagonize the MTV executives. The solicitation to cable operators was sent out a day prior to the Nickelodeon-MTV stock offering, which was to be called the MTV Network Inc.

Wall Street was watching closely. Mara Miesnieks of Smith Barney commented: "It's certainly not good timing for MTV. It raises some questions: What is, or could be the competition? . . . Knowing Turner's reputation for being hardnosed and getting things done quickly . . . it's not positive, and it's not clear how much it will hurt the [MTV] offering."

Turner's offer of a free service also coincided with MTV contract renegotiations with some of its affiliates, involving over one million households. Margaret Wade and Dorene Lauer, MTV's press relations people, refused to comment on the move. Rumors abounded. One view was that Turner was throwing a monkey wrench into MTV's public stock offering. *Advertising Age* implied that Turner failed to come to "terms with Drew Lewis, Chairman of Warner-Amex Cable Communications, on a merger of TBS' news services and MTV's music and children's channels." This time the street rap was correct. Lending institutions did force Turner to talk to MTV. Turner's economic situation was not as solid as his successes might indicate. One observer told *Cable Vision:* "Somebody is going, through instability, it's not MTV." A record company publicist noted, "The marketing people here are very reluctant to say something to irritate MTV." The source added that Turner's proposal was a "good deal." Miles Copeland, president of IRS Records, commented: "MTV is a phenomenon because it has no competition. If it had competition, we would see a very different industry. We would not see new groups breaking it. If somebody wants to play music videos, somebody is going to hit MTV square on." IRS was not a major play in the music video game.

Advertisers seemed leery. Ad money was essential to Turner's project, as he promised cable operators a five-year freebie. Several BBDO executives openly were critical. Arnie Semsky said, "It's going to be cut throat and somebody is going to get hurt." A fellow vice president, Bill Weiner, added, "I don't know how Turner can provide a quality service with only advertising revenues." He reasoned that Turner would eventually charge for the service if the music channel would survive. Prophetically, Steve Leff, executive vice president at Backer & Spielvogel, noted, "I wouldn't be surprised if you see one of these guys acquiring the other." Few Madison Avenue insiders were betting on Turner's challenge.

Ad people had reason to be cautious. Cable operators were not flocking to Turner's offering. While twelve-channel cable systems have been correctly labelled "dinosaurs," in 1984 the majority of systems used them. This meant a limitation of available services. MTV had already penetrated most of these markets, with over twenty million households. Many expressed the view that carrying two twenty-four-hour music networks was impossible. A majority already had contracts with MTV. A few hoped that Turner's entry into the business might force MTV to lower its rates. MTV executives didn't quite see it that way. President John F. Kennedy's father's slogan "Don't get mad, get even" permeated MTV.

MTV was not idle. MTV Networks heralded the signing of the nation's two largest cable companies (Tele-Communications Inc. and American Television and Communications) to long-term contracts. Neither party would comment on the stipulations of the concords. Secrecy was becoming an MTV trademark.

One MSO operator mused, "Turner [has to prove his] legs before dumping MTV for a rival service." Storer Broadcasting, a major broadcasting chain especially in the Midwest, complained, "Turner doesn't have much to show us yet in terms of format." Another operator was more blunt: "He's the devil you do know. He shocked a lot of us when he raised his rates for CNN after buying out SNC." It was a riverboat gamble and everyone had a few cards up their corporate sleeves.

Janet Foster, of Group W Cable, had some encouraging words. She told *Ad Age,* "Fantastic and marvelous. I'm surprised that it's taken this long for someone to compete with Warner." Obviously MTV folks didn't concur, even in light of Bob Pittman's statement that only one other music channel could survive in the cable market. In an April symposium WASEC's chief operations officer observed to *Cable Vision,* "But of course there will be other formats. What will we do then? I don't think the market is sufficiently large yet—one, with the cable operators; two, with the record companies; three, with the artists; and four, with the potential consumers to support other types of music. When the time comes, I'm sure that if we don't try it, someone else will." He was prophetic. "Terrible Ted" entered the picture four months later, which upset Pittman's game plan. The battle lines were clearly drawn.

Turner only fueled the flames. He repeatedly called MTV "sleazy" in a press interview. Explaining the characterization, he said, "I was referring to the management of MTV, which was running those violent clips."

This was no longer a matter of economics, it was becoming very personal. Despite his physical appearance, Bob Pittman was a fighter, as Turner would soon discover.

The son of Atlanta's outdoor advertising tycoon was a winner. His accomplishments made him a public, however notorious, figure. The Cable Music Channel from the beginning was beseiged with problems. The televised opening and the one-arm victory salute would be the high points of what revolved into a thirty-four-day nightmare.

Good intentions did not transcend the counterattack by MTV, demographics, and the media. One TBS employee said, "The little coverage we got was in the trades and most of it negative."

MTV enjoyed a lock on the younger segment of the twelve- to thirty-four-year-old audience. Turner seemingly avoided a dilemma plaguing radio programmers: the attraction of the 25+ age groups whose musical involvement psychographically was a mystery. The "Big Chill Generation," as Jon Sinton, then research vice-president of Burkhart/Abrams, calls them, are a tough audience to grab unless "Stairway to Heaven" or "Hey Jude" are on the air.

MTV enjoyed a multitude of advantages. It earned $15.4 million in Madison Avenue revenues. It had 21.8 million households as subscribers. A.C. Nielsen rated the channel as the most watched advertiser—supported—"Basic"—service during an average day. Even before the five label exclusivity arrangement, artists and record executives recognized the force of the network.

Turner's public pronouncements had created problems, especially his characterization of Warners and its choice of video clips.

The Downfall

As MTV was flexing its power, MVN, now soon to be CMC, was losing a good deal of credibility with advertisers and operators. *Cable Vision* reported: "TBS stated that it 'expects' its Music Video Network to have five million subscribers by its October 26 start." Executives generally refused to substantiate the figure or unveil the format. Cynicism abounded. Leaks in the cable and music trades hinted that the household numbers might be misleading.

There were more contradictory statements. One source claimed a targeted 12 to 24 demographic base that would appeal to the forty-year-old market. An Atlanta publicist told this writer that the network would go for the 18 to 34 demographic. Others had the figures expanded to 18 to 54. It was blatantly apparent that, unlike Pittman, TBS had not done its homework, even with Burkhart/Abrams as consultants. In an age of psychographics, somebody erred.

The format issue was equally confused. Scott Sassa told a reporter: "Contemporary hit radio gets a big part of its listening audience from the 18 to 24 age group. But when you take heavy metal music out of the format, you will get people much older. Our format is going to vary, so that different dayparts [time slots] . . . have maximum appeal with the available audience at the time." The CMC executive went on to suggest that the network planned a sixty- to eighty-video playlist a week. Sassa, for the first time, provided a general, but accurate model of the format. The damage control appeared to have worked for several days.

Arthur Sando, vice president for TBS, said two days later in *Satellite TV Week* that he was not "quite ready to delineate" the mix of the music channel.

Intercompany communications, across the nation, have been criticized for years in the record industry due to the time zones. Still, TBS appeared to be developing the Coastal confusion into an art form:

> In short, Cable Music Channel provides the best service of its kind, with quality programming targeted at a broad-scale television audience.

A week prior to the Los Angeles startup, CMC finally issued a press release as to the format. It was CHR—the format Sassa dismissed. For many cable operators the statement—by the time it was published—was too late.

TURNER BROADCASTING SYSTEM'S FOURTH MAJOR CABLE NETWORK, Cable Music Channel, will be beamed via satellite, 24-hours-a-day, beginning at NOON (ET) on Friday, October 26, 1984, as cable's newest, free ad-supported music video channel. It is unique because of its broad suburban appeal matched to the demographics of cable homes passed.

Cable Music Channel features cross-over music from the POP, ROCK, DANCE and COUNTRY charts. Its format is that of Contemporary Hit Radio (CHR), the number one radio format in the U.S. today. Based on a rotation of 60–80 music video clips per week, a typical Cable Music Channel programming block is as follows:
- First song: a music video rising on the charts.
- Second song: a new release.
- Third song: a recurrent (past hit) or novelty video.
- Plus Prime-Time Special Events and Concerts.

Within Cable Music Channel's CHR format, dayparts are adjusted for the basic, corresponding viewing audiences.
- 6–10 AM: Morning Drive flavor. Quick paced. DJ voice overs.

- 10 AM–3 PM: Softer hits, targeted for people at home during the day.
- 3–8 PM: Upbeat Rock & Roll, targeted for teens and young adults.
- 8–11 PM: Prime Time, featuring Top 40 rotation, plus more; straight forward.
- 11 pm–6 AM: Progressive CHR format, targeted for late-night audiences; some heavy metal.

Cable Music Channel employs the latest in computer graphics and film animation, coupled with LIVE voice overs to provide intros, strong continuity and outstanding on-air presence. On-camera Video Jockeys were rejected due to unfavorable audience research indicating poor acceptance of their intrusions.

Cable Music Channel also plays more music videos per hour than any other service, rating 15–20% more than its closest competition. The network draws upon over 80% of all existing music videos plus 60 new ones produced monthly. Cable Music Channel will reject about 10% of all music videos due to gratuitous sex and violence and under 10% will not be used due to temporary unavailability.

Turner's concerns on the flight back to Atlanta were justified. The daily press coverage virtually ignored the channel. One Midwest writer observed: "Many of the artists and clips will be familiar to MTV viewers. Prince, David Bowie, Corey Hart, Tina Turner, Chicago and other old faces and clips were aired the first day." The all-important trade papers, more involved with economics than fans, were much less kind.

Three days later *Cablevision* and other trades began to run feature stories on CMC's "actual numbers and finances." One cable operator said, off the record, "He should have brought the PTL, and knocked off all this demographic hype."

Billboard broke the story. Turner's channel would have to pay for some broadcast material. MTV's exclusivity lock was obviously hurting the network. "I can talk until I'm blue in the face about whether that's a good thing or not," Sassa noted. "But rhetoric doesn't do it, lawsuits don't do it. It's going out there and showing that you're an effective way to market records." In light of the newly exposed numbers—CMC now claimed 2.5 million homes, half of the previously stated figure—record companies were leery. Sassa, the most candid of the TBS team, continued: "Cable service can't survive until they get to ten million homes because they just don't have the advertising base." He was correct, but CMC in actuality had less than one-third of a million—a fact that would not surface for weeks.

CMC had projected an annual increase to ten million homes by July

1985. Now the number was halved. This was only the first layer of the emperor's clothes to be stripped away. Investigative reporters began to look into the situation. Their findings, along with economic realities, would eventually sink the musical experiment.

Cablevision followed suit. It's "Leading the Week" item by Simon Applebaum, headlined "Cable Music Channel Launches with 2.5 M Less Subs Than Hoped." The story went on to list a myriad of major MSOs that refused the service, including some that originally had been very positive.

A spokesperson claimed that CMC aired with 2,309,874 households, a figure less than reported. The numbers quickly deteriorated. Ten 'major" MSOs had signed with CMC, including Storer, Group W, and eight others. In mid-November the TBS people still kept a stiff upper lip, negative news reports notwithstanding.

Even Turner's "CNN Headline News" broadcast November 11 underscored the problems. It was reported:

> The new cable channel, competition for MTV and owned by Turner Broadcasting, is performing for fewer viewers now than was first announced. The Cable Music Channel was launched to try to attract older viewers. Company officials said it had 2.5 million subscribers. New figures released by a Turner spokesperson show 400,000 watch the MOR round the clock performance. TBS corporation public relations man Arthur Sando says, "there is no guarantee the channel will survive! The venture could lose $5 to $6 million its first year." There is no explanation as to how the first subscriber figure was determined.

A cynic might indicate that CNN foresaw the forthcoming *Billboard* story on the low viewship and TBS' attempt to raise money to pay off debtors. The stipulations of the loans were such that CMC had little chance of survival. Arthur Sando suggested it was "too early to pull the plug," but admitted the situation was "disappointing." The handwriting was on the wall. Many observers wondered whether the channel would go under or if there was a corporate "white knight" in the wings. CMC's last trade ad appeared in cable trade magazines reading:

> NOW AVAILABLE
> The creators of cable's top-rated Night Tracks and Chartbusters bring you the service that's programmed to take music videos to mainstream America.
>
> Cable Music Channel is more music, fewer commercial interruptions with live off camera video disc jockeys. And, it's free of excessive sex and violence.

Cable Music Channel offers you a tremendous opportunity to create new excitement, add real value to Basic, and increase local advertising dollars.

In the fourth week of November Ted Turner told Arthur Sando, "Well, it just isn't going to make it." He blamed the cable industry. He elaborated: "We continue to believe that Cable Music Channel is a top-quality music service, but we have not had enough support from the cable industry for it to become a viable service." The decision was made to cut TBS' losses and bail out. "Pain?" said Sando, "No not really . . . it was a business decision; these things happen in corporate life."

MTV has since its early days been very secretive regarding its business dealings. Bob Pittman made a brief statement on how a $1.5 million deal with TBS evolved in late November. "The Turner organization decided they wanted to shut CMC down," he told a reporter. "They asked if there were certain assets that we would be interested in acquiring. Since we were launching VH-1, we were interested in those assets which we thought we could use—say, converting CMC subscribers to VH-1 subscribers."

The takeover was made public on November 28, less than two days prior to CMC's 11:59 P.M. (EST) shutdown. CMC was purchased for $1 million. MTV agreed to buy an additional $500,000 of advertising time on TBS' remaining networks. One aspect of the buy-out labelled "certain assets" was generally ignored. The victorious network also acquired channel 15 on Sat Com 3R (F–3), previously "CNN Headline News' " "back-up" feed. It would become VH-1 at 6 P.M. (EST) New Years Day at a start-up cost of $7 million, which included the acquisition of CMC's assets and required time buys.

The final half hour of the dying channel was filled with bitterness and insider comments, and song selections. Elton John's "Why They Call It the Blues" played. The female voiceover followed with, "We're all losing when it comes down to it." Billy Idol's—not one of Turner's favorites—"Eyes Without a Face" led into another commentary: "Blink your eyes and we could be gone." Julian Lennon's "Valotte," containing the line "Do you know there is something wrong," was followed by a voiceover of: "Reap what you sow, baby" to introduce Big Country's "Where the Rose Is Down." Commercials followed, promoting WTBS and Paramount Pictures.[2] The female voice struck again: "I'm going to take all my musical toys back to 'Hotlanta.' " Missing Persons' "Surrender Your Heart," a surrealistic clip, was followed with "Sometimes you see it, but you don't get it . . . the Cable Music Channel has escaped you now!"

The innuendo's became more overt with the last two songs and the commentaries. Quartermaster's "Take Me to Your Heart" was obvious, with lines such as "You're gonna see me wherever you go/You're gonna hear me on the radio." The remarks that followed left little doubt that some fifty people were about to lose their jobs. "Take me and somebody's got to do it. Here's to . . . Bob and Ted and the whole gang in Hotlanta. These are the people that made it possible and somehow impossible. You gotta love 'em for that. It's like being your buddy and not being your friend. I was just kidding," the voiceover continued. "I love Atlanta and Ted Turner. I love the Cable Music Channel. . . . I want to make a little statement. I want to thank all the people that made our brief stay possible. . . . Hey!"

Another unidentified sexier voice followed. The words were bittersweet. "From downtown Los Angeles this is the big goodbye. You know what I mean, some days you get the canyon; some days you get the rapids; some days you get the elevator; and sometimes you get the shaft. I had a wonderful time though. I thank you all. You know we never really disappear. Television is always here. Some days we go up in space then we wait to drop back down" (an obvious reference to Turner's satellite system).

The channel, musically, ended as it started with "I Love L.A." The clip was perfect for the CMC employee farewells. The Newman video starts from skid row to the glamour spots of the city with residents waving at the singer in his classic maroon 1950s Buick convertible. Segued into the clip were fifty-two CMCers, including Scott Sassa, most of whom were about to be pink slipped. A majority went along with the farewell wave. Two didn't. John Williams feigned a tear while Helen Davis tore up the logo. With the partings done the network signed off with, "It's not really goodbye, no darlings, we'll always be there somewhere so watch this space. Say goodbye y'all now." A male voice did just that "Goodbye y'all." Silence followed. Then someone said into an open mike, "Goodness it's over with and CM. . . ." Static. CMC was no more.

The postmortems were quick in coming. Few insiders or journalists disputed the simple facts, but the interpretations were another matter. The "white knight" ironically was the MTV Network. Even Sando admitted that CMC did not have much of an economic chance. Cable operators do not subscribe on the basis of morality. "MTV went out and made a lot of deals," he said, and exclusivity, both formal and informal, was the name of the game. Turner told *USA Today,* several months later, "I really don't know [the losses] . . . but I think it's less than $2 million. . . . That probably would not include the corporate overhead that went into analyzing it." He added: "Probably the best thing that happened is our decision to get out of it as quickly as we did."[3]

Ted Turner and some financial analysts took the position that "take your losses and run" was a wise move. "We feel that the discontinuance of the service now and the sales arrangement with MTV Inc. are in the best interest of the company," said Turner. Tom Keaver, *Cable TV*'s economic correspondent, concurred. The journalist noted that the arrangement would recoup anywhere from 10 to even 50 percent of TBS' failed musical endeavor. Lee Wilder, a cable watcher with Robinson Humphrey/American Express, felt Turner received "a great price." She went on to suggest that the takeover could put TBS in the "break even" category as early as the fourth quarter of 1984 or, at least, in the first quarter of the following year.

Other observers, including TBS' Arthur Sando, took the position, "If you're first, you've got a great position in this field." MTV's subscriber base was too large. A record company executive ruefully observed, "You can't really say it was competition."

Each argument had merit. Turner took on the Goliath on moral grounds more than business sense. CMC's inflated audience share, estimated at some 90 percent, turned off many industry people. Then there were the loan restrictions that handcuffed the operation.

Shortly after the selling out, "Terrible Ted" addressed 700 members of the Academy of Television Arts and Sciences at the Century Plaza Hotel in Los Angeles. He refused to discuss CMC, but did say that television needed a social conscience. "What good is it if you win the ratings battle and wreck your country by polluting the young people's minds?" he asked.

"Why did he do it?" was a common question. Several former CNNers offered an explanation. Reese Schonfeld recalled, "Ted has always had an enormous drive for power . . . sex and money was a distant third." Knocking off MTV fit that mold. Already a darling of the conservatives, his antirock stance suited a burning ambition to "someday be president of the United States." "He must constantly go on to ever-greater gambles, ever-greater achievements," said newsman Daniel Schorr, "and that's what I think motivates him." Few people were aware of Turner's next project. A takeover bid for a major television network.

Turner's failed experiment in music programming raised some concerns at the lavish hotel. Was the 25+ market ready for a diet of nonstop music? The MTV Network was going after the same audience. Bob Pittman admitted that the VH-1 viewers "are the people who don't like MTV, who don't like the music. . . . I think they are looking for something much softer, much more melodic." The statement was made to a CNN reporter. Pat Creed of Rockamerica, a music video promotional service, was unsure. "The next big video trend is kicking in with a vengence. Call it what you will—'Lite Video,' 'Low-cal Video,' 'Old Folks Video,' or just plain dull video; it is as trendy as long white T-shirts sporting silly slogans." The observation would prove prophetic. At the apparent close of the TBS conflict Pittman had his MTV and Turner his cable news monopoly: "Cable's most important network!"

Turner's skirmish with MTV would have been a humbling defeat for many enterpreneurs; it wasn't for Turner. In 1985 he temporarily dominated the news by attempting a costly takeover of CBS Inc. and by purchasing MGM-UA films.

In April 1986 Turner was asked about his feelings toward video music. The following exchange took place at the Atlanta Hilton:

> AUTHOR: What do you think of the state of music videos?
> TURNER: Oh, I don't know. I haven't been watching music videos very much lately.
> AUTHOR: Do you still think video music is a negative force?
> TURNER: Depends on what the music is!
> AUTHOR: What about heavy metal?
> TURNER: (abruptly) To tell you the truth I'm not into heavy metal.

Music video may have left a bitter taste in Turner's mouth. He does not like losing. The staff of "Night Tracks" was developing a direct assault on the weekend late-night music ghetto. The strategy was described by Eric McLamb, TBS public relations manager: "We are attracting the young audience [18–34] which normally have to be up early the next day, but on Saturdays and Sunday they don't have to get up early. They are going to watch television. . . . So it's not something just to fill time. . . . We are attracting a certain audience because you have to remember that our lead in, the Super Station [WTBS], are the movies or sports-watching crowd. And we pull from that crowd as well as we do the MTV watching crowd." That's the demographic "certain" audience "Night Tracks" is aimed at.

The production team as well as McLamb brag about their numbers. "Chartbuster" (debuted May 19, 1984) and "Power Play" (October 4, 1985) have respectable numbers, skewed by massive WTBS cable hookups with 36 million households. While denying any competition with MTV, producers Lynch and Biller proclaim their Nielsen's would exceed MTV in head-to-head combat. To accomplish this task in 1986 McLamb and Bill Chapmen planned an August 1 promotion campaign. "On-air promotion, press kits, tape mailings, special events, contests—we will have to fly some to a concert and to spend time with a road crew," said McLamb. A New York festival was in the works and a new logo featuring a prowling black cat "stalking the night" reading "Only 'Night Tracks' captures the late-night audience you're looking for." The first quarter 1985 Nielsen's are also featured (see Figure 8.1). A short promotional video clip was also made especially for potential time buyers.

Summing up, one WTBS executive said, "I don't know exactly the figure but we just committed quite a sizable sum to the promotion of 'Night Tracks' over the next year [1987] and we're going to kind of culminate in a 'Night Track' Festival we will have."

While Turner's attention was diverted to his MGM-UA property and the diversification of the CNN networks, Lynch/Biller Productions in Hollywood and McLam were covertly creeping, just like the new prowling cat logo, on their perceived weakened adversary—MTV (see Epilogue).

MTVN had overcome most of the obstacles of 1984. Now it was time to stage another New Year's Eve Ball in the four time zones and launch VH-1 at 6:00 P.M. (EST).

MTV's 1984 Nielsen ratings were strong. They finished the fourth quarter with a 0.9 rating, with an average viewship of 229,000 watching throughout a twenty-four-hour broadcast period. Overall, MTV placed second to Turner's WTBS, which had an annual rating of 1.0. The excellent "numbers" were attributed to the success of the long-form Michael Jackson clip "Thriller." They had something to celebrate New Year's Eve.

The fourth annual shindig was staged at the Manhattan Center in New York's Pennsylvania Station neighborhood. A thousand plus people milled around trying the imported cuisine and hoping to be interviewed or actually listening to UB40, General Public, the Eurogliders, John Cafferty and the Beaver Brown Band, and Joan Jett and the Blackhearts. Frankie Goes Hollywood made a "guest" appearance singing "Relax," joined by Duran Duran's Simon Le Bon and John Taylor. According to a journalist, guest veejay David Lee Roth "stole the show with his sardonic sense of humor and the premiere of his 'California Girls' video."

Kevin Koffler of *Rock Video* indicated there was more going on "off the stage than on." He wrote:

Offstage, the people who thought they were elite sat upstairs, while the real circus took place on the dance floor below. Peter Wof walked around looking extremely bored, while The Earons sweated to death in their astronaut outfits. Record company executives, groupies, and a myriad other invited and uninvited guests partied with the likes of Cyndi Lauper, The Cars, Bon Jovi, Dee Snider, and Foreigner's Mick Jones.[4]

Cable subscribers viewed routinized performances and veejay "interviews." In several hours it was time for the birth of VH-1.[5]

Notes

1. Even the acronym "CMC" was ill-planned, as the title belonged to CMC television Network and its subsidiaries, such as the California Music Channel.
2. Paramount had signed a specialty deal with TBS.
3. *USA Today*, February 5, 1985, p. 2B.
4. *Rock Video*, June 1985, p. 62.
5. As a postscript, CMC was the beginning of a series of media tragedies to befall Turner. *Newsweek* reported: "For Captain Outrageous, those [glory] days are over. Turner's purchase of M-G-M, the fabled Hollywood movie studio, has all but scuttled Turner Broadcasting, his flagship company. Sinking under $1.2 billion in debt" (February 9, 1987, p. 46).

8

"Old Folks Video": VH-1 and Hit Video USA

[They] have jumped headfirst into programming for the lucrative upper demographic market, all hoping to come out smelling like roses.
Pat Creed, Rockamerica

Too Old to Rock 'n' Roll
Too Young to Die.

Jethro Tull, © 1976 Chrysalis Music (ASCAP)

On New Year's day madcap WNBC morning deejay Don Imus prepared the VH-1 sound check prior to going on air at 6:00 P.M. [EST]. The MTVN brass gathered to view the electronic unveiling. Privately, some were uneasy with the project. A number of clones plus alternative weekend programs had proliferated. The climate had improved considerably since 1981, but the 25+ psychographic was mercurial. The so-called Yuppies were a paradox to Madison Avenue as well as political pundits.

By innovative conceptualizing, timing, and luck, MTV had originally tapped into the youth culture written off by the television industry. Conditions and personnel had changed considerably in forty-one months, although some of the major players at Fort Lee (such as Fred/Alan Inc., commissioned to do the logos) were still involved.

VH-1, as noted, aided in sinking Ted Turner's violation of the "Rules of One." There exists a body of opinion, despite denials, that VH-1 was conceived for the sole purpose of sabotaging CMC. The counteroffensive was a resounding success.

Hastily commissioned ORC and Nielsen concept tests lent some credence to the viability of a twenty-five- to fifty-four-year old music video audience. Nobody, however, was betting on the outcome. The "Big Chill Generation" had a myriad of entertainment distractions besides music television.

193

Reactions on Madison Avenue were skeptical. Ron Kaatz of J. Walter Thompson USA noted, "It's going to be a much harder advertising sell because the target that MTV currently reaches is hard to reach any other way. They're mobile, they don't read, and they don't watch traditional TV. But, that's not the case with twenty-five- to forty-nine-year olds. There are lots of other ways to reach them." "I don't know," said Steve Leff at Becker & Spielvogel, "that older adults have as much time as teenagers to sit in front of the tube or whether they will be as entranced by music videos."

BBDO's Arnie Semsky expressed mixed feelings. He concurred that the desired demographic was reachable with other media, but added, "There definitely is an audience out there that is older and likes music videos but is not satisfied by MTV." Other time buyers felt music videos had reached the saturation point and adopted a "wait and see" posture.

Recording industry executives, while welcoming alternatives to MTV, lodged reservations. Music consumership declines with age. They harbored doubts over the number of proposed new music video ventures.

"Is there room for four services?" questioned Arista's video manager Peter Baron. "I don't know if there's going to be enough programming to cover twenty-four hours for four channels." Kris Puszkiewicz at Island Records stated that new networks would have to be "very imaginative" to succeed in the increasingly competitive market. "At this point it's unproven that, that audience cares, and wants to watch videos. I'm trusting that MTV knows what it's doing and it's going to work. But at this point we're not running and specifically signing artists and making videos for those upper-demographic categories," said Epic's Harvey Leeds.[1] Leed's major concern was that the 25+ record buyers have traditionally been "very passive." This demographic unit repeatedly shows musical preference being much higher than record buying percentage or ratio. Cable operators, true to form, moaned about channel incapacity, adding the possibility of low consumer demand. Mark Weber, Sammons Communications, noted: "Personally I don't think the older audience would watch a music channel like the young kids do." Some cable operators welcomed the clash of music video services, hoping downlink rates would fall.

Outspoken deejay Scott Shannon voiced reservations about the neophyte network, which employed him. When asked if the Yuppies would sit and watch music videos, he responded: "That's a dark area that I don't think even Bob Pittman knows the answer to."

A gray test pattern appeared on transponder 15 beamed from Sat

Com B, previously a Turner news signal. It read: "Watch for the premiere of VH-1, Video Hits One, at 6:00 P.M., EST Today." A brief pause of a blank screen greeted an unintelligible sound check by Don Imus, uncomfortably sitting in a control booth.

The first few seconds introducing the name New York deejays filled the air with static. The feed was "snap, crackle, and pop," which signed into the opening. The network, aired on time, although one might well question the choice of launch hour in light of the postseason Bowl games, which have considerable appeal with VH-1's targeted market.

Footage of slain soul artist Marvin Gaye singing the national anthem, complete with Marine honor guard in the background, filmed at the 1983 Philadelphia NBA All-Star basketball game, began the musical programming. It was nostalgic and symbolic. VH-1's opening act was black—a star best remembered from the glory days of Motown Records in the 1960s. Diana Ross, followed with "Missing You," a tribute to Gaye. Her clip contained shots of Gaye and the old Berry Gordy owned "Hitsville U.S.A." at 1684 West Grandia in Detroit. The current remake of the Righteous Brothers' "wall of sound" classic "You've Lost that Loving Feeling" by Hall and Oates, purveyors of blue-eyed Philadelphia soul, appeared. John Lennon's clip "Nobody Told Me," visually featuring Yoko, continued the uninterrupted top of the hour. The overall ambiance was that of nostalgia, a far cry from the immediacy of its sister network.

The channel identification, with the now familiar uplifted index finger, greeted "Have you driven a Ford?"—VH-1's first time buy. A Big Red chewing gum ad rapidly pursued the automotive commercial. A Colossus promo animation titled "VH-1 Presents the History of Video Music: In the beginning . . ." plugged the network, including an Archie Bunkerish couple throwing their arms up in despair at the sight and sound of MTV. "Now there's VH-1 [the voiceover trailed on] . . . the right sound for the right one." A fiftyish jingle repeated. An uneasy Imus finally reappeared in the control booth. This time the sound distortion was gone. "Olivia Newton-John and ah 'Shaking it.' She just got married you know, the guy's ten years younger than she is! It's sick isn't it. No, that's nice. Hi! I'm Don Imus and this is VH-1, Video Hits One. We've got live one-minute interviews every hour and in twenty minutes we'll talk to Kenny Rogers. Right now, headline with VH-1 'People News.' "

"People News" consisted of printed bulletins. The first informed the viewer that "Supergirl" Helen Slater is signed for two sequels if *Supergirl* is a success. She is now filming a teen drama, *Fair Is Fair,* in

Texas. Another dealt with Tina Turner's completion of *Mad Max,* and the comeback star's video cassettes. Al Jarreau maintained the middle-of-the-road adult contemporary format with "After All."

Logos by Fred Seibert and Alan Goodman were animated by Drew Takashashi's nine-member staff at Colossal Pictures to be part of a sixties quality. Goodman explained that VH-1 was "for people with memories of growing up, goodness, unlike MTV, which is for those who are still growing up. We'd been talking about using video jingles for two years, and then this project came about and we went through a solid week of late-night meetings with the VH-1 people figuring out who their viewers would be and how to speak to them. We realized that jingles were an important element of their language, the language we all remember from the sixties which has only recently resurfaced with the advent of hit radio. But even though the VH-1 jingles sound like the mid-sixties and have the same graphics style, it's all extremely 1980s."

LPG/Pon stressed the targeted window. Their promotional network identifications emphasized the "*your* kind of music" theme. One frequently mentioned promo declared, "Welcome to the neighborhood with nice people, big back yards, and lots of fresh air; welcome to VH-1."

WNBC-AM's Don Imus, the first "personality" hired for VH-1, appeared unsure of himself, which was highly unusual for a deejay known for his on-air mockery of artists and generally termed "outrageous." Imus' opening barbs were reserved for the Jacksons: "Coming up in just a few minutes Rebbie Jackson, who is yet another member of the Jackson family. I don't know how many people are in the family. All have videos, all are talented. She's Michael's grandmother I think [raised eyebrow]. No, maybe she's his older sister, I'm not sure." After the clip he added: "That's 'Centipede,' that by the way was written by Michael and he produced the thing and that's pretty good. I'm Don Imus and this is VH-1." After misprounouncing and slurring Dolby, part of the network identification, he turned his attention to another Jackson: "Coming up now. Let's take a look at Jermaine Jackson. We got another Jackson. Oh good. A successful family, they just came off their Victory tour [laughs], which we're all very happy about." More laughter. A *Village Voice* critic described Imus' television presence as having "the deteriorating look of a former lounge lizard, his face surrounded by a relentlessly bad perm." Imus lent support to the description, blowing the introduction to Barry Manilow's "Let's Hang On" from his playlist. An off-camera voice yells out the title. During his four-hour stint Imus commented, "This is longer than I've ever done anything in my life."

Rick James got on MTVN. "Ebony Eyes" with Smokey Robinson and "Standing on the Top," joined by the Temptations, appeared. Randy Owen and Alabama had "Fire in the Night" presented. Imus termed them "one of my favorite groups."

A survey of Video Hits One's twelve opening hours found 120 clips programmed, featuring 92 acts, mostly from the adult contemporary and Top Forty formats.[2] One-third of the acts were black crossover artists. An industry spokesperson remarked, "That's one way to check the Black Entertainment TV music numbers."[3]

BET's Robert Johnson concurs:

> I think both MTV and VH-1 have had to respond to BET. As we get into major urban markets and start going head to head with them they are going to have to respond more and more so. I think you will see more black videos on VH-1 because of BET. I think throughout, for the next three to five years, VH-1 and MTV are going to have BET in the background.

The motivations for VH-1 transcended instant profitability. "The operation is being kept small and as inexpensive as possible," a source told *Billboard*. "VH-1 will continue to be supported by profits from MTV until the channel can stand on its own." An insider was more pessimistic: "I really just don't think they want to give it a shot, because they're too scared of what is going to happen to MTV . . . that's a very wrong attitude." Johnson added: "It remains to be seen how much support in dollars MTVN wants to put in VH-1. If they want to keep putting dollars in it to keep it growing it will stay around."

The network launched with a 3.4 million subscriber base and 28 charter ad buyers. VH-1 charged $300 for a half-minute commercial. Local operators had two minutes available for bartered four minutes.

After seeing the opening hours, a media critic restated the case that VH-1 was taking aim at BET's programming since the Discovery Music Network remained in the blueprint stage and CMC was relegated to the scrapheap of television history. The journalists' speculations have some merit. BET programmed twelve to sixteen hours of music videos. BET's concentration on music videos as of October 1984 has been applauded as a major innovative alternative. "What's really exciting about BET is their program format change made," said Janet Foster, vice-president of programming for Group W. "They went to an urban contemporary music video approach. It's expanding them beyond just a black service. It's making a more mainstream audience available to them because it's a contemporary music form, not just a black format." The mix of artists was one-quarter white. The remainder were black, including crossover artists. Talking to Jim Bessman, Robert Johnson said, "Once we get head to head with them in numbers, we'll beat them both. . . . black radio can outpoll white radio formats, even though the advertisers say they don't have the right demos. Same with us—we may not get the dollars that MTV gets, but we'll get the viewers."[4] On another occasion he added: "Once we get in the markets with MTV and VH-1 and the awareness of BET's 'Video Soul," and particularly 'Vibrations,' goes up I think there are going to be some very interesting results that will show I think that BET will cut very, very deeply into MTV's audience and VH-1 will have a smaller audience than both services."

Mystery Theater: The Origins of VH-1

The evolution of Video Hits One (VH-1) resembled a mixture of Bud Abbott and Lou Costello's skit "who is on first base" and the Watergate period press conferences. The motive behind the creation of another music video outlet was obvious: the Rule of One. Yet, for some still unexplained reason, the most Bob Pittman and his associates would say originally was, "Obviously, Ted Turner has affected our timing" to announce.

Cablevision invited music video representatives to its Park Avenue bureau to discuss the future of the new genre. Bob Pittman sat in the editorial conference room fielding questions. *Cablevision*'s Victor Livingston asked, "Wait a minute Bob . . . what about another service?" Resorting to real or mythical data, Pittman replied, "We've done the research on it, and if we thought it existed, we'd launch one tomorrow. We have the transponder capacity and certainly the financing. You mentioned Barbra Streisand, Neil Diamond, Kenny Rogers; mention ten others for me. You're dealing with a very narrow group of people."

As of mid-April 1984, Pittman rejected the notion of a VH-1 concept. Ted Turner's invasion of the turf changed the picture. Bob Johnson comments: "I think VH-1 is a service that was first launched mainly as a way to block Ted Turner from getting into the business and sort of slicing off MTV viewers. I don't see it as over a long period of time a successful enterprise."

Ted Turner generated some typical Orwellian "double speak." MTVN proclaimed the new channel two weeks *after* Turner made his move in Atlanta. David Horowitz, former head of MTVN, indicated that Turner did accelerate the development of an adult contemporary network, "but the new service *had been* on the back burner ever since

MTV was launched three years ago (emphasis added). Bob Pittman repeated the corporate line: "When MTV was launched we looked for four possible channels, each with a separate and distinct audience: country, R&B, adult, and rock. We chose rock because we thought it had the best shot. Teenagers are the quickest to jump on anything new. But we saw a significant other audience as well." Most executives present at the creation of MTV disagree. One, preferring anonymity, stated, "Who's he kidding? The original idea was rock music. Lack wanted urban contemporary, also, not Pittman." A major player in the development of the music channel noted: "AC was never mentioned while I was there." Supporting these observations is the MTV Networks Inc. *Prospectus* dated August 10, 1984, addressed to potential stock purchasers, which excludes any mention of a second adult-oriented music channel. Under the "New Product Concept" heading the document read, "Widespread consumer demand for MTV is a relatively recent development. There can be no assurance that this demand will continue."

Six weeks following the August announcement of a new music channel MTVN began slowly providing some details. A spokeswoman told Fred Dawson, "We referred to MTV prior to its premiere as album rock video, but that didn't really give any impression of what the service turned out to be. The truth is the service created its own unique category of music video programming, and that's what Video Hits One will do." Declining to be more specific, the publicist indicated that VH-1's playlist would be culled from various *Billboard* charts. At the time of the statement the trade magazine featured eleven working charts ranging from adult contemporary to urban contemporary. Would there be veejays? The answer was that an on-air "personality" would be part of the mysterious format.

Several days later a press release appeared. VH-1 was characterized as having a "unique and recognizable style." The vagueness of the release colored all the statements emanating from Rockefeller Plaza. David Horowitz said: "The success of MTV . . . has opened the doors for further music programming innovations at our company. As a result, we have been investigating the development of a second all-music channel. Today, we are very pleased to announce the launch of that channel." Robert Pittman added very little information: "The development of this new cable music service was stimulated by our success wtih MTV and by the need expressed by cable operators, advertisers, and the record industry for a second, differentiated all-music service." The only concrete facts to emerge were that VH-1 was targeting upward to age fifty-four, debuting January 1, 1985, and airing twenty-four hours per day. Most editors would not even consider the material worth a sidebar on the entertainment page. A few facts discriminately were released. The concept test conducted by ORC found that 78 percent of the respondents were in favor of the "idea." The network would use Dolby noise reduction for the "truest stereo." The system would cost cable operators $800 to upgrade their MTV analog to digital stereo. MTVN's engineering head Andy Setos commented, "We've been studying this system for a long time, and believe it's the best way to transmit stereo sound via satellite. In fact, we are going to use it for MTV as well."

Domenick Fioravanti, a former senior vice-president and general manager, announced on October 23 that veejays would be employed on the proposed network. Don Imus, the WNBC personality, was the first veejay chosen. "We feel Don Imus has developed a faithful following, has been a stand-out success throughout his radio career, and will bring VH-1 a wealth of experience and strong personality that will benefit this new channel."

The man fired and rehired by Bob Pittman described the position as a "wonderful opportunity to be not only heard, but seen too. Music videos are the new thing, and I am particularly excited about working for a channel that will be programmed by the same people who developed MTV." This was overhype, as the Lacks, Schneiders, Steinbergs, Bakers, and others were distant memories—if that.

In a follow-up interview with *Billboard*, Imus admitted, "I haven't had a chance to sit down with them and find out what they do want."[5] He did not see any transitional problems as his style "worked well in radio, and I'm sure it will work well in television. . . . I really think I can manage to offend as many people on television as on radio. I promise to give it my best effort." (He had already "offended" people on "Imus Plus," a briefly syndicated ninety-minute talks show in 1978).

The Imus hiring prompted Bob Pittman to elaborate on the concept of VH-1. The new channel would have four veejays and was "not going to be a video jukebox . . . [it would be] stable, comfortable, and folksy." Pittman went on to describe the network as "a softer Top Forty mix," including crossover artists from "the R&B genre," country, and "really the soft rock segment" exemplified by Barry Manilow and Air Supply. In broadcasting parlance, this was adult contemporary (or dentist office music).

The hiring of Scott Shannon added another piece to the VH-1 puzzle. Imus' competitor at New York's WHTZ-FM with "The Z-Morning Zoo" was an adult contemporary drive-time personality. "I am really looking forward to being involved with everyone at MTVN and VH-1. When I first got into radio, Don Imus was one of my idols, so I'm excited about working with him, too." Shannon's comment was as expected, but the Imus remark attracted some attention in New York radio circles. Rumors abounded concerning a personal animosity between the ratings rivals. The "Zoo Keeper" used as a promotional stunt car radio converters called "Imus Busters." Nationally, Shannon was better known beyond the New York City market, as host of a weekly syndicated three-hour radio show called "The Rockin' America Top 30 Countdown," which was distributed by Westwood One to 450 U.S. affiliates.

Any question regarding the direction of VH-1 was answered by the addition of Frankie Crocker—"radio personality" *par excellence*. His off-mike activities were more colorful and controversial than merely introducing urban contemporary hits at Inner City Broadcasting's flagship station WBLS-FM (New York).[6] One of his better known escapades was riding up to the Studio 54 disco on a white horse following a two-year hiatus at the University of Southern California studying acting and directing. He mused, "The Knight who comes to save everybody rides a white horse." WBLS at the time was in a state of ratings distress.

Crocker's stay in California was not voluntary. Allegedly involved in a payola scandal in 1977, he was contesting a perjury charge connected with the incident. The case ended in a mistrial.

Upon his return the deejay was swept up by discomania. At the time he told Doug Hall, "This town has gone disco crazy. When rock started it went rock crazy. Disco is definitely replacing rock. . . . It's a musical revolution that transcends color and age groups." However, Crocker noted, "I would hate to see the time come when you couldn't get into a ballad." After riding the crest of the short-lived "disco disaster," as program director he did improve the WBLS audience share in New York City.

John "Bowser" Bauman, best known as the keyboard player with Sha Na Na, was the last veejay to be chosen prior to the launch date. Unlike his colleagues, Bauman's experience in broadcasting involved hosting "The Pop & Rocker Game" and several guest shots on game shows.

Commenting on the choices, Bob Pittman said, "We were looking for personalities who could bring a point of view about topical issues. . . . A lot of people think that adult [contemporary] means sedate, dead, boring. That is not true. Shannon and Imus come across with material that relates." A critic would later call it "Valium Video."

Manhattan Cable rejected VH-1. A press conference for the New York media was staged with a preview reel of material to be aired on New Year's Day. *Cablevision*'s Robert DiMatteo attended: "As the mellow sounds of soft rock, soft R&B, and pop country filled my head, I have this image of a stooped, wizened old man doddering up to Bob Pittman and yammering: 'I want my MTV!' "[7]

In late January LPG/Pon displayed the first VH-1 advertising drive in the Phoenix, Des Moines, and Denver secondary markets. The thirty- to sixty-second spots resembled their famous "I Want My MTV" commercials. The television spots featured recognizable stars, such as Barbara Streisand, Lionel Richie, Olivia Newton-John, Smokey Robinson, and others. They were portrayed telephoning name artists proudly proclaiming, "My music's on cable TV." Stevie Wonder's "I Just Called to Say I Love You" clip interrupted. At the fade-out acts on the adult contemporary video channel are clustered by the VH-1 logo loudly shouting, "Mr. cable operator, we want music." The campaign reportedly was costing MTVN a cool million dollars.

New Year's Resolutions

A popular analogy between the two networks was comparing VH-1 as equivalent to *People* magazine while MTV was akin to *Rolling Stone*. A valid contrast, however, was that *Rolling Stone*'s readship transcended the 25 + demographic. The *Village Voice's* Elvis Mitchell echoed a sentiment shared by many: "VH-1 makes being over 30 humiliating. Somebody ought to tell these folks that the *Big Chill* generation still craves rock 'n' roll." A scene from the *Big Chill:* Mourning the suicide of their activist college cohort, the group gathers in the living room. The host picks up an album, gently places it on the turntable, flicking the on switch. "You mean you still listen to that music?" asks a friend. He looks up. "There is no other music."

The proposition that Yuppies somehow gravitate to lush soft rock, soul, or country arrangements is a broadcasting assumption based on sand castles. One morning drive-time deejay remarked, "I don't think they give a damn about the music. It's weather and news they listen to, and the way it's presented."

The new music channel did have one card up its corporate sleeve. As a *Cable Television Business* survey of operators indicated, the average system's manager was thirty-five years of age—the heart of the VH-1 demographic. This finding was highlighted by the market penetration achieved in nineteen of the twenty major cable markets. Manhattan Cable signed on for a March 1 debut, adding 200,000 households to the viewership toll. The Manhattan Cable premiere found some MTVN executives and VH-1 veejays assembled at Tower Records' uptown store. Inside a huge sign exclaimed, "Celebrate the Launch of VH-1: The Best New Video Music Channel."

VH-1's impact on record sales was murky. An employee in the Sam Goody chain indicated that VH-1's effect was imperceptible. A New York merchandiser said, "It's hard to say specifically that they're doing anything." A Richmond, Virginia, retailer argued that he could not tell if the interest in urban contemporary artists was generated by BET, MTV, or VH-1. In a *Billboard* call-out poll, Alabama was frequently cited as greatly benefiting from the exposure of "Fire in the Night."

In the closing week of January VH-1 released its playlist, divided into three categories: heavy, medium, light. The chart contained thirty-two titles basically culled from the *Billboard* Top 100. "I have no particular desire to play only 30 currents, believe me," said the demographic wiz of programming, Steve Casey. "Look at how few country stars have videos available."

VH-1 Programming[8]

Heavy Rotation

Alabama, "Fire in the Night"; Chicago, "You're the Inspiration"; Jermaine Jackson, "Do What You Do"; Elton John, "Neon"; Kenny Rogers, "Crazy"; Diana Ross, "Missing You" and Stevie Wonder, "Love Light in Flight.

Medium Rotation

Ashford and Simpson, "Solid"; George Benson, "20/20"; Kim Carnes, "Invitation to Dance"; Culture Club, "Mistake #3"; Sheena Easton, "Strut"; Billy Joel, "Keeping the Faith"; Kool and the Gang, "Misled"; Melissa Manchester, "Thief of Hearts"; Barry Manilow, "When October Goes"; Barry Manilow, "Paradise Cafe"; Midnight Star, "Operator"; New Edition, "Mr. Telephone Man" and Temptations, "Treat Her Like a Lady."

Light Rotation

Cast of *Cats,* "Rum Tum Tugger" (soundtrack); Janie Fricke, "First Word in Memory Is Me"; Siedah Garrett, "Do You Want It Right Now"; Lonnette McKee, "Ill Wind"; Michael Murphy, "What She Wants"; Rodney Salisbury, "Look What She's Done"; S.O.S. Band, "Just the Way You Like It" and Janey Street, "Under the Clock."

Many cable operators felt that VH-1's launch was poorly timed and too low key. A spokesperson at Cablevision System in Long Island reported "nothing special so far." Other carriers complained that the second MTVN channel wasn't offering co-op money (shared expenses) to publicize the availability of the service. Instead, the limited advertising dollars being spent were in selected major markets with television and radio time buys. Ad executives were ambiguous about VH-1. Cable analyst Ira Tumpowsky was bothered by the "very low profile" of the visual adult contemporary offering, noting: "Obviously they're trying to keep expenses to a minimum."

Bob Roganti, vice-president of MTVN's advertising sales, announced: "We're very encouraged by the initial reaction of clients toward the channel. . . . All of the so-called top-of-the-line product clients." He cited sixty-six clients, up from the twenty-eight at launch date. A rate change was promised: thirty seconds at $400 the second quarter of 1985. By year's end, Roganti hoped to double the exposure fee. One bright spot was the assertion that soft rock might deliver women consumers. Would housewives watch MTV? "Absolutely," replied Bob Pittman.

Other insiders privately grumbled about a perceived absence of support. In juxtaposition to MTV, the VH-1 veejays were rapidly becoming the network's magnet, especially Don Imus. A *Newsweek* reviewer summed up: "VH-1's programming is a mishmash of soft rock, oldies, soft country, Sinatra, and soft rhythm and blues. Mostly, this diet of music is so bland that viewers might snooze through it if someone like Imus didn't occasionally jolt them into semiconsciousness by suggesting that John Denver be sent up on the space shuttle— and kept there."[9] Critics, and some subscribers, perceived the music fare as a video tranquilizer. Consequently, as L. Kevin Metheny, vice-president for music production, relates, "We placed the burden of entertainment more heavily on VH-1's veejays." "The veejay will be the focal point . . . the Johnny Carson or Phil Donahue of music," added Pittman.

After a shaky start, Imus slowly injected some of the zaniness of his top-rated WNBC morning show. MTVN gave him considerable leeway. Imus, according to Metheny, enjoyed "as close to carte blanche as it can get."

Reassured, Imus began to zing artists and VH-1 on and off camera. "We have an exclusive interview coming up. You know, that's where we talk to one of those dopey rock stars and ask them all stupid junk about their private lives." Introducing a Paul McCartney clip he mused, "If I could only get Linda McCartney to wash her hair."

On March 1 the network held its first promotional contest: VH-1's Lush Life with Linda Ronstadt. Elektra Records had been pushing the contest to expose the forthcoming album to the "people who are intrigued by promotions of MTV but wouldn't want to be part of that." The winner of the contest would receive an all-expense paid flight to New York City, two nights in a penthouse suite over a weekend, $1,000 a day in spending money, a full-length fur coat, a Lincoln Continental, and a "private" meal with the singer. Robin Sloane of Elektra corrected the announcement to state that "Linda will be available to do this dinner, but it will be a dinner for about ten people." Label executives, publicity people, and the vocalist's management would also be present. Imus took full advantage of the month-long contest, telling viewers it really wasn't worth the effort as no sex would be involved. However, he urged females to send in snapshots, as *he* might be available that weekend. Dale Hinman of Port Crane, New York, was the "grand prize winner."

Talking to the press, Imus was less inhibited. He told *Newsweek:*

> I think the neatest trick that these artists pull is to do these home movies, and we play them as videos. I mean we have a video of the Oak Ridge Boys where they have fifty of their *fat relatives,* really—and their dirty kids with ice cream and watermelon smeared all over them. And they took a Panasonic eight-millimeter out there and they sent the video to us and we play it. I mean, I can barely tolerate the Oak Ridge Boys and their family. I mean, I hate their family. No one wants to see their *fat family,* you know.[10]

Less inconoclastic than Imus, Bauman satirized the promotional campaign with, "Carly Simon's father was one of the founders of Simon and Schuster. Which was her father?" Senior vice-president John Sykes, once romantically linked to Simon, didn't think it was so funny. Shannon, Crocker, and the newly added veejay, Rita Coolidge, left the video horseplay to Imus and Bauman.

Singer Rita Coolidge became the fifth veejay. The daughter of a Tennessee Baptist minister, the native Cherokee Indian established herself as a vocalist on radio jingles in Memphis. Delaney and Bonnie heard one of the jingles and recruited her as one of their back-up singers.

The tour ended in Los Angeles, where she quickly broke into the session scene with Eric Clapton, Graham Nash, and Leon Russell, who reportedly wrote "Delta Lady" about her.

She went on the now infamous Mad Dogs and Englishmen tour. "It was a circus," she says. "It was an incredible time. . . . There was no time for anything . . . some didn't make it." The reference, of course, is to Joe Cocker. In the interim, she met and married Kris Kristofferson. The union, now ended, produced a child, Casey, and two Grammys for Best Country Vocal Performance by a Duo for "From the Bottle to the Bottom" (1973) and "Love Please" (1976). As a solo performer, under the tuteluge of producer David Anderle, she abandoned rock music. "I realized I didn't need rock and roll to move an audience. I found my strength lay in ballads, songs. I came out of that searching period learning you could touch people's hearts and it could have as much impact as making them dance in the streets." This attitude and a little film and TV experience landed her a position in the VH-1 "personality" rotation.

The media's emphasis on the flamboyant Imus downplayed his cohorts plus the VH-1 format. John Lack, now co-owner of seven radio stations, summarized a pervasive rock broadcaster's attitude: "When you look at these guys of VH-1—Don Imus or Frankie Crocker—they're terrible, they don't understand the role . . . you're there to move the music you're not there to interrupt it, you're not there to upstage it, you're there to move it along. You're only there to keep this thing flowing."

Leads and subheads such as "Music Video for Housewives" (*Rolling Stone*), "VH-1 Seeks Old Folks at Home" (*On Cable*), "Music Video Grows Grayer" (*Satellite TV Week*), and "Are You Old Enough for VH-1?" (*Cablevision*) were unflattering. *Cablevision*'s Simon Applebaum, who covered VH-1, summed up the early months by suggesting, "It's going very well . . . growing very well over the first three months. MTV's revenues were designed to tide VH-1 over the start-up while experiencing some difficulties in ratings, and enthusiasm."

Changes

By economic standards, 1984 was MTV's most successful year. Yet, at the Billboard Sixth Annual Video Music Conference, held in the plush Sheraton Premiere Hotel in Universal City, industry executives were decrying the network's fare. Robin Sloane, Elektra's director of video, noted: "Three years ago, MTV had a certain spirit, a certain sense of adventure. . . . Now it's a passive medium." Jeff Ayeroff, now with Warner Brothers, concurred: "I think that what we're producing is the lowest common denominator product, because the medium we're producing for demands that standard."

Debora Iyall of Romeo Void complained, "It seems like it mirrors the Top 40 and sort of Midwest taste. And so perhaps they've sort of changed their idea of who they want to reach. . . . I think it's much more geared toward the Midwest heavy metal temperament and music rather than what's new." She admitted, "I don't watch TV at all."

"It's almost like a comic book with music," observed a label executive, referring to heavy metal. Quiet Riot's Kevin DuBrow says, "You have to be a kid at heart to understand this music. When you finally grow up, you simply lose touch." Heavy metal has been a stable substream in the rock world since the days of Iron Butterfly, Steppenwolf, Blue Cheer, Deep Purple, and especially Led Zeppelin. One merchandiser said, "They're solid, earthly, and blue collar and have nothing to do with vogue."

Heavy metal resurfaced as a prominent force in 1983 with Quiet Riot, Motley Crue, and Def Leppard on MTV. "I hate to start all my conversations with the market of MTV, but video is the key to success with a heavy metal band," noted Elektra's Lou Maglia. "You get a Motley Crue on MTV and you get that mass exposure immediately." *Rolling Stone*'s Deborah Frost concurred: "Without the twenty-four-hour-a-day cable channel, most of the new metal acts . . . would still be grubbing gigs in local bars."

MTV resurrected heavy metal, airing clips set in dungeons and torture chambers with black-leathered figures writhing in the midst of fog machines. This approach had originally worked for Billy Idol's "White Wedding," but by the fall of 1984 heavy metal was rapidly becoming a caricature of itself. Broadcasters were bemoaning "overexposure" and blatant attention-getting devices and gimmicks. Doug Podell, host of Detroit's "Beat It," suggested that some acts have taken animated album covers "too far" to exploit and promote a record.

Looking at the January Nielsen meter, Bob Pittman became uneasy. He disliked the demographics and the marginal ratings decline to a 0.9 from the 1984 average of 1.0. This meant a loss of 849,000 TV households (the Nielsen 0.9 characterized the first quarter of 1985).

In mid-February Pittman announced, "We've pulled way back on heavy metal." Talking with *Rolling Stone*'s Jeffery Graham, Pittman elaborated:

> People either love it or hate it. And people who hate it, hate it with a passion. . . . We want to play music that's on the cutting edge [such as Talking Heads]. . . . I don't think anyone would say that heavy metal is the most creative element in music today. It's a quick, crass, easy buck for record companies. These guys don't deserve to dominate the channel. They're not as popular as the Police or Mick Jagger.

He denied any influence by moral entrepreneurs on his decision, remarking: "If that had been the case the time to have cut back would have been nine months ago." What happened in April 1984 to prompt that response was a frequently asked but unanswered question. MTV spokesperson Dorene Lauer said, "We're not worried," referring to Dr. Thomas Radecki's National Coalition on Television Violence (NCTV). Pittman further contended, "We don't allow gratuitous violence and we don't allow nudity. We do allow people with purple hair and some people are quick to label such styles as bad."

Record labels quickly responded. Epic's Harvey Leeds said, "It doesn't bother me. A hit record is a hit record, whether it's metal or cocktail music." Labels with a greater stake in the genre were not quite so blasé about the cutback. Polygram's Randy Roberts told *Billboard,* "We are very concerned as a company. . . . MTV had a lot to do with a lot of bands breaking." The Scorpions, plus Def Leppard, were Polygram artists.

Artists and directors were shaken. "Ironically, it was MTV who gave the form a kick in the pants," said Gene Simmons. "That's where you heard new groups like Black & Blue and Helix. Now they're [MTV] starting to toe the corporate line, and that's too bad." Dee Snider of Twisted Sister proclaimed, "It's a drag. MTV was responsible for the resurgence of heavy metal. . . . It will just have to go back to the road." This option was unappealing to video clip directors as well as the labels. "Video is the key to success with a heavy metal band. In the past, you'd develop a band on tour, and the first LP would sell 100,000 and the second a quarter of a million and the third 500,000."[11] With MTV the reaction was immediate, as more people watched a clip than attended a concert. "Yes, it does hurt," said one executive, "but keep in mind a vast number of metalers live in the unwired urban cities of the Midwest . . . where MTV doesn't go."

Producer/director Martin Kahan appeared more alarmist. "It's a precursor to the death of rock 'n' roll. The one place where you could find the original spirit of rock 'n' roll is in heavy metal video: the outrageousness. The 'I don't care what you think, this is how I am' attitude. Now the anti-this and anti-that forces have won." *Rock Video*'s Jim Bessman bemoaned MTV's conservatism: "Not that I'm such a big fan of heavy metal, but it has given us plenty of great songs and videos, and I'm sorry to see MTV cut back on anything because in the end it just means more of the same." Despite the industry groans, Pittman's data proved prophetic as the "antis" were planning a full press media blitz aimed at MTV and rock music (see Chapter 10).

Heavy metal fans were treated to "specials," even on MTV, but their favorites were absent from the music channel's heavy rotations. "Night Flight" did several "Take Off" segments on this genre. Bessman was proven correct as MTV entered a state of institutionalized blandness. Warner's Jo Bergman commented, "I think that there's been a lull over there. . . . We've got to be interested in what we're doing in terms of creating material. It all starts to look like a retread. It's got to get back to the sense that it's being at the cutting edge again, and I think they're aware of that." Bob Giraldi told *Esquire,* "The things I did in 'Beat It' don't look very different right now—everybody's done it. It almost looks old-fashioned."[12]

The pulling of heavy metal was controversial as some of the clips done tongue-in-cheek were more in the Road Runner cartoon or Three Stooges slapstick idiom than overt violence. Twisted Sister's Dee Snyder, of "We're Not Gonna Take It," was MTV's version of Don Imus.

In the midst of the wailing and gnashing of teeth, an important piece of history was ignored. Much of MTV's success was due to external events. The original selection of video clips was based on availability. The Buggles, Squeeze, Bow Wow Wow, and a plethora of others were aired more from the need to fill time than name recognition in the early days of the music channel. Michael Jackson was literally forced onto the MTV playlist. By 1984 the MTV Acquisitions Committee exercised more control. Not only had the volume of videos increased, the network's status in the music industry had as well. The basic fact remained, however, that MTV was still dependent on the record companies and to a lesser degree to artists' management for the submission of clips. Pittman acknowledged this dilemma: "All the big records get released in summertime and at Christmas. There's very little new exciting stuff out now."

Still smarting from the heavy metal decision, Kahan went public in *Billboard*. His views were not unique. Most had repeatedly been expressed privately by record company executives, artists, directors, and management firms all in fear of "Buzz's Basement" or the infamous "lunar" rotation. He told the sympathetic Jim Bessman:

> I don't want to say that MTV is a big bad wolf because it's in a very tough spot. It can no longer afford to be the gadfly when it has to please its stockholders and advertisers.
>
> But we're now working in an atmosphere where we have to cater to the Tuesday morning MTV acquisition meeting. It used to be just go out and make a creative piece, but now, because MTV's playlist is so tight and formulated, people are responding to the realities of getting played and not their own creative voices.
>
> What I'd love to see happen is a constructive encounter session between the video makers, MTV, and the record companies, to get rid of the

misplaced expectations we all have about MTV. The bottom line is that MTV is not records but videos—they respond to record sales and radio play, but they don't play records, they play videos.

This was Kahan's explanation for the lull.

MTV was becoming rather testy about the press coverage of the ratings decline. *Rolling Stone*'s observation that MTV "viewship average dropped twenty-five percent in the last year" evoked a barrage of counterclaims and explanations. Robert Pittman wrote a letter to *Rolling Stone* demanding a retraction. In the May 23 issue *Rolling Stone* published Pittman's letter.

> Contrary to assertions in your April 11th issue, MTV has experienced neither plummeting ratings nor "a fairly drastic drop in the network's ratings" ("Heavy Metal on the Outs at MTV," *RS* 445). In fact, during 1984—MTV's first full year of metered ratings by the A.C. Nielsen Company—MTV: Music Television was the *Number One* basic-cable network for the year, with an average twenty-four-hour rating of 1.0. [One rating point equals 246,621 television households.] While ratings vary from quarter to quarter, depending upon programming available (e.g., Michael Jackson in 1983 and early 1984), it's *significant* that no basic-cable network had a higher rating than MTV in any quarter except the first quarter of 1984.
>
> Even though our network is deliberately designed to appeal to a discrete audience—those who enjoy rock music—it gained a higher total-household rating than such mass-audience cable channels as the USA Network, ESPN, and CNN. While we are *not* all things to all people, those who do like MTV watch with intense loyalty.
>
> MTV's success is the result of tireless efforts by our innovative programming group, dedicated to creating a video-music network that is true to the ideals, energy, and attitudes of the music we play. By blundering with the facts and creating misinformation, you compromise the integrity of our staff, the musicians we bring to the public night and day, and your loyal readers.
>
> > Robert W. Pittman
> > Executive Vice-President and Chief
> > Operating Officer, MTV Networks
> > New York, New York

> We stand corrected: MTV has not suffered a "drastic" drop in its ratings in the last year as we reported. While there was a twenty-five percent decline in the network's ratings for the fourth quarter of 1984 compared with the same period in 1983, MTV's overall ratings for the two years were almost identical. As Mr. Pittman's letter states, MTV is more than holding its own among other cable networks.—ED.

The reply was surprisingly docile considering the hostility between Pittman and the magazine's publisher, Jann Wenner.

Dorene Lauer, now senior account executive at Howard Bloom, was the MTV publicist. She said: "Let me explain what happened. . . . The fourth quarter of 1983 was 1.2, which has been our strongest quarter, and that was pretty much contributed to by *Thriller* that ran like crazy during that quarter, and that was a very, very successful thing for us."

Marshall Cohen and Bob Pittman pointed to *Thriller* as artificially distorting the ratings. "We were able to mask the problem with *Thriller*. Michael Jackson was a phenomenon and a new face," said Pittman. Marshall Cohen echoed the sentiment: "If it is said 'MTV ratings down—due to no *Thriller*,' it would be correct."

The second quarter ended with a 0.8. Les Garland stated, "We're healthy and fine. I think you'll see the 0.8 rise." The vice-president was partially correct. Bob Geldoff's mega-event Live Aid would temporarily add a point to MTV's Nielsen share.

As the MTV summer doldrums continued, VH-1 was adding two million subscribers. Ron Kaazt, of the Thompson agency, remained optimistic. "It's a service I think a lot of people would like to watch if they had the chance, and I think there's a market for it . . . we'll read more about it later on when it gets on cable systems in big cities."

To achieve this goal VH-1 courted the adult contemporary radio medium and resorted to promotions. "We are seeking to create a fantasy opportunity for the viewer. It gives us a sense of being bigger than life, and provides an interactive sense with the audience," explained Kevin Metheny. The contests were similar to those seen on MTV during the early years. The Ronstadt "Lush Life" campaign was the first. A "Cats" contest followed. Katy McCormack of Toledo won a weekend in New York with the usual limo, paid hotel rooms, $1,000 in spending money, and naturally tickets to the Broadway musical. To promo the network and John Denver's album *Dreamland Express* a summer contest was introduced. Patty Peavy, a thirty-six-year-old mother of three from Novi, Michigan, was flown by the singer in a Lear jet to his Red Rock concert. The usual limo, spending money, and hotel accommodations were provided. An avid fan, Peavy had sent 150 postcards to the network, which received a total of 80,000 entries. This would be her twenty-ninth Denver concert. Runner-ups won cassettes of *Dreamland*. The post-Ronstadt campaigns were basically low-budget operations.

VH-1 sponsored a tour featuring Air Supply. "I think this is going to help sell an extra million records," said the group's manager Don

Arden. He credited VH-1's heavy rotation of the Australian act's "Making Love Out of Nothing" with turning some 200,000 units. Metheney had reservations about the promotional tour aspect, which had worked well for MTV because the sister network viewers were "more aggressive music fans." He wasn't sure that adult contemporary artists had enough supporters in the 25+ demographic to justify more tours.

Another ploy contributing to the increase in downlinks was VH-1's cultivation of adult contemporary radio outlets with advertising monies and mutual promotions. LPG/Pon spots were strategically placed in test cable markets. John Denver's July 6 appearance was employed as a promotion in four surrounding markets. Adult contemporary programmers were positive. A Phoenix program director said, "I encourage my jocks to watch the channel to see if there are any artists we've missed." Another added, "It may help popularize AC music in general." MTVN's Kevin Metheny saw the new network as a breaking ground for artists: "ACs are healthy but still terrified that they are being overwhelmed. The story may well be that new AC artists will emerge by the virtue of VH-1 exposure. . . . We observe success on various country, R&B, and pop charts with an emphasis on industry AC lists."[14] The channel's format could by mid-year be labeled "adult crossover."

Street Pulse Group, a market consultancy, in an August sample found that 82 percent of the wired homes in the selected market could receive VH-1. Ninety percent of the respondents—25–34, record consumers—had the second MTVN channel. Two-thirds watched the adult contemporary channel. President Michael Shalett concluded, "VH-1 viewers are active record buyers. . . . Where it is carried by local cable operators, the data suggests strongly that VH-1 sells records to baby boomers." The key, of course, is "where it is carried"![15]

MTVN's first quarter net income jumped 81 percent over the previous year. In 1984, during the first profitable quarter, the net was $1.4 million. In twelve months this figure increased to $2.5 million. David Horowitz credited some of the leap to "nationwide enthusiasm" for VH-1.

Director Martin Kahan saw VH-1 as providing a "creative shot in the arm" to music video, especially in light of MTV's perceived institutionalization. The September 9, 1985 issue of *Cablevision* reported its annual affiliate and subscriber figures. VH-1 enjoyed 547 operators with a subscribership of 7,003,000. After nine months, VH-1 had outdistanced MTV's early numbers of 6,750,000 subs after thirteen months of broadcasting. MTV, as of the fall of 1982, did have more cable systems: 825.

MTV-Money TV: Viacom

By the spring of 1985 media merger mania had become an epidemic. One business magazine described the electronic media as resembling a "giant auction block." Capital Cities, with a revenue one-fourth of ABC-TV's, purchased the giant network. Roone Arledge characterized the takeover as "the canary eating the cat."

Media stocks soared as rumors abounded concerning the intentions of hostile raiders T. Boone Pickens, Ted Turner, and Australian-born newspaper baron Rupert Murdock.

Turner, despite a humiliating defeat at the hands of MTVN, had his eye on the CBS Group. His attempt—"the ultimate in financial mirrors"—failed. The "Mouth of South" eventually settled for the MGM-UA properties and their film archives of over 500 motion pictures.

Warner-Amex was a prime target for a corporate absorption. Wall Street media analyst Nathan Sugarman observed, "It's clear that the partnership will dissolve—Warner wants cash and American Express wants out." The tom-toms of Wall Street intensified.

WCI was economically wounded by the attempted Murdock raid, the Atari failure, the metro cable franchise overcommitments, and Chris-Craft Industries' (CCI) "white knight" agreement.

Viacom International, originally a CBS subsidiary as a syndicator of television cablecasting, established Showtime in January 1979 as a pay-film service. The operation was a co-venture with Westinghouse's Group W cable system. Viacom bought out Westinghouse's 50 percent interest in November 1982 for $75 million. Viacom then approached Warner-Amex regarding a possible arrangement involving The Movie Channel. WASEC executives generally opposed the proposed venture. "I didn't want to [sell] but it doesn't matter how I felt about it," said Schneider, the former WASEC president. "They want to sell the company, they sell the company." Lack was not as sanguine. The preliminary corporate discussions signaled a retrenchment by the Warner-Amex principals. His concerns came to fruition.

On September 2, 1983, a merger of Showtime (4.5 million subscribers) and TMC (2.5 million house leases) was disclosed. WCI paid Viacom $40 million in cash with a promised $5 million per year for "consulting services." The "services" were for a six-year period. The transaction totalled $70 million. Warner-Amex traded its interest in

TMC in exchange for a 19 percent share of the merger. A closer examination of the deal shows the following breakdown:

Showtime/The Movie Channel

Vicaom	50%
WCI	31%
Warner-Amex	19%
	100%

In reality, WCI controlled 40.5 percent since American Express, half owner of Warner-Amex, was reduced to 9.5 percent of the film services. Viacom, having effective majority control, said: "When two organizations consolidate into one there are bound to be some changes." WASEC personnel, who ran The Movie Channel, were the most likely candidates for "changes."[16]

American Express' 1983 projected earning's were to decrease by 10 percent due to Fireman's Fund's (their subsidiary) "silly philosophy of being all things to all people in all places," according to president S.I. Weill. On Wall Street American Express' stock dropped $4.25.

As MTV and Nickelodeon were about to enter the world of profitability, the parent WCI was challenged by a hostile raider. Controversial media czar, Rupert Murdock, was buying up Warner's stock. By December the Australian mogul had amassed 7 percent of the corporation's stock. WCI quickly informed Murdock of the "cross-ownership" provision that prohibits a 5 percent control in cable franchises plus newspapers or magazines in a specific market. As owner of the *New York Post* and *Village Voice,* should he acquire 5 percent of Warner-Amex he would violate that stipulation in New York City. Spokespersons indicated that Murdock's main goal was to obtain Warner's movie operations and sell off the remaining holdings.

In the interim, Viacom strengthened its industry position. Showtime/ TMC signed an exclusivity deal with Paramount Pictures. *Flashdance* would be the first world premiere on The Movie Channel on February 12. An industry consensus of the $400 to $700 million arrangement was "this signals that they're definitely a major competitor."

Warner Communications found a "saving" white knight in Chris-Craft Industries Inc. A stock transfer was announced, effectively designed to block Murdock's News International Corporation takeover. Chris-Craft gained a 19 percent interest in WCI, trading a 42.5 percentage of their BHC television subsidiary.

Murdock vented his anger in the pages of *Business Week:* "There is a question about whether those people can run TV stations. I'm not sure they could get a casino license. . . . After all, Warners was voted one of the least-admired companies. I don't think it was well run. Look at the results, I don't know whether it is bad management or lack of management, but it is run by dealmakers rather than managers."[17]

WCI chairman Steve Ross, a proven street fighter, retorted: "I'm not interested in what Murdock says about our ability to manage. Our record speaks for itself. Last year [1983] was bad, but the twenty prior years were fantastic." Included in the CCI-WCI concord was a "poison pill" clause. Warners would be required to buy out Chris-Craft if any party gained a one-third share of WCI's stock. Should this eventuality occur, WCI's cash supply would be depleted. Ross doubted the "pill" would be necessary.

"The big problem there has been all the corporate adventuring," said Murdock. "The move into Atari, all the wheeling and dealing. I think that the profits in Atari caused a complete loss of a sense of reality at the corporate level." WCI was looking at a half-billion dollar 1983 loss in the video game business. *Business Week* quoted an Atari executive who stated, "No one in their right mind would buy it."

Warner-Amex that same year suffered a $99 million deficit after taxes. Ross commented: "You have two choices, you can either build or acquire. We are building for the future. If we lose $40 million, that is because we have invested money that will bring $80 million several years down the road."

Murdock would take his profits and withdraw, but refused to be "a patsy that can be run over and disenfranchised in this way."[18] The press media tycoon exacted a considerable cash profit from the sale of WCI stock.

Drew Lewis, chairperson of WACC, had the unenviable task of cable franchise damage control. His controversial handling of the air traffic controllers, while secretary of transportation, would prove a mixed resource.

Warner-Amex Cable, along with other MSO chains, was retreating from the high-powered commitments of the early 1980s. Lewis' approach was heavy handed. An unidentified cable operator told *Broadcasting,* "Everyone is renegotiating. That's normal. The only difference in the case of Warner-Amex is that it is bringing the whole to the press. That's a tactic to make the cities appreciate that some changes are necessary." Cox Cable's publicity spokesman said, "You don't have to ruffle feathers. . . ."

Lewis confronted the Milwaukee market. "There simply aren't enough entertainment programming services available or contemplated to fill more than forty channels," he said. A mere glance at *Satellite TV*

Week's listings refuted the assertion. The local director of Milwaukee's cable operations, Robert Welch, described the action as an "unconscionable affront to the people."

In the meantime WACC and Viacom Cable were discussing a joint venture to merge the fourteen suburban and metropolitan services.

Lewis repeated the Draconian belt-tightening message at a Dallas City Council meeting (partially rebroadcast nationally on MacNeil/ Lehrer's PBC evening news-magazine). Lewis observed, "There's one thing that's clear—we're not going to stay in Dallas and lose $20 million a year for the next twenty years." Industry spokespersons were rapidly distancing themselves: "Cable must not be painted with the brush of what is happening in the major urban centers."

Abruptly, on January 24 the QUBE Network ended. Six interactive systems became a TV blizzard. Vice-president Scott Kurnit announced: "Warner-Amex remains committed to interactive programming and to QUBE [but] . . . we should not be investing money in projects that don't have a foreseeable return in the investment."

WASEC was the *only* viable property in Warner-Amex's portfolio. Stock analysts agreed that "the time might be ripe to capitalize on MTV via its market value." As noted, on August 10, 1984 MTVN became a public stock offering. The value of the stock, temporarily dormant, shot up in 1985.

American Express, in another indication of its growing disinterest in cablecasting, acquired Lehman Brothers et al. for $360 million. The financial service would be named Shearson, Lehman/American Express. It would be second only to Merrill Lynch and Co. An American Express bailout from the joint venture was surely a matter of time and opportunity.

David Horowitz, CEO, admitted that the parent companies "invested considerably more than they had planned." In the euphoria of cablemania, overextension was common. In Wall Street jargon, American Express went in as a "cash cow." WCI was riding the crest of Atari and QUBE's perceived potential. The stark economic realities of wiring America, merger mania, and social trends impacted on the partners, especially Warners.

Drew Lewis, after addressing an 1985 MTVN shareholders meeting, said Warner-Amex's options were to "go public with the company, sell it, or split it into two pieces." Stock analysts questioned the division of Warner-Amex, as the venture was "not as attractive without MTV."

In mid-May Warner-Amex reportedly received numerous proposals for a complete or partial takeover. MTVN's David Horowitz, Robert Pittman, plus Boston Ventures Limited offered a leveraged buyout of

Warner-Amex's two-thirds share of MTV and the common stock available.

Vicacom International expressed an interest in the entire venture—MTVN, Showtime, and *possibly* the battered cable division. An unidentified source told *Billboard,* "It's unlikely that Viacom will prevail in getting all of Warner-Amex. The individual managers, particularly at MTV Networks, are saying to the board, 'We don't want to go with Viacom or anyone else.' At MTV, management has quite a bit of clout, as it's such a people-oriented business. In the case of the Warner-Amex cable system, people may not be such a factor, and Viacom could have a better chance there."[19] The source gave the inside track to the Horowitz group; however, Viacom had the cable system chip. Other rumored bidders included Telecommunications (TCI) with Time Inc., American Television and Communications (ATC), and Drew Lewis, who denied the report.

TCI/ATC joined with American Express in offering to buy out Warner Communications' half of the coventure. WCI, awaiting a stockholders meeting in June, had no immediate response. Ownership of ATC by Time Life Inc. did create antitrust problems in light of Warner-Amex's half-interest of Showtime/TMC.

Negotiations continued into August. A WTC counteroffer to American Express was rumored, heightened by an offer of $470 million by Forstmann Little and Company (FLC). The offer assumed that WCI would purchase American Express' interest in the joint venture. Forstmann had replaced Boston Venture, with the Horowitz-Pittman team, as most likely to gain control of MTVN.

On August 9, 1985 Warner Communications rejected the Forstmann bid because WCI: was denied "a voice in management," despite an offering of a 20 percent interest. Theodore Forstmann, in a press release, objected that WCI "had approved our offer . . . subject to receipt of American Express consent . . . [however Warners insisted that FLC] not take certain actions . . . that could be damaging to MTV."

Viacom International was victorious. On August 24, 1985 an agreement was entered into with Warner to acquire Warner-Amex's two-third interest in MTVN plus sole possession of Showtime/The Movie Channel. Viacom planned to buy the publically held one-third of MTVN at $33.50 per share. Besides money, Warner had the option to purchase over two million shares of Viacom. The bottom line for Steven Ross was control of the cable system and ammunition in the battle with Chris-Craft's Herbert Siegal for Warner's future.

Viacom senior vice-president Ronald Lightstone informed journalists, "We're still interested in Warner-Amex Cable, if Warner wants to sell" On programming he added, "We're always coming up with possibilities . . . So I wouldn't be surprised if there would be some sort of *synergy* there with MTV" (emphasis added).

Many MTVers were anomic. Since February 1983 15 percent of the WASEC employees had been let go. Warner's financial and internal political escapades had affected MTV. Schneider's removal was but one example. Viacom's role was amorphous and there were other problems to wrestle with.

After a two year hiatus Dale Pon was charged with developing a new television campaign for MTV. The "I Want My MTV" slogan was dropped. In its place four video promos were developed, ending with the motto "MTV: Some people just don't get it." The motif was a two-edged sword mimicking the network's critics and as an image-enhancing, ratings-building vehicle. The campaign spotlighted a fundamentalist televangelist, a conservative businessman, a Fidel Castro look alike who wants to be a veejay, and a Soviet commissar standing in front of the Kremlim wall condemining MTV. The criticisms were interspersed with brief lines from video clips.

The Soviet spot commenced with Cheech and Chong's "Born in East L.A." A uniformed Russian official appears: "This stupid rock 'n' roll and idiot little film." A musical reply. "Original video on MTV, America gets weaker." (A favorite theme of the radical Right going back to David Noebel's *Communism, Hypnotism, and the Beatles* pamphlet of 1965.) "So America keep watching." Diabolical laughter follows.[20] Bryan Adams appears with, "Some people just don't get it." Mick Jagger closes with a line from "Back in the USSR," ducking into an apartment. John Cougar Mellencamp and Andy Taylor were also recruited to express the new punch line.

Cable operators were no longer the problem. It was the shrinking viewership. Tom Freston explained that the three-and-a-half week TV blitz "talks more to the sensibility and personality of MTV in a general way." Time buys were scheduled for "Miami Vice," "Saturday Night Live," "Hollywood Beat," and "Hill Street Blues."

The drive was aimed at wired households to improve the music network's declining numbers. The Nielsen's for the third quarter of 1985 indicated an 0.9 rating with a 3 percent share. Although an improvement over the 0.8 of the second quarter, it was viewed as an aberration due to the success of Live Aid in July.

The million dollar plus campaign was not just image-building as Freston claimed. The clever ads failed to stem the ratings slide. MTV was in a state of siege in the fall of 1985. Their reaction, in Watergate terminology, was "stonewalling." Frequent critic Tom Shales of the influential *Washington Post* wrote, "MTV is run like a fortress. Inquiries from the press are met with chilly officious evasiveness." Shales' difficulties were understandable as the publicity department's function is to avoid "bad press." Shales and Dave Marsh were notorious MTV bashers.

Topics of a controversial nature generated a similar response. Jana Dozier of *Houston Style* magazine reported, "When asked whether any legal disputes have actually arisen because of them [exclusives], Kluger said he didn't know and would check with the legal department and call back. He didn't." It is highly improbable that Kluger was unaware of the DMN suit or the Justice Department query into the "exclusivity" deal."

Writers and journalists merely seeking interviews with some MTV executives or veejays were treated with disdain. One incident aptly illustrates MTV's attitude toward the press. A writer from a cable company requested an interview with Bob Pittman. The answer was "no." The publicity person added, "I'll get Johnny Sykes for you. He's good enough for the Midwest." Sykes proved to be a highly fruitful interview. Still, the attitude was insulting to the reporter and the senior vice-president. The individual involved has excited the network.

Barry Kluger, current director of press relations, has followed in the footsteps of his predecessors. Fortress MTV treats friend and foe with total equality. Media reaction was predictable. MTV's coverage, with the exception of the trades, proved fairly negative, as writers were generally forced to rely on secondary sources (and nurse bruised egos).[21]

This public relations strategy proved disingenious when problems and controversies surfaced. Inquiries were either dismissed or met by a short statement by an unnamed "spokesperson." These comebacks added little in the way of credibility for MTV's case.

In late October 1984, MTV expanded its rotations from the traditional to seven. Les Garland of MTV explained that the network was airing 107 clips daily and "there's no way three categories can handle it." The new rotation began as of November 10.

Garland provided *Billboard* with this rationale: "They will more accurately reflect how many clips we are playing and how we are looking at the number of clips we are playing." This was viewed as a possible reaction to the exclusives agreements with the "must play" provisos.

Garland described the categories and their meanings:

New: "The testing ground for acts' brand new videos. Clips can move right out of there and go on to be a hit." New will probably be "less than seven plays per week." Garland added that "so far they [the record labels] have been very, very happy about this."

Light: "A testing ground of the 'new' category" (three to five plays per week).

Breakout: "Where any potential hit song can break without a need to get any increase in rotational exposure. . . . seen more than enough to prove itself within the normal four-week cycle." Breakout will be a place for "potential hits."

Medium: "These are established hit records. Still on its upward climb towards its peak, but not top 10. Probably top 25 on its upward swing."

Active: Confirmed hits not yet megahits . . . gives us a place to go if we get a nibble, if we get a feel on something."

Heavy: A place for "monster hits."

Power: "Sneak preview videos"—a rotation made up for clips "only seen on MTV. . . . Time anchored airplay. All of them to be seen at the top of the hour. They will make it easier for us to standardize the continuity of promotion, pre-promoting them well in advance, almost making them major events."

The most prestigious slot, power, would be rotated four to five times per twenty-four-hour period and would generally be world premieres. Power videos would appear at the top of the hour because a majority of viewers "tune-in to MTV and all other shows" at that time. Garland claimed that they planned to "get one every hour, twenty-four times."

Music Video Services (MVS) watches MTV for their record company clients. President John Persico elucidated MVS's purpose: "It's similar in concept to those companies that hire people to see when and how often commercial spots run. We see the need for somebody to do this, because it's important for a record company to know how much their product is being played" and when. "It's not a problem with honesty," he maintained, "but with MTV's new playlist categories; sometimes that important precise information just isn't clear. The information developed will help better coordinate marketing and promotional efforts by providing data which will better coordinate expenditures on videos. . . . [They] will know how many people they are accessing with the video they spent $80,000 for. They then will be able to determine whether that $80,000 was justified." The idea made some sense since MTV admitted that specific plays each day would be difficult to determine.

This seemingly harmless notion created sparks in June 1985 when

MVS's monitored numbers disagreed with MTV's. MVS by implication discovered that MTV's numbers were inflated. The MVS data from June 26 to July 3 noted discrepancies. Firm's video in the power rotation by rights should have been aired at least twenty-eight times. Instead, according to the Atlanta-based firm, Jimmy Page's group was on only five times. One report indicated that of eighty-eight videos tracked the inflation rate was 25.4 percent. This was embarrassing, as the exclusives contracts in some instances had clauses as to the amount of exposure the categories would guarantee. *TV Guide* ran this reply:

> "We stand by our reported plays," says an MTV spokesperson. "We challenge their reporting. When we checked their research last February, we found whole blocks of time where they failed to monitor us."[22]

The response had nothing to do with the MVS timeframe. No further explanation for the discrepancies was given. Senior executives were unavailable for comment.

"Who Are Those People?" Sherman/Clayton Acts Versus MTV

The dark-suited corporate legal eagles, already reeling from the reams of Viacom documents and government filings, were greeted with an unexpected second antitrust suit. The DMN litigation was pending. Their original response was, "Who are these people?"

New York attorney Curtis V. Trinko, backed by colorful Texas trial lawyer Richard "Racehorse" Haynes, entered the U.S. District Court of Texas on October 10, 1985 and filed suit against MTVN, WACC, and WASEC charging noncompliance with sections 1 and 2 of the Sherman Act and four violations of the Clayton Act.

The plaintiff was the Wodlinger Broadcasting Company, the owner of Hit Video/TV5, a low-power, all-music VHF station in Houston. The audience reach of the operation was officially a mere fifteen-mile radius. A press release stated that on a clear day "it will be receivable up to 50 miles away with an outdoor antenna." The suit, assigned to federal magistrate James DeAnda, charged restraint of trade and denial of "access to advertising coverage on many of the channels carried by said cable systems." Damages of $205 million were requested, accompanied by a reversal of the CMC buyout.

The crucial issue of national importance, said Trinko, "relates to MTV's exclusivity contracts with most major record companies that produce the vast bulk of the popular music videos. Such contracts restrain trade through a course of conduct which denies competitors—including Houston's Channel 5—access to vital, unique and otherwise unavailable product." Record companies were cited as "coconspirators." Trinko, the long-time Wodlinger family attorney, with an unmipressive antitrust success record, continued: "Corporate giants have moved against Channel 5 with the clear intent of eliminating it [TV5] as a source of competition . . . by exercising all of their power and economic leverage against the local station."[23] Haynes issued a statement that TV5 "is being systematically denied access to coverage by the Warner-Amex Cable System in Houston, as well as all other major cable systems in the Houston area. . . . [TV5] is even being denied the right to buy advertisements on other channels carried by Warner-Amex Cable system and other cable companies . . . due to pressure being exerted by Warner Amex."

Mrs. Connie Wodlinger, company president, added: "It is the entertainment outrage of the electronic age . . . denying this station the ability to reach an astounding 42% of the households . . . accessible only by cable TV."

Many MTVers privately scoffed at the litigious action. Wodlinger, however, was not to be taken lightly, as past and future endeavors illustrated.

Connie Wodlinger, an attractive thirty-four-year-old reddish blond, has been correctly described as a "rare animal," "one sharp lady," "very aggressive," and lucky. Her professional background verifies most of these characterizations. Her self-portrayal lends support to these perceptions. Wodlinger's view is as that of an "overachiever," and "I've always been very ambitious, single-minded, and just real career-oriented." Her professional climb began at Bonner Kansas High School with the school paper. During the summers she attended journalism courses at the University of Kansas at Lawrence, which was the home of a biweekly newspaper called the *Outlook*. In 1968, as a senior Connie wrote features for the paper. Upon graduating high school she was offered the position of news editor. The *Outlook* purchased two nearby papers—the *Oskalooosa Independence* and the *Winchester Star*. Eighteen-year-old Connie was appointed editor of both, at a salary of $60.00 a week.

"I started at the University of Kansas that fall and thought I could go to college and retain my newspaper job . . . it was just a means to further my career," she recalls. Course requirements and classmates proved a problem. "They were kids and all they wanted to do was drink beer." During the Thanksgiving break of 1969 she joined her Air Force boyfriend, later to become her first husband, in Colorado

Springs. She got a job as copy editor for the *Colorado Springs Sun,*
part of the Greenspan chain.

She married and had a child. After her husband's Viet Nam tour they
moved to Kansas City. Failing to find a newspaper slot, she went to
work for ISC Industries, a holding company with a broadcast division.
Her position was in the public relations department as the editor of the
corporate newsletter, magazine, and press releases. The job proved a
bore. "I was continually looking for something of interest, and decided
to do a story about the broadcast division."

ISC owned a television outlet and several radio stations. Mark
Wodlinger had recently been hired to run the ABC affiliate Channel 9.
Wodlinger is a telecasting veteran having experience with Metromedia
as well as ABC. Mark and Connie's first joint media adventure began in
1974. They purchased KBEY-FM, a low-rated progressive rock bas-
tion. The front money was borrowed. After repeated refusals they
found a bank willing to loan them the money on the value of the
license. "Fortunately this bank had some broadcasting experience and
was aware of the value and the potential, but we were obviously on a
spot. It was make it or break it time."

Mark Wodlinger's contract at TV 9 had an additional year to run.
Connie took over the operation of the station. "I had never been in a
radio station in my life, but without question, management and operations come naturally to me. . . . I was just like a fish in water. I loved
it." The call letters and format were changed to Top 40-oriented
KBEQ-FM. "Everybody said we were crazy and that it couldn't be
done and so forth." The partnership was corporately ideal. A broadcaster merged with a public relations writer and editor. The partnership
had other benefits. "He likes to do the wheeling and dealing and the
negotiating. He likes to buy and sell stations and look at new industries, lobby for the industry, but just in general. I'm the management
operations person. I run the property."

They married in 1974. Mark was twenty-nine years older than
Connie. This union added another child to the household. Three years
later the radio franchise was sold for $5.1 million. With the profits they
"lived the good life" boating and traveling. By 1979 jet setting became
tedious. "We had to determine to retire, manage our investments, and
be happy with that or make the decision to build our own little
broadcasting empire, and go for it." Splitting their time between
estates in Maples, Florida, and Kansas City, the Wodlingers began
shopping for broadcasting properties. In 1981, they purchased KCLO-
AM and KTRO-FM. The AM property was left as a country and
western station broadcasting from Leavenworth. The Kansas City

FMer became KZZC or ZZ-99 with a new contemporary hits radio (CHR) format. In 1981 CHR, a first-cousin to Top Forty, was the rage in radio circles.

In February 1981 the couple entered into a battle for the Miami market license of WMJX, which had its FCC license contested due to fraud charges. The competition for the franchise was fierce. Mark and Connie bought out the competition. The frequency was back on the air in June 1985 as WCJX. Connie Wodlinger explained: "It was my station and CJ are my initials." At the same time they were in the process of building their FCC winnings in Houston.

Barry Garron's *Houston Star* column of July 10, 1984 led with "Wodlingers Are Winners in TV Lottery." Mark and Connie had "won" the FCC drawing for a low-power television franchise in the booming Texas community.

The FCC, overwhelmed by applicants, had altered its traditional policy of extensive hearings and raffled off valuable licenses. The Wodlingers tried for all that were available. They got Houston, then one of America's fastest growing cities. "If I were to take my applications and choose the one I wanted to get," observed Connie Wodlinger, "Houston would be at the top of that list." Despite its limited range of fifteen miles, the market size exceeded a population of over 3.2 million viewers.

The competition consisted of the normal network affiliates, a PBS outlet, plus three independents with the customary clutter of syndicated sit-coms and vintage movies.

In May 1985, Connie announced the launch of KHU-TV, Channel 5, an all-music video, twenty-four-hour-service. "I was looking for commercial viable," she says, "not to be another independent and run 'Leave It To Beaver' reruns and 'Mr. Ed.' There were already three independents and they don't have anything worth seeing to show. So there certainly wasn't anything else out there. If it's worth seeing believe me it's already on the air. I love the music industry, having been in it and coming from it."

The rationale for the format was familiar: low-cost clips, promotions, and wire service "rip and read" news. "Essentially we will have an MTV-style format, along with feature-interview segments, vintage videos, and contemporary hit radio music," she said at the time. The call letters were changed to KO5HU (TV5). "There may come a time when cable will pick us up, but we will always be a free service on the air waves," the president maintained.

Houston Style's Jana Dozier pressed Connie Wodlinger on the MTV comparison. "I take a different approach to on-air talent than other music video channels do . . . we looked for 'real people,' people that you can relate to. I was very adamant about that. The most important thing we have to offer is that we're a Houston station, originating 100 percent of the time out of Houston. There isn't another station doing that."[24]

Ad rates ranged from $125 to $400 per thirty-second spot. Six minutes on the hour were allocated for time buys. *Billboard* would list TV5 on their ignoble "video red ink" list (September 9, 1985). Local provincialism and pride realistically could not offset MTVN's cable impact nor impress record labels or suppliers of music video programming. Program director Mike Opelka disputes this contention, saying "community-mindedness" provided TV5 with a local window that transcends the nationalism found on MTV. This view severely contradicted Bob Pittman's *Rolling Stone* quote: "People in Podunk, Iowa, think it's more theirs than it is mine, it's a cult." Ms. Wodlinger didn't quite accept that view: "I think that within the next ten years you're going to see every major city will have its own local music channels just like the radio listener does today. You are going to have the choice of any format you would like." By 1987 local music video programs were on a severe decline replaced in many instances by the home shopping phenomenon.

Curiously, TV5 first aired on July 12, 1985 at 6:00 A.M. (CDT) with "Born in the U.S.A."—at the same time the Live-Aid mega-event was scheduled for MTV. A local critic noted, "Houston tuned in to watch TV5's debut." Connie echoes this parochical view: "We were only going up here in Houston, so whatever they were doing nationally was irrelevant to us." (So much for McLuhan's "global village.") Unfortunately neither had any ratings to substantiate the claim.

MTVers credit Bob Geldof's "the day the world rocked" as one of the few Nielsen bright spots during 1985. Their audience ratings rose a full share point the third quarter.

TV5's president, when questioned on the timing, explained:

> That was a simple matter. We were actually scheduled to go on air July 1. . . . I could have gotten an extention, but according to my license I was granted for my construction permit on July 12th, 1984 . . . I had one year to put it on the air. So July 12th of '85 was the final day that I could go on without applying for an extension. I wasn't able to go on July 1st because a piece of equipment came in and we weren't able to get it installed. Moreover . . . well, it was purely coincidental, and I'd do it again in a minute because it really didn't matter one way or the other. We wanted to get up and get on as quickly as we could and like anything else it was something brand new that hadn't been done, and there was not a prototype for really a local music channel but we were gonna do it, so we

wanted to get up and run and get the wrinkles out. We had run, dry run close circuit for about five days before we went up but until you're actually on air there are a lot of things which you don't find, but it was just purely coincidental.

"Houston Hit Video," TV5's logo, encountered criticisms familiar to the MTV veejays. A *Houston Post* critic said the on-air personalities "don't seem to have read the trade publications to find out what's going on in the music business. Their laid-back approach to their air breaks is simply a lack of needed preparation." Joe Pogge of KKBQ cited the problem as one of "building a corps of veejays from Houston. And it's difficult, because where do you look for video hosts in a market where there have never been any." TV5 ignored George Santayana's admonition concerning the repetition of history. Connie Wodlinger noted: "There's no research available that says it will work, but it's my feeling that Houston is the best market in the country to try this concept. The demographics are good—Houston is a young city." The target window was generally the 18 through 34 market. This lack of psychographics would only evoke moans from the Steve Caseys, Marshall Cohens, and other statistically minded executives at MTV headquarters, 1775 Broadway.

The weeks following the localized take-off of TV5 evidenced a significant growth in the station. Twenty-five veejays were employed. Seven were local radio personalities in the VH-1 mold. This was an unusually large number of announcers for a station the size of TV5. The format was strictly CHR genre. The Wodlingers enjoyed considerable success with the format in Kansas City. The early morning "shave and shower" segment—drive time in radio terminology—mirrored the usual news, weather, and familiar hits pattern. The ten o'clock "cookie cutter" slot was termed "Video Kaleidoscope," followed by an aerobic "Video A Go-Go." The afternoon was nearly visual radio with "lighter" material. "Video Feud," a page out of the "Battle of the Bands" or "Basement Tapes," was next. The remaining programs parroted the standard contemporary hits radio format, and the British-based "London Times Video "featured the mandatory new music. The night shift was aptly titled "The Danger Zone," emphasizing basically heavy metal bands. Occasional interviews and promotions interpreted the proceedings. TV5 was a very impressive low-power VHF or overground station with a total CHR rotation clock.

When the suit was filed there was a mixed reaction. Most MTV spokespersons dismissed the Wodlingers. "I don't know much about the whole operation. I know they're local, I've got some information on their talent, on their demos, and a few other things, but I really don't know what the motivation is behind it. They wanted to succeed. But, I really don't know what their motivation is for the tack they're taking. We think of law suits, there's no merit to it," said one executive. A few suspected method behind an apparent madness. MTV, a proven institution, could easily withstand a suit filed by a station with a fifteen-mile radius. MTVN and Viacom merely stated, "The company intends to vigorously defend the law suit."

One observer did take the Wodlingers seriously. He said, "They're a lot shrewder than most people think. Turner is a megalomanic, but these Texas folks are doing pretty much what he attempted. You watch, they're tenacious enough to actually challenge MTVN. I wouldn't be surprised if they were to go head to head, especially with all the publicity the law suit has generated. Remember MTV has made a lot of enemies over the past couple of years. Then there's the [cable] rate issue. . . ."

Ms. Wodlinger said, "Don't tell them. . . . I want to sneak up on them." Her timing was impeccable. MTV was preoccupied with Viacom and ratings. Having met the requirements of the Hart-Scott-Rodino Act, the FCC approved the Viacom purchase of WCI's interests in Showtime/TMC and MTVN. The sale would be closed on November 15, 1985. After the close a cash merger with MTVN would occur with a follow-up offer to buy outstanding shares in the company for $33.50 a share.

Some MTVers wondered about the fate of president David Horowitz, viewed by most as a Steven Ross loyalist. One senior executive observed, "Without Ross, he's lost his power source."

Viacom in the meantime was planning a stock offering of some 2.5 million shares to repay a portion of the money spent on the WCI deal. The total package, according to Wall Street analysts, would cost the media conglomerate $694 million.

Rumors persisted that Viacom was turning its corporate attention to securing a percentage of Ted Turner's interests in his newly acquired MGM/UA studios. As the weekly news magazines were again suggesting in earnest, mergermania was running rampant in the media world. The big shock would be the General Electric-RCA wedding.

David Horowitz "resigned," a few hours after Viacom officially took over. Ironically, this was the man who told *Esquire*, "I became MTV's steward and no matter what you might hear, I'm the world's oldest teenager."[25] He and Pittman had attempted to gain control of MTVN in the summer of 1985. Pittman, in part, suceeded. He became MTVN's president and chief operating officer in December. Few MTVers openly remarked on the changeover. Marshall Cohen would merely say, "I'm really sorry that Horowitz isn't going to be here."

Pittman's ascendancy to the top spot at MTVN and *Esquire*'s December 1985 description of him as having ignited "not just a television concept but a cultural revolution in contemporary style" evoked considerable off-the-record comments from present and ex-coworkers. One former collaborator said, "Bob's strength is not as a programmer, it's as a promoter. . . . Bob wears the suit that fits. When he has to wear the numbers suit he wears it. He's very glib. He understands how to use words toward an end, but he's the kind of person who will only use the numbers to tell you anything he wants at any given moment. He just looks at them, gets a general feel, and it's close enough. . . . Bob is too ambitious to waste too much time, that's all. . . . He doesn't want to be objective, he wants to be ambitious." A previous WASEC employee observed, "Music is certainly not his primary interest."

These sources could be dismissed as cases of envy or sour grapes. However, a number of the anonymous spokespeople had nothing to gain from Pittman bashing. Several merely desired to "set the record straight." The *Esquire* article by Joseph Dalton triggered more negative reactions than the promotion.

Earlier in the year VH-1 programming director Steve Casey complained, "Look at how few of those country stars have videos available." Record labels opinioned that the Nashville Network (TNN) was inadequate in exposing artists. MCA's Kay Shaw bluntly stated, "If anything remotely approaching MTV comes up the video clip production would increase. Rick Blackburn, general manager of CBS, added: "After all, the growth of pop music sure wasn't tied to the radio; it was MTV that made it explode." "Videos in country are an expense, not an income. It will be a long time before they are income-producing items, and it's questionable whether they'll ever play the role they do in pop music," noted RCA's Joe Galante. In one voice nearly all country executives questioned the exposure value of TNN. TNN's C. Paul Corbin objected, "A year ago [1984] only about 50 quality country videos were available." The debate was fundamentally one of "which came first the chicken or the egg." In January 1985 TNN announced two new video shows, *"Country Clips"* and *"Video Country."* Companies remained skeptical. Several months after the debut of these additions a Cincinnati merchandiser told *Billboard*, "I've seen sales from both TNN and Country Music Television, but TNN's impact has been minimal in terms of MTV's power."[26] Group W, a co-owner of TNN, claimed, "We estimate TNN sold 1.1 million albums in 1984."

This statement made by sales president Peter Weisbard was met with disbelief by label executives.

VH-1 saw an opportunity to exploit the small, but loyal, country market. The network sent a delegation of senior executives and talent relations people to the Country Music Association (CMA) awards show in late October. Garland, Sykes, Metheny, and publicist Sue Binford headed the staff, which included Rita Coolidge. Coolidge was quite familiar with the Nashville scene and conducted interviews for the one-minute personality spots.

"We want them to understand that VH-1 is a twenty-four-hour environment with a country commitment equal to other genres. . . . People who think they don't like country music in fact like Willie Nelson, Anne Murray, Barbara Mandrell, who has an all-star quality but has actually been 'too country' at radio." Metheny continued his pitch contending a quarter of the videos on the network were C&W: "We've always found the lines between musical spectra to be blurry." CMA's Judi Turner applauded the argument, saying the MTVN network promised "the greatest hope for exposure to country videos."[27] A media cynic wondered out loud if this wasn't "an attempt to neutralize TNN."

In Texas the Wodlinger saga became more bizarre. Three weeks after the filing of the highly publicized suit, speculation surfaced that TV5 was planning a satellite-delivered national music video network. Constance Wodlinger promised an announcement in mid-November. In a matter of days a press release confirmed the rumors.

The release was greeted by general disbelief. Observers were puzzled. No concept testing had been done. The Wodlingers invested $4 million without any significant cable operators subscribing to the service. The report did suggest some possible explanations for the staff size of the low-power Texas station and perhaps the legal action. As with DMN, several MTVers indicated that the suit could very well have been an attention-getting device. A cable industry observer contended that the employment of the high-powered New York public relations firm of Lou Gordon Associates to manage media coverage of

Figure 8.1
NIELSEN NOVEMBER 1985 FRIDAY NIGHTS

"Friday Night Videos" (NBC)	4.1
"Night Flight"	1.0 at 11:00 P.M.
"Night Tracks"	1.0 at 12:00 A.M.

Main audience: young adults 18–34. Numbers courtesy of Horst Stipp, director social research NBC-TV.

the antitrust case was designed to hype or garner national consideration.

The December 2, 1985 issue of *Cablevision* carried a full-page ad with an emboldened Born Free on a black backdrop.

Hit Video USA would appear on December 16 on Sat Com 4 as a "PG-rated" service. Mike Opelka would supervise a staff of fifty, employing a format of interviews, top 10 countdowns, and the usual MTV-type material.

At 12:05 P.M. (EST) Hit Video USA became a reality with a test signal announcing the network. A clean-cut veejay—a la Alan Hunter—introduced the service. He was arrogantly standing in a doorway, hands on hips, clad in a preppie red sweater covering a white dress shirt, in proper gray jeans, surrounded by modern art. The set was subtly attractive. "TV5 in Houston has just become Hit Video USA. My name is Kris Kincade and we'll be playing the best of contemporary hit videos twenty-four hours a day. . . . Glad you could tune in a whole lot. We're going to kick off the hour right now with the rock 'n' roll anthem. Seems only appropriate that we play Bruce Springsteen's 'Born in the USA.' " The same song used to launch TV5 in July.

"The Boss" was followed by VH-1 staple Lionel Richie in "Say You, Say Me." A veejay promo titled "Everybody" flashed across the screen. The first of four soundtracks appearing in the first hour was "Spies Like Us" by ex-Beatle Paul McCartney. The hour was pure CHR, running the gambit from Stevie Wonder, "Miami Vice" theme, to C&W singer Deborah Allan's "Rockin Little Christmas." The maiden hour closed with Wham. Kincade introduced Mark Goodman look-alike Darren Byrnes, the host of the two-hour "Danger Zone." The title song from *Live and Die in L.A.* by Wang Chung opened this segment, with Sammy Hager on next. Both veejays asked for requests and implored, "Give us a call" and "tell a friend." It was difficult to distinguish the opening hours of Hit Video USA from VH-1, although the veejays had learned to "shut up and play the music."

The Wodlingers had come a long way from winning the FCC lottery to gambling $4 million on a network without any cable commitments. Reportedly three small CATVs in the Houston area aired the downlink. The official explanation was: "We wanted to be up and on before the marketing push, so that operators could look at us and figure that we intend to be around. Many people attempt to pre-sell an idea before they debut, but as things turn out, the service never happens or they just last a short time." The reference was obviously to Ted Turner's unsuccessful attempt at music video.

The fate of Hit Video USA is firmly in the grip of the cable operators. Ted Turner's CMC went under with 350,000 subscribers. During the holiday season the Wodlinger's, according to a spokesperson, had none signed. There is a shroud of mystery surrounding the entire venture. Was the MTVN law suit a publicity smokescreen? MTV, however, does have the answer to the question, "Who are these people?"[28]

While skeptical, some media analysts were qualifying their state of disbelief. Rumors began to spread as to a new strategy for MTV. There was also some circumstantial evidence that VH-1 was perceived by the new owners as an economic liability.

Speaking to *Rolling Stone* Viacom's Ron Lightstone said, "We've taken programs developed for cable and put them into broadcast syndication."[29] "The Annual MTV Awards Show," produced by Chlmeyer Communications, had been made available for syndication through LBS Communications.

Viacom changed this posture. A mid-December release indicated that a one-hour, MTV-produced version of "Top 20 Video Count-down" would be syndicated to local overground commercial stations by April 1. Viacom's attempt to "synergize" MTV would run into difficulties. The CBS Record Group opposed the plan. When the spin-off countdown show was cleared on seventy-six stations in March (with Pittman predicting 75 percent acceptance by launch date in the country's markets), CBS was still discussing the strategy and voiced concerns of overexposure. The thrust of the objection was the myriad of countdown shows already available, ranging from "Friday Night Videos" to programs by Casey Kasem and Dick Clark. In light of the perceived glut, CBS executives viewed yet another similar service as having little promotional value. Pittman countered indirectly that the actual video clip time would involve "about forty-five minutes" allow-ing for ads, station IDs, and other breakaways.

The show would announce the top twenty songs, but air clips only from labels with licensing agreements. As Steve Dupler of *Billboard* correctly wrote, Viacom would lose many artists on MTV's rotation list and in the trade magazine's top twenty, such as the Hooters, Bruce Springsteen, Ozzy Osbourne, Sade, and others. Other labels, including WEA, merely acknowledged that talks with Mr. Pittman were "contin-uing."

The first coproduction took place January 3, 1986 with arch-rival "Friday Night Videos" on NBC. The "Year End Review" on the commercial network featured Paul Schaeffer as host with appearances by two MTV veejays—Mark Goodman and Martha Quinn. They integrated interviews with the "top ten" videos of 1985.

In mid-December VH-1 announced a one-hour program of "alternative music" to be called "Quiet Storm." This synergized genre, called "new age," would come from some of the more esoteric labels like Private Music, Windham Hill, and ECM. New age music has been defined as an echo of the traditional guitar state of the art techno-rock electronics, which hint at the course of the future. It is instrumental, going two or three steps beyond some of Jan Hammer's compositions for "Miami Vice." (One of the better examples of the genre are found on Mark O'Conner's *Meanings of* album).

Kevin Metheny, speaking to a trade reporter, indicated that he wanted to "let people in the industry know our intentions to showcase this kind of music and for them to help us amass an adequate programming inventory to get it off the ground. . . . We're looking to get this up to four, five, or even six hours per week. . . . As that type of programming gets broad-based legs we'll be prepared to place it in regular VH-1 rotation." The previously ignored labels were delighted, but cautious. Steve Backer of Windham Hill said, "It makes producing clips on these artists more worthwhile." "This is definitely going to broaden our market," noted Doreen D'Agostino of Private Music. "Their demographic is our demographic, and it was a matter of time until VH-1 opened the doors to image videos." The speciality style certainly lent itself to the visual genre, as Francis Ford Coppola's *Koyannasqatsie* illustrated. Ironically, as MTV appeared to be stagnating, the second music network was planning to explore new uncharted waters.

In a year and follow-up study the Street Pulse merchandisers research group found that VH-1 did impact on black music sales. Mike Shallet, the firm's president, reported that the adult contemporary network "benefitted greatly" such acts as Freddie Jackson, Whitney Houston, the Pointer Sisters, and Chaka Khan. "There's no way in my mind that I see Freddie or Whitney having the success they had without VH-1," he said. He went on to imply that the year-old network was appealing to the 24 + demographic. VH-1 had a base of 3.5 viewers in 10 million households. One surprise was the percentage of female teens sampled in some fifty retail outlets. "The teenage girls were looking for the black music they heard on top 40 radio but weren't seeing on MTV." MTVN vice-president Kevin Metheny was elated: "We proved that older people want to watch videos." Shallet was even more optimistic. "VH-1 will lead a new radio format, a mix of country, AOR, black, oldies, adult contemporary, and new age," he told Jefferson Graham.[30]

Mike Shallet's annual summary proved only half true. Compact disc unit sales increased by an impressive 291 percent over 1984, with 22.6 million CDs sold, surpassing the 5.8 million figure of the previous year. Record sales declined. Jan Hammer's *Miami Vice* soundtrack released to capitalize on the holiday season was one of the few bright spots of 1985, selling over four million units. Musically, 1985 was described as being "flat."

VH-1's significance as a promotional channel would be strongly questioned by merchandisers and record company executives. Harvey Leeds of Epic's video promotion, a favorite media source, indicated that CBS's in-house research found that VH-1 viewers continued to be modestly involved in record buying and were not influenced by that network to buy product. He told *Billboard,* "A year ago we were hoping that VH-1 would help us cross over certain artists faster and to increase their sales base. . . . unfortunately, we can't say the channel has done that."[31]

Several label executives restated the earlier argument that MTVN was not promoting the station as a promotional tool. "I don't think there's any awareness of VH-1 in the consumer mind the way there is about MTV. They need to do some heavy advertising and promotion," said Elektra's Robin Sloane. At Atlantic, a vice-president parroted the "more aggressive promotion" stance but acknowledged that "the book is still open on VH-1."

MCA and Artista were more optimistic, having a larger stable of adult contemporary artists. Peter Baron noted, "We think it is an important area of exposure for us."

Merchandisers were on the negative side. A regional manager for Tower Records said, "Does anybody even watch it? I don't think the folks who would are record buyers anyway." "I was really hopeful that it would do something when they first introduced it," said Randi Swindel, "but I don't think it's lived up to its promise."

Grabbing for the printouts, Tom Freston countered that Nielsen research found the VH-1 viewer to be 31 percent more apt to consume records and cassettes than nonviewers. According to the Opinion Research Center, 47 percent of the audience had an influence on purchasing activity. Moreover, they bought 3.4 records in early 1986. Viacom's annual report described VH-1 as the "fastest growing" channel with eleven million households in thirty-nine of the top MSOs. Labels and retailers remained skeptical as to MTVN's intentions and VH-1's affectibility in the marketplace.

Robert Johnson remained confident that BET could compete with VH-1, especially when major urban markets such as Cleveland, De-troit, Baltimore, and the nation's capital had cable service. The Nashville Network (TNN), with some 3,500 CATVs and 23.8 million subscribers, seemed unconcerned with VH-1's attempt to lure away some of its viewers. A spokesperson indicated that the network was pleased with the adult contemporary exposure and that "they'll motivate the labels to make more and better videos."

Now chief honcho of MTV Networks, having bullied his way up to the top by a skillful self-promotion campaign, Pittman may have reflected on the state of MTV. While all the results were not in, 1985 had been a rough year. Despite his ascension to the presidential office, he had lost the takeover battle to Viacom. Still in the formulative phase, Viacom's projected plans would dilute the MTV format, which Pittman so rigidly adhered to in the early years of MTV.

The high points of 1985 were unique events, such as Live Aid and the annual awards broadcast, but musically the original excitement was evaporating. There was no *Thriller*. Potential threats were cropping up like crab grass. "We're going to see a lot more competition for that concept, and that's a problem. . . . MTV is beginning to recognize they've got to do more than music videos," said Mike Drexler, vice-president of media and programming for Doyle, Dane, Bernbach, a New York ad agency.

MTV, prior to Viacom's entry into the picture, had expanded its music news division, and joined with a New York rock club to produce "Live at the Ritz" on a "seasonal basis." The Ritz was, according to MTV acquisitions director Chip Rocklin, "the right showcase" for new acts. MTV and the showcased artists' label would share the expenses.

The IRS Records monthly "Cutting Edge" program was showcasing cult groups on location in underground clubs in cities such as Austin, Winston-Salem, and Los Angeles. The label's creative services director Carl Grasso said, "We're trying to connect the dots between the country's music cities. We are in the business of putting records out and making money, but we do care a great deal about the music scene in general."

In August, MTV violated the "impressionistic mood," as defined by Pittman, with a British "sit-com," aired at 11:30 P.M. (EST), Sunday night—a time slot "Monty Python" previously occupied on PBS. "The Young Ones" has been described as "a sort of whole earth hitchhikers' guide to everything you ever wanted to know about surviving as a hippie in the 1980s." The central character, Neal, played by Nigel Planer, consistently denounces "horrid technological change"—especially computers and music videos. Some rock acts such as Chris Difford and Motorhead and Madness occasionally appear on the original shows. "Even though there are only fourteen episodes," says John Sykes, "we find viewers getting more and more excited about the show." He stressed, "We were initially hesitant as we didn't want to just present the traditional type of rock 'n' roll humor, that always just misses the mark." (Within months the "Monkees" series would grace the MTV program schedule.) Atlantic Records' in early 1986 would release a musical comedy, *Neals Book of the Dead,* based on the series.

Toward the waning months of 1985, MTVN senior executives began to fall as the leaves of autumn. After the move from Rockefeller Plaza to fresh quarters at 1775 Broadway, general manager Domenick Fioravanti and publicity people Don Bridges and Dorene Lauer were "not with us anymore." One executive described the situation as a game of musical chairs. Once secure MTVers were cautiously examining future employment options. A competitor said, "They're covering their corporate ass."

The ratings picture for 1985 was mixed. After the first quarter flap, MTV's ratings dropped to a 0.8 in the second quarter, while the audience share jumped 3 percent. Ira Tumponsky noted, "Ratings are just part of the story." "If you look at share, it's up; they're delivering many more households," observed Robert Alter of the Cable Advertising Bureau. "The ratings for the second quarter," said Marshall Cohen, MTV vice-president, "were tied with Christian Broadcast Network [CBN]. If you went no further than the rating and share, you could conceivably extrapolate that MTV and CBN have the same viewing audience. They most certainly do not, and the variations in the quantitative numbers show where those differences lie, which mean the most to advertisers." Cohen was referring to the Nielsen profile where MTV led its basic cable counterparts. The sampling found MTV leading with percentage of households with pay-TV, households with viewing members twelve to thirty-four, and in groups with a $20,000 income. This type of data appeals to psychographically minded observers on Madison Avenue. The third quarter would further balloon the "numbers." The fourth would send rumors throughout MTV, but those would come after the New Year's festivities which began earlier each year.

MTV began its pre-New Year's programming at 1:00 P.M. (EST) with the "Top 100 of 1985"—a ten-and-a-half hour countdown of the most popular videos of the year. While airing clips the veejays attempted to create the proper aura for the fifth New Year's Eve Rock and Roll Ball to be staged at the Manhattan Center. The selections were made on the basis of the staying power of a clip on the "Top 20 Countdown" Saturday night show.

Statistically, forty-three American bands were featured, with the United Kingdom exhibiting thirty-eight. Ten were Anglo collaborations, with six emanating from north of the American border. There were thirty-seven male solo artists, a mere nine female solos, forty-six bands, seven duos, and one instrumental (the theme from "Miami Vice.")

As the countdown continued John Cougar Mellencamp's "Lonely Ol' Night" was number four. Mark Goodman attempted to heighten the "suspense." "Broken Wings" by Mr. Mister ranked third. Grace Slick, about to headline the ball, introduced the runner-up—the Starship's "We Built this City," denying it was an ode to San Francisco as popularly believed. Finally, the top clip of 1985 was "Money for Nothing" by Dire Straits. The clip was a natural, with all the visual texture of MTV. The lyrics ("You play the guitar on the MTV/That ain't workin the way you do it") are underscored by claymated figures, with cuts to a television set airing the network logo and concert clips with rotation categories thrown in.

At 11:30 Goodman took his champagne bottle to the Center. The four-and-a-half hour live event began with a scene from a commando-secured, dog-patrolled warehouse "somewhere" in Queens that contained the postcards for the "Million Dollar Give Away."

A parody of the "Miami Vice" opening followed, complete with shots of the snake-infested Florida everglades and animated pink flamingos. Martha Quinn and a reserved Nina Blackwood hosted; the other three veejays were scattered backstage and other places. Howie Mandel was the roving "comedian" or "social director."

The Starship opened with several verses from "We Built this City" segued into the sixties classic "Somebody to Love." The energized semi-medley promised a typical Starship performance. However, with each ensuing number the set deteriorated. The inclusion of colorful Dee Snyder of Twisted Sister on "Rock Myself to Sleep" was of little help. The rendition of "White Rabbit" was a shadow of the original. Grace Slick obviously had tired of the song, speaking some of the lines, and her range was limited. Mercifully, the set ended with the rest of "This City."

The Hooters, who escaped the relative obscurity of the Philadelphia music circuit with their Live Aid set, highlighted the broadcast. They began their segment with "Day by Day," and followed with the anti-teen suicide song, "Where Do the Children Go," and "All You Zombies." They outshown the other artists. The Hooters were voted the best "New American Band" by the contributors to the *Rolling Stone* Readers Poll by an impressive 47.6 percent—twice the figure of the runner-up (Viacom would use the *Stone* poll for an "MTV Presents" syndicated show coproduced with the rock magazine).

Noting the appearance of seventeen-year-old sideman gone solo, artist Charlie Sexton, Martha Quinn told Nina Blackwood: "Every New Year's Eve we've seen a new artist play the Rock and Roll Ball and go on to achieve success. Cyndi Lauper, Duran Duran, The Thompson Twins, Billy Idol. . . ." She neglected to mention that the three acts on the first New Year's show belong in the rock trivia category. Sexton, doing his first major gig, received a lukewarm reception. After "Be So Lonely" he yelled at the crowd, "Happy New Year . . . come on now!" Martha and Nina hyped the Triplet's first album. They had won first prize on "Basement Tapes" earlier.

The Australian heavy metal band The Divinyls were the last of the officially scheduled acts, doing "Pleasure and Pain" amongst other unfamiliar tunes. Martha Quinn, referring to Howie Mandel, said: "He has the pulse of this party." Unfortunately, she was almost correct.

Mandel's major chore was to identify the winner of the Nabisco-sponsored "Million Dollar Giveaway," which attracted 3.5 million entries. Faye Ballantine of Florence Alabama won. The prize was awarded after an elaborate plot interspersed during the ball with "Lester Mowgli" acting the role of an accountant who travels to a Queens warehouse guarded by an army of Ramboish types. He finds bag 499, grabs a postcard, is handcuffed to a steel strong box, and returns to the Manhattan Center stage to have Howie read the name of the person about to win an original installment of $85,000 with $32,000 per year to follow for the next quarter century. Ms. Ballantine also acquired a Porsche Targa, and vacations to Rio de Janeiro and Paris. The contest unveiling, network IDs, and the Hooters partially made up for the many shortcomings of the telecast.

The MTV logo was altered to have the small "v" being transformed into a pink flamingo. Animated pink flamingos frequently graced the screen. The connection with "Miami Vice" was inescapable.

Mark Goodman and the other veejays replayed their highly criticized performances of Live Aid and past New Year's shows. At the top J.J. Jackson told viewers, "This is live. They have to remember words and notes to everything." Mark Goodman kept asking, "What are you looking forward to in 1986?" A typical exchange or "interview" with the Cars' Gary Hawks went: "What's the coolest thing that happened in 1985?" Hawks' reply: "When I got air-conditioning in my car." Goodman: "What will be the coolest thing in 1986?" Answer: "1987." China Kantor, daughter of Grace Slick and Paul Kantor, was queried, "Do you write?" "Yeah, I write songs," she told Goodman. More pink flamingos. Nina Blackwood said little, avoiding a host of banalities and references to rock history books, misinformation, or introductions like

Alan Hunter's "Somehow they found time to play Live Aid," referring to the Hooters who later pointed to the benefit as providing their big break.

Goodman should have asked Robert Pittman the standard question. The reply might have been interesting in light of what was happening. The ball, first under Pittman's presidency of MTV, did not auger well for the future as subsequent events would demonstrate.

Five days after the ball, MTV revived their multimillion dollar consumer advertising campaign, the largest to date unveiled by the network. Roger Daltry and Phil Collins were enlisted to join Adams and Mellencamp to tagline the four "antitestimonials" with "MTV: Some people just don't get it." The commercials were to appear on "Miami Vice," "The A-Team," and "Family Ties" during a four-week period.

While the 1984 fourth quarter Nielsens may have created a storm at MTV, the 1985 numbers generated a full-blown hurrricane. The downward slide was severe enough for Nielsen vice-president William Hamill to suggest in a December 20 letter addressed to Robert Pittman that the ratings service would investigate its sampling techniques as "we have not seen declines in any individual demographic segment as large as these for MTV." He went on: "This is the first time a demographic fluctuation this large has happened." Reportedly, the original findings showed a 0.8 in 1985, suggesting a drop of some 35.5 percent as opposed to the previous year. The fourth quarter twenty-four-hour rating was down to 0.7. More significantly, segmental declines by age were 20 percent in the eighteen- to twenty-four-year-olds and a horrendous 25 percent in the twelve- to seventeen-year-olds. An unidentified spokesperson for MTV responded, "Any projected ratings are invalid, and anyone who projects a rating obviously does not understand the nuances of ratings and sample designs." A dramatic drop of this kind could have dire consequences. Jack Hill of the Cable Advertising Bureau, however, told *Billboard* that MTV "has no real direct competition" and will probably "remain a major vehicle for delivering teens and young adults. Even with such a large drop in those areas, that's still where the bulk of their audience is." Overall, he noted, "The effect of a demographic drop of this scale could be disastrous. Networks live and die by these numbers." Pittman demanded a reevaluation. These numbers may have affected Viacom's decision to syndicate "Countdown" and may also have sealed the fate of WCI eleven-year veteran executive David Horowitz. Syndication could serve as a profit-making device and as an advertisement for MTV.

MTV's deterioration may have been due to a general "lull" in the record business. There were only nine gold singles produced in 1985, the lowest figure since 1964. Albums were strong, but individual hits are the forte of the music network.

The explosion of the shuttle Challenger on January 28, 1986 claimed seven lives and shocked the nation. A less significant casualty was Fred Seibert's highly acclaimed moon-landing MTV logo. On February 5, seven days after the tragedy, Tom Freston announced: "A week has come and gone and it's obviously just too painful to use [the NASA space footage logo] as a channel identification."

The protocol of "MTV presents the 1985 *Rolling Stone* Readers Poll," hosted by Michael Douglas with some segments introduced by Jann Wenner, was surprising if not shocking. *Stone* reporters, collaborating with MTV directors and producers, stretched the imagination. During the broadcast spots were run promoting the two Viacom pay-cable movie networks and MTV. Nickelodeon and especially VH-1 were conspicuously absent. Michael Goldberg's appearance interviewing John Fogerty and the closing credits—Executive Producers: Robert Pittman *and* Jann S. Wenner—boggled the imagination. Goldberg has been a frequent critic of MTV. It was equally common industry knowledge of the longstanding animosity between Pittman and Wenner. The explanation lay in the final credit: a "Viacom Presentation."

Pittman's stubborn positions regarding oldies and new music were evaporating with each new press release. "Economics makes for strange bedfellows," said a source. Dale Pon's new slogan—"MTV, some people just don't get it"—began to take on an entirely new meaning not intended by the ad agency.

MTV's decision to delete the moonlanding logo, whatever the reason, was symbolic of the end of an era. Reluctantly, MTV was forced to accept the Nielsen findings despite their protestations that the network's target audience was underrepresented in the sample. In this instance trade papers and magazines were not accused of inaccurate reporting of the "numbers.'"

MTV is an international institution that affected nearly every facet of American popular culture in the 1980s. Comedian Bob Hope's closing theme seemed appropriate—"Thanks for the Memory."

Notes

1. *On Cable,* January 1985, p. 21.
2. *On Cable*, January 23, 1985, pp. 1, 31, 61.
3. Ibid.

4. *Billboard*, March 30, 1985, p. 30.
5. *Billboard*, November 3, 1984, p. 4.
6. Inner City Broadcasting was behind the abortive Black Music TV cable project. *Billboard*, February 3, 1979, p. 30.
7. *Cablevision*, February 4, 1985, p. 27.
8. February 1985. Approximately one-fifth of the titles were found in the MTV rotation.
9. *Newsweek*, July 15, 1985, p. 51.
10. *Newsweek*, July 15, 1985.
11. This discussion is an expansion of the author's "Heavy Metal Music May Be Rusting," *Sentinel-Tribune*, April 29, 1985, p. 17.
12. *Esquire*, December 1985, p. 387.
13. *Billboard*, March 23, 1985, p. 30.
14. *Billboard*, June 15, 1985, p. 16.
15. *Billboard*, August 17, 1985, p. 16.
16. Two WACC systems totaling 21,000 basic hookups were sold to Centel and Marcus Communications for an undisclosed amount.
17. *Business Week*, January 23, 1984, p. 106.
18. *Business Week*, January 23, 1984, pp. 106–08.
19. *Billboard*, May 25, 1985, p. 4.
20. Commercials lampooning the Soviets in the fall of 1985 were in vogue on Madison Avenue. Good examples are Wendy's Russian "fashion show" and the comic Yakov Smirnoff, a supposed defector, saying, "I love America because there's plenty of Lite beer and you can always find a party. In Russia, the Party always finds you."
21. This writer was, after a period of time, able to develop several "moles" within the network. Another source of information were ex-MTVers, of which there are many who are more than willing to discuss internal events and politics, usually "off the record."
22. *TV Guide*, November 3, 1984, p. 42.
23. In a letter dated February 18, 1986, Assistant Attorney General Douglas Ginsburg of the Antitrust Division indicated that "this investigation is still open."
24. *Houston Style*, October 1985, p. 45.
25. In another strange twist of fate it was Horowitz in the same interview who credited Pittman with the founding of MTV—historically a totally inaccurate statement that infuriated a number of those actually present at the creation of the network.
26. *Billboard*, March 30, 1985,, pp. 52, 56.
27. *Billboard*, November 2, 1985, pp. 43, 46.
28. As of August 1, 1986 Hit Video USA remained on Sat Com 4. Some of Viacom's machinations with MTV may well heighten CATV's interest in the fledgling music network.
29. *Rolling Stone*, October 10, 1985, p. 12.
30. *USA Today*, December 30, 1985.
31. *Billboard*, April 12, 1986, pp. 1, 84.

9

"We're at the Hub of It All": The Impact of MTV

*The people who make video are
cutting-edge visual literates of our
time. They may not have read
everything, but they have seen
everything.*

—Tom Shales, critic,
Washington Post

*"Miami Vice" is so rock 'n' roll
influenced. . . .*

—Ted Nugent, singer

*"Miami Vice" was really Hill and
Renko with a music-video feel.*

—Brandon Tartikoff, programming
president of NBC-TV.

Few objective observers would dispute MTV's influence on the American popular culture of the 1980s. Bob Giraldi claims, as have others, "It saved the record industry." It transformed many segments of the entertainment and news print media with its style, *film noir,* mood, and abbreviated span of attention.

The "mood" or ambiance has been discussed by Robert Pittman on frequent occasions. "What we've introduced with MTV is a nonnarrative form. As opposed to conventional television, where you rely on plot and continuity, we rely on *mood* and *emotion.* We make you feel a certain way as opposed to you walking away with any particular knowledge." This was a restatement of his McLuhanesque view stated in the *New York Times:*

> You're dealing with a culture of TV babies. . . . What kids can't do today is follow things too long. They get bored and distracted, their minds

241

wander. If information is presented to them in tight fragments that don't necessarily follow each other, kids can comprehend that.[1]

He provides an example: "I think, personal theory, that was one of the things that led to the split over the Vietnam War. You had one generation, my parents', who were listening to the newscasts and listening to the words. You had my generation, who were looking at the pictures and forming an impression and a different understanding than was conveyed by those words." This was sensory versus linear perception.

Discussing film critic Gene Siskel's portrayal of this approach as "junk," Pittman says, "I think what they're going to find is those people will read faster, they will get to the essence of the information . . . they may not pick up all the adjectives as well . . . they may not pick up necessarily the writer's flavor. But they'll pull the information out in a much more concise way—and perhaps even understand the information a little better."

Several people have indicated that this concept of "mood" is a reflection of Pittman's personal lifestyle. After interviewing Pittman, Toby Goldstein, a publicist and freelance writer, wrote: "This is a man who says he learns about the news from skimming headlines and is proud that his attention span is so brief as to render him incapable of reading a publication like the *New Yorker.*"[2] A long-time associate responded: "He has a goal. His attention stays as long on something as is necessary to reach his goal. We all waste a lot of time. Bob is too ambitious to waste too much time."

USA Today and numerous weekly news magazines such as *U.S. News & World Report* plus *Newsweek* now use short-form items that require the attention span of a hummingbird. While some in the "pencil" medium decry the trend, the syndrome is very much a part of the social construction of reality in fashions, television, and film. The working title of the highly successful "Miami Vice" was "MTV Cops." A plethora of films owe their success to thematic video clips aired on the music network. Fashion designers plague rock stars to wear their designs while performing in concert clips. Automobile and clothing commercials frequently are indistinguishable from MTV clips. Many are made by the same directors and producers. Bob Giraldi is the director of the Miller Lite beer commercials as well as Michael Jackson's famous "Beat It" video.

"The Clip Was Better Than the Movie"

Harry Warner is reported to have responded to a question after the premiering of the historical *Jazz Singer,* "Who the hell wants to hear actors talk. The music—that's the big plus about this." Beginning with Al Jolson's audio and visual interface movies, the dominant medium of that period became the genre to expose music. The 1930s were characterized by a plethora of musicals of the Busby Berkeley variety and singing cowboys.

Berkeley's musicals revolved around the Brill Building, home of ASCAP, and the Broadway stage. The scripts were generally simple. It was the musical extravaganzas that highlighted the films.

Westerns of the 1930s took a break to hype a song as the usual black and white hats fought their predictable way to justice. The stock plots also found time for dubbed harmonizing. The campfire shot with full orchestra was an ideal setting. As Robert Shelton, formerly of the *New York Times,* would write, western actors nearly all echoed the same lines: "Them bandits have beaten mah mother, ravished mah girl, burned down mah house. . . . Ah'm agonna get 'em if'n it's the last thing ah do—but first, folks, ah'm agonna sing ya a little song."

The low-budget, grade B sagebrush action film legitimized country music outside of its then predominantly rural market.

"Shorts," or three- to five-minute film clips, were employed to highlight the talents of musical performers from vaudeville and radio. The "Singing Brakeman" Jimmie Rodgers starred in a "short" prior to his untimely death.

The Big Band era upgraded the "showcase" film, which acted as a vehicle for name swing performers. The plots were almost identical: "rags to riches" stories providing a recording artist the opportunity to play their musical material. Benny Goodman did *Hollywood Hotel,* Tommy Dorsey did *Las Vegas Nights,* and Artie Shaw did *Dancing Co-Ed.* With the exception of Glenn Miller's *Sun Valley Serenade,* critic George Simon described the swing films as "every one of them forgettable."

The motion picture was an effective medium for singer/actors, such as Bing Crosby and Gene Autry, who used the big screen to introduce songs. "White Christmas" by Irving Berlin came from *Holiday Inn.* Some considered it an "ideal" wartime song. "Back in the Saddle" was the title song of an Autry action flick.

By the mid-1940s, there was little dispute that film-introduced songs did sell. Despite the 78 rpm technology, *The Jolson Story* turned a million units in 1946 with a charted hit "The Anniversary Song." Still, the technology was absent.

CBS's Peter Goldmark's main purpose for developing the long-playing (33⅓ rpm) record was uninterrupted symphonic music. CBS' earliest LP releases were in that genre. Jazz, "mood music," and Broadway shows were added to the catalog in order to appeal to an older affluent audience. Soundtracks became top sellers due to their universality. They attracted people that rarely bought records. *An American in Paris* (1952), *Oklahoma!* (1955), and *The King and I* released in 1956 did very well by LP standards.

Rock "showcases" proliferated in the wake of the success of "Rock Around the Clock," the theme from *Blackboard Jungle*. Sam Katzman led with the drive-in hit *Rock Around the Clock*, followed by *Mister Rock 'n' Roll*. Elvis Presley's *Love Me Tender* or *Loving You* lacked a story line except to set up musical numbers. *The Girl Can't Help It*, starring the late Jayne Mansfield and a stellar cast of singing stars, worked as a total picture. It remained a showcase. The Presley effort *King Creole*, based on Harold Robbins' semiautobiographical *A Stone for Danny Fisher*, had the rare dramatic impact. Even in the Robbins' story the music predominated. Only Presley's film scores were made available to record buyers, usually in the EP (extended play) 45 rpm mode.

The rock "showcase" LP rarely was released, due to licensing difficulties and the assumption that adolescents didn't purchase albums.

The Sound of Music reached the *Guiness Book* and remained there for over a decade following its 1959 "gold" certification. (The platinum designation was introduced in 1976.)

Million-selling soundtracks in the 1960s included *Goldfinger*, from the James Bond adventure film, theme sung by Shirley Bassey; *My Fair Lady; Mary Poppins*, a staple in the "kiddie" market; and the Beatles' *Hard Day's Night* and *Help*.

With the advent of the "Fab Four" and the acid-rock scene, the importance of singles was rapidly diminishing. Free-form radio, later titled and formulized album-oriented rock (AOR) by Mike Harrison, altered buying habits.

RSO's Robert Stigwood manipulated the film/record landscape. His *Saturday Night Fever*, which sold 22 million units, supposedly augured a trend. *Newsweek*'s cover heralded: "Disco Takes Over." The lead paragraph stated: "Roll over, rock. Disco is here to stay." The Bee Gees-dominated soundtrack had several hits prior to *Saturday Night Fever*'s release in movie houses on December 14, 1977. It sold 850,000 copies prior to the premiere of the film. RSO's philosophy was to release segments of the soundtrack to hype the movie. In several instances the marketing campaign worked, and then came *Sgt. Pepper*. The film, universally condemned by critics, sold more Beatles' albums than the soundtrack featuring the Bee Gees, Peter Frampton, and Aerosmith. The movie LP "stiffed." The verdict on soundtracks was revitalized by a country and western version of *Fever*, again starring

John Travolta: *Urban Cowboy* sold more western-styled clothes than records.

Urban Cowboy, a double-album set listed at $15.95, was bottom-lined at $100,000. The production costs were modest by recording industry standards. Becky Shargo, music supervisor on *Urban Cowboy,* told *Mother Jones:* "A lot of our production cost were absorbed by the film. . . . We did a lot of songs very quickly, too; many were recorded in a single day." A number of cuts had nothing to do with the film. Still, Johnny Lee's "Looking for Love" was a platinum single. The *Rolling Stone Record Guide* described the music as an "uneven soundtrack collection of country-rock tunes for the John Travolta flop." As of May 1981, the album sold over three million units. Elektra/Asylum reportedly grossed $23 million on the nonsoundtrack.

Mark Hunter, a freelance writer, observed: "Many people in the industry now point to cable TV, which often features short promotional films of rock bands, as an emerging ally."[3] This was stated four months prior to the debut of MTV. MTV's original time buyers were film studios primarily targetting the teen psychographic. Rather than packaging a sixty-second commercial, film companies focused on video clips, highlighting portions of the movie with potential hit songs. In August 1982 *Variety* headlined: "Clip Tunes Help Sell Pix and Records."

Flashdance was the prototype. Cinema analyst Richard Corliss for *Time* summarized the situation in the May 9, 1983 issue:

> If *Flashdance* looks like a 95-minute "video" for MTV, the cable music channel, it should be no surprise. For one thing, Director Adrian Lyne is another in the long list of British mannerists (Alan Parker, Ridley Scott, Hugh Hudson) to have graduated from TV commercials, and to bring their techniques and attention span with them. For another, the film's "production numbers" were designed, or at least marketed, with MTV in mind. Paramount began running two-minute commercials on MTV a full three weeks before the movie opened. "The MTV audience likes music, movement, dancing," notes Weaver. "We hoped the movie and MTV would make a happy marriage. And it happened."
>
> This week MTV will begin airing two *Flashdance* videos featuring Beals, the 19-year-old Yale freshman who was chosen over 4,000 other applicants. Beals has a sweet-sad face, a lean, expressive body and enough sultry energy to bring heat and humidity to her role; but in fact she is just one more erotic element in Lyne's fantasy of smoke, strobe lights and soft focus. Given the exposure, Beals may not mind. Neither do her Big Brothers on Hollywood Boulevard, who could be laughing all the way to 1984.

Two video clips promoted the movie on MTV: Irene Cara's "What a Feeling" and later Michael Sembello's mega-hit "Maniac."

MTV was now the major exposure medium. Its competitors were still in the research and development phase.

Staying Alive, a sequel to *Saturday Night Fever,* pushed the soundtrack, despite poor reviews. Polygram's Harry Losk told *Variety,* "We realize that it's not a great movie, but we're hoping that the power of John Travolta will start a run to the box office, not to mention record merchandisers." Several cuts did fairly well, underlining the soundtrack video clip ethos. *Staying Alive,* a shadow of *Fever,* did generate hits in the Bee Gees' "The Woman in You" and Frank Stallone's "Far from Over." At this time several of the brothers Gibb were publically dissociating themselves from the discomania that revitalized their careers.

The success of mediocre films such as *Staying Alive* and *Flashdance* prompted *Rolling Stone*'s Debry Miller to write: "MTV and video clips are a strong new force in movie advertising." A survey of MTV watchers found that 68 percent attended specific films on the basis of a video aired on the channel.

The film industry was convinced of MTV's impact on box office receipts. Leonard Goldberg, producer of *War Games,* noted: "If you have a really hot soundtrack and you can get MTV playing it all day long, you're in business."

Not all participants were enthused with the MTV/film connection. Frank Stallone barely appeared in the video clip of "Far from Over." John Travolta received a majority of the footage.

This mode created problems. Gordon Weaver of Paramount Pictures relates:

> That's because the original intent of these music videos is to promote the movie, although there's spillover benefit to the record when the movie is played. . . . We work with the label, but we both have separate functions. [Paramount Pictures distributes the clips to MTV and other television outlets, as well as locally to clubs.] We do this through our offices in New York and our 43 advertising agencies around the country. . . . It's a godsend. The demographics are so perfect with music video.

Don Simpson, coproducer of *Flashdance,* says getting on MTV with the videos was "a priority." " 'Maniac' was on MTV before the movie came out; *Flashdance* itself was inspired by MTV."

Danny Goldberg, of Gold Mountain Records, wrote in *Billboard:* "The film business is in the process of taking giant steps in our direction. MTV and other music video programs will transform the film business even more than they are alternating the record industry. The economics of film distribution depends totally on 'opening' a picture—

doing decent business in the first weekend. And the right kind of music video is the best way of pre-selling a film." More emphatically, Colfax's Gary Le Mel, who was involved in the contrived Monkees' material, told *Variety* in April 1984: "There was a period when you said 'soundtrack album' [post-RSO's *Sgt. Pepper*] and the record companies would jump behind the door. Now, A&R guys are calling me, asking what pictures are coming out."

Paramount's Gordon Weaver, whose company had spent nearly $3 million in promoting *Flashdance,* provided: "We incorporated the music into all of our radio and TV spots. If you have a single . . . [Irene Cara's "What A Feeling] playing on the radio, the spots are like cross-pollination." MTV was supplied with four short-form videos—"What a Feeling," "Imagination," "Maniac," and "Romeo." Polygram's Jack Kiernan reported that the album had gone platinum in a matter of weeks. In sum, the album and film were marketed to "sell one another."

Flashdance, according to MTV's Les Garland, was "the picture that brought all the studios into the music video field." Columbia Pictures' Colfax division executive Gary LeMel says, "Hollywood sees a way to get a lot of [free] advertising and marketing for its target audience. The target audience for MTV is the same target for pictures. You need the 12 to 25 demographic."[5]

Flashdance was the prototype; *Footloose* was the trend setter. *Footloose* provided a number of successful singles despite a universal view that "the clips were better than the movie." Harking to the monetary success of *Flashdance,* the *Footloose* campaign was on an overkill level version of hype. Al Teller, now CBS's Record Group president, noted that releasing five video-supported singles from the film was more than justified: "If we had followed the conventional staggered release pattern, we could have put out singles for a year." The overall quality of the movie motivated the following rationale: "We wanted the singles to be out while the movie was out."

Teller knew the visual, but the content of *Footloose* was weak. CBS capitalized on the movie's summer momentum. Kenny Loggins' title piece from *Footloose* was aired on MTV three months prior to the film's debut. CBS filmed Bonnie Tyler's "Holding Out for a Hero." *Footloose* created a number of hits by synergizing the visual audio aspects of the vehicle.

The film's promotional campaign spanned a spate of imitations. At the time, video costs ran $50,000 on average and MTV's ad rates were $2,000. A short-form clip (three to four minutes) would quickly pay for itself in exposure and ad rates.

There were economic difficulties, however. The budget for *Footloose* was $30,000 per song, which included licensing artists from competing labels. Shalamar and Sammy Hager were "rented" from WCI by CBS. One observer noted, "It was a smart ploy. After all WCI had control of MTV." And, as one advertiser maintained, "MTV's audience is the movie-going audience."

Trade magazines such as *Variety* were raising questions. A Richard Gold article was subheaded, "Some Fear Genre Overkill." An executive was quoted as saying, "I just read a script from a top studio about a corporate business falling apart and they wanted a rock 'n' roll soundtrack." The motion picture's subject did not warrant the talents of Phil Collins, Kenny Loggins, or Joe Jackson. "A video should enhance a song, not dominate it," wrote the once-feared ex-MTV director of programming Ronald "Buzz" Bindle of "Buzz's Basement" infamy.[6]

More MTVish films were born, in the hopes of emulating *Saturday Night Fever, Flashdance,* and *Footloose.* The outcomes were mixed. *Beat Street, Breakin,* and *Stayin' Alive* created havoc in film and record labels' accounting departments.

"When Doves Cry" by Prince introduced his pasted together video clips entitled *Purple Rain.* Once again film critics, visual and print, panned the movie. The album sold over ten million units. The strategy was to release the film three months after the hit "Doves" *single.* It worked. The film and music trade in the summer of 1984 highlighted the soundtrack phenomenon. Al Teller told *Billboard:* "The key marketing aspect has been the video trend. It can't be overestimated. Unlike records, which the public can sample over the airwaves, with movies you either see them or you don't. With the cost of advertising being what it is, the chance to put segments of films on the air is an important break from that limitation."[7]

"Underscoring used to be the key goal for music in films," said Russ Regan of Polygram. "The new generation of film makers aren't intimidated by music, and they realize that [music] can enhance a film rather than threaten it."

Other label executives were less optimistic. Some released album tracks prior to the movie release to dissociate the LP from the movie. Rick Springfield's *Hard to Hold* and *Against All Odds* were cited as tracks superior to the movies. But, they suffered from the theater-based response. RCA's Paul Atkinson, a general *zeitgeist,* summed it thusly: "I don't think we can market films, and I don't think [films] can sell records." Folks at MCA and Polygram certainly dissented from this view. Atkinson's remarks had merit. There exist a plethora of soundtracks that cannot stand by themselves. The *Chicago Tribune*'s Tom Popson raised an interesting question:

> Having gone to a movie theater and seen a film you enjoyed, it is always a pleasure to later encounter a soundtrack album from the film. Played during moments of leisure, the record summons up once again memorable scenes from the movie and sometimes even stirs the same emotions you felt in the theater. Two fine examples of this would be the soundtrack music from *Chariots of Fire* and *Rocky*.
>
> However, this experience of reliving a film by playing a record often is available only to those who attend movies that are either good or average. Those people who take pleasure in seeing really bad movies frequently find there is no soundtrack album they can play. This is understandable.
>
> Bad-movie fans, while certainly enthusiastic in their preferences, are a relatively small brigade greatly outnumbered by good-movie fans. If you were a big record-company executive, which audience would you try to tap with a soundtrack album?[8]

The answer, of course, was the largest psychographic market possible (i.e., MTV).

Ry Cooder's score to *Paris, Texas* stood alone minus the video. The *Miami Vice* TV compilation depended on the NBC services (more to follow). Soundtracks such as *Moscow on the Hudson,* a mix of country and western plus jazz, was a "stiff" lacking any continuity. Paul McCartney's *Board Street* visually was a distraction. The album, conversely, was far superior, if one excluded "Eleanor Rigby" (it was an aesthetic disaster when compared to the original).

The clip to promote Ray Parker Jr.'s video version of "Ghostbusters" included notable personalities *not* in the film. The clip reportedly boosted theater attendance by 20 percent. Frank Price, Universal Pictures president concluded, "There's no question that music as a promotional tool for pictures is going to be around indefinitely."[9]

Record labels are having second thoughts. The leasing of videos to market films has been a loss-leader, especially if the tune is a certified gold or platinum hit. Numerous labels, acknowledging the exposure value of films, also note the promotional expenses of video clips associated with the motion picture. "They're getting devious," said one "bizzer." "We're supposed to promote in some cases junk with expensive clips for acts that don't need it."

The marriage between the film and record industries was becoming fiesty. One was grumbling about licensing fees, the other about box office disasters that did nothing for an album. The saga of *Eddie and the Cruisers* is an illlustration. MTV, HBO, and TMC transformed a flop into a platinum hit.

John Cafferty and the Beaver Brown Band was an eleven-year-old band living off the frat bar East Coast circuit. They earned platinum wall hangings while still playing in clubs and beer-flowing Greek gatherings.

The Beaver Brown Band, led by John Cafferty, originated in 1973. They did Top Forty hits and the oldies: Fats Domino, Chuck Berry, Mitch Ryder, and Dion and the Belmonts.

"We kinda modeled ourselves after the energy of the J. Geils Band," says Cafferty. "Every song was about ninety miles an hour. For the first three years we were together I don't think we even knew a slow song!"

In 1977 Michael "Tunes" Autunes joined the band. He was the only member of the unit to actually appear in *Eddie and the Cruisers*. Autunes says, "They put a full-court press on me!" He became the sixth member of the Beaver Brown Band.

The group paid their dues. "We played every bar you could play in Rhode Island for a long time," said Cafferty, a short and slight man, sort of a leprechaun with a Kirk Douglas jaw and lengthy sideburns. "Then we branched out to Cape Cod and Boston, and basically just stayed around the area for four years. Finally, we got a job in New Haven, Connecticut. Somebody saw us there."

"There's an old show biz saying 'You gotta be great every night' because you never know who's in the audience," Caffety told *The Washington Post*. Cafferty recalls: "Kenny Vance was in the audience in the Other End one night about nine years ago. He never introduced himself." The stranger would play a large role in their future.

The film critics were not especially kind to the film. Comparisons were constantly made to Bruce Springsteen. Others found the plot thin or invoked the symbolism of the late Jim Morrison or the poetry of Bob Dylan. Mired in the teen-scream flood of summertime films, *Eddie* grossed an unimpressive $4.7 million, which in film terms is a loss. The soundtrack sold poorly. The album moved about 175,000 units—a figure that does not evoke or cause joy in the corporate boardrooms of record companies.

Enter the infant world of music video and cable television. The film was a flop. Renting unsuccessful motion pictures to cable networks is a tried-and-true method of regaining at least a part of a producer's loss.

Norman Hunter of the 152 Record Bar chain indicated that the cable exposure for *Eddie* jumped sales from twelve units to 4,581 albums in a period of four weeks.

Trade pieces on *Flashdance* and *Footloose* received attention at the NBC-TV West Coast headquarters. Brandon Tartikoff made the now famous notation "MTV Cops" on his memo pad or cocktail napkin, which ever story one accepts.

"MTV Cops": Miami Vice

"Friday Night Videos" on NBC-TV satisfied a baby-boom audience hungry for music clips. The cableless half of America could now see what they had been reading about.

Pittman's "mood" fascinated Brandon Tartikoff, the network's programming head. A bona fide Yuppie, he saw potential in a cop show series with an MTV atmosphere. Speaking with an *Esquire* writer, Tartikoff recalled, "I decided they were doing something special and after a week I overdosed on MTV. After I'd done that I called Anthony Yerkovich and Michael Mann and told them to put cops into it. The working title was 'MTV Cops.' "[10] He added, " 'Miami Vice' was really Hill and Renko with a music-video feel. That was where the idea began."[11]

The "MTV Cops" concept originally appeared on the executive's now famous memo pad, where "Cheers" and "The Bill Cosby Show" also originated, according to NBC publicist Brian Robinette. The actual storyboard details of the birth of the highly rated show are partially truth or fiction depending on the source.

Tartikoff is a product of the sixties. A liberal arts major in English, he graduated with honors from Yale University. One of his professors, Robert Penn Warren, suggested: "Have you ever thought of going into television?" He did. Beginning at a New Haven TV station, he connected with Chicago's WLS-TV and through Lew Erlich got an introduction to Fred Silverman. Silverman elevated Tartikoff to manager of dramatic development in 1976 at ABC-TV.

In September 1977, he was appointed an NBC director of comedy programming in Burbank. He became and served as protégé of Fred Silverman. Silverman, the man "who turned ABC around," experienced a stormy tenure at NBC. His "Super Train" brought Grant Tinker in as NBC head. Being in the Nielsen ratings' basement, Tinker and Tartikoff approved shows like "Hill Street Blues," "Cheers," St. Elsewhere," and encouraged producer Stephen Cannell to create TV's version of *The Dirty Dozen,* "The A-Team." The success of these programs was Tartikoff's patience. He frequently said, "Don't worry, we'll give it time."

The "MTV Cops" would differ from "Hill Street" or "Starsky and Hutch" because: "It will look so old-fashioned to you and you won't be able to figure out why. Then you'll realize that the reason it looks old-fashioned is that it's moving so slow." As he told *Washington Post* TV critic Tom Shales, "It'll be totally derivative, yet seem fresh. I use the term 'fresh' rather than 'original.' "

Tartikoff approached Kerry McCluggage, a Universal Television executive. He was the conduit to former supervising producer/writer of "Hill Street Blues," Anthony "Tony" Yerkovich. Some dispute the musical account, particularly Michael Mann, the executive producer, who has said: " 'Miami Vice' is set apart from other TV shows by its music. I've been asked if we are doing the same thing as MTV. We're not. If the whole video approach—stylized film along with song—is considered a movement, which it is, then you could say we're first cousins."[12] "MTV re-educated and expanded people's capacities and brought a new style of story-telling to the small screen," replied Yerkovich. Mann's characterization of Tony Yerkovich caused a minor furor in the wake of a *Rolling Stone* article.

Joel Sarnow, the show's story consultant, wrote: "As his weekly 'created by' credit indicates, Tony established the characters, narrative style, and the format of the show in his pilot script. Your assertion that Yerkovich was brought in to write a 'rough draft and teleplay' of the pilot is misleading and unfair to this fine writer."

Steve Bochco, "Hill Street" ex-producer whose tenure was on the cutting edge, joined producer Jeff Lewis in writing: "No one is more intimate with Tony Yerkovich's writing than we are . . . and you may rest assured that 'Miami Vice' was his creation, his script, his sensibilities." The name "Sonny Crockett" came from a "Hill Street" episode written by Yerkovich. The character, now played by Don Johnson, was a vice squad cop on "Hill Street." *Rolling Stone* apologized, noting that their story was based on the Michael Mann interview. *Esquire, TV Guide,* and the Burbank publicity people support the "MTV Cops"–"Hill Street" connection. The implementation is another matter. At Universal Pictures, Yerkovich was *the* creator of the successful Friday night show.

Yerkovich, after supervising the original five programs, explained to Denise Worrel:

> Even when I was on "Hill Street Blues," I was collecting information on Miami. I thought of it as sort of a modern-day American Casablanca. It seemed to be an interesting socioeconomic tidepool: the incredible

number of refugees from Central America and Cuba, the already extensive Cuban-American community, and on top of all that the drug trade.
There is a fascinating amount of service industries that revolve around
the drug trade—money laundering, bail bondsmen, attorneys who service drug smugglers. Miami has become a sort of Barbary Coast of free
enterprise gone berserk.

He provided the story line and environment, but Mann filled the
atmospherics. As director Lee Kazin said, "The show is written for an
MTV audience, which is more interested in images, emotions, and
energy than plot and character and words."[13]

To accommodate the music video audience, album cuts from groups
like the Rolling Stones, Foreigner, and artists such as Phil Collins, Tina
Turner, Glenn Frey, and Bob Seger were rented. The licensing costs
ranged into the five-figure range, depending on the status of the act.
Fred Lyle explained: "The people making these shows and watching
them are people in their late twenties, their thirties, who grew up on
rock and roll. Music is important in their life and so it's been incorporated into movies and TV." Bob Pittman couldn't have said it better.

Yerkovich sat down at his typewriter and constructed a two-hour
pilot he originally titled "Gold Coast." It aired Sunday, September 16,
1984 as "Miami Vice." The premiere episode found the two protago-
nists, Sonny Crockett (Don Johnson) and Richardo Tubbs (Philip
Michael Thomas), being brought together in pursuit of a drug kingpin,
Calderone. Tubbs, a New York detective, is after revenge for the
slaying of his brother on the streets of New York City. Crockett is an
undercover vice cop after the Colombian dealer. The subplot revolves
around Crockett's marital dissolution. In one of the most revealing
scenes he phones his estranged wife asking, "Once upon a time . . .
what was between us . . . it was real, wasn't it?" A long pause and
Caroline answers, "You bet, Sonny." Phil Collins' "In the Air Tonight" further enhanced the light-drenched public booth and the halt-
ing conversation given meaning by the crisp dialogue segued by
Collins' song. This would be one of the five episodes written by
Yerkovich for the series, concluding with "Calderone's Demise,"
which very effectively featured Tina Turner's "What's Love Got to Do
with It?"

Millions of Americans in the advertisers' magic 25 to 49 demographic turn on the TV set to "Miami Vice." An NBC spokesperson
characterized the show:

"Miami Vice" dramatizes police action unlike any other TV series.

Blending eye-catching imagery with a music-video score, the innovative series caught the collective attention of the television press even before its two-hour premiere in September, 1984. The consensus? "Miami Vice" takes chances in its stylized film technique, pace, storylines, acting and casting, all of which made it television's hottest new program.

The two stars, Don Johnson and Philip Michael Thomas, portray Detectives Crockett and Tubbs, respectively, two vice cops in Miami, FL, who form an unlikely team. Crockett, whose idealism is camouflaged by his burned-out sense of the reality that confronts him daily, is a former all-star football receiver at the University of Florida who now lives on a moored sloop with a dyspeptic pet alligator named Elvis.

Tubbs, a New York City transplant, is more even-tempered but equally enterprising in his detective work as he adjusts to the vibrant Miami scene.

Co-starring are Edward James Olmos (who joined the cast during the season) as the stoic, enigmatic Lt. Martin Castillo; Saundra Santiago and Olivia Brown appear as a female undercover team; and Michael Talbott and John Diehl play a more unconventional undercover duo.

A consensus of critics is that the appeal of "Miami Vice" revolves around the utilization of MTV imagery, *film noir,* and the employment of the rock genre aimed at baby boomers.

Driving his car, Mann heard ex-Eagle Glenn Frey's "Smuggler's Blues." The song was transformed into a storyboard. The award-winning musical video was then scripted by Michael Pinero and directed by former "Starsky and Hutch" costar Michael Paul Glaser. Frey was enlisted to appear in the episode portraying a pilot embroiled with Crockett and Tubbs in unraveling a drug-running ring.

The promotional value of the show was readily apparent. The single of "Smuggler's Blues" on May 7, 1985 was bulleting up the national charts, with the album, *The Allnighter,* close behind.

TV Guide critic Kenneth Turan expressed reservations, writing characters are "stuck with songs that don't particularly lend themselves to visual equivalents or . . . all the creativity went into the writing of the song, with the video version being kind of a throwaway afterthought." "We get the song that fits the scene, we don't try and jam Madonna down people's throats," disagreed Fred Lyle, associate producer and music coordinator.

Miami Vice did more than merely expose music. It became an instant fashion trendsetter and provided a vehicle for rock stars' acting aspirations. "The show has taken Italian men's fashion and spread it to mass America," Kal Ruttenstein, vice-president of Bloomingdales, told *Time.* "Sale of unconstructed blazers, shiny fabric jackets and light as colors have gone up noticeably." Fashion houses overtly and covertly marketing the Crockett and Tubbs look.

The impact of "Miami Vice" paralleled that of MTV as rock stars, athletes, and even Gordon Liddy, of Watergate infamy, have appeared on the program. Ted Nugent, who played a drug dealer on one episode, commented that the show as a platform was "a great opportunity for someone who wants to pursue acting, especially in my position because I'm rock 'n' roll and I can also infiltrate the music side of the show. But it's a show that utilizes the spirit of rock 'n' roll to help mold a mood in different scenes, as rock 'n' roll is certainly meant to do."[15]

MCA Records, under the same corporate umbrella as Universal Pictures, has prospered with soundtracks. "Miami Vice" was a natural. Composer Jan Hammer recalls, "Ever since the first episode I've gotten letters asking where people could buy the music. I've gotten letters from people in Nebraska, places you wouldn't think of as being hip, saying they love the music." The letters pushed the proper buttons.

Producer Danny Goldberg approached Michael Mann with the argument, "You're showcasing all this music. Why not create some original music and have a hit record?"

As "Vice-mania" escalated, the project was undertaken for a holiday season release. MCA Records in November 1985 announced:

> No television series has ever so immediately electrified audiences as "Miami Vice." Its riveting power flows in no small part from its producer's realization that mood and texture are as potent as plot and character to audiences whose lives are continually awash with nonverbal imagery. From abstract art to political "photo opportunities," from advertising to MTV, the message of form is recognized as equal to the message of content. There is nothing startlingly new in these observations, but the responsiveness of audiences to "Miami Vice's" high style underlines their accuracy.

> The series' style owes a great deal to its innovative use of popular music, both in Jan Hammer's sizzling instrumental themes and in the hit songs by established stars that stud each episode. MCA Records' *Miami Vice* Soundtrack collects the best of each into a package that thoroughly documents the show's groundbreaking aural power. Included are three never-before-heard songs from the series' season that begins in Fall 1985: Glenn Frey's "You Belong to the City," Chaka Khan's "Own the Night," and Grandmaster Melle Mel's "Vice." From the series' debut season, you will find Frey's "Smuggler's Blues," Tina Turner's "Better Be Good to Me" from her Grammy-award-winning *Private Dancer* LP, and Phil Collins' "In the Air Tonight."

The major guru behind the *Vice* soundtrack was Jan Hammer, the "Henry Mancini of the Eighties." In his 150-year-old farmhouse in upstate New York, working eighty hours a week, he wrote and recorded twenty minutes of original music. Included in the soundtrack album were three superlative examples of the scoring he has provided, "Flashback," "Evan," and "Chase," as well as two versions of the series scorching "Miami Vice Theme."

Hammer emigrated to the United States in 1968 from Czechoslovakia to attend the prestigious Berklee School of Music in Boston. Two years later, he was playing keyboards in the Sarah Vaughn Trio. He came to wide prominence as a member of the precedent-shattering Mahavishnu Orchestra, a jazz-rock fusion ensemble also featuring John McLaughlin and Billy Cobham. He has since earned several gold and platinum albums recording with the likes of Jeff Beck, Al Dimeola, and Neal Schon of Journey. He recently appeared as a sideman on Mick Jagger's debut solo album. "He is one of the most respected electric keyboardists in the world today and is acknowledged to be among the finest rock drummers as well. His musical skills incorporate those of a first-rate producer, engineer, composer, and arranger, talents that appear to make him uniquely qualified to score, produce, and arrange the music for each episode of "Miami Vice," announced MCA.

Besides his high-tech operation, Hammer with Fred Lyle also had the money to license atmospheric contemporary songs, ranging from $10,000, for the mood of the cop show.

"We treat the music we use with respect," notes Fred Lyle. "It's never gratuitous. Instead of doing the whole show and letting Frey's song tell all the pain and the anguish of being a smuggler at the end, over the credits, like you'd expect on TV, we're using the song maybe eight times throughout the show. You're in a scene, and all of a sudden up comes Frey, singing, 'It's the lure of easy money. It's got a very strong appeal.' And you're out again. It's like a Greek chorus." A press release further exclaimed: "The highly charged songs underline the emotions conjured by the narrative and compliment the glamorous fashionable pastel palette of the series' now-famous 'lock.' They also match the mature, often ambiguous moral themes that 'Miami Vice' so often confronts. The show offers few black-and-white judgments; its peacock colors are an ironic veneer over the grayish half-light in which much of its action takes place."

Another view comes from Thomas Carter, who directed the two-hour pilot film:

> What I wanted to do was not to use music as just background but as psychological subtext, if you will. What I felt was happening to Crockett at one point was he had lost touch with reality. His marriage had fallen apart, and he had discovered that his ex-partner was leaking information to the bad guys. So I said, I want to do a sequence with Crockett and

Tubbs in a car, lay some music over it, and I think they should drive somewhere. I came up with the idea of using a Phil Collins tune, "In the Air Tonight." That is probably the prototypical "Miami Vice" sequence.[16]

As MTV was contesting the 1985 Nielsens, TV executives were seriously looking at "Miami Vice" costs. As of spring 1986, Universal was considering utilizing the local southern California environment for filming to reduce expenses. The film company was receiving $950,000 from NBC for each "Miami Vice" segment. Universal's budget called for $1.4 million; four episodes ran near $2 million while Mann was away filming *Red Dragon.* Universal's deficit had doubled since the opening in September 1984, according to a studio spokesperson.

Tartikoff's response to a *Los Angeles Times* reporter to the possible site change was, "What's left unsaid here is that Universal has to get a little better at their business. And I don't know if that's their problem anyway—the expense of doing it in Miami. It's an expensive show no matter where you did it."[17]

On April 11, 1986 an unusual announcement followed the drama: the show would be renewed for a third fall season and produced in Miami, dispelling the industry and media speculation. The low-rated, but quality show, *Hunter,* renewed at the same time, did not receive similar treatment. The principals were unavailable for comment. One insider suggested that the success of the soundtrack was a potential gold mine, not to mention the various merchandising strategies already in the pipeline. There was also the question of syndication.

"Miami Vice's" fortunes may well be tied to its mid-wife MTV, a network reportedly losing $7 million in advertising. One observer gave "Miami Vice" high grades over MTV, saying: "MTV's short-forms have no continuity, whereas "Miami Vice" has a plot with attractive characters on a major network." "They need more shows," the source remarked. MTV expanded: "Just as this series is in the creative forefront of today's television, the music contained on the *Miami Vice* Soundtrack album is representative of the very finest popular music. The range is wide, from the bittersweet musings of Glenn Frey to the furious street truth of Grandmaster Melle Mel, but the impact is always direct and irresistible. A hundred years from now, when they inquire about the music of the '80s, this album will stand as an extraordinary sampler."

Several imitators were briefly aired unsuccessfully by ABC-TV: "Hollywood Beat" and "The Insiders," a quasi-*Rolling Stone* saga of two hip reporters. Neither ran longer than the initial option pick-up period.

The longevity of the "Miami Vice" series appears to hinge on script quality (many insiders want Yerkovich to return) and the charisma of the cast, especially Don Johnson. Only time and the "numbers" will tell.

They Wear What They Watch: MTV and Fashions

MTV is "almost a subliminal fashion show," said Judy McGrath, creative director. "Rock stars are always on the cutting edge. They incorporate signals of what's coming." "Michael Jackson, Cyndi Lauper, and Boy George are fashion plates. They create new looks," noted CBS' Eliot Hubbard. Larry Levanthal, editor of *Kids Fashions*: "MTV has had a big impact on children's clothing. It has saturated the maket. Kids are becoming more sophisticated."[18] Merchandisers and designers couldn't agree more, pointing to the influence of MTV. "Preschool children know fashion. They're exposed to MTV and Madonna even before they can walk and talk," added Sally Fischer of Benetton. "With video, it's an era of instant communication," observed Ilene Abata, fashion director of Woodward & Lothrop, a department store chain. "Kids see what the stars are wearing tonight, and they want to wear it tomorrow."[19]

Children's fashion advisor for J.C. Penney Debra Chambliss noted: "Rock video is really driving the children's market right now. . . . Whatever the rock stars are wearing, kids are trying to emulate them. For girls, the rock video fad means neon brights and lots of layers, parachute pants with zippers, grommets and hardware. . . . For boys, we're seeing parachute pants in shiny fabrics. Red fleece tops with black insets—even for the eight-year-olds."

The emulation of entertainment media celebrities is nothing new. The hair styles of Veronica Lake and Rita Hayworth were copied by millions of female filmgoers in the 1940s. Music in the 1950s created some mini-fashions or fads, such as the Elvis Presley duck-tail (D.A.) haircut. Elvis' infrequent television and costumed appearances in films and guest shots did little for the fashion industry. The popularization of clothing fads is a creation of visuals, albeit in magazines, films, or television.

"Shindig," "Hullabaloo," and "Laugh-In" during the mid-1960s brought Twiggy-like mini dresses and bell-bottom trousers to the fore. It wasn't the music itself, but the screen image. Paul Kantner, then with the Jefferson Airplane, recalled: "We were never in the fashion, but we were conscious of what we wore. That's part of the fun of rock and roll: to surprise and shock people." The group's paisley shirts became the "in" thing. Fads such as London's Carnaby Street, Mary Quant, and Twiggy faded with the advent of the 1970s. David Bowie's persona was revolutionary. His androgynous look was at least a decade before its time, until the advent of Boy George and Michael Jackson. T-shirts and jeans were the teen uniforms of the 1970s, prior to *Saturday Night Fever* when disco clothing—white suit, black shirt—hit the department store racks.

Vivienne Westwood, an ex-school teacher from the northern part of England, and rock manager and promoter Malcolm McLaren collaborated in a boutique to create the "punk" look. McLaren managed the infamous Sex Pistols. Their creations stressed nihilism and anarchistic designs. The fashion, more precisely fad, did not cross the Atlantic with a great deal of acceptance. The punkish designs fared as badly as the Pistols' aborted tour. Only in New York or Los Angeles, particularly, did they garner much support.

Several years later Westwood introduced the "pirate" look popularized by Stuart Leslie Goddard (a/k/a Adam Ant), who was an early fixture on MTV. Bow Wow Wow, who appeared on the first New Year's Rock and Roll Ball for the music network, another McLaren client, also sported the roguish clothing. In 1983 the "Buffalo Gals" appearance underscoring preindustrial society with sheepskin vests began to infiltrate music videos.

The return of heavy metal and the ever-present Billy Idol on music video clips moved black leather out of the "outlaw" C&W environment into the metalers' domain. Chains and studded collars purchased at pet shops were equally part of the regalia. Jo Bergman, discussing a visit to London, says: "Everything looked familiar. I'd seen it all on MTV." The sales value of music video was not lost in the fashion world. In January 1983 *Men's Wear* warned, "It's a trend traditional retailers can't afford to ignore. The best advice is to test—and watch MTV." Ironically, the fashion industry trade realized the merchandising value of the music channel before some record labels and Madison Avenue.

"I Keep Looking At You" appeared on "Basement Tapes" in May 1983, two months after the debut of the contest show. The over-the-transom video professionally done by Spectrum Associates depicts a fashion show, models displaying a new line of clothing. The contestant was designer Lloyd Allen, known in the garment industry for his sportswear creations. The tape was picked up and rotated on the normal MTV playlist. Epic released the song as a single.

A more surrealistic vision of the fashion milieu, reportedly, appeared on the playlist produced by Leslie Allen. Her husband's song was "We

Keep Pumping." An MTV spokesperson told *Ad Age,* "The channel is advertiser-supported. The bottom line for consideration of any submission is always the music. There is no place for 'just fashion.' " Lloyd and Leslie Allen were ideally qualified for the clips. She was a television producer and Lloyd had played guitar since the age of twelve. Allen's MX clothing line was aimed at MTV viewers. Leslie Allen cautioned competitors that video clips were expensive. She was in a position to bring in a video for about $40,000. Designers without television industry spouses would have to travel the usual production route with all of the inherent costs involved.

Leslie Allen's caveat was generallly ignored. Norma Kamali showcased her swimwear with four videos produced for in-store display. "Fall Fantasy" was a quarter-hour long-form clip directed by Francis Kenny, best known for "Can't Stop Dancing," and his work with Cyndi Lauper plus Huey Lewis and the News. "The Shoulder Pad Song" from the video was being considered as a possible submission for the MTV rotation. It never got past the Acquisitions Committee. Despite this minor setback, Kamali continued with videos, corraling Carly Simon, a client, to perform six songs for her seventh video for the fall 1985 line.

Just as shopping mall boutiques blared AOR music in the late 1960s for atmosphere, music videos began appearing at the "point of purchase." Talk of an MTV-style cable show was being discussed. Ted Turner reportedly was planning a pilot of an MTVish video show tentatively titled "Images," supported by Williwear and other "houses." CNN was already doing as interview and runaway fashion show called *"Style with Elsa Klensch."* The program, however, was traditional "show and tell" endemic to the all-news cable network. A *Newsweek* reporter noted, despite the cost of videos—some in the $150,000 range: "Just a few years ago music videos helped revive a sluggish record business. Now, with the apparel industry suffering from heavy price cutting and consumer malaise, designers hope their tapes can provide Fashion Avenue with the same life."[20]

The marketing ploy was adopted by many of the major designers, such as Willie Smith of Williwear, Henry Grethel, Ralph Lauren, Daniel Hechter, Jeffery Banks and of course Ms. Kamali. The settings for the short- and long-form videos were as exotic as those in Duran Duran or David Bowie clips. Senegal, Kenya, and foggy London were employed as production sites. The short-forms were basically for CNN news bites and the Klensch Saturday morning half-hour show. The long-forms were aimed at clothing stores with a theater and cable television potential.

The fashion industry was planning four thirty-minute TV programs with eight selections by a division of the Ohlmeyer Ad agency. In charge of the fashion section was Sandy Pittman. Mrs. Robert Pittman told *U.S. News,* "We make it worth the designer's while to produce videos because we've got the air time." She went on to indicate that videos for CNN and other cable networks or syndication were in the preparation stage. Merchandisers were fairly enthusiastic. "Fashion videos are going to become a major part of selling," said a Bloomingdale's executive. "There has been a tremendous rise in business where videos play continuously," noted Pat Papock of Anne Klein II.[21]

The Associated Merchandising Corporation urged its member retailers to feature "MTV boutiques." Macy's in New York opened shops titled Madonnaland and Girls Just Want to Have Fun, named after the Lauper video hit. When Madonna closed her national tour in New York Macy's sold out her licensed garments and jewelry in two days. Fashion magazine scribes in early 1986 were predicting a return to the psychedelic styles of the days of the counterculture of the 1960s. Judy McGrath of MTV concurred, pointing to videos by the Dream Academy and The Cult. The influence of MTV-inspired videos will be tested by these predictions as both acts are being rotated on the network and have albums on the *Billboard* charts. There is no doubt that MTV was the prototype for a marketing strategy on Fashion Avenue. Karla Alexander, manager of internal media in an Ohio Hudson's store, cautions: "Whether it's a fad or a marketing tool remains to be seen."

In March 1986 *Newsweek*'s fashion critic provided partial answer, quoting designer Jasper Conran: "After looking into a closet of outrageous clothes for so long, there comes a time you just can't face it anymore."[22]

"You Play the Guitar on the MTV": The Artists

Prior to the famous Warner-Amex brass meeting on the founding of the music television network, the second annual Billboard Music Conference was held in Universal City. One of the panels, "Recording Artists Who Are Shaping Their Own Video Future," dealt with the value of music videos in career development. Notably absent were American pioneers such as Todd Rundgren, who made a long-form video to promote *The Hermit of Mink Hollow,* and Mike Nesmith, the ex-Monkee with *Elephant Parts.* Participating were Mike Cotton of the Tubes, Leon Russell, and Bob Geldof of the Boomtown Rats. Their reactions to video clips were mixed. "There is a problem with musicians handling video," said Cotton. "Some don't have much to say musically, let alone visually. There's little hope for video albums or video shows. They lack the essential feeling of immediacy. You look at a tape, you get bored after two or three showings." The Tubes' view related that of much of the artistic community in regards to television in general. Bob Geldof, referring to the RCA plan for video disks, observed: "A year ago I thought video albums might be as important as the talkies were to the silent movies. I no longer see that as absolutely true. I will listen to audio time and time again. But I can watch a video only three or four times. . . . I don't want to sound too pessimistic to you business types. . . . Video won't be that effective for promo." Russell, with a Burbank video studio, was cautiously optimistic. He noted the historical importance of videos: "I've always wanted to capture events as accurately as possible. Elvis was a dance. If we were left with the 'Ed Sullivan Show,' we wouldn't know that."

These arguments would be echoed when Lack, Sykes, and Pittman blanketed the labels pitching MTV as a "promotional" vehicle. The record companies' original response was "Why Free?" videos. CBS was the hardest sell, but Lack was able to use some contracts to persuade Black Rock to supply the videos, although Al Teller remained skeptical. "Record companies are still unconvinced about a visual medium," summed up Jo Bergman. "Period."

Following the Fort Lee debut field reports found artists showcased on MTV selling in markets not serviced by AOR playlists. Reports from the network test markets and trade magazine reports promoted the artists and MTV. *Billboard* headlined, "MTV Cable spurs Disk Sales of Artists Aired" (October 10, 1981). Similar stories appeared frequently in the music trades throughout 1982. MTV's credibility was eventually established when the network finally broke the cable barrier in Manhattan and Los Angeles by early 1983. Rumors of groups such as Styx taking acting lessons abounded. By August 1983 labels and artists were singing the praises of the channel. Brian Setzer of the Stray Cats told the *Washington Post,* "College radio and MTV were the only two sources that were hip to us: promoters couldn't understand why we had no airplay and were selling out on our first tour" (November 25, 1982). MTV's Les Garland couldn't agree more: "Their manager told me he even plotted their tour by the markets MTV serves, and they sold something like 200,000 records without any significant radio exposure. Once radio kicked in, they took it that much further." Singer Bob Welch, formerly with Fleetwood Mac, said:

"MTV sure makes a difference in visibility. I've had kids come back after a concert and tell they were first exposed to my music on MTV."

"If you're not on MTV, then to a large share of music consumer, you just don't exist," reported Polygram's Len Epand. He originally opposed the promotional value of MTV. Even Epic Records credited the success of Adam Ant to the network. Artists heaped piles of praise on MTV, some of it politically inspired, no doubt.

The cost of videos was beginning to impact on the performers, as labels were increasingly requiring groups to foot 50 percent of the production costs as recoup money. Hall and Oates' manager Tommy Motolla viewed MTV as boosting album sales by 40 percent and "concert interest is stimulated as well." Daryl Hall expressed reservations: "Over the past year, the tail has started to wag the dog. The importance of the visual has begun to overpower the music."

"I write and try to create something that's complete. Once the record is done to me I've told the story," says Billy Joel. "The mood is complete. I've created the whole picture. A lot of times having to come up with a video idea is sort of defacing my own art."

Other artists began to express reservations about videos. The *tour de force* came from Joe Jackson, whose "Steppin' Out" video, produced by Steve Barron, was a hit. In a *Billboard* "Commentary" of June 16, 1984, Jackson outlined his reasons for "not making a promo video." "What it's become, in my opinion," he wrote, "is a shallow, tasteless and formulized way of selling music which, often, can't stand on its own." He went on to chronicle a number of perceived grievances:

> Things which used to count, such as being a good composer, player or singer, are getting lost in the desperate rush to visualize everything. It's now possible to be all of the above and still get nowhere simply by not looking good in a video or, worse still, not making one.

> Also, many artists lose their credibility and/or self respect by coming across as bad actors rather than as good musicians. One result of this is that artists are now being signed for their video potential rather than for their musical talent.

Dan Beck of Portrait Records, a member of the CBS Group, confirmed this to the *Wall Street Journal:* "Cyndi [Lauper] was signed because she'll be a great film performer; she has the dynamics to create interesting visuals."[23] Madonna, Grace Jones, and others partially were signed because they could "project an image."

Jackson equally objected to the impact of video on live performances where the artist could not duplicate a video clip's technical embellishments. Chicago film critic Gene Siskel said: "I think that they're affecting even live performances—someone who books live acts in clubs . . . said that the music videos are disappointing people when they go and see the live performers, because the performers live aren't as interesting. I think this is distancing people from people."

The costs and demands of videos also raised Jackson's ire:

> I was recently told that had it not been for the success of my last album, I would not be able to release a single in Australia unless there was an accompanying video. This is now standard record company policy. More established artists who have not built careers on videos are also affected as they are pressured to compete, often with disastrous results.

> As videos get more and more expensive, a "play-it-safe" strategy becomes more evident. No one wants to break the formula, and it will only get more difficult for anything different or innovative to break through.

> I am not attempting to put down all videos. There are a handful that I even like! Nor would I deny visually oriented artists a vital means of expression (if I could dance like Michael Jackson I might be making a video right now). What I object to is the way desperation and greed are blowing the importance of video way out of proportion.

> Voicing these opinions to various people in the music business, I've met with some surprisingly nervous reactions. I'm made to feel like some sort of heretic. Many people agree with me, but are afraid to buck the system and maybe make less money.

> Fear and greed are not good bases for a creative artist to work from.

Says Bob Dylan, "I know they're thought of as an art form, but I don't think they are." He strongly objected to the content: "They're on and they're over too fast." Cost was another factor. He added, "I never know what anybody's doing with me. . . . When I saw a shot of me from my mouth to my forehead on that screen. I figure, 'I got somethin'? I'm paying for that?"[24]

Rock 'n' Roll Confidential supported Jackson, as did some readers of *Billboard*. One expressed the feeling: "Record companies are courting MTV as though it were the mind of every kid in America. They must be saying, 'This is what you must think of when you hear this song.' Who would have known that Big Brother in 1984 would turn out to be MTV?" Jon Small, Billy Joel's producer, concurred, although not for quite the same reasons. "MTV is like muscle TV," he told Tony Seidman. "We love them" for starting the music video mania, but he resented the network's power.

Jackson's letter uncorked the genie from the bottle. Ricky Tripp of the Tripps Brothers Band, without a record affiliation, wrote: "Let's remember that *Thriller* sold 35 million [sic] *records* not *videos*." Tripp neglected the obvious statistic—only 15 million VCRs were in use in 1984.

MTV was surprisingly silent on this issue. Having just fought the "exclusivity" battle, they were not anxious to cross swords with disgruntled artists. They expected and received support from the makers of music videos. Len Epand of Polygram contributed a lengthy reply to the "Commentary" page (July 7, 1984). The label's general manager attempted to refute Jackson's charges:

> I make my living in MV, yet I agree with Jackson on certain points. There are many ill-conceived, badly performed and socially offensive song videos. But Jackson draws the wrong conclusions and errs in damning an entire nascent medium with sweeping statements that miss what is really going on—even if he does allow that there are some videos he likes. . . .
>
> More to the point, visuals don't distract or detract from music; they do the reverse. They heighten music's impact, demanding more attention on the song and performance; hence, a great record that may have gone unnoticed has much greater chances of success if properly promoted as a hot video. Hence, too, a terrible video interpretation could murder it. MV remains a music-driven medium.
>
> At MTV, one of our most critical avenues of exposure (if you're not on, that means millions of people may not know you exist), programming is determined as much by a record's radio and chart success as by the audience's response to its visual niftiness. (Which explains, too, why an average quality video occasionally may receive a disproportionately high amount of play.)
>
> Lastly, there's the success of MV-styled and promoted feature films. Here film has grown more dependent upon music, now relying increasingly on record people to program its audio components. Reverse devaluation? No. The synthesis is yielding a growing percentage of hit records and films because a good marriage of music and imagery augments the potency of each.
>
> After considering all of this, my reaction to Joe Jackson's comments turned sanguine. I have to be pragmatic. With our roster of artists beating down the doors to make videos and get them shown, we need every available TV slot. Thanks to Joe, we'll have a few more.
>
> But I also appreciate Jackson's courage, which does MV the biggest favor of all—it helps take it down from its sacred cow status, a needed step towards its maturation.
>
> I look forward to the day when MV is no longer primarily the bastard child of marketing, when MV artists and a community of creative

professionals will prosper in a fun, satisfying business, a business that entertains its own audience with a diversity of affordable, high-value video records. It'll happen just as surely as radio gave way to television and yet remained a healthy and purposeful medium.

In the same way, MV and music will continue to coexist and feed off each other with vitality long after the media hoopla has eloped with the next big thing.

At the Sixth *Billboard* Video Music Conference held in Pasadena artists frequently seen on MTV lent their support. They praised music videos and MTV, with some qualifications. Martha Davis of the Motels commented, "Being able to act out vignettes is wonderful." "I try to have fun with my video work. I try not to take it seriously," said fellow panelist Grace Slick. "Weird Al" Yankovic, whose music successes can be directly linked to videos, noted: "I think video is a cool thing."

The Motel's spokesperson disapproved of "exclusives." Ms. Davis noted: "Many places do not receive MTV. Personally, I would like those locations to get a chance to watch my new single." One member of the audience mumbled, "Note David Benjamin" [producer of 'Friday Night Videos']. NBC-TV was the only telecommunications avenue capable of penetrating most of the national markets.

Commenting on VH-1 ex-Doors member Ray Manzarek said: "Adult contemporary? What does that mean? Less sex . . . I'm an adult, so give me something hot, I can take the heat."

MTV's February 1985 decision to curtail heavy metal clips aroused considerable protest. Artists complained long and loud to *Heavy Rock* (originally titled *Rock Video*) and *Hit Parader* magazines.

A more significant dissent came from Wilfred Jung, EMI's Music Ltd. managing director for central Europe—the cradle of music video. He wrote in the "Commentary" section of the April 2, 1985 issue of *Billboard:*

> I think it is about time that the record industry kissed video clips goodbye and concentrated on the job of producing good records.
>
> That may sound like heresy or sheer naivete in this audio/visual age, or maybe it will just be construed as heretical by the television companies.
>
> Could there be some record company executives out there who, while accepting that music videos are an expensive fact of life, would nevertheless not shed a tear if they could opt out of the video rat-race for good?
>
> After all, who really needs these massively expensive and highly ephemeral productions? It occurs to me that good records always managed to sell in the past without the aid of video clips, and the most imaginative,

ingenious and staggeringly expensive clip in the world won't make a hit out of a bad record. Or at least, I am not aware that such a miracle has ever occurred.

The problem, like so many business problems, is that nobody is going to take the lead in jumping off the bandwagon. "As long as my competitors are wasting prodigious amounts of money, I have to do the same" is the contemporary philosophy we all seem to embrace.

What keeps the video myth intact is that nobody can really measure to what extent a music video stimulates the sale of any given single or album. What certainly can be demonstrated, however, is that television companies love music videos and are not noticeably dismayed by the fact that the cost of producing them is borne by the record companies.

I am sure the record industry would be able to survive and prosper without video clips, and so can the true artists. I am aware that there are some acts who see themselves not merely as musical artists, but also as actors of epic caliber.

On the other hand, there are artists who deplore the music industry's current preoccuption with music videos and would prefer to concentrate on presenting their music in the—dare I say it—old fashioned non-theatrical way.

One final grumble about the video age: Isn't it unsatisfactory that music videos inhibit the consumer from building his own thought pictures around a song? Wouldn't it be better to let people exercise their own individual imagination?

Jung's viewpoint had considerable merit when applied to the United Kingdom, the Commonwealth nations, and the European continent. These nations, with a limited number of government controlled TV outlets, exhibited music programming akin to the restrictive Top 40 AM singles-oriented radio stations of the mid-1960s in the United States.

Many American record executives and artists privately saw MTV in the same light. However, MTV served two functions: propelling exposure—and hopefully sales—plus rejuvenating the artist's faith in the label's marketing and promotional abilities. Despite the grumblings and dissatisfactions expressed, there is little doubt that MTV did "break" a number of artists, especially in the early days. Veejay Martha Quinn's boast that MTV exposure aided Cyndi Lauper, Duran Duran, The Thompson Twins, Billy Idol, and others has considerable merit.

Success on "Basement Tapes" provided groups such as The Triplets with an audience base and a record contract. Lloyd Allen used the same program to sell himself and a fashion line to a label, and the MTV rotation. MTV's original pre-Pon slogan "You'll never look at music the same way again" was valid, at least in the early years. For artists,

MTV maintains its exposure clout in over 27 million households. Could it do the same for societal betterment?

Charity and Promotion MTV Style

Over the years MTV aired a number of public service announcements (PSA) ranging from the "Feel the Power" campaign to antidrug and cancer drives. The causes were laudable and helped MTV's image.

MTV launched a voter registration push in 1984 from September 9 through the first week of October. Contributing over $1 million in ad time, thirty-second spots stressing the slogan, "Feel the Power," were aired featuring Cyndi Lauper, Huey Lewis and the News, the Motels, and others. Crosby, Stills, and Nash performed a special song, as did Peter Wolf, and the Pointer Sisters recorded a political adaption of their hit "Jump."

Promoter Tom Sexton observed, "What we created were voter videos [with] very strong messages, nonpartisan ones." Sexton and Goldmine Records' Danny Goldberg took this concept to Les Garland. He concurred. Goldberg stated: "Most of the credit has to go to Les and to MTV . . . we could have sat around idealizing until we were blue in the face." Some 200,000 900-number calls were received requesting voter information.

Starting November 14, one-minute drug abuse spots were aired twice daily using characters from the *Gremlins* film. The ads ran for two weeks until Thanksgiving.

MTV Rock 'n' Roll To Go, a record anthology released in January 1985 and heavily promoted by the channel, promised $2.50 per unit in charitable contributions for cancer research. This project was the brainchild of Elektra's Bob Krasnow and Robert Pittman. Fourteen major labels and artists participated in the campaign and more than 350,000 copies were sold.

A cosponsor in the PSA programs suggested that artists had discovered a new social awareness, although he did admit that the music industry as a whole was "a little irresponsible" and "jaded."

Band Aid, USA for Africa, and Live Aid

Irresponsibility was put aside in the several attempts to aid the starving population of famine-struck Ethiopia.

One of the chief functions of mass media is agenda setting. As Will Rodgers once equipped, "All I know is what I read in the papers." So began the Ethiopian artistic crusade.

The drought in Ethiopia had been acute for years prior to Michael Buerk's October expose on the BBC-TV. The footage of skeletonesque dying children shocked viewers. One was Bob Geldof, a brash leader of the Irish punk rock group the Boomtown Rats. He recalls an image on the broadcast of an emaciated child with flies buzzing around his eyes. "That one image is what made me do the whole thing," he says. The Boomtown Rats had rehearsed "It's My World." The lyrics were changed during a taxi ride in a short twenty minutes. The new title was, "Do They Know It's Christmas/Feed the World." Midge Ure of Ultravox cowrote the tune to a medium-fast rhythm reminiscent of Eddie and the Hot Rods. Geldof said: "If the Rats had done the same record, it would have been a hit. So I have to get the stars."

Geldof recruited forty British artists by "moral blackmail." Present at the all-nighter were Phil Collins, Paul Young, Boy George, and Simon LeBon, among others. The single grossed $10 million. It received extensive MTV rotation despite the controversial line, "Well tonight thank God it's them instead of you." U2's Bono, at the hurried London session, asked, "Are you sure this is what you want me to sing?" *Village Voice* critic Robert Christgau characterized the line as "appalling." "There'a bit of irony," retorted the fiesty Irishman, "you would not wish this on anyone."

NBC-TV telecast the BCC footage with forceful results, particularly during the prime news time dinner-hour schedule. The wheels were in motion for what would become the United Support of Artists for Africa (USA for Africa).

The historic "We Are the World" session took place at the A&M studios located on the Charlie Chaplin sound stage, beginning at 10:00 P.M. (PST) January 28 after a pep talk from Geldof, following the American Music Awards telecast. The session ended after ten hours. The result was a single and several videos.

Geldof had considered the idea but due to his poor American credibility decided he couldn't pull it off. "From their point of view, it's like Joe Blow calling up, and they figured, as John Lennon said, you get benefited to death! They don't know me, but if Ken Kragen calls up they know it's kosher. They know that Lionel and Quincy will be there and that you're gonna have a good show."

In America Geldof was perceived as a hot head with a "big mouth." This he acknowledges came from the first Rats tour in the States. "We had done very well, thank you, around the rest of the world," he recalls, "and in my youthful arrogance I assumed America would fall. But I was stupid! I was moaning about radio, I was moaning about the press, I was being rude, and the Americans just told me to fuck off."

Geldof, who had his CBS record contract cancelled in late 1985 after being nominated for the Nobel Peace Prize, was the inspiration, but it was Harry Belafonte who ignited the "We Are the World" venture.

Belafonte, following in the footsteps of the late Harry Chapin, was devoted to the cause of eradicating world hunger. He had visited Ethiopia, posing as a Caribbean. Returning to the States, Belafonte decided some action must be undertaken. "After the success of Band Aid, and particularly Bob Geldof, it was obvious that USA for Africa was an idea whose time had come. The power of artists is unlimited," he said. Harry wanted to do a benefit concert with black performers. He called promoter Ron Delsener. Delsener suggested he contact manager Ken Kragen.

Kragen, "the event organizer," who had represented Chapin, re-called: "This all started with a phone call from Harry Belafonte . . . Harry and I discussed the concert idea." Kragen was apprehensive. A concert would not raise a great deal of money. "I suggested an American version of Band Aid. No one had a license on this concept . . . in fact we felt that Band Aid had broken the ground and made it much easier for us to do it now." He contacted his client Lionel Richie and wife Brenda. "They loved the idea," said Kragen. "They had been thinking about doing something for several weeks."

The recruiting process began using the nucleus of Kragen's roster of artists:

The next day, Brenda [Richie] was in a store shopping for Christmas gifts. In walked Stevie Wonder, who asked her to help him pick out some things. She said, "Not until you call my husband." They got Lionel in the doctor's office, and Stevie agreed to work with Lionel on the song. In the meantime I called Quincy and asked him to produce. Quincy then called Michael Jackson to see if he would appear on the song, and Michael said he wanted to work with Lionel and Stevie on writing it as well. (As it turned out, Stevie didn't write the song with Michael and Lionel, because he had to go away. But he has stayed involved all along.)

I called Harry back about 36 hours after his initial phone call to me, and I said, "I have a song by Michael Jackson, Lionel Richie and Stevie Wonder, produced by Quincy Jones. Kenny Rogers and a couple of my other clients, Lindsey Buckingham and Kim Carnes, have agreed to participate. Now I'm going to start looking for other people." Harry said, "I can't believe it!"

Deciding to do the recording on the night of the American Music Awards, Jan. 28th, was perhaps the key decision that I made. It was a perfect way to make sure that I could get the maximum number of artists to take part. I knew that a number of key artists would be at the American Music Awards. I also knew that there were certain artists who would attract the others into the project: Michael, Lionel, Stevie, Bruce Springsteen.[25]

Getting "The Boss" was pivotal. "The turning point was Springsteen's commitment. That legitimized the project in the eyes of the rock community," said Kragen. "He has tremendous credibility, and I really think that helped attract a lot of other artists." The event organizer pulled the usual organizational strings. Still Kragen credits Geldof with instilling the power of social change in the rock industry. He remembers a comment of Geldof's: "We in the music business have made drugs fashionable; we've made wild hair styles fashionable; we've made unusual clothes fashionable." Now the task was consciousness raising about world hunger, especially in southern Africa.

Belafonte and Kragen set the wheels rolling. Forty-five unpaid artists would have to create "We Are the World." The actual song has been described by critics as "more moral than musical" *(Los Angeles Herald Examiner)* and "No more than lowest-common denominator AOR dignified with a religious tinge and put in the service of toothless one-worlder do-goodism" *(Village Voice).* Quincy Jones, who produced the record, summed up the event in a short full-page *Billboard* letter. It read:

> A special thank you to the singers, musicians, organizers and crew
> • for checking your egos at the door and filling the studio with immense love and talent.
> • for giving so much to those whose needs are so great.
>
> It is no accident that you are considered the very best.
>
> In my 35 years in the business, nothing will ever top this for me.
>
> I love you all,
> Quincy Jones

Basically, Jones' letter captured the event as well as *Making of "We Are the World."* Some ego-mania did surface, however, as to row placement and the nonappearance of Prince. Geldof lived up to his reputation of having an enormous Irish temper. "He didn't come. Why not?" he railed at reporter Michael Goldberg. "That's the question. Has he got other things that are more important than trying to save people's lives? Going to a disco?"[26]

Several publicity people explained Prince's notable absence by saying, "He's a very, very private person." In a rare interview with Neal Karlen, he was asked about missing the taping. "No. I think I did my part in giving my song [for the album]. I *hope* I did my part. I think I did the best thing I could do."

By July 1985 the two all-night sessions generated a gross of over $60 million for famine relief and other projects.

MTV played a major role in exposing the video material from "We Are the World" and "Do They Know It's Christmas?" Pittman was happy to describe the network's role, with a tinge of self-promotion thrown in:

> Many of you have heard me talk about MTV—and how exposure on MTV can help sell records. Our viewers are intensely loyal—they care about the best video music—but their caring goes much further than that. They care about their world and want to be involved in decisions about their future.

> So today we're proud to be using MTV's exposure to help in a different way, for another purpose—a purely humanitarian purpose. It's all part of a massive, coordinated effort from the music industry called USA for Africa, developed to send famine relief to Africa. From artists to technicians to distributors to record industry executives and employees to radio to MTV—everyone is giving what they can to help this cause. When each person gives a little, the result can be synergistic—much greater than the sum of its parts.

> MTV's donation to the campaign revolves around a substantial amount of national air time. First, we presented the world premiere of the USA for Africa music video, "We Are The World," on March 11. The video then went immediately into MTV's heavy rotation, which maximizes audience exposure to and awareness of the cause, and which generates direct contributions to the fund as well as sales of the "We Are The World" record, the profits of which all go to USA for Africa.

> Following the MTV world premiere came our donation of time for a saturation campaign of public service announcements, asking for direct donations to the relief fund.

> Next, MTV Music News further elevated audience awareness levels and created event status for the USA for Africa project via the News' devotion of one segment every hour for four days to this project—followed by other news stories throughout the campaign. These news segments included exclusive behind-the-scenes footage of the "We Are the World" recording session plus interviews with participating artists.

> In addition, MTV is making special USA for Africa merchandise available for purchase on the network. All profits are donated to USA for Africa.

HBO paid some $2 million for the rights to the *Making of "We Are The World,"* which premiered on May 1. MTV announced a promotion for the competitor's one-hour "rockumentary" of the session in return for exclusive rights to the shorter form of the video of "We Are the World."

In the successful aftermath of the Geldof and Kragen records and other merchandising tools, the irrepressible Irishman approached English promoter Harvey Goldsmith with a seemingly grandiose proposal. Geldof told the thirty-nine-year-old promoter that he wanted to do an international telethon. "Is it possible?" asked Bob. "Nothing's impossible," replied Goldsmith. Later he would say to the *Rolling Stone,* "That's when the nightmare started."[27]

Tatparanandam Ananda Krishnan is a man well known in financial circles. An oil baron, head of Excorp, with an M.B.A. from Harvard, he decided to expand his horizons. His new interests fit perfectly with Geldof's vision. He read a story about "Do They Know It's Christmas?" and Band Aid. He was intrigued. He contacted Geldof and offered his assistance. Broke, as usual, Geldof accepted Krishnan's underwriting of the operating costs and salaries for the Band Aid Trust.

Having been encouraged by Goldsmith, Geldof repeated to Krishnan this dream of an international mega-event to raise money. Ironically in pursuing his broadcasting sports concerns the oil man had been in touch with Michael Mitchell. Mitchell was involved in the logistics of staging the 1984 Los Angeles Olympics. Krishnan contacted Mitchell in hopes of staging a similar event. The 1982 World Soccer Cup championship games had attracted some 1.2 billion viewers on a global scale. Mitchell was skeptical. The two did form Worldwide Sports and Entertainment, which would have the capabilities of duplicating the "global village" aspect of the Soccer Cup competition and the Los Angeles Olympics. Their goal was to be able to amass a worldwide audience of over 1.5 billion.

Krishnan brought Geldof and Mitchell together. In May the two met in New York for an hour and a half and concurred on the concept. Krishnan put up $750,000 in start-up money, accompanied by a $1 million letter of credit. Harvey Goldsmith admits it was at that time that "the jigsaw [pieces] fell into place."

Goldsmith booked the 72,000 seat outdoor Wembley Stadium, just outside of London, for Saturday July 13, 1985. A similar sized site was needed in the United States.

Ken Kragen was contacted, but stuck to his original view of low grosses and monumental logistical problems. He declined to get involved. With Kragen out of the picture, Geldof needed an established, well-connected American promoter. He called rock impressario and mega-promoter Bill Graham. "How those two ever cooperated is beyond me," sighed one observer. Graham contacted Philadelphia talent buyers Larry Magid and partner Allen Spivak. They agreed to promote the American side of the concert and scheduled the John F.

Kennedy Stadium, which holds 100,000 if the fire marshall is absent. "In the beginning, a lot of people doubted our ability to pull it off, but there were a few things going for it that nobody realized. One great thing we had on our side was a lack of time. We had thirty-five days from start to finish, so there wasn't a lot of time for bulls**t or overanalyzation."

Mitchell and Geldof began to set up the broadcasting aspect for the dual concerts. Mitchell resolved to bring in the major nations with television capacity. These included the British Commonwealth nations, Western and parts of Eastern Europe, and Japan.

In the United States the obvious and most important outlet was MTV. The commercial, noncable-based networks were unlikely to drop their usual Saturday sports fare for rock music. There was also the question of the "locals." An affiliate can choose an old movie or syndicated show underwritten by local sponsors rather than accept the network feed.

The international haggling over licensing and broadcast rights, especially in West Germany and France, went on. The USSR made a hollow indication that the state-owned network would air at least part of the concert. (They didn't.) The American situation was more complex than expected.

Mitchell approached the MTV brass with his scheme. They negotiated the rights to telecast the all-day mega-event in exchange for the use of the channel's production studios and transmission facilities. No cash was to change hands. The veejays would do the commentaries on the transatlantic concert and also promote the network. "We were there from the very beginning," a spokesperson told reporters. "We want to cover the entire thing."

Reportedly CBS and NBC nixed the idea. Mitchell approached ABC, indicating that their competitors were considering a telecast. ABC agreed to a three-hour, prime-time Saturday night excerpt. Once the commercial network came on board the fur, according to Harvey Goldsmith, began to fly. "MTV didn't want ABC, and ABC didn't want MTV," observed the British promoter. Mitchell's organization intervened, contending that the Live Aid cause was more important than intramedia bickering. MTV denied any objections to ABC's coverage. One MTV staffer did qualify the official proclamations by noting, "Of course, it would have been great to carry it as an exclusive."

Some 107 independent stations linked to syndicated programming carried the first eleven hours, but were required to terminate their coverage two hours prior to ABC's national three-hour, prime-time show to be hosted by Dick Clark. It was only when Dick Clark Productions moved in their eighteen wheelers and set up for 8:00 P.M. (EDT) that cableless rock fans returned to the festivities. The fan reactions in some quarters were grim. The ABC agreement with Worldwide Sports and Entertainment motivated some to call their local cable operators and indignantly demand "I Want My MTV."

Clark and ABC appeared to be the villains, but as Mike Mitchell noted, "ABC is picking up most of that [union wages] cost." This did not make disenfranchised viewers any happier. Some resented Clark's involvement. He was an interloper climbing aboard a train long after it had left the station.

Negotiations on the broadcasting front were progressing, now came the task of booking artists. Geldof recalls that many of those participating in "We Are the World" were not terribly interested in another benefit: "Some said, 'We've done our bit, and it's not gonna make any difference if we play the concert or not.' " Geldof was frustrated. "He started calling me regularly in May, when he was finding that there was difficulty getting the key black acts." Ken Kragen informed *Rolling Stone,* "I told him, which is the truth, 'Bob, I would be happy to help you. . . . Everybody is kind of acting like they already gave.' " The black artist issue, like the MTV "Billie Jean" incident, would come back to mar some of the original publicity for Live Aid. Press conferences have plagued Bob Geldof throughout his career. On June 10 he announced a "global jukebox [where] you put your money in, punch your selection, and that's it." The jukebox would feature a virtual who's who of rockers to perform at Live Aid. The following roster was presented at the press conference as confirmed for the extravaganza:

London

Adam Ant, Boomtown Rats, David Bowie, Boy George, Phil Collins, Duran Duran, Bryan Ferry, Elton John, Howard Jones, Nik Kershaw, Paul McCartney, Alison Moyet, The Pretenders, Queen, Sade, Spandau Ballet, Status Quo, Rod Stewart, the Style Council, Sting, U2, Ultravox, Paul Young, Wham! and The Who.

Philadelphia

Bryan Adams, The Cars, Eric Clapton, Phil Collins, Elvis Costello, Dire Straits, Duran Duran, Hall and Oates with the Temptations, Mick Jagger, Waylon Jennings, Judas Priest, Kris Kristofferson, Huey Lewis and the News, Billy Ocean, Robert Plant, Power Station, Santana, Paul Simon, Simple Minds, Tears for Fears, Thompson Twins, Stevie Wonder, and Neil Young.

The press conferences, held in London and New York, immediately raised questions. Many of the names mentioned had *not* confirmed (Mick Jagger, Waylon Jennings, Paul Simon, and Tears for Fears). According to reporters present it was strongly hinted that Springsteen, Jackson, Richie, and several other superstars might participate. Stevie Wonder, through publicist Ira Tucker Jr., expressed displeasure. He had declined to be involved due to recording commitments. Huey Lewis also declined. Geldof had oversold the bill with suggestions of artist appearances and also messages of support from cold warriors Gorbachev and Reagan. Sometime later Bill Graham explained the announcements as "honest mistakes" due to overzealousness. The roster hype was not discovered until later, but the exclusion of black artists on the bill was immediately noticed by reporters.

A journalist asked "Why so few?" Geldof replied, tactlessly, "I've been trying to book all the major black acts for six [sic] f**king months. I've been trying and the end result is what you see. I not only asked them, I went to their personal friends, I went to people they were ghostwriting books with, I went to their video people. We invited everyone. If someone isn't there, draw your own conclusions." Geldof could have diplomatically harkened back to his conversations with Kragen, instead the promoters of Live Aid were reliving MTV's 1983 experiences.

Robert Pittman told *Billboard,* "Never before in the history of rock 'n' roll has such an ensemble of artists gathered, nor have television and radio networks cooperated so fully in support of a cause."[28] MTV's chief operating officer no doubt was promoting the telecast, but the statement came at a time when Bill Graham, Larry Magid, and others were fielding questions like, "Are you suggesting black artists won't or can't perform?" Several rock publications such as *RRC* jumped on MTV, lumping the channel with the selection of artists. Geldof, again, made matters worse with his comments.

Live Aid organizers only fanned the flames with statements of black artists asked to perform. Rick James, Dionne Warwick, Donna Summer, and others denied any contact with Geldof or Graham. Reminiscent of some of Bob Pittman's statements during the Michael Jackson polemic, Geldof reportedly told the Philadelphia *Daily News,* "There aren't that many black top artists, that's a fact of life. . . . You've got to book acts for TV, that people will recognize from TV."[29] *RCC* editorialized: "The concept that *all* the popular black acts in America turned down the possibility of 22 minutes of exposure on MTV is preposterous. . . . [Live Aid's] a basically white show designed for an 'up beat' white audience, shown in its entirety on a network (MTV) that seldom airs black music . . . it is not an accident."

In light of the controversy some black acts, especially Teddy Pendergrass, were added. This was an important move as Philadelphia remained a racial tinderbox in the aftermath of the police bombing of the MOVE headquarters, which left eleven dead and 250 neighbors burned out of their homes.

In an interview five months after the historic event Geldof merely brushed aside the issue saying, "There were a lot of reasons, but basically I felt they just didn't want to do it." This has to be the height of understatement from one of the most outspoken individuals in the music industry.

On July 13 all the verbal battles and disinformation were forgotten. *Newsweek* characterized Live Aid as "Woodstock, meet MTV." *Rolling Stone* called it "The Day the World Rocked."

In a mobile control booth, MTV's director and crew started work at 4:00 A.M. Friday adding network logos, commercials, and prerecorded veejay spots with a "live" look. Perhaps Andy Setos, an MTV founder, anticipated the veejays' spontaneous abilities.

Following the initial hiatus, Bill Graham had ninety or more acts to choose from and only half that number could be accommodated. Each artist was restricted to four songs or twenty-two minutes. The promoter was in an awkward predicament. Turning down a name act could "end the relationship." He reportedly politely declined the services of Yes and Foreigner. Having made the selections the jockeying for time slots began. One manager is quoted as saying, "There are ulterior motives for over 75 percent of the acts. They forget what the cause is about—'I want prime-time viewing. I'm not playing with him. I'm not following that person. I've got to be on between eight and eleven for the ABC network.' " ABC-TV did leave Graham with an excellent cop-out. They had insisted on certain artists for their prime-time segment.

At 9:00 A.M. Joan Baez opened the gala with "We will reach deep into our hearts and our soul and say that we will move a little from the comfort of our lives to understand their hurt." Adding, "This is your Woodstock, and it's long overdue." Joan's former cohort Bob Dylan, who would appear later in the program, did not quite concur with the analogy. "The kids are getting a raw deal. Nobody's telling them anything through music anymore."

Graham's scheduling appeared to be working. Ms. Baez, Black Sabbath, Run-D.M.C., the Four Tops, and Judas Priest were done before noon.

At Wembley, Goldsmith arranged for Prince Charles to open the ceremonies. Phil Collins did "Against All Odds" and joined Sting for several duets. Collins then left the stadium, hopped on a Concorde, and flew to finish up in the "City of Brotherly Love." The program exhibited numerous high points: the reunions of Led Zeppelin; The Who; Crosby, Stills, Nash, and Young; and Black Sabbath; duets such as Mick Jagger and Tina Turner sensuously playing with "State of Shock" giving the song a new meaning.

During the concert Ken Kragen approached Mitchell saying he had been wrong about the concert aspect of fund raising. Kragen participated in the finale, which appropriately included Lionel Richie and Harry Belafonte. "We Are the World" rang out from JFK Stadium, however off-key. Seven miles outside of London the Wembley contingent closed with Geldof's "Do They Know It's Christmas." Many of the artists needed photocopies of the lyrics, which Sting passed around.

The bottom line depending on whose figures are used was sixteen hours of entertainment, seen by at least 1.5 billion viewers in 160 countries, with sixty pop stars performing. The estimated gross was $40 million with another $10 million expected to come as many potential donors were believed unable to make their pledges.

By most accounts the two concerts were nearly perfect for those in attendance, except for the loss of audio on Paul McCartney's "Let It Be" and a breakdown in satellite transmission on The Who's opener. Considering the magnitude of the project the mega-event more than exceeded most people's expectations. Prince Charles applauded Geldof's organizational abilities: "He surely missed his vocation. He should have been a general. The concert was marvelous, brilliantly organized." Some television critics and viewers were not so generous in their assessments.

Media critics in the major newspapers objected to portions of MTV's coverage of Live Aid. The *New York Times* saw the telecast as "relentless self-promotion."[30] The brunt of the criticisms were aimed at the MTV veejays.

Cablevision's Robert DiMatteo wrote that they were "repetitive and insipid . . . considering that they've had four years of experience, the MTV V-Js still have not learned the value of under-statement: when they're at a loss for words, they just gush a little louder; when they want to seem personable, they strain for hipness."[31]

The most devastating attack predictably came from the typewriter of *Washington Post* analyst Tom Shales. The writer described the hapless veejays as "gigglingly delerious" hosts and as interesting as a "drenchingly wet blank blanket on the proceedings." He provided examples of McCartney's "Let It Be" being interpreted by "reaction shots of the MTV veejays watching on monitors. . . . This was just what nobody in his right mind with the possible exception of the veejays' parents wanted to see."

Those present at London's Wembley Stadium justified the video disruptions as due to sound failures. Viewers, however, had no inkling of the cause of their ire. The columnist admitted this sound problem, but added "to have hyped the ex-Beatle/Wing's infrequent public appearance and destroyed it with frequent shots of Martha Quinn and Mark Goodman gettin' real goovy seemed a new definition of exploitative hubris."

During REO Speedwagon's "I Can't Fight this Feeling," which Shales claimed was interrupted by "achingly facile blab," he found "Quinn, in a tipsily giggling state, and Goodman, bubbling to beat the bands."[32] Goodman replied, "I didn't know I was on camera. I was participating in the event." This lame excuse supported the critics' complaints.

"The most important part of the presentation is what the audience thinks," says Garland. "It was a unanimous success . . . and that's what really counts." This observation was based on callouts to 200 MTV viewers in eight cities. The veejays were rated by 89 percent of those sampled as "excellent, very good, or good." Sixty-four percent labelled them as "informative." As always using the "numbers" Pittman told *USA Today:* "I don't think those guys have to be defended. The raps they took were totally unjust. . . . The thing I think was the most important was that Live Aid made more aware [those sampled] of what's going on in Africa.[33] Garland claimed that MTV had not received any negative letters. The two executives basically ignored the printed complaints.

There was little question, the mega-event was the high point of the 1985 music scene, and it momentarily restored some of MTV's original "mood."

Notes

1. *New York Times,* May 8, 1983, p. 43.
2. *Creem,* April 1982, p. 37.
3. May 1981, pp. 56–57.
4. *Billboard,* January 25, 1984, p. 10.
5. *Variety,* February 22, 1984, p. 108.
6. *Billboard,* November 30, 1986, p. 10.
7. *Billboard,* June 30, 1984, p. 3.
8. *Toledo Blade,* March 18, 1986, p. P–4.
9. *Newsweek,* March 11, 1985, p. 78.
10. *Esquire,* December 1985, p. 385.
11. *Esquire,* March 1986, p. 72.

12. *Rolling Stone*, March 28, 1985, p. 62.
13. *Time*, October 8, 1984, p. 80.
14. *T.V. Guide*, August 10, 1985, p. 14.
15. *Hard Rock Video*, June 1986, p. 15.
16. *Time*, September 16, 1985, p. 63.
17. Reprinted in *Toledo Blade*, March 11, 1986, p. P–4.
18. Cleveland *Plain Dealer*, September 1, 1985, p. 1–B.
19. September 20, 1984, p. 18. Louise Mandrell's video clip was barred from MTV and TNN due to the presence of a recognizable soft drink container.
20. *Newsweek*, January 7, 1985, p. 37.
21. *U.S. News and World Report*, September 30, 1985, pp. 68–69.
22. *Newsweek*, March 31, 1986, p. 61.
23. *Wall Street Journal*, October 17, 1983, p. 1.
24. *Rolling Stone*, December 5, 1985, p. 53.
25 *Billboard*, April 6, 1985, USA–3.
26. The rest of Geldof's remarks are in the March 14, 1985 issue of *Rolling Stone*.
27. This section on Live Aid relies heavily on interviews with Bob Geldof and others that appeared in the August 15 and December 5, 1985 issues of *Rolling Stone*. Some participants interviewed essentially repeated the material in this section in almost the same precise language.
28. *Billboard*, June 22, 1985, pp. 1, 74.
29. *RRC*, July 1985, p. 1.
30. The observation would prove mild when contrasted to the Nashville Network's self-hype on Farm Aid.
31. *Cablevision*, August 5, 1985, p. 30.
32. *Washington Post*, July 15, 1985, p. B–2.
33. *USA Today*, July 26, 1985.

10

"MTV: Some People Just Don't Get It"

*First it was Elvis, then the Beatles,
and now it's MTV.*
MTV's "anti-anti" spot

*They're sex songs, out and out. I
loathe what they're doing in many of
these lyrics.*
Frank Sinatra, singer

*What good is it if you win the ratings
battle and wreck your country by
polluting the young people's minds?*
Ted Turner, president WTBS

*It's music videos . . . the cause of
drug use.*
Rev. Jesse Jackson on "Night Line"

"We really integrated the most powerful forces in our two decades,"
says John Sykes, senior vice-president of MTVN, "TV and rock and
roll." These combined elements would further agitate those societal
forces that viewed each as corrosive to the fabric of American traditional values and morality.

Historian Richard Hofstadter called it "the revolt against moder-
nity." In 1964 the Civil Rights Act was passed, thousands of young
people were going West with "a flower in their hair," the feminist
movement was taking root, and a "dirty little war" was underway.

Conservative values, theological and political, were being trampled
by the forces of "secular humanism," "hedonism," and the communications technology that appeared to make it possible. At least, that was
the view from the pulpits of rural America and the New Right. Right-
wing political fund raiser Richard Viguerie in 1976 foresaw a perfect
union in the making. He commented, "The next major area of growth
for conservative ideology and philosophy is among the evangelicals."
Frustrated by the perceived moral erosion of America, many fundamentalists agreed with the notion that "it is time for Christians to crawl
out from under their pews" and influence institutions in "establishing

and maintaining the moral principles of Scripture." This tenet of the Moral Majority's "Christian Bill of Rights" was quickly aimed at the electronic media. As Cal Thomas, public relations vice-president of the organization told *Time,* "The revolutionaries always take the radio station first. They get the presidential palace later."[1]

Prior to the mid-1970s evangelicals were a fairly passive lot. They were isolated in the South and sections of the Midwest. Their societal protestations were scoffed at by those not sharing in the "born again" theology. The occasional book and record burnings were dismissed as aberrant manifestations of traditional "know nothingism." The archetype of the 1924 Scopes monkey trial was deeply ingrained in the American psyche outside of the old Confederacy.

Ministers and preachers decried the "decline" of the American family unit. They totally concurred with Plato that "our children's amusements must be strictly controlled, because once they lose their discipline, it becomes impossible to produce good orderly citizens."

"Television is more than a passing entertainment medium, it is as much a part of society as electric lights. Those of us who have seen it change in the last few years know how it's changed, but the kids see this and think that's the way the world is," said John Hurt, originally of the Clean Up TV campaign. "There's a lot of immorality in the U.S., but not to the extent that it's shown on television."[2]

In a house some ten minutes away from the birthplace of Elvis Presley, the Reverend Donald E. Wildmon gathered for an evening of television viewing with his family during the 1976 Christmas season. The thirty-nine-year-old United Methodist minister recoiled at what he saw. "On one channel, there was sex. I told my child to change channels," he recalls. "He did. On the second channel, there was profanity. I told him to change it again. He did. And on the third network, there was violence." He was enraged and determined to alter the television landscape. Wildmon resigned his Tupelo ministry to devote his time to expunging sex and violence from the nation's airwaves. Singlehandedly he founded the National Federation for Decency. By 1979 he claimed 10,000 subscribers to his newsletter and $50,000 in contributions. He set up a system of volunteer monitors to rate the fare emanating from the networks. These watchdogs also kept track of the time buyers on offensive shows.

In Joelton, Tennessee, at the Church of Christ John Hurt began his own crusade in 1979. "If you ever plan to take a stand for moral decency, now is the time, while hundreds of thousands of others are moving in the same direction," he informed his flock. The congregation contacted other Church of Christ parishes, asking for a list of the five most "morally" repugnant television shows. The list included "Saturday Night Live," "Dallas," "Soap," "Three's Company," and "Charlie's Angels."

By March 1980, Hurt organized a boycott of the sponsors, as they are the "Achilles' heels" of the networks. Wildmon was employing similar tactics. The two joined forces with Jerry Falwell's blessings. Wildmon headed the Coalition for Better Television.

The coalition's drive received some lip-service from advertisers, but most echoed Kathleen MacDonough of General Foods: the fundamentalists "have arrived at standards that reflect their views, but we don't believe they reflect the views of society as a whole." Several companies, such as Sears and Warner-Lambert, withdrew support, but three of the objectionable programs were in the Nielsen top ten. "Dallas" was number one. Madison Avenue does not relinquish a market share of that size unless the protesters number in the millions.

NCTV began rating "violence" on August 20, 1980, finding the sci-fi show "Buck Rogers" as the main culprit, followed by the teen favorite "The Dukes of Hazzard." Radecki's organization appeared a natural ally for Wildmon's Coalition for Better Television. Invited to join the corporate boycott zealots, the Illinois psychiatrist backed off explaining: "We are limiting our area of concern to the TV-violence issue, and to issues where there is widespread bipartisan agreement—and also valid research findings. . . . We are also troubled that there is so much disagreement—even within the Christian community—as to what is, and what is not, appropriate 'sexual' portrayal."[3] Appearing as the academic voice of reason, Radecki using "scholarly" measurements provided the material that any boycotter needed to justify their questionable activities.

While not embracing the fundamentalists, NCTV did rate and monitor prime-time television for "violent" content.[4] Radecki notes:

> I think we have become desensitized to violence. We've learned to use violence as a way to entertain ourselves to get an excitement. We haven't heard the message of the surgeon general and the recent U.S. Attorney's Task force on Family Violence that the evidence is overwhelming that violent entertainment increases the tendency towards loss of temper and violence in normal children and adult viewers. We need to hear that message and turn the channel.

Social scientists were skeptical. Who was doing the monitoring? *Rock Video,* hardly an objective source, noted that the judges received "lodging in the NCTV co-op, board, health insurance and $50.00 a month."[5] The most asked question in academe was, "Who are these monitors?"

Content analysis depends on random sampling. The methodology was flawed, as nobody knew the value set of the jury. Their names were published (five in all), but their credentials were undisclosed. While evaluating commercial programming, NCTV began rating MTV in October 1983.

The first NCTV report concluded that 18 percent of music video fare was violent. Phil Galli, NCTV's project director, observed: "Rock video's combination of lyrics and images adds a new dimension to television violence. Many of the videos added violent imagery that wasn't even present in the lyrics. We found large amounts of violence present in every viewing hour with the exception of a fund-raising concert for Kampuchea." Dr. Radecki stated:

> The heavy use of violence in a very appealing format by the leading rock movie stars clearly has a strong harmful effect on young American viewers. The message is that violence is normal and okay, that hostile sexual relations between men and women are common and acceptable, that heroes actively engaged in torture and murder of others for fun. Michael Jackson's "Thriller" video, banned in Australia, features a very appealing young hero having fun terrorizing his girlfriend with horror violence. The Rolling Stones' video, "Under Cover of the Night," banned in England, features intense automatic weapon violence with Keith Richard and Mick Jagger heavily involved, including a violent lawless execution. Billy Idol's "Dancing with Myself," filmed by the producer of *The Texas Chainsaw Massacre,* has a naked woman struggling in chains behind a translucent sheet.

> Sadistic and sexually sadistic violence of a very intense nature is common on MTV, worse than any other TV channel except possibly HBO and other pay-cable movie channels. "Fight Fire with Fire" by Kansas features slave torture and sadist women. "Murder Weapon" by T-Bone Burnett features the stalking of a woman to kill her with a gun. Golden Earring's "Twilight Zone" included slow-motion murder and repeated interrogation torture. MTV has women boiled alive while other women are portrayed as cold-hearted and enjoying torturing men. "Street of Dreams" by Rainbow has a psychiatrist dominating a man through hypnosis intermixed with male-female violent fantasies including a bound and gagged woman.

Galli notes that the programming features a fantasy world where there are no laws, anything goes, people's music heroes are all-powerful and do anything they want. NCTV's monitoring of violent music found sixty groups with names of explicit violence, including the

Dead Kennedys, 3 Teens Kill 4, Sadist Faction, Pseudo Sadists, and Rash of Stabbings.

Radecki went on to state:

> MTV and Warner push very violent sadist and hate programming into the American home. This telecasting is very similar to the material researched at the University of Wisconsin which caused major increases in desensitization towards violence in normal male viewers and major increases in their willingness to rape women. This programming clearly incites imminent violence. Not even political speech inciting imminent violence is protected by the first amendment, let alone the gruesome sadism of MTV. Yet, this problem [sic] can be corrected without even challenging any constitutional question.[6]

After bashing TV in all media formats, he did tell a *Cablevision* reporter, "We have not said that MTV is *more* violent."

In a Janus-like manner Radecki told the conservative *U.S. Press* that MTV's message was that "violence is normal and okay, that hostile sexual relations are common and acceptable, that heroes actually engage in torture murders for fun."[7]

NCTV completed one year of monitoring rock music videos. The level of violence in October and November 1984 was virtually identical with the same months in 1983 (i.e., 17.9 versus 18.0 instances of violence per hour). They noted that 36 percent of all videos contained explicit violence and another 10 percent contained anger and suggestions of violence. Half of all violent videos contained violence between men and women, with each attacking the other with about equal frequency.

NCTV praised five groups whose videos featured primarily prosocial themes: John, Sean, and Julian Lennon, The Romantics, Donna Sommers, U-2, and Missing Persons. NCTV's study completed in early 1984 noted that rock music from 1963 contained far fewer violent lyrics than in 1983, 54 percent fewer to be exact. Of interest is that John Lennon and his sons and Paul McCartney have produced primarily nonviolent and prosocial videos while the "modern" heavy metal groups dominated the high violence category.

NCTV's monitoring covered some 300 hours of music videos, primarily on MTV and WTBS. The levels of violence on both were virtually identical during October and November 1984, both averaging 17.9 instances of violence per hour. NCTV found that 40 percent of MTV videos fell in the violent or suggestive of violence categories, while 43 percent of WTBS's fell in these categories. Conversely, 5 percent of MTV videos were prosocial or featured the educational use of violence, while 3 percent of WTBS's featured these themes.

NCTV expressed great concern over the increasing popularity of violence in rock music. Heavy metal groups predominate in the very high violence category. Michael and Jermaine Jackson, ABC, Ronnie Dio, Berlin, Def Leppard, Ratt, Billy Idol, KISS, Duran Duran, Scorpion, Stray Cats, Quiet Riot, and Rick Springfield led in violence. Twisted Sister, Dokken, and Motley Crue also produced two very violent videos each. One video by Twisted Sister is reported to have led to an imitation murder in New Mexico earlier this year. NCTV's monitoring found a close association between the presence of studded metal jewelry with torn clothing and a theme of violence in the videos. Dr. Radecki, NCTV chairperson and director of the music video monitoring research, expressed great concern about a "growing culture of violence" in rock music. He stated:

> I have already seen several cases of young people in my psychiatric practice with severe problems of anger and anti-social behavior who are deeply immersed into a sub-culture of violent rock music. They each own several dozen tee-shirts with violent images of various heavy metal groups on them and wear varous types of metal-studded jewelry and barbed-wire necklaces. It is plainly obvious that they are heavily immersed in fantasies of violence that also is affecting their way of thinking and their behavior in an anti-social direction.

Although members of NCTV were frequent guests on religious talk shows and generated considerable press attention, many social scientists were unconvinced. They found holes in the October 1983 to November 1984 rating system.

The ranking system as explained by NCTV appeared as follows:

> The groups with 3 or more music videos in NCTV's monitoring project are ranked below from most prosocial to most violent. A positive weighting was given for prosocial videos or ones that used violence in an educational manner. A negative weighting was given for suggestions of violence or violent videos with extra weighting given for violence between men and women or for the portrayal of sadistic violence.

> Although NCTV's objective scoring of incidents of violence in each video does not perfectly reflect the harmful impact of that video, it avoids some of the pitfalls of a totally subjective system and is a fairly good representation of the amount of harmful effect. Thus, although videos with higher numbers of incidents of violence are not necessarily always worse than every video with fewer incidents, in general, videos with more violent images are worse than those with fewer. Also, by only ranking groups with at least 3 videos, it is hoped that the impact of any one video will be less important than the general message of the group's videos overall.

The ratings criteria are:

> Songs titled alphabetically within each category.
> V = Violence, I = Intermediate, NV = Nonviolent, PS = Prosocial.
> *V = Sexually Related Violence
> **V = Sadistic, usually Sexual Sadistic Violence
> V(Educ.) = Educational Use of Violence
> "lyrics" = violence in lyrics only
> "video" = violence in video only. Note: many records are not listed "lyrics" or "video" due to late addition of this designation.
> Format = Band, *Song Title,* Record Company—instances of violence.

Radecki summarized NCTV's findings:

> The tremendous violence of MTV parallels the extreme violence of recent Hollywood movies and the dramatic increase in sadistic violence in pornography. The fault for this disgusting and destructive violence lies with the U.S. Congress and the White House. The legislative and executive branches of our government have taken a hands-off and anything goes attitude toward violent entertainment no matter how harmful or destructive. Mark Fowler, chairman of the Federal Communication Commission, said that he hopes that the FCC will do nothing about TV violence. Congress has refused to take even the smallest action to correct this problem after 10 congressional hearings over two decades and admissions of harmful effects from three Surgeon Generals. Entertainment and real-life violence just keep growing.

NCTV called for *required counteradvertising* to correct the misinformation of $1 billion worth of advertising promoting violent entertainment. NCTV also called for a mandatory *nonviolent alternative cable movie and music video channel* whenever violent ones are offered. In addition, Radecki insisted that ratings should be made of all programs and videos on broadcast or cable TV; those programs deemed to have *extreme adult violence should be restricted from TV* and available to adults only in theaters or on videocassettes, since these programs incite imminent violence.

> MTV and other violent TV networks are out to guarantee that the second television generation will be more violent than the first, which turned out to be the most violent generation of Americans on record. The fact that 1 out of 3 women in her lifetime will be raped and that twice as many women are raped by husbands and boyfriends as by strangers shows that we have taught ourselves to be a barbaric and violent society. We must shake off the domination of our Congress by the TV and film industry and demand corrective action.

This NCTV press release illustrated the fervor of the group.

Considerable attention was given to Michael Jackson's mega-seller, *Thriller,* both the album and the video cassettes. MTV had a fifteen-minute long-form exclusive video of the title song. Bob Pittman said, "We played it at the time Vestron Video released the 60-minute home video version of *The Making of "Thriller."* Six weeks later . . . it went on Showtime."

Stressing their concern for social issues, the New Christian Right and some well-meaning youth-oriented organizations transferred their focus from television back to rock music. A youthful evangelist from Lafayette, Louisiana, Jacob Aranza, in *Backward Masking Unmasked* observed: "Sex has always been a seller on TV . . . but in recent years [six] even so-called pop singers have begun to use sex as their seller."[8]

Rock music from its inception has evoked generational and theological protest. "Rock Around the Clock," the first major generic hit, was the theme from a movie, *Blackboard Jungle,* which depicted juvenile delinquency. The same year the Supreme Court handed down the historic *Brown* v. *Board of Education of Topeka* school desegregation decision. Rock's black heritage found white citizens in the "Bible Belt" attempting to ban the genre. In the North the music was perceived by some as a threat to public safety and morality. Elvis Presley merely underscored parental concerns. Various ordinances, the payola scandals, and record burnings could not alter the growth of the music.

The "British Invasion" and the San Francisco psychedelic scene again generated the predictable outcries, especially from the Radical Right and even a vice-president of the United States. Rock still held the allegiance of the young.

Most adults dismissed rock as an adolescent phase and shouted, "Turn that noise down!" Spiro Agnew's caveat, "Have you heard the words of some of these songs?" in reference to drug lyrics fell on deaf ears, except at the FCC.

A series of conservative fundamentalist preachers all but made a living condemning folk music and then rock and roll. Originally, David Noebel and Joseph R. Crowe cited rock music as part of "the Communist movement" to incite or pacify American youth. Frank Garlock, Bob Larson, the Peters Brothers, and a host of others wrote and held revival meetings railing against the sexuality and Satanism of the musical genre. They preached to the converted.

The advent of MTV, especially in one television set households, raised some parental eyebrows and ire. "What are they watching?" became a common complaint.

"Born again" rock lecturer Rob Lamb told *U.S. Press:* "MTV has done something that has never been done before in rock's history on a consistent level, which is to add visual imagery to the lyrics. What this does many times is to make very clear what the song lyrics are talking about. They run 350 [sic] videos a day, 24 hours a day." The link was established. Even Dr. Radecki would find the subject irresistible. Television and rock and roll—a union that fit Plato's warning in the *Republic:* "The introduction of novel fashions in music is a thing to beware of as endangering the whole fabric of society."

The Greek philosopher's admonition historically has been and continues to be accepted as part of the conventional wisdom, despite little undeniable proof to support the statement. The Athenians feared the power of art, aesthetics, and music. In the contemporary world the print and electronic media were to be feared. The wedding of rock music and television inflamed the traditional critics and the uproar spread to other segments of the society.

While John Lack and associates were in the process of audience building, the new Christian Right was busily attacking "Dallas" and other "objectionable" prime-time network offerings. Wildmon and the coalition would "claim" credit for the cancellation of "Soap" and "Charlie's Angels." ABC responded that the cancellations were a normal practice due to the declining ratings of the shows. Personnel changes in the Angels trio probably had more to do with the decision than the threats of sponsor boycotts.

Televangelists took to the air to refocus concern on rock music. In 1982, the PTL (Praise The Lord) Network began the campaign.

The so-called "backmasking" issue surfaced on January 14, 1982 on the evangelical talk show hosted by Paul Crouch with a statement by William H. Yarroll of Applied Potentials Institute in Aurora, Colorado. The self-styled "neuroscientist" contended that rock stars were in league with Anton Levey's Church of Satan and were placing hidden messages on records in reverse so that the subconscious mind could grasp the "secret" or subliminal communications.

Monika Wilfrey, a twenty-year-old housewife from Lancaster, California, saw the PTL segment. She rotated rock records backwards with the index finger and heard the demonic utterances. "We threw away a lot of records and tapes and such. It was really frustrating," she told AP. "Some of them were new." Ms. Wilfrey reportedly contacted conservative California assemblyman Phil Wyman. Bill A.B. 3741 was introduced by Wyman in the California legislature as "a consumer protection stature warning of subliminal messages." In a widely publicized press conference, holding up copies of ELO's *Face the Music* and Led Zeppelin's untitled *(TV)* Wyman contended that rock records "can manipulate our behavior without our knowledge or consent and turn us into disciples of the anti-Christ."

A meeting of the Consumer Protection and Toxic Materials Committee heard Yarroll's testimony and a tape of "Stairway to Heaven" played in reverse. Audiologists and psychologists were openly critical. Marcel Kinsbourne, affiliated with Harvard University, called the Yarroll thesis "fantasy," adding that "there's no reason that supports" the subliminal reception of "hidden messages."

Assemblyman Wyman appeared on the "Behind the Scenes" program to promote his antibackmasking bill. Congressman Robert K. Dornan (R-California) issued a statement: "It is especially important that parents and their teenage consumers be alerted that several major selling rock albums contain messages glorifying Satan." The technique for transmitting the satanic messages was "backward-masking." Backmasking, a misnomer, was a recording technique used "whereby a message can be heard audibly by playing the record in reverse, but the same message is *also* subconsciously registered when the record is played forward."[9] The Congressman continued, "How widespread this practice is, I don't know. But I do know that it is dangerous, deceptive, and consumers should be warned."

The conservative Congressman generated national media attention. The issue, outside of fundamentalist circles, soon became yesterday's news. His proposed legislation died on Capitol Hill. It was the psychiatric community that fired the first salvo in the "war on MTV."

"A decision has been made to ban the music television station (MTV)," announced an internal memo distributed to the staff of the Institute for Living, a Hartford, Connecticut, mental hospital. "Just as the hospital makes choices about what movies are shown at evening entertainment, similarly we feel it necessary to regulate cable TV when we believe its effects are detrimental to the hospital milieu and and patient care. In addition to the fact that there have been several complaints by patients about this particular channel, we have observed ill effects on certain of our patients as a result of viewing MTV." The "ill effects" were not specified. The memo, signed by Dr. Richard M. Bridgberg, concluded: "Thus as of 8:00 A.M. Monday, August 2, we expect that MTV will no longer be viewed on any unit in the hospital."

Billboard columnist Roman Kozak decided to pursue the story. He posed several questions to Robert Fagan, spokesman for the hospital. If popular culture is denied inside institutional walls, "how can the hospital ever expect patients to make any sort of adjustment once they get out into the real world?"

Fagan agreed to the premise, but described MTV as "too inciting," as opposed to the radios and records allowed the residents. "These patients are very vulnerable and we have to be very careful with them and we try to monitor what they see. Many of them are hallucinating. And when you have scenes of people regurgitating or decapitations this kind of thing is detrimental. Some of the rough edges have to be smoothed out for our patients. MTV is too much."[10]

Kozak closed his piece, "Caution: MTV May Be Hazardous to Your Mind," by noting that Institute detainees were allowed to watch the evening news. Many defenders of MTV's programming have suggested that there is more violence on newscasts than on music videos. "On any night you watch TV," says Bob Giraldi, "there's more sex and violence than there ever is in a week of watching MTV or rock video." Comedian Bill Cosby once termed adolescence as a "state of temporary insanity." Many parents reacted to MTV in a manner similar to Dr. Bridgberg and Mr. Fagan.

As MTV continued to penetrate rural cable outlets, individual and organized campaigns were mounted. CATV operator Roger Wise recalled the local reaction: "I've heard not only obscenity but . . . the use of instruments in certain fashions, and violent production techniques where it is back lighted and rear projected. Yet we've had some serious objections."

These objections come not only from concerned parents, but also school teachers and even some university people. A typical letter to the cable company was: "MTV is completely disgusting and a waste of our money. If people want to watch it they should pay extra. It is suggestive and offensive for young children." The same writer labeled the channel as basically a "negative influence."

The cable company experienced few "turns" (disconnects) due to the appearance of MTV. The northwest Ohio community lacked an organized anticampaign. Emporia, Virginia, was another matter.

Pembroke Cablevision added MTV to its subscriber fare in the summer of 1983. A teenager in the community of 4,800 was surprised, "I thought they would never get it in Emporia, it's so far back in the boondocks." Adolescents in the rustic community were delighted with the addition. They wanted their MTV. One commented: "MTV is new. There are not that many new things that come to Emporia."

Unfortunately for the youngsters of the city, a supervisor of youth activities at the Calvary Baptist Church, Roger Wilcher, did not share their enthusiasm for the music channel. "I find it vulgar and distasteful," he told a UPI contributor. "We as adults must guide our young people. We must make some moral guidelines."

Wilcher led some of his fellow parishioners to petition the city council—before the FCC decision on local regulation of cable content—to remove the offensive network. Domenick Fioravanti wrote to the council and the cable operator noting, "Our programming is intended to entertain and inform—not to offend." The MTV vice-president's explanation proved only partially persuasive. In a compromise the council voted to restrict access to MTV by moving it from a "basic" service to the "pay-tier." The 1,659 subscribers would be required to contribute an extra $120 annually for the privilege of seeing MTV.

Few people were satisfied with the outcome. Wilcher and his followers wanted MTV banned from the system. Adolescents objected with resigned indignation. One said, "They messed up. It won't hurt. It was helping us." "If they want to take off MTV there's no reason they shouldn't take off all of television," noted another. "You can't justify taking off a channel for teenagers when there isn't that much to do anyway," retorted a sixteen-year-old.

A survey found that only 283 respondents of the 28 percent answering wanted the service changed; 186 had no objections. One of these, D. Scott Fisher, an insurance agent, observed: "I think the kids are the losers. You can't create a controlled environment for your kids to grow up in."[11]

Other communities serviced by Pembroke Cablevision made no fuss about MTV. Occasional reports of anti-MTV protests did reach the news media. Leo Weidner, a Mormon bishop and partner in an apartment complex in Provo, Utah, catering to Brigham Young University students, banned MTV from the housing units, labeling music videos "pornographic." According to a report in the March 1985 issue of *Rock 'n' Roll Confidential,* he had never seen the channel. In July 1984 a petition circulated in Weymouth, Massachusetts by "born again" Christian women who saw MTV as "decadent, morally degrading, and evil" compelled the local cable operator to make available a "black out" device for the music channel.

Surgeon General C. Everett Koop told a southern medical school audience: "Violence and pornography are at a crossroads now. One place they are crossing is in these rock video cassettes that have become so popular with young people." He warned that youngsters have become "saturated with what I think is going to make them have trouble having satisfying relationships with people of the opposite sex . . . when you're raised with rock music that uses both pornography and violence."[12]

Koop's comments, picked up by the media, were without any

scientific substantiation but were widely quoted by antirockers. Rob Lamb for one used the remark as another "MTV liability."

"Darling Nikki" Goes to Washington: The "Washington Wives"

A twelve-year-old preteen walked into a Cincinnati record outlet and purchased Prince's *1999* as a birthday gift for a girlfriend. The adolescent would begin a furor that partially legitimized the New Christian Right's campaign against "objectionable" media. The recipient's mother heard the lyrics and found they were "sexually explicit." She complained to the *Cincinnati Inquirer*.

Members of the Delshire Elementary School PTA discussed the allegations and proposed a ratings system similar to that used by the movie industry. Twenty chapters of the Cincinnati Parent Teacher Organizations (PTA) endorsed the dictate and vowed to carry their campaign to the group's national convention to be held in Las Vegas in mid-June of 1984.

In the midst of gambling casinos and seminude stage shows the statewide body passed a resolution asking record labels to voluntarily rate their product on the basis of content. The statement read that the parent-teacher lobby would "urge record companies to put a label on record, tape, and cassette covers rating the material contained within with regard to profanity, sex, violence, or vulgarity."

A Washington official would explain to *Billboard*'s Bill Holland: "We are just asking the record companies about this; we want to encourage."

The Recording Industry Association of America (RIAA) originally replied with a terse "no comment" to the Ohio PTA's proposal. Pursuing the story, Bill Holland spoke with Stanley Gortikov, the amorphous industry group's president. He indicated that the association had not been contacted by the PTA. "I can surely understand their feelings about this, about children," he said diplomatically. "All I can say at this point is that we will seriously consider any proposal the PTA brings to our attention." He added a qualifier as to the problems of rating records as opposed to films and asked, "Who would be rating the ratings?" No mention of music videos or MTV was expressed.

In October, Elaine Stienkemeyer, National PTA president, finally mailed the resolution to twenty-nine record companies. A spokesperson for the PTA indicated:

> We suggested the record companies establish a panel to evaluate the material for themselves. We feel they're in the position to do this, as they have already in many cases stickered albums and tapes that they feel

may be considered offensive to certain groups. . . . This is more a statement of concern than a threat of action. Certain individual chapters around the country have contacted us, asking what kinds of action they might take if the proposal is not adopted by the industry. But so far, nothing is planned on a national level by the PTA.

The 5.6 million member organization was difficult to ignore as opposed to the televangelists and the record-burning circuit riders. The RIAA privately repeated, "We're not the Motion Picture Association of America (MPAA) and a ratings system is out of the question." An RIAA spokesperson cautioned, "I find it a dangerous kind of precedent. It's not censorship per se, but it certainly does open a Pandora's box of unpleasant possibilities."[13] This observation would prove prophetic, as the RIAA and the industry would painfully discover.

Most product with warning labels graced the covers of comedic albums by George Carlin and Richard Pryor. Radio stations received albums cautioning, "Some Selections May Not Be Suitable for Airplay," to avoid difficulties with the FCC. (The Tubes' "White Punks on Dope" contained a caveat of this type.) Insiders were displeased with the entire proposal. In chorus-like unison executives in New York and Los Angeles voiced the "artistic freedom" argument, always adding: "The movie industry has to deal with less than 400 submissions a year. We have over 25,000 songs. It would be impossible to rate that number." The RIAA membership chose to ignore the resolution.

The PTA at the leadership level was uncomfortable with this grass roots campaign. The New Christian Right had evoked internal havoc in the organization with their social agenda of school prayer and scientific creationism. They did not welcome another issue with obvious First Amendment implications. Educators in general were cool to the image of being censors while arguing "academic freedom," especially for sex education courses. Moral entrepreneurs, however, make for bizarre political alliances.

As the RIAA membership was mulling over the PTA proposal *Billboard* ran a commentary by Lou Alfano, the operator of Oldiesmobile, a disk jockey service for night clubs operating from Sterling, Virginia. Alfano took the PTA position, but applied it to MTV and "its clones." Using the parental control of the TV set argument, the self-proclaimed deejay claimed that MTV was losing its promotional value because "I am far from alone in prohibiting my youngsters [ages four and nine] . . . from watching MTV and other music video shows." He suggested that video producers should show self-restraint or MTV should telecast "G-rated clips during hours when young kids are most likely to be watching, and progressively add those rated PG-13, PG, and then R as the hours get later. Here is the challenge: Please make it safe for my kids to watch MTV. Let's not permit the zealots of the world to stage a music video burning party." No industry response appeared in the trade magazine.

MTV remained publically silent on Alfano's opinion, but the network executives were contemplating a playlist revision that would negatively affect the heavy metalers—seen by many watchdogs as the prime purveyors of moral decadence. (Ironically, Prince, Sheena E., and Madonna were hardly following in the footsteps of Led Zeppelin or Black Sabbath.) Pittman refused to engage in the debate. In several interviews he did acknowledge the "irritation" aspect of heavy metal. As noted, the strongest statement emanating from Rockefeller Plaza was, "We do allow people with purple hair, some people are quick to label such styles as bad." A close associate of Pittman's noted:

> He figures there are ends of the spectrum . . . but there are things either to the hard side or the soft side that so offend the opposite end of the listening spectrum that they can be real negatives to the overall program-ming strategy of the channel. So, for instance, if you put on Kenny Rogers on a rock station it is so offensive to the heavier rock listeners while it is not offensive to the larger public that you lose a big opportu-nity in viewing and listening. I think there was a growing feeling as the research came in that while the heavy metal viewers were a louder and more vocal group than anyone else in the listenership that as MTV expanded its audience base, not necessarily its numbers, but its audience base, that the heavy metal clips were causing them more problems than they were helping.

On February 4, 1985 RCA Records president Robert Summer ad-dressed the Anti-Defamation League's Music and Performing Arts Division. In his remarks, without mentioning the PTA or the New Christian Right, Summer voiced the opinion:

> The great artist, the creator, is by nature a driven, uncompromising creature whose creative passion makes him a formidable, even danger-ous, power. Although he is not always God's messenger, he is his own voice. We need not follow, but we must guarantee that he is heard. . . . We, the men and women of the entertainment industry, must serve as an aware and ever-present force wherever and whenever freedom of the spirit and the mind is challenged. It is a matter of life and death.

This speech was widely distributed to the news media in the fall of 1985.

The same month, the PTA held a seminar in Los Angeles to discuss rating the home video market. Rudy Neely of the Video Software

Dealers Association noted, " We're not doing business with the children, but with the parents." Again, music videos were left untouched.

Sony's "Video 45" series did on occasion add the citation "Note: Contains partial nudity. Parental discretion advised" to video cassettes such as Duran Duran, which included the uncensored version of "Girls on Film." Conversely, the same company released a Devo "Video LP" with "Whip It," frequently cited as the *first* controversial clip, minus any labelling.

As the famous pink blossoms in the nation's capital emerged, "Tipper" (Mrs. Albert) Gore's eleven-year-old daughter was playing a song from Prince's soundtrack album *Purple Rain*. "Darling Nikki" caught the Tennessee senator's wife off stride. The filler song, never released as a single, was about genital arousal. "I was shocked when I heard the words to one of the songs," she recalls. " 'Darling Nikki.' It describes masturbation by Nikki, who is called a 'sex fiend.' " Treasury Secretary James Baker's spouse, Susan, reportedly heard "Like a Virgin" on her clock radio. Washington socialite Pam Hower was offended by "Let's Get Physical" and other tunes accompanying her aerobics class. Mrs. Gore told *Rolling Stone*, "We got together and said you know, these things were happening to us *in our homes*."[14]

A letter signed by Mrs. Baker, Gore, Packwood, Thurmond, and others was sent announcing a meeting at the prestigious St. Columbia's Episcopal Church on May 13, 1985. The note, dated April 16, partially read: "Some rock groups advocate satanic rituals, others sing of open rebellion against parental and other authority, others sing of killing babies."

Five senatorial and cabinet rank wives formed the Parents Music Research Center (PMRC) on May 5. (Only the founding members are listed.)

As a mailing list was being compiled from the D.C. social register, Kandy Stroud, a singer of "sacred songs" with the elite Coral Arts Society, revived the term "Porn Rock" (the designation originally appeared in David Devoss' "Aural Sex: The Rise of 'Porn Rock,' *Human Behavior*, July 1976). It reappeared in *Newsweek*'s "My Turn" space published in late April.[15]

Stroud's opening was repetitious standard. She heard "Darling Nikki" played by her fifteen-year-old daughter (sound familiar?). She reacted, "Unabashedly sexual lyrics . . . compose the musical diet millions of children are now being fed at concerts, on albums, on radio and MTV." She maintained that "legislative action may be needed, or better yet, a measure of self-restraint . . . [thus] a diet of rock music that is not only good to dance to but healthy for their hearts and minds and souls as well." Asked about this initial salvo, Tipper Gore indicated to *Rolling Stone* that Ms. Stroud was a PMRC consultant, an "unofficial member." A question of chronological significance was when did Stroud get involved with the "Washington Wives," before or after the "My Turn" piece? The guest column presented the PMRC scenario with the usual illustrations. (Coincidence?)

MTV pulled the Rolling Stones' "Under Cover of Night" (after two weeks of rotation due to "viewer complaints").

Hit Parader and *Hard Rock Video* (the only music magazine to arrive in an unmarked brown envelope) attacked the RIAA action. *Rock Video,* since its inception, had been publishing a series by Jonathan Gross titled, "What You Can't See on MTV," with graphics. The magazine was furious. "Masturbating with a magazine never hurt anybody," wrote Donald Lyons, "but repression kills. . . . It's up to us, the metal public, to fight censorship by patronizing only those businesses that do not go along with it."[16] The tactics, regardless of the cause, would appeal to the Reverend Wildmon's National Federation for Decency.

"What You Can't See on MTV"[17]

Film Editing Requested
Queen, "Body Language"
Joe Perry Project, "Black Velvet Pants"
David Bowie, "China Girl"
Duran Duran, "Girls on Film"
Joan Jett, "Bad Reputation"
Golden Earrings, "Twilight Zone"
Berlin, "Sex"
Frankie Goes To Hollywood, "Relax" (4 edits)
Rolling Stones, "She Was Hot"
Dwight Twilley, "Girls"
Elvis Brothers, "Fire in the City"
Frankie Goes to Hollywood, "Two Tribes"
Cars, "Hello Again"
O'Bryan, "Lovelight"
"Streets of Fire" (soundtrack clip)
DeGarmo & Key, "Six, Six, Six"
Ramones, "Psychotherapy"
Peter Godwin, "Images of Heaven"
Mel Brooks, "Hitler Rap"

As in the "racism" debate, MTV's Achilles heel was in media relations. Revealing their "call-out" research, which indicated that many so-called "objectionable" videos were absent from the MTV playlist, would have saved considerable aggravation. The timing of playlist changes to reach a demographic above the age of fifteen—the core of heavy metal fans—could have aided the channel's cause. Historically it is correct that demographic upgrading did occur prior to Tipper Gore's stumbling onto *Purple Rain*. Much of this data was not available until after the actual controversy. Pittman's remark that the videos were merely "humorous" only fueled the polemic.

The senior executives at MTV believed in stonewalling, usually to their detriment. This ploy may have been valid in 1984, but it was totally counterproductive in 1985 (see Epilogue.)

Present at the PMRC meeting was Jerry Link, a self-styled authority on rock, who had been condemning the music's lyrics and influence for over six years in the Washington area. He presented a slide show endemic to antirock preachers. (Most of it would be redone for the benefit of the PMRC husbands at a Senate hearing.) He read from Motley Crue's *Shout at the Devil,* then "If the Kid Can't Make You Come" by Time, featuring Morris Day, another Prince *Purple Rain* film spinoff, plus an obscure album by the esoteric Impaler band titled *The Rise of the Mutants*.

Link, who would become another consultant for the PMRC, sold his audience a bill of goods, using a highly misrepresentative sample designed to further inflame the passions of the "Washington Wives" *and* their husbands. In a revealing comment Susan Baker recalled, "Listen, I grew up bopping with Elvis . . . Chuck Berry . . . lost my thrill on Blueberry Hill . . . Of course, *now* I know that song was suggestive, *but then I didn't* (emphasis added).[18] A number of broadcasters and scholars compiling thematic lists of songs omitted Fats Domino's "Blueberry Hill" from their "sexuality" category.

Without questioning Link's credentials or assumptions the "Washington Wives" embarked on their crusade. The PMRC debut garnered little attention. An item buried in the back pages of the *Washington Post* was all the media coverage the event generated. The outcome of the meeting was a letter sent to record companies, the signatories again using their formal married names. "We just hit them on the head with the biggest plank we had," Tipper Gore told the *Wall Street Journal*.[19]

No stranger to politics, Tipper Gore was more than conscious of the industry's interest in snaking through a tax on blank recording tape equipment prior to the planned retirement of Senator Charles Mathias. Mathias shepherded the original legislation tied to the "Save America's Music" campaign prior to the *Universal* v. *Sony Betamax* Supreme Court decision. The failure of the drive had been a humiliating defeat for Gortikov after years of bombarding the industry and media with the evils of "home dupers." The blank tape tax legislation would hang over the negotiations between the PMRC and the RIAA in the future. Susan Baker in an August interview told a reporter there was no connection: "I don't even know the contents of those bills." She well may not have, but Stan Gortikov certainly did.

The PMRC letter to industry presidents and CEOs stressed a ratings system, thus allying the wives with the PTA. The letter also graphically described the lyrics to "Darling Nikki," Judas Priest's "Eat Me Alive," and Sheena Easton's version of "Sugar Walls," written by Prince. "I don't think Prince has any idea how much trouble he's caused," said an executive. "He's really their Exhibit A." With the possible exception of Twisted Sister, Prince was one of the few nationally known rock stars to appear on the "Washington Wives" list of the filthy fifteen."

Artist	Song	Rating
AC/DC	"Let Me Put My Love into You"	X
Black Sabbath	"Trashed"	D/A
Cyndi Lauper	"She Bop"	X
Def Leppard	"High 'n' Dry"	D/A
Judas Priest	"Eat Me Alive"	X
Madonna	"Dress You Up"	X
Mary Jane Girls	"My House"	X
Mercyful Fate	"Into the Coven"	O
Motley Crue	"Bastard"	V
Prince	"Darling Nikki"	X
Sheena Easton	"Sugar Walls"	X
Twisted Sister	"We're Not Gonna Take It"	V
Vanity	"Strap on Robby Baby"	X
Venom	"Possessed"	O
W.A.S.P.	"(Animal) F**k Like a Beast"	X

The PMRC, besides being married to the powerful, was media-wise. Mrs. Gore, Mrs. Thurmond, and others had campaigned with their husbands. Their media blitz began in earnest with appearances on talk shows and through press releases.

Operating from a donated office suite at the Metropolitan Square, the PMRC press releases began on May 14 as the founders surfaced on radio and television talk shows. Tipper Gore appeared on the network morning "news" shows. Their coup was the July 17 appearance of Tipper and Susan on the "Donahue Show," which generated 5,000 letters, some with donations, in a twenty-four-hour period.

The press, especially Washington columnists, joined in the campaign. George F. Will, William Raspberry, and David Gergen (former Reagan communications chief) decried the content of rock lyrics. In *U.S. News & World Report,* Gergen paraphrased the PMRC press release and concluded, "Presumably, if an album were X-rated, most radio stations and video programs would drop the worst offenders. . . . A growing army of parents is ready—and anxious—to join the campaign."[20]

Edward O. Fritts, head of the National Association of Broadcasters (NAB) contacted 806 members. He wrote: "The lyrics of some recent rock records and the tone of their related music videos are fast becoming a matter of public debate. Many state that they are extremely troubled by the explicit and violent language of today's songs." The open letter concluded, "It is, of course, up to each broadcast licensee to make its decision as to the manner in which it carries out its programming responsibilities under the Communications Act."

Broadcasters' responses were ambivalent. Some concurred. In highly competitive major markets, Z-100 (WHTZ New York) and VH-1's Scott Shannon expressed the prevailing opinion: "Our basic policy is to play what listeners demand. We don't try to impose our own rules." WHTZ had dropped "Sugar Walls" after a two-week rotation due to audience reaction.

In the ratings-conscious Boston market Sonny Jo White (WXKS) told a trade publication: "Thanks to TV and MTV, teenagers are more aware of everything today." He went on to indicate, "Are we trying to fool ourselves by not showing what's up with radio?" He didn't see contemporary lyrics as a *problem.*[21] Boston's local music video TV station V-66 was concerned. In a suburb, Weymouth, MTV was eventually "off cable TV" due to New Christian Right petitions. V-66 avoided "sexual or violent" material.

On May 31 Fritts mailed a letter to forty-five record labels requesting the lyrical texts of their product. Again, the NAB president denied any attempt at censorship: "We believe with your help we can play a constructive role by assisting broadcasters in making reasoned programming choices." He cited "the sheer volume" of product and the inherent difficulties of monitoring the matter.

A vast majority of label executives voiced a thundering "No comment!" in response. Arista's Clive Davis, no stranger to controversy, went public indicating he would warn broadcasters by letter when "there might be a problem . . . so they could use their own discretion." Conversely, "I don't mean to diminish the concerns of parents' groups or the PTA—but numerically, it's a fraction, less than 1 percent of songs released by record companies here. And there's also the risk of censoring artists who have just as much right to be heard as a novelist or a playwright."[22]

Gortikov, while attending a press conference for the American Copyright Council, a "public educational" lobby group, on Capitol Hill, agreed to talk with the PMRC. Following the meeting described as "door opening," by Pam Hower, it was indicated that the RIAA desired to leave discussions to the individual labels. Gortikov was aware that there was little consensus regarding ratings or warning stickers within the association's membership.

Bruce Morrison, a Connecticut Democratic congressman, and ten cosponsors introduced the Home Audio Recording Act of 1985. Filed June 17, H.R. 2911 would require soft and hardware manufacturers to compensate the copyright holders with a royalty fee. The recommended payments would range from 10 to 25 percent of the price of audio recorders, and one cent per minute for blank tape. Blank video cassettes were excluded from the bill. Opponents, such as Michael Blevins of the Audio Rights Coalition, countered that all people would be hurt by this. The record industry would be the only one to benefit. The record industry's congressional successes have been few. The RIAA would require all the support it could muster on what was generally viewed as anticonsumer legislation.

Shortly after the bill's introduction, Gortikov wrote to record company executives warning, "I cannot escape continuing dialogue with the PMRC in view of its Washington links." The letter went on to suggest that the association's attempt to get the unpopular bills through the national legislature would be jeopardized by a lack of a compromise on the lyric warning stickers. "Are we expected to give up Article One [of the Constitution] so the big guys can collect an extra dollar on every blank tape and 10 to 25 percent on tape recorders?" asked Frank Zappa.

Shortsightedly, MTV ignored the campaign with its usual posture of "there's no problem." The nation's capital did not have a cable system, consequently the music channel was generally overlooked. (Most of the "offensive" songs lacked an accompanying video.)

The Songwriter's Guild was not quite so sanguine. The organization's president, George Weiss, envisioned a storm brewing. In several forums he called for self-restraint. Repeating the Platonic thesis in a *Billboard* "Commentary" Weiss argued that producers of culture should use their influence in "shutting off the spigot of tasteless, blatantly sexual lyrics, and the shockingly graphic videos saturating the TV channels. There is surely enough violence in our society without glorifying it in the music aimed at our youngsters."[23] Weiss' letter evoked a response. There was some industry support, but others dissented. One Ohio broadcaster objected, "While I realize that the lyrical content of some of today's songs is suggestive, I don't consider them pornographic, or I wouldn't play them on the air."

The PMRC media campaign continued and snowballed. The catalyst was the "Donahue Show" appearance. On the talk show Tipper Gore and Susan Baker ran through the familiar litany of the excesses of rock lyrics. Finally a member of the audience asked, "Are we saying that drugs and sex, and pornography that's depicted on MTV, is fine? I don't hear any outcry about that." Christopher Connelly, a former *Rolling Stone* associate editor, fielded the question replying, "MTV is not the same as rock 'n' roll. MTV is a series of commercials. Promotional videos that are designed to create image for the product . . . if people skip buying the records they'll stop doing those videos. We don't like a lot of the videos either." Tipper Gore explained the PMRC's neglect of videos: "You have to start somewhere and they use the public air waves to sell their product, and MTV and rock videos are the wave of the future. Kids are saying, 'Have you seen Michael Jackson's new song?' They are seeing it and the images are very powerful when they're on the screen and it's having an impact on younger kids. The point again is that it's younger and younger kids that are being exposed to these mature themes." From the broadcast it became abundantly clear that the PMRC was more interested in the record companies than MTV or other rock outlets. Pack journalism followed.

The financially oriented *Wall Street Journal* covered the issue with other publications in close pursuit. The usual arguments were voiced. Record companies generally caved in. The shadow of the Morrison bill proved more significant. One executive said, "They are going to prevail," referring to the PMRC.

In August it was totally unclear how the industry would react, despite Gortikov's suggestion of a "generic labelling" akin to film ratings.

There was no united front. Publicist Robert Alschuler of CBS noted: "Any sort of rating system would be fraught with inequities." Merchandisers echoed Ross Solomon, coowner of the Tower Record chain, who said: "It's just plain dumb."

Off the record, NAB and RIAA members uniformly expressed the view that pending congressional legislation transcended the labelling issue.

After a wave of correspondence and two meetings, Gortikov proposed a printed inscription on albums to identify "blatant explicit lyric content." His August 5 letter suggested a "PG: Explicit Lyrics" label.

Several days later, the PMRC replied. The thrust of their counterproposal was that there should be an "R" label, to be determined by a "panel including all aspects of the business (artists, songwriters, producers, distributors, executives, broadcasters, retailers, et cetera), as well as a representative group from the community at large, to come up with specific guidelines."

The "Washington Wives" did offer to abandon their original ratings typology, but Mrs. Gore and associates felt "PG" wasn't strong enough and "R" would be more appropriate. The impasse would lead to the intervention of Senator Danforth, who announced information hearings on the subject. A staff source conded that the informational event would also "bring some pressure on the groups involved."

As PMRC and RIAA discussions dragged, postponed by Stan Gortikov's hospitalization for a blood disorder, the Danforth Senate communications subcommittee announced a September 19 hearing on "porn rock." The PMRC's "consciousness raising" had prevailed. The motivation for the subcommittee hearing is difficult to substantiate. Despite details, the PMRC did spark the controversial hearings characterized by one senatorial member as a "media event."

There exist several interpretations for the calling of the hearing and individual involvement. Steve Hilton, Senator Danforth's press officer, recalls: "There were three factors: one was the interest of the PMRC expressed to the staff of the commerce committee; two was the interest of Senator Gore in the issue; and three was Senator Danforth's interest, as the father of children, in the issue."

The ornate Senate chamber forum was packed. All four major news networks were present. Standing in the back were obvious heavy metalers. Outside the Capitol members of the Moral Majority picketed against "porn rock." Officially the hearing was labeled "Contents of Music and the Lyrics of Records."

The first witness was Senator Paula Hawkins (R-Florida). She, after opening statements, quickly expanded the discussion to music videos. "I am not sure how many of my colleagues get much opportunity to watch any of the music video shows now available on cable and free TV." Hawkins then proceeded to show segments of Van Halen's "Hot for the Teacher," followed by Twisted Sister's "We're Not Going to Take It." She concluded, "I think a picture is worth a thousand words.

This issue is too hot not to cool down." Susan Baker appeared after Senator Hawkins. She complained about an MTV promotion involving Twisted Sister.

Senator Hawkins appeared more concerned with music videos than the subject of record labeling. The exchange with Susan Baker went this way:

HAWKINS: Well, it is my understanding it is no longer possible to have a successful rock album without a video; that MTV is widely viewed by children, whether their parents are home or not. Has your group met with representatives of the TV industry?

MRS. BAKER: Yes we have, and MTV was originally begun to promote records. . . . And there have been some really fun things done with MTV and some really awful things done. So we have talked with them, but we will meet with them again.

HAWKINS: What was their response?

MRS. BAKER: Well, their response was that they already had standards in place. We had thought that their standards should be a little tighter for a younger viewing audience. But we will be asking them to label videos that have violence or sexually explicit material in them, so that parents will know.

Baker repeated her stance that MTV should cluster the disagreeable clips and indicated that a second meeting with the MTV brass would be forthcoming. Ironically, MTV executives were not invited to testify. An unsigned letter for the Congressional Record was submitted. MTV's letter to the subcommittee contained the usual "standards" motif. The anonymous writer (Les Garland) advocated:

As in an art gallery, MTV presents exploratory and imaginative art forms, the interpretation of which may occasionally generate honest disagreements among individuals who respond differently to their messages. The review process demands difficult, subjective judgments which reflect sensitivity and concern. Yet, clearly it will be impossible for everything to appeal to all people at all times.

A PMRC spokesperson denied any knowledge of Mrs. Danforth's involvement with the organization. Tipper Gore told *Rolling Stone* that the chairman's wife was "connected with" their organization.[24]

The "Washington Wives" did receive the attention of the record industry, as the scheduled witness list indicated (see Table 10.1).

The dialogue continued. The RIAA rejected a ratings system. The PMRC desired more than the previously offered "PG" designation.

The PTA, not yet officially connected with the PMRC, was becoming

Table 10.1
SENATE COMMITTEE ON COMMERCE, SCIENCE, AND
TRANSPORTATION
Witness List*
Hearing on Record Labeling
Thursday, September 19, 1985, 9:30 a.m.

Senator Paula Hawkins
Parents Music Resource Center, 300 Metropolitan Square, 655 15th Street,
N.W., Washington, D.C. 20005
Mr. John Denver, Post Office Box 1587, Aspen, Colorado 81611
Frank Zappa, c/o Daniel C. Rosenberg, Esq., 4th Floor, Wilshire Palisades
Building, 1299 Ocean Avenue, Santa Monica, California 90401
Mr. Dee Snyder, Twisted Sister, Freefall Talent Group, 40 Underhill Blvd.,
Syosset, New York 11791
Mrs. Millie Waterman, National PTA Vice-President for Legislative Activity,
5256 Corduroy Road, Mentor, Ohio 44060
Mr. Stanley M. Gortikov, President, Recording Industry Association of Amer-
ica, Inc., 888 Seventh Avenue, Ninth Floor, New York, New York 10106

PANEL
Dr. Joe Stuessy, University of Texas at San Antonio, 12854 Castle George, San
Antonio, Texas 78230
Dr. Paul King, 2911 Brunswick Road, Memphis, Tennessee 38134
Mr. Eddie Fritts, President, National Association of Broadcasters, 1771 N
Street, N.W., Washington, D.C. 20036
Mr. William Steding, Executive Vice-President, Central Broadcasting Divi-
sion, Bonneville International Corporation, 12700 Park Central Drive, Suite
512, Dallas, Texas 75251
Mr. Robert J. Sabatini, Jr., WRKC-FM, King College, 4508 Cedell Place,
Camp Springs, Maryland 20748
Mr. Cerphe Colwell, 11117 Waterman's Drive, Reston, Virginia 22091

* Not necessarily in order of appearance

increasingly concerned. "We're uncomfortable with the fact that
[PMRC] is asking record labels to 'carefully consider' their contacts
with artists whose material is sexually, or otherwise, explicit, and we
feel that borders on abridging First Amendment Rights," said Tari
Marshall. The PTA spokesperson was correct. Even Tipper Gore,
commenting on the hearing, said, "We aren't seeking legislation or
regulation."

Artists, producers, and others remained unconvinced. Trade magazines and ABC's "Nightline" found dissenters. Manager Cliff Burn-
stein told *Billboard*, "If you don't fight every little incursion of
freedom of speech, this is the kind of thing that's going to happen. It's
all well and good to say they're just targetting obscenity and violence;
the next thing you know it will be 'Romeo and Juliet,' or the equivalent

in music." Auguring the future he maintained, "All artists, managers, and producers should be calling the record companies they do business with to tell them, 'Don't cave in, not even a little bit.' It's very important for all to be heard on this issue, because it could just creep in very quietly. . . . They take one or two examples and say this is what the popular music industry is all about."

Motley Crue's comanager noted, "I guess they don't like 85 percent of our material. We've had record burnings, and we've played dates in the Bible Belt where religious groups have put pressure on radio stations and colliseum managers who were working with us."

"Where do you start and stop?" queried Sheena Easton's manager. "Does 'Puppy Love' mean bestiality? Does 'On the Good Ship Lolli-pop' mean a psychedelic trip? There's no place to stop."[25]

Appearing on "Nightline" Kandy Stroud responded, "Nobody's talking about taking away anybody's First Amendment rights." "This is censorship," complained Frank Zappa, a leading critic of the PMRC. The rock innovator went on to point out the Shopping Mall Association's threat to cancel leases if "you rack hard-rated albums." Ted Koppel characterized the September 13 show as an "interesting discussion," which would continue on Capitol Hill in six days. The stormy late-night news program would prove to be a mere warm-up.

Coincidentally, the Mathias Senate copyright subcommittee promised to introduce an audio blank taping bill in late September. The RIAA was further torn between potential increased revenues and "artistic freedom." Most record labels, predictably, went with the profit motive.

The cablecasters ignored the debate. In June, MTV made a presentation of their "standards" code "to assure they were aware of the differences between us and other generic music video shows." "Often, although it may appear that we are running the same video as another show, we are actually showing an edited version," said MTV's "standards" person, Michele Vonfeld.

The music video telecasters were fairly blasé about the entire polemic. A majority of Jeffery Link's selected examples had never been visually aired. David Benjamin of "Friday Night Videos" said: "We have always worried about the moral sensibility ties of the great American public." He did admit to increased pressure from NBC and its affiliates. A BET producer, airing Sheena Easton and Prince, told an interviewer: "We don't feel the community is offended by our programming."

Local overground show executives repeatedly stated that their playlists mirrored "community standards." Linda Rosenfeld of Los Angeles' *Video 22* program said: "We generally don't offend people, but we do want the kids to see most of what's out there." She dismissed "extremists and alarmists."[26] "We have local programming here and producers who stop some of the videos and the violence going on TV," says Doug Podell of Detroit's "The Beat."

On Wednesday, September 11, the PMRC and the PTA joined forces. The coalition remained adamant in opposing the RIAA's generic warning, but conceded that "full disclosure" of lyric on jackets would suffice. This was a minor retreat from the "ratings" system. The seemingly more rational lyric proposal, as Gortikov would soon point out, was impractical. Record labels in many instances lacked copyrights to publish lyrics. There also existed the problem of increased costs if the PMRC/PTA proposal was adopted.

Music industry insiders considered 1985 as relatively "flat." There was a lull in contrast to the previous year of unprecedented grosses. Even Prince could not repeat the sale success of *Purple Rain*. Both viewpoints would surface before the Danforth committee.

President Reagan, addressing a Republican fund raiser, rhetorically entered the fray by telling the party faithful: "Music and media flood their children's world with glorifications of drugs, violence, and perversity—and there is nothing they can do about it, they're told because of the First Amendment." Judicially, the chief executive was correct; however, the RIAA was very conscious of Congress' actions concerning privacy and blank tape legislation.

There exists a strange symbiotic relationship between the key components of the music industry. They need one another, but the basic interests are quite dissimilar. Merchandisers (NARM) and broadcasters are dependent on "hit" product. Labels want to "break" new acts.

In legislative actions since 1909 (the passage of the original Copyright Act) rarely have these parts united in a common front. Keeping with trade the NARM board of directors dissociated from the RIAA on record labeling. After citing the usual artistic freedom slogan and the minute number of controversial songs, the directors suggested artistic reasonability. They must "be made to realize that, in addition to the moral issues, lyrics which are objectionable to the general public will cause the song to suffer. Air play will lessen and retailers and distributors will have concerns about attempting *to sell such songs*" (emphasis added). The board rejected ratings, adding only "voluntary efforts" can solve the dilemma.

A prevailing attitude at NARM was that they "didn't want to turn off buyers,'' face mall evictions, or support the proposed blank tape tax. (NARM was the last to join in the ''Save America's Music'' campaign, only after considerable arm twisting.)

Disregarding NARM's opposition, the RIAA and the PMRC/PTA announced an accord at a Washington press conference on the first Friday of November. The truce proved a trade-off. In a press release twenty record labels, including all the ''majors,'' stated they would ''identify future releases of their recordings with lyric content relating to explicit sex, explicit violence, or explicit substance abuse. Such recordings, where contractually permitted, either will be identified with a packaging inscription that will state: 'Explicit Lyrics–Parental Advisory' . . . or such recording will display printed lyrics . . . [this will meet] the concerns of parents of younger children and to achieve a fair balance with the essential rights and freedom of creators, performers, and adult purchasers of recorded music.''

The PMRC/PTA agreed to ''support and defend the lyrics and labeling policies and the companies which implement them, and to appeal to the remaining companies for cooperation.'' All parties agreed to suggest that the Danforth committee desist from governmental action.

The Mathias committee began hearings several days earlier on the home-tape legislation—a mere coincidence no doubt. Veteran manager Ron DeBlasio shrugged, ''I realize the politics of it, and I think everybody else does as well. The industry had to give up something. But since they had to do it, let's hope it stops here, and let's get on to something else.''

''Honestly, I think we're all bored with it and want to get back to our jobs,'' said Charley Prevost, president of Island Records. He was an opponent of the accord. The outspoken Tower Record chain and NARM secretary Ross Solomon felt the agreement would boast sales of ''albums with racy lyrics.''

Regarding music video, the merchandiser told a reporter, ''I have felt from the beginning that it's a non-issue. If something is so patently objectionable, then it will be seen to be non-broadcastable and won't be recorded in the first place.''[27]

Following the arrangement, the industry refocused on more pressing internal issues. Heavy metalers were unhappy. *Hard Rock,* a teen-oriented magazine, cried: ''Cave-in in D.C.: Liberty Smothered by Greed.'' Donald Lyons in a three-page piece accused the PMRC of censorship and the desire to ''kill rock and kill joy; they are the new witch-burning Salem Puritans.''

MTV Acquitted?

The dialogue during "The Donahue Show" and the Danforth hearings suggested that MTV would be the next victim on the PMRC hit list. In press interviews the congressional wives made little secret of their concern with music videos. Talking with Don Lyons, Susan Baker said on August 6 that MTV was "blatant and offensive" and "should have a visible rating mark that should stay on the screen throughout the video. And it'd be a good idea to have a daily period, say from 2 to 6, when only benign music videos would be played." Her colleague, Tipper Gore, was more adamant: "I'm disturbed by the portrayal of women and the graphic violence on MTV. An older person or teenager can look at this and see the humor in it, but an eight- or ten-year-old isn't anesthetized yet. Power images on television, whether it's MTV or "The A-Team," have a strong effect on younger kids." Continuing the *Rolling Stone* session, she pointed to Van Halen's "Hot for the Teacher" video to support her argument. In discussing the popular clip "Thriller," Susan Baker repeated the argument that visuals "should also have [a warning] noted before the videos are played."

MTV's response was the existing content guidelines: "We think our standards are stricter than the networks," regulated by the FCC. The publicist's point was well taken, as NBC-TV and WTBS did air clips unedited that were rejected by MTV. MTV added that most of the "filthy fifteen" did not have supporting videos. "Or if they do, we have either declined to play them or played them only after they were sent back for editing," said the usual anonymous spokesperson.

MTV had fortified its programming. The PMRC was invited to a presentation in June designed to educate the group about the "differences" between us and other generic music video shows," said Michele Vonfeld. "Often, although it may appear that we are running the same video as another show, we are actually showing an edited version."

Sue Binford, vice-president for publicity, told *Rolling Stone:* "We think we do a very fine job of balancing the sensitivities of the cable distributors, the advertisers, the consumer, and the music industry." A legion of heavy metal mavens would hardly concur.

David Benjamin of "Night Night Videos" responded: "The clips that the PMRC played on "Donahue"—that was the first time I'd seen most of those videos. Where they came up with this stuff is beyond me. As far as I'm aware, there has never been a complaint about any video we've ever shown. And NBC keeps a very close eye on that." Cynthia Friedland, the mother of a fourteen-year-old and coproducer of "Night Flight," says: "I am not in favor of a rating system, and I feel that many parents are shirking their own responsibility by relying on labels . . . putting a label on a record isn't going to make anybody, not a kid anyway, not buy a record. If anything, it's going to tempt them." As ideo-theology was faced with reality, Donny Osmond—hardly in the Dee Snyder category—concurred: "I'm going to have to try like crazy to avoid a G-rated album . . . in no way is Donny Osmond going to be coming out with a G-rated album."

Underlining Osmond's economic argument was MTV's Second Annual Video Awards show where David Lee Roth, described in a *People* magazine cover story as a caveman and sexual chauvinist who "has offended parents everywhere," was nominated in six categories. He failed to win a single statue.

MTV did not take the PMRC too seriously. FCC regulations, upheld by the judiciary, banned any form of censorship. Sue Binford was correct that the "masters of MTV" were not in Washington. The "Wives" lacked any organizational constituency transferable into lobbying activities or single-issue balloting.

Music video programmers publically denied any impact. Les Garland countered complaints from "offensive" acts and their managers. He said, "Rock videos have replaced cartoons and 'The Three Stooges' after school. Who do they think is watching? It's definitely not the twenty-year-olds." Radio programmers followed suit, pointing to their mandate from the FCC.

MTV's smugness proved misguided, as their ratings should have proved. Still, the direct impact on the channel could be dismissed; in Les Garland's terms, "We just put the paintings on the wall." The flaw in the argument was that the quality of the art was becoming bland and for many viewers repetitious. The problem was quite simple: as the PMRC placed political pressure on the RIAA, with twenty-three consenting companies, and the NAB, the quality of the video clips would become stupefied. Viacom's takeover would not improve matters. By 1985 few, outside of the MTV publicity department, were calling Robert Pittman "a video *wunderkind.*"

Attacks continued. Television preachers, circuit riders, and the heavy metalists continued to take aim at MTV and broadcasting media.

TV Guide editorialized: "Diligent research reveals that a momentous event affecting youngsters of high school age occurred in August 1981—MTV was inaugurated. Since then SAT [Scholastic Aptitude Tests] scores have been on the rise. Could it be that the two phenom-

ena are related? Could MTV be the reason for . . . no, let's not even
think about it."[28] Columnist and "Nightline" correspondent Jeff Green-
field made the same argument: "Don't Blame TV."[29]

Newsweek's year-end issue ended on an objective note. They ran an
article titled "MTV's Message: Parents Worry About the Sex and
Violence in Music. Are They Really Bad for Our Kids?" Their ultimate
conclusion, after a survey of some national authorities in the social and
behavioral sciences was: "Nobody knows exactly what MTV is doing
to us."

Speaking before the New York Television Academy, Pat Robertson
took time out from his quest for the presidency to lambaste MTV. The
founder of the "700 Club" and CBN told the gathering, "Major rock
groups are singing about drugs and every kind of sex, from Prince's
'Darling Nicki' [sic] to Sheena Easton's 'Sugar Walls.' Rock groups
don't care about free speech. They're just trying to see what they can
get away with. They need to be told that they can't go any further than
a certain point on radio and television." (He neglected to mention
"Darling Nikki" had no MTV video play.)

Adopting a tactic from the Rev. Wildmon, Robertson indicated that
advertisers should boycott MTV. "They're bringing in $80 million in
basic revenues a year. That's higher than we get in commercials and
that of ESPN. And yet, they're showing music videos depicting one
guy killing his father with an ax [sic] others depicting sadomasochism
and the occult. Advertisers aren't being responsible in the ad placement. Can't we have some sense of responsibility, to strengthen our
cities, to strengthen our young? Wouldn't it be a prudent time to take
action?"

MTV's anonymous spokesperson replied, "The allegations leveled
at MTV with regard to its programming content are totally unfounded
and anyone who would take the time to watch an hour of MTV would
arrive at the same conclusion."[30] Cynthia Friedland was correct when
she said, "I don't see MTV taking any issue with it, or doing anything." The reason for the low profile was simply that MTV executives
view the standards procedure in place as fortifying the channel from
most assaults.

Rob Lamb, the "well-known expert" cited by the ultraconservative
U.S. Press, may have attacked the wrong artist in the person of Ronnie
James Dio. Pointing to "Holy Diver" Lamb said, "There's a lot of
demonic imagery. Witches and different objects like that come at you
during the video constantly. And so, a person really gets demonic
feeling from watching videos like that." Dio, who is not a satanist or
into the occult, told Anne M. Raso: "I think it's wrong that they want

to go after our videos. . . . And as far as violence goes . . . aah come on. It's all done tongue-in-cheek really, isn't it?" Doug Podell, among others who have spoken with Dio, does not see him in Lamb's perceptual framework.

MTV: Mephistophelian/Murderous Television?

Since its inception MTV has used a standards philosophy and a two-tier monitoring system for advertisers and video clips. "No gratuitous sex or violence" is the rule, although "gratuitious" is highly interpretative and subjective. The channel originally prohibited time buys for hard liquor, advocacy of gambling, smoking, birth control devices, dating services, drug paraphernalia, and X-rated movies and video products. The statement indicated: "Based on the standards and practices set forth herein, MTV will rightfully accept, decline, or revise" content.

In the beginning months these standards were basically applied with vigor to advertisers, but the video clips were another matter. Bob Pittman noted: "It's not the Barry Manilow channel. Some songs are unhappy. Some have a dark message. It's the essence of rock. It mirrors the issues of people moving from adolescence to adulthood [but we don't] show naked women running around or throwing babies out of trucks." Les Garland, one of the original members of the then three-member review committee said, "Censorship is not a word we like to use around here." On another occasion Garland indicated that the name recognition of an act was more important than the clip content.

As MTV grew in popularity the volume of "review" clips increased tenfold. The Acquisitions Committee was expanded to ten members meeting at 10:00 A.M. Tuesday morning. Ten percent of the aspirants were rejected for unsuitable content or substandard production techniques. The committee was expanded to fifteen members in early 1984. The video then goes to the "program-standards" person. "MTV's standards are as stringent as broadcasting standards," says Sue Binford. Our nameless spokesperson added, "And because we are in people's homes whether they like it or not, we have a certain responsibility to our affiliates and cable operators, who in turn are responsible to their community." "We would have to be very short-sighted not to take these factors into account. The trick is to get the video on MTV or on shows like 'Friday Night Videos' without compromising the creativity and integrity of the band," Elektra's Robin Sloane maintained.[31]

"Balance" for MTV is tricky business. One observer pointed out:

"They have to keep in mind who they're dealing with—the artist, label—without turning off the audience or antagonizing the moral watchdogs too much."

Misogyny, Exploitation, or Just Fun

Since the advent of the feminist movement various women's groups have been at odds with the music industry. The most notable confrontation occurred in the latter part of the 1970s when the Women Against Violence Against Women threatened to boycott Warner Communications Inc. product due to album cover content. David Horowitz, later president of MTVN, mediated the dispute.[32] Some clips shown on MTV rekindled the attack.

An organized feminist campaign against MTV has yet to be mounted. Occasional press salvos have been recorded, however. The barbs started flying in 1984.

The *New Leader*'s television critic, Marvin Kitman, was adamant: "I shudder at the thought of analyzing Billy Idol's 'White Wedding,' with the wedding ring of thorns that makes the bride's finger bleed, the chorus in black leather shaking their derrieres at the camera, the coffins, the exploding kitchen appliances. This one would have made the Marquis de Sade's top 40 chart."[33]

"Women are depicted in many videos as bitches, teases, castrators, and all-around sex-things," wrote Elayne Rapping. "Even female performers are often forced to play out these roles in order to get on MTV. The Waitresses' 'I Know What Boys Want' is only one of scores of videos by female singers in which tight skirts, garish make-up, and street-hustler poses are standard." She singled out Michael Jackson's "Thriller" as especially offensive because of the "women in danger" motif.

Dr. Tom Radecki added, "Rock stars are role models for kids, so it's not hard to imagine young viewers, after seeing 'Thriller,' saying 'Gee, if Michael Jackson can terrorize his girlfriend why can't I do it too?' "

Newsweek joined some of the critics. "Several clips feature women in leather gear acting out scenes of torture, bondage, and violence, and Billy Idol's 'White Wedding' includes Nazi-style salutes. MTV seems to follow network television's hypocritical policy of severely restricting nudity while giving violence a comparatively free hand; a Nazi-style salute from Idol's tape appears in one of MTV's own on-air promotions."[34]

Idol's video raised the ire of Kristine McKenna in the *Los Angeles Times*: "Sexual stereotyping comes to a glorious head in Billy Idol's

'White Wedding' video, which opens with a chorus line of women in black leather waving their fannys at the camera."

Without directly responding to these criticisms Idol defined his role: "They expect it, but they don't like it . . . they want excitement, as long as it's not at their own expense. They don't mind if someone's outrageous with somebody else. . . . We were making fun of rock 'n' roll." Many feminists and others didn't find Idol's clips especially "humorous," to use Bob Pittman's description.

In an interview with Leslie Ridgeway, Pittman elaborated: "I think video clips *spoof* sexism. . . . I think people are playing with the theme and making fun of it. We accept total responsibility for what we play. We wouldn't show a sexist clip."[35]

Sue Steinberg contradicted her former boss saying, "The emphasis on certain images contributes to the illusion of violence and sexism. They seem to see how far they can go. And it's getting worse." Similar sentiments were expressed at the September 19 subcommittee hearing, especially concerning Judas Priest's "Eat Me Alive" and AC/DC's "Let Me Put My Love into You."

The argument was not one-sided. While not apologizing for some of the excesses, a number of observers suggested that the role of women in music videos on MTV and elsewhere was an extension of the liberation movement. Holly Brubach in the *Atlantic* pointed to Cyndi Lauper's "Girls Just Want to Have Fun" noting, "Men begin to look like an awful self-important, dull bunch. Whether or not girls just want to have fun, they appear to be the only ones who know how."[36]

Dan Sperling of *USA Today* conducted an informal poll of social scientists concerning the role of women in music videos. Nearly all the responses dismissed the impact of MTV on change. However, Harvard psychiatrist Dr. Paul Laffer added, "In some ways it's natural as a by-product of the liberation movement that they have their say in that department as well." "Whatever the songs themselves may be saying, the women are portraying themselves as having many options," said psychologist Ann Weber. Another practitioner, referring to Lauper, Tina Turner, and Madonna, observed that it is "more consistent with the 1980s image of a woman. It's definitely away from the 'Cinderella-Prince Charming ideal.' These women represent part of the independent stature of women."[37]

David Gergen, an ally of the PMRC, dismissed these opinions writing, "Some sociologists say the music doesn't make an impression on teenagers. Others think nothing can be done. Nonsense." Lisa, age fifteen, said: "I hate the way, like, people think, like that all teenagers are stupid and just, like, watch MTV. I watch it, but I watch other things too. But sometimes the videos are better than a lot, like, other shows."

Renowned child psychologist Robert Jay Lifton perhaps best summed up the entire polemic over MTV and music TV by saying, "If anybody says he or she knows, I don't believe it, it's too new."

Notes

1. *Time,* December 15, 1980, p. 24.
2. *Baltimore Sun,* November 7, 1980.
3. *TV Guide,* April 18, 1981, p. 10.
4. "We use the definition of violence as the intentional and hostile use of force by one person against another to intentionally inflict harm upon the other person or try to inflict harm on the other person either physically or mentally," replied Radecki.
5. *Rock Video,* June 1985, p. 49.
6. From a January 10, 1984 press release.
7. *U.S. Press,* August 7, 1984, p. 9.
8. Jacob Aranza, *Backward Masking Unmasked* (Shreveport, Louisiana: Huntington House, 1984), p. 25.
9. See Michael Walker's "Backward Messages in Commercially Available Records," *Popular Music and Society* (185), 2–14.
10. *Billboard,* September 11, 1982, pp. 10, 60.
11. Wire service UPI release, May 15, 1984.
12. Wire service UPI release, May 16, 1984.
13. See *Billboard,* July 7, 1984, p. 4; October 27, 1984, p. 70.
14. *Rolling Stone,* November 7, 1985, p. 17.
15. *Newsweek,* May 6, 1985, p. 14. The news magazine is dated about nine days postdeadline.
16. *Rock Video,* November 1985, p. 30.
17. Examples are from Jonathan Gross' series in *Rock Video* (April 1984– February 1985); reappeared in *Hard Rock Video* (November 1985).
18. *Hard Rock Video,* January 1985, p. 29.
19. *Wall Street Journal,* July 31, 1985, p. 19.
20. *U.S. News & World Report,* May 20, 1985, p. 98.
21. Quotes from *Billboard,* June 8, 1985, p. 78.
22. *Billboard,* June 15, 1985, p. 73.
23. *Billboard,* June 29, 1985, p. 10.
24. *Rolling Stone,* November 7, 1985, p. 64. However cryptic, Steve Hilton's statement does appear to square with events.
25. *Billboard,* September 7, 1985, p. 68.
26. *Billboard,* September 21, 1985, p. 36.
27. *Billboard,* November 16, 1985, pp. 69, 75.
28. *TV Guide,* November 2, 1985, p. A–3.
29. *TV Guide,* January 18, 1986, p. 5.
30. From a document addressed to potential advertisers and record labels in *Cablevision,* March 24, 1986, p. 12. The patricide illustration is a fabrication. Robertson, no doubt was referring to Twisted Sister's "We're Not Gonna Take It." The slapstick video has no ax being wielded, and the

militaristic antirock father survives his ordeal in the best "Road Runner" fashion.

31. *Rolling Stone*, November 10, 1985, p. 18.
32. *Victimology* (1977–78), pp. 510–24.
33. *New Leader*, January 9, 1984, p. 20.
34. *Newsweek*, April 18, 1983, p. 96.
35. *Satellite Week*, February 3, 1985, p. F–4.
36. *Atlantic*, July 1984, p. 1000.
37. *USA Today*, March 14, 1983, p. 30.

Epilogue

Hey, hey, we're the Monkees. . . .
Come and watch us sing and play
We're the young generation
And we've got somethin'
to say. . . .

© Screen Gems/EMI

While the 1984 fourth-quarter Nielsens may have created a storm at MTV, the 1985 numbers generated a full-blown hurricane. The downward slide was severe enough for Nielsen vice-president William Hamill to suggest in a December 20, 1985 letter addressed to Robert Pittman that the ratings service would investigate its sampling techniques, as "we have not seen declines in any individual demographic segment as large as these for MTV." He went on: "This is the first time a demographic fluctuation this large has happened." Reportedly, the original findings showed a 0.8 in 1985, suggesting a drop of some 35.5 percent as opposed to the previous year. The fourth-quarter twenty-four-hour rating was down to 0.7. More significantly, segmental declines by age were 20 percent in the eighteen- to twenty-four-year-olds and a horrendous 25 percent in the twelve- through seventeen-year-olds. An unidentified spokesperson for MTV responded, "Any *projected* ratings are invalid, and anyone who projects a rating obviously does not understand the nuances of ratings and sample designs" (emphasis added). A dramatic drop of this kind could have dire consequences. Jack Hill of the Cable Advertising Bureau, however, told *Billboard* that MTV "has no real direct competition" and will probably "remain a major vehicle for delivering teens and young adults. Even with such a large drop in those areas, that's still where the bulk of their audience is." Overall, he noted, "the effect of a demographic drop of this scale could be disastrous. Networks live and die by these numbers." Pittman demanded a reevaluation. These numbers may have affected Viacom's decision to syndicate "Countdown" and also sealed the fate of WCI eleven-year veteran executive David

317

Horowitz. Syndication could serve as a profit-making device and as an advertisement for MTV.

MTV's deterioration may have been due to a general "lull" in the record business. There were only nine gold singles in 1985, the lowest figure since 1964. Albums were steady, but individual hits are the forte of the music network.

The explosion of the shuttle Challenger on January 28, 1986 claimed seven lives and shocked the nation. A less significant casualty was Fred Seibert's highly acclaimed moon-landing MTV logo. On February 5, seven days after the tragedy, Tom Freston announced: "A week has come and gone and it's obviously just too painful to use [the NASA space footage logo] as a channel identification."

January was far from being totally bleak for the channel. The Discovery Music Network's antitrust suit was settled out of court for what MTV characterized as a "nominal fee." Joel Bennett, Discovery's attorney, announced that the agreement "basically covered all Discovery's legal fees."

"MTV Presents the 1985 *Rolling Stone* Readers Poll," hosted by Michael Douglas with some segments introduced by Jann Wenner, was surprising. *Stone* reporters, collaborating with MTV directors and producers, stretched the imagination. During the broadcast spots were run promoting the two Viacom pay-cable movie networks and MTV. Nickelodeon and especially VH-1 were conspicuously absent. Michael Goldberg's appearance interviewing John Fogerty and the closing credits—Executive Producers: Robert Pittman *and* Jann S. Wenner—boggled the imagination. Goldberg has been a frequent critic of MTV. It was equally common industry knowledge of the longstanding animosity between Pittman and Wenner. The explanation lay in the final credit: a "Viacom Presentation."

Pittman's stubborn positions regarding oldies and new music were evaporating with each new press release. "Economics makes for strange bedfellows," said a source. The ratings fall provided the Viacom hierarchy with the ammunition to combat hard-core resistance to synergizing MTV. A number of executives privately feared a drastic format change. Pittman was playing the usual corporate game as CEO, but others expressed the conservative position: "Stick with the format, it works." The so-called conservatives lost. Dale Pon's new slogan— "MTV, some people just don't get it"—began to take on an entirely new meaning not intended by the ad agency.

MTV's decision to delete the moonlanding log, whatever the reason, was partially symbolic of the end of an era. Reluctantly, MTV was forced to deal with Nielsen Cable Activity Report findings despite their protestations that the network's target audience was underrepresented in the sample. In this instance trade papers and magazines were not accused of inaccurate reporting of the "numbers." This downturn characterized the entire industry.

1986 opened on a sour note for the music business. RIAA numbers would confirm that the success of 1984 was not repeated in 1985. Outside of the *Miami Vice* soundtrack, which was number one for eleven weeks, a precedent, there were few "monster" albums. Artists like Dire Straits and Phil Collins did well, but the charity mega-events such as Live Aid did not produce soundtrack LPs. There were no *Thriller*s or Springsteen sensations. MTV's ratings plummeted downward. While the panic button wasn't yet pushed, the original tenets were overlooked. Personnelwise a scorecard was helpful. MTV was entering another phase.

The RIAA released the bad news on March 25, 1986. Despite a 9 percent increase in LP releases, the number of units shipped slipped four points since 1984. Cassette shipments climbed only a miserly 2 percent in contrast to double-digit leaps in the past two years. (Gross economic figures are misleading as a label can raise prices to compensate for lower unit volume.) The RIAA press release indicated that the limited number of compact discs saved the year economically from the declines in albums and cassette sales. The usually optimistic RIAA described 1985 as being generally "flat." Singles shipped dropped 8 percent from the previous year. This did not augur well for MTV, as cutbacks were definitely in the offing; also, the "flatness" of 1985 explained the dearth of quality clips during the year. One executive at "Night Tracks" said, "We are prisoners of what the labels provide."

Not surprisingly three of the major winners at the second annual MTV Video Music Awards were Tina Turner's "What's Love Got to Do With It?" Phil Collins' "Easy Lover," and Glenn Frey's "Smuggler's Blues." All were prominently featured on "Miami Vice." "Miami Vice," an NBC show, was proving a significant exposure vehicle feeding back to MTV. It would have proved interesting if the awards had an instrumental category to add to the existing fifteen.

A small town in New Mexico held a "Dress-Up Day" where students came in the regalia of their favorite television performers. A few white and black gloves were present, but the green and turquoise "Miami Vice" influence predominated. The school principal, Ray Swinney, was amazed: "My son and all his friends know all the songs and what the ["Miami Vice"] characters say and what happens. I don't think you can begin to understand the impact."[1] A year later a syndicated columnist criticized: "The music was throbbing and compelling. It seemed to propel the plots." Roger Simon elaborated: "The show seems to have descended into the cold, dark depths of someone's [Michael Mann?] troubled soul." The ratings decline supported this negative perception. The progeny of MTV was having a greater teen impact than the musical parent, at least in a small town west of Albuquerque.

Even "Miami Vice" was experiencing difficulties, however. The cost overruns were a vexation at Universal. NBC was paying Universal Pictures $950,000 per episode. The costs frequently surpassed the $1.5 to $2 million range. Don Johnson, the costar, was earning $1.5 million per year for the series as of 1986. Philip Michael Thomas raked in $30,000 for each segment. Universal hoped to recoup their investment through future syndication.

The record industry was beginning to sour on MTV's synergism. Clive Davis was the point man expressing the feelings of many afraid to publicly criticize MTV. On several occasions the flamboyant Artista president lambasted the entire gatekeeping media for their conservatism (shades of 1981!).

While addressing the second annual music symposium on May 2 Clive Davis said: "There are large and vital areas of modern music that are being disenfranchised by all radio formats who, it seems to me, have made arbitrary and narrow decisions about what listeners will and will not accept." He compared the industry's "play it safe" attitude to "the conservative menace in the forms of the PMRC and the Moral Majority and the other guardians of public taste."

"You can count on one hand the number of heavy-rotation AOR acts whose roots don't go back to at least the seventies and very often the sixties," said Davis. "Why? There is no shortage of exciting new rock." Yet, he added, programmers "continue to play it safe, to revert to 'classic rock' formats, to pound the same cuts and the same artists over and over. . . . It took MTV to program the new and the different sounds, and it then forced the hand of the establishment-oriented stations to get with it."

In a *Rolling Stone* interview Davis decried the state of gatekeeping in the 1985 period: "The last time something like this occurred, MTV picked it up and started programming Duran Duran, Culture Club, and a number of English artists who couldn't get arrested except in two or three cities. Now MTV is pretty well reflecting radio. I don't think they're any more or less adventurous."[2] Pittman and associates were trying to address the flatness of 1986 with programming changes.

MTV's and Robert Pittman's agenda for 1986 was threefold: rejuvenate the network, raise ratings, and deal with Viacom's strategy. Some of these endeavors were by their very nature somewhat contradictory. Viacom's corporate philosophy of synergizing MTV and Pittman's view of narrowcasting were incompatible on the surface. "MTV is a paradox," said Bart McHugh, vice-president at Doyle Dane Bornbach Inc., a heavyweight on Madison Avenue.

The ratings situation bedeviled them, although the drop had no real external effect. The objections voiced by network executives were repeats of sentiments expressed by industry people and social scientists for years, especially when applied to certain demographic units in the society. MTVers were predominantly upset by the Nielsen description of declining youth market viewership. Youth were underrepresented compared to older generations and rural dwellers. Marshall Cohen said: "Kids are bad diary keepers."[3]

This *was* a significant decline, if Bob Pittman's earlier assessment was correct: "We will reach 90 percent of them in any given household. You'd have to be a social outcast not to watch."[4] The ratings indicated that the number of "outcasts" was growing. In direct response Pittman told *USA Today:* "I think the ratings have been blown way out of proportion in the press."[5] Once again the messenger was blamed for the situation. Most articles merely quoted Les Garland and others concerning the shortcomings of the Nielsens.

Pittman and senior vice-president and general manager of advertising Bob Roganti at least publicly pointed to unspecialized networks as the prime victims of ratings plunges. Pittman said: "We don't sell ratings. People come to us because they want the environment." Roganti was more specific, telling *Cablevision:* "What brings an advertiser to sit down and talk with us is that we're the only game in town with this demographic." He continued, saying MTV has been "the number one channel in terms of ad revenue for the past two years." The gross in 1985 was $86.3 million. Estimates were in the $97.2 million range for 1986. "It's still one of the few ball games in town with something that focuses on the young adult market," said Ron Kaatz, vice-president of the J. Walter Thompson agency.

Record industry executives, conscious of ever-escalating video clip costs, were not quite as supportive. One expressed the view that "MTV is in danger of being this year's Cabbage Patch Doll."[6] An Atlantic Records vice-president told Brian Donion, "They must universify programming in order to maintain viewer interest."[7] Some folks at MTV were hesitant. Tom Freston noted: "We will be producing more one-hour or ninety-minute music specials and more weekly music series." "Why paint the car when you've got a good color already," Martha Quinn told a reporter (she would be gone by the end of 1986).

The answer to the rhetorical statement was the ratings situation and Viacom's business ideology.

Video clips, even prior to MTV's launch, were termed the "building blocks" for the channel. Production costs were beginning to erode the blocks. With sales declining, record companies were becoming increasingly skittish about financing video clips. "We all went video crazy for a few years," said Arma Andon of CBS Records, "right up until this year [1986]. Now, we're just being more sensible. What you're seeing now is not so much a drop-off as a return to a sensible and practical level of clip production." The CBS Group was curtailing its involvement with videos. At Polygram, one of the last holdouts in 1981, Len Epand repeated the argument "We are definitely more selective now than we've been."[8] A&M stressed that the label would be more "careful" and "selective" in the volume of videos being made available. RCA and Warner Bros. planned no policy changes at the time. Jeff Ayeroff at Warner Bros. said, "To say that videos doesn't work for us is foolish, because it can and does."[9]

Disavowing company pressure, Journey announced they would follow Van Halen's lead and forgo visual support for their *Raised on Radio* album. The band's manager told Steve Gett, "They [video clips] didn't have any significant impact on the life of the records."[10] Herb Herbert was referring to previous hits with MTV exposure. Both bands enjoyed best-selling albums without MTV.

Bob Pittman saw the writing on the proverbial wall. Cost-conscious labels could follow the CBS model. The format already altered by "The Young Ones," "120 Minutes," and "The Monkees" required further tinkering. He hoped future additions would generate as much interest as the Monkee revival.

The Times They Are A-Changin'

David Fishof, a thirty-four-year-old talent agent specializing in athletes and concert tours, such as the highly successful "Happy Together" package, was motivated to have a twentieth anniversary Monkees summer tour. Given the sellouts of the Turtles (Flo and Eddie), the Association, Buckinghams, Gary Lewis and the Playboys, and others, a reunion of the Monkees, suggested by their older fans, did not seem totally absurd. Fishof, headquartered one floor below the MTV suites, engineered a reunion of three of the original members. Mike Nesmith declined, preferring to continue with his Pacific Arts projects. Reportedly, MTV executives were simultaneously considering reviving the group's late sixties NBC episodes purchased from Col-Gems.

In mid-February Tom Freston, MTV general manager, called for a "Monkee-thon" or "Pleasant Valley Sunday" for February 23 which would feature continuous "Monkees" programs, 45 in all. This twenty-two-and-a-half-hour special would reintroduce the Michael Nesmith-led Beatles-imitation group. In March, MTV proposed two "Monkees" episodes per day—one at noon and the other in prime time: 8:00 P.M. Freston told *Cablevision,* "The Monkees had a seminal influence on rock video. They were the first TV video band and a lot of their songs have lasted on the oldies charts.[11] Speaking to *Rolling Stone* he said: "We all made fun of their music back in the sixties, but they're classics."[12]

"They're hoping to attract the Yuppie nostalgia crowd. Their ratings are in trouble and they want to try something different. It's an interesting way to respond to their ratings difficulties," said Dave Marsh.

The "Pleasant Valley Sunday" telethon would be the second all-day MTV special, following in the footsteps of the July 12, 1985 Live Aid seventeen-hour extravaganza. The reasoning for the acquisition of 58 "Monkees" shows made little overt sense as nostalgia. The Yuppies were targeted by VH-1. Many media watchers felt that the nostalgia craze in television, with the successful "Perry Mason," "I Dream of Jeannie," and "Leave It To Beaver" revival specials, might warrant the resurrection of the "schlock" rock show. Author/critic Greil Marcus believed the decision was made to attract the younger end of the demographic scale—those too young to remember the original series, which was finally cancelled in August 1968.

Geraldine Laybourne, vice-president at Nickelodeon, appeared to support this view. She contended that the Monkees were "very attractive," as the minus-fifteen age network could air the episodes as well in prime time. She said, "We're not doing this just out of nostalgia," adding considerable weight to the Marcus thesis.

A further ploy to boost ratings was a viewer request call-in, "Dial MTV." This idea was certainly not new, although less expensive than the HIT Video USA number. The 900 prefix only cost 50 cents, as opposed to a long distance call to Houston.

The critics were proven partially right. Tom Freston said: "We've never received such a volume of mail. We were dumbfounded by the whole thing." Robert Pittman's psychographically determined obser-vation was revalidated: "At MTV, we don't shoot for the fourteen-year-olds—we own them." In response to the viewers' reaction to the vintage group, March was promoted as "Monkees Month" and April became "More Monkees Madness," exhibiting three segments per day. On April 18, MTV announced an end-of-the-month five-day special "I Was a Teen-Age Monkee: A True Story." Highlights consisted of Peter Tork and Mickey Dolenz discussing the NBC years, the tours, and the feature film *Head*. Jerry Barry and Jerry Goffin, who wrote many of the groups' early hits, were interviewed. Older fans explained their devotion over the years. Even Frank Zappa briefly appeared.

Although planned prior to the "Pleasant Daily Sunday," Rhino Records would release all of the original Monkees albums. Arista Records, denying any linkage, released a greatest hits album, which surfaced at 180 on the *Billboard* chart on May 3. *Then & Now . . . The Best of the Monkees* went platinum after staying on the charts over fifty weeks. Five Rhino reissues were on the "Top Pop" albums list of 200. The summer tour proved a guaranteed sellout, with local promoters fighting over the bookings. The tour was expanded into the fall with talk of the trio doing concert dates abroad. Rumors also abound concerning "The New Monkees," an NBC prime-time series featuring as in 1966 four unknowns. *Newsweek*'s Jim Miller credited MTV with the phenomenal comeback.[13]

In the spring of 1986 MTV introduced a two-hour show, "120 Minutes," as a vehicle to expose new acts. Les Garland noted that the network viewers expected to "see new music aired on the channel." Record executives objected that the weekly Monday night program would be broadcast at 1:00 A.M. (EST). "Anything on at one o'clock in the morning is tough. I would think they'd be trying to reach the thirteen-to-eighteen-year-olds, and they're all sleeping by that time on the East Coast," said Arista's Peter Baron. Epic's Harvey Leeds added, "To me, it shows their lack of respect and commitment for what labels do for a living. Still, least it's on at 10 P.M. in Los Angeles." In usual fashion, Garland retorted: "We're not afraid of the time slot. One o'clock in the morning for a two-hour special is a logical place on the East Coast. Letterman is on at one in the morning [sic] and he had a great audience." Garland neglected to address the East Coast demographic issue. Letterman's appeal is to the Yuppies, not teens. Despite MTV's denials, many felt the lunar program was a peace offering to increasingly disgruntled record executives, managers, and artists. One manager noted, "Why should artists pay for a show where half the target market is sleeping? How many music directors are up that late on Mondays?" He seriously questioned the exposure value of "120 Minutes" as scheduled. There were, of course, the VCR owners.

Older young people were tiring of the standard fare on MTV. This ploy *might* have regenerated some of the early excitement—"anything can happen"—of 1982 and 1983. Cautiously, MTV's Liz Heller told *Billboard,* "I think the show is a great idea—it's guaranteed exposure for those acts you're worried will get any air play at all." Garland couldn't agree more: "The audience has, over the past four and a half years, grown to expect new music [artists?] on the channel."[14] That was correct, but "Is this the right format?" some would ask.

Basking in the glow of the well-received Monkees campaign, MTV's spirits were dampened by the Nielsens. Due to advertiser pressure the polling organization finally made public the 1985 fourth quarter cable numbers. Research vice-president Ned Greenberg maintained, "While we at MTV are not convinced of the accuracy of the NCAR ratings for MTV, the data released ends previous unfounded speculation about low ratings and provides advertisers with the specific Nielsen data they need.[15] The National Cable Audience Research (NCAR) arm of television's "Bible" found MTV with an 0.6 share. The figure indicated a drop of 30 percent from the previous year. It confirmed that the 12 to 17 demographic was down 25 percent. It was hoped that "The Monkees" would turn this around. The number of eighteen through twenty-four-year-olds declined some twenty percent. One insider suggested that VH-1 may have fragmented the audience, thus accounting for the slump.

The July 1986 Nielsens showed a one-point gain. Each point reflects 859,000 cable households. The upturn, seemingly slight, found MTV tied with the Turner-owned all-news channel CNN and the USA Network featuring "Night Flight." While a direct link to "The Monkees" or "120 Minutes" could not be established, MTV showed the following gains:

1986	Affiliates	Households
January 6	3,385	27.8 million
March 31	3,385	28.0 million
July 7	3,400	28.2 million
September 1	3,556	29.0 million

Source: *Cablevision*

MTV's growth in another "flat" year could prove Jim Miller correct, at least as a hypothesis. The music networks, as noted by a Turner executive, are "prisoners" to what is available for broadcast from the suppliers, notably the record labels.

The fate of "120 Minutes" is unknown, especially in light of the cost containment policies of the labels. MTV's diversification did not end with these additions and changes. Shows such as "The International Hour," a monthly showcase; "The MTV New Video Hour," highlighting the latest releases; "The MTV Music News Viewers Poll," and the request line "Dial MTV" were added or in the planning stages.

Viacom's plans to syndicate a cut-down version of "Top 20 Video Countdown," scheduled for April, ran into label resistance. Notably, the CBS Record Group refused to supply slips for the show. The issue was royalty payments. Overexposure was the concern. "You've got a glut now with 'Friday Night Videos,' " a CBS source told *Billboard,* "which has essentially become a countdown show, Dick Clark, and others."[16] Robert Pittman did not see this as a problem as the show, subtracting commercials, station identifications, and other local filler, would actually be forty-five minutes in length featuring "about seven or eight videos." All of the titles would appear on the program hosted by Mark Goodman, but some labels would be absent. The loss of Springsteen, the Hooters, Sade, and in the future Michael Jackson clips augured poorly for the project.

Joseph D. Zaleski, president of the Viacom Domestic Syndicate, announced an April 12 debut on 104 stations encompassing 81 percent of national market. Ratings information on the venture are unavailable. A Viacom spokesman, Michael Gerber, expressed the view MTV should add a weekly movie, taking a page out of the "Night Flight" format book. Tentatively the "MTV Presents" film would fit the strategy: "We're looking for synergies with our properties."[17]

A May 30 MTV press release announced the debut of a new veejay— the first new on-air personality since 1981. Julie Brown, a pop music correspondent from the British breakfast show "TV AM," began the morning slot on June 9, a Monday. MTV's publicity department, in keeping with tradition, neglected to mention the departure of J.J. Jackson and Nina Blackwood, two of the originals. Blackwood quickly migrated to the syndicated weekly TV offering "Solid Gold" to do short interviews as their "music reporter."

Unlike the founding five video jocks the twenty-six-year-old Ms. Brown had considerable television and acting experience hosting MTV's European counterpart "Music Box." Tom Freston commented: "Julie's expertise in rock and roll and television, coupled with her versatility and great sense of enthusiasm, makes her a terrific addition to MTV and we're excited to welcome her to the channel."

The exiting of "Triple J" and especially Nina Blackwood evoked some critical responses. Jim Bessman, contributor to *Billboard* and *Rock Video,* lamented her firing: "I regret that Nina has left the MTV VJ ranks. As far as I'm concerned she was the only real person they had before the cameras." *Satellite TV Week* reported, "MTV management said her image was too steeped in an earlier era, a polite way of saying 'no more laid back ex-hippies.' " Off the record, a critic observed: "They canned the wrong people. Julie Brown's image is tarnished already—a black woman replacing them—that just takes the sting out of letting JJ go." In the *New York Times* Tom Freston denied race was a factor: "The girl was head and shoulders over everyone else we looked at. . . . It is true that we're more aggressively evolving than may be we have in the past. At least, it's being noticed now."[18] Carolyne Heldman would be the next addition later that year. In July John Sykes, vice-president of programming, a key figure in the history of MTV, quietly accepted a position with a Los Angeles talent agency.

MTV celebrated its fifth anniversary by replaying the New Year's concert, as in previous years. *TV Guide* and some trades made note of the five-year success story. *TV Guide*'s Howard Polskin acknowledged MTV's "hub" with a Pittman quote. The three-page article closed citing the ratings controversy and cutback in available video clips (August 23, 1986). The September 7 issue of *Cablevision* did a cover story on the network. The piece stressed the paradoxical theme of revenue and ratings.

"The rumors are like that every corporate takeover. There are at least a dozen different rumors on every possibility that you could think of. . . . I've talked with him [Pittman] and he gave me another five," said Fred Seibert in early 1986. In August the same year the dominant rumor became fact. Robert Warren Pittman resigned. The original reason given was that the MTV CEO would form a new record label in a joint venture with MCA and Viacom. Reportedly he would be cleaning out his desk by the end of the year. Allegedly Les Garland would accompany his boss to the West Coast.

Sidney Sheinberg, president and CEO at MCA, said: "We see him as someone who will try to remain at the cutting edge of cultural evolution, not just fixed on teenagers." The new project was described by Pittman in *Cablevision* as a "broad-based, diversified communications company, with involvement in many facets of the business."[19]

As expected, speculation abounded as to Pittman's motives. One school contended that Viacom had gone too far in restructuring the MTV format. Pittman's continued association with the communications conglomerate belies this argument. A more plausible scenario is that he lost a power struggle with Showtime's Neil Austrian for the chairmanship of Viacom's Networks Group.

On September 25 the lame duck CEO announced a major management shuffle at MTVN: "I am pleased to appoint two senior MTVN executives to newly created positions within the company. These appointments represent a consolidation of our organization with focus on the specific constituencies served by each executive, and recognize the outstanding achievements and enormous contributions of each to the growth and success of MTVN. The new management structure, combined with the strengths of the entire management team, position MTVN to continue its outstanding record of innovation and growth." Tom Freston became president of entertainment and Bob Roganti president of operations. Freston would handle the "nuts and bolts" while Roganti took over marketing and creative services and research.

Kenneth F. Gorman, whose position Pittman supposedly coveted, said: "The appointment of Messrs. Freston and Roganti are reflective of our ability to draw on our extraordinary pool of management and creative talent at MTVN." Of the original five, only methodologist Marshall Cohen survived, being appointed senior vice-president of research and corporate services in October by Roganti. Andy Setos became a Viacom engineering executive.

One of Cohen's more recent accomplishments involved investing several million dollars in AGB's National Television Audience Measure firm or "the People Meter." AGB was touted as a replacement for Nielsen to go on line in September 1988. MTV had not forgotten the Nielsens of the previous year.[20] Discussing the People Meter with *Billboard* Les Garland scolded, "Under Nielsen's current methodology, less than 10 homes [sic] across America determine MTV's ratings out of an audience of 30 million homes. That's what I call a ratings problem. . . . How can you believe a 0.8 or 0.7 rating, when you run a contest and get 500,000 entries?"[21]

In Search of . . . VH–1

The machinations at MTV were designed to maintain status, market share, and profitability. VH-1, a year after its launch, still had to establish an identity acceptable to the 25 + demographic. The candid Michelle Peacock noted that the channel had a "hard road ahead of them, just like MTV did—there are no believers at first." Epic's Harvey Leeds was one of the VH-1 agnostics: "Our research shows that VH-1 viewers are relatively light record buyers, and the majority say VH-1 has no effect on their purchasing decision. . . . I don't think

Sade's success could be directly attributed to VH-1. Let's face it—radio broke Sade. VH-1 has nothing like the kind of impact that MTV had on an act like 'Til Tuesday.''[22]

Billboard surveyed other labels and merchandisers and found a similar response. Tom Freston disputed the trade magazine's conclusions: "We have research from Nielsen saying the VH-1 viewer is 31 percent more likely to purchase albums and tapes than the nonviewer." (Had Nielsen suddenly become reliable?) "The Opinion Research Co. says that 47 percent of VH-1 viewers report that the channel has influenced their album and tape purchases," he went on. The adult contemporary television viewers reportedly bought 3.4 million albums in the past four months. Freston's data were not terribly convincing. VH-1 viewers by their very nature were "heavy" music consumers as opposed to nonviewers. Merchandisers countered that radio was the initial point of contact. A few saw the AC channel as, perhaps, visual reinforcement.

Despite the rebuttals VH-1 was planning changes. Kevin Metheny, the network's senior officer, resigned in late March. In a departing interview with *Cablevision* he acknowledged that "New Visions" would be only one of planned content alterations. "Some of the things that I wanted to do would have cost as much as one-half million dollars, but I don't know which of those they adopted," he said. Metheny described his leaving as "amicable" and said, "I'm tired. It was enough." He planned a long vacation.

On April 10 Lee Masters took over. Masters, a radio veteran, was an old cohort of Robert Pittman's, having worked as a deejay at WNBC beginning in 1977. He cohosted the syndicated "Album Tracks" on NBC affiliates with the MTV CEO. "Lee brings an exceptional breadth of experience to his new position," said Freston, "along with a track record that demonstrates both entrepreneurial talents and a strong ability to produce results. His expertise in both programming and management makes him exceptionally qualified to lead VH-1 into its next phase of growth and development." One cynic commented, "They brought in one of Pittman's buddies because they didn't want to spend the kind of money Kevin was urging."

In mid-1986 VH-1 expressed two goals: profitability and audience expansion to the Nielsen ratings level. The latter objective could be negative in light of the channel's number of households—11.9 million as of June was not impressive.

"If they approach and promote the service properly," said Sam Kaiser at Atlantic Records, "it could be a winner, but people are slow to change. They have to show a proper financial commitment to it."[23]

Lee Masters was aware of the problem of external perceptions, which became the reality. "We are in a sense experimenting," he said. One promised change would be to end the lag time of over two weeks in taping veejay segments. A set design alteration was in the works. Masters explained the slow start in contrast to the sister channel by claiming that adults did not "jump on the bandwagon so quickly for something new the way kids did with MTV."

In a follow-up interview with *USA Today* Masters elaborated that VH-1 would be entering Phase 2 under his tutelage. "We've had a chance to talk to viewers," he said, "about the ways they would like to see VH-1 improve."[24] He announced the airing of a twelve-hour Farm Aid II concert to be aired on July 4, and the addition of a sixth veejay. In September 874 affiliates reported that VH-1 had 13 million subscribers. January 1987 witnessed an increase to 1,189 CATVs with a potential 14.1 million viewers.

MTVN attempted to strengthen VH-1 by shifting much of the adult contemporary material submitted to MTV over to the sister channel. Not all labels were terribly happy with this strategy. Les Garland said: "Labels push all their videos for MTV, but we see a lot of them as being right for VH-1." Technically he was right, but record executives didn't always concur.

November and December found several new veejays being added to the staff. One was Tim Byrd, an ex-deejay who had hosted a dance show in Cleveland on WKYC-TV. After several radio positions he moved to New York's WKHK-FM. "Coming to New York wasn't originally one of my goals" he said. "The only time I'd been there, when I was 21, I'd been in a cab accident, so I wasn't anxious to come back." He migrated to WNBC-AM, becoming another MTVN alumnus.

Roger Rose was the next acquisition. An actor/comedian by profession—"Knight Rider," "Buck Rogers," and "Air Wolf"—he garnered some radio experience cohosting a drive-time show on Magic 106 and KFI. These were typical comedy mixed with music adult contemporary vehicles. By the end of the year, Masters had his on-air roster and 14 million subscribers.

Moves at MTV

As VH-1 continued into Phase 2, MTV altered its format, or at least claimed a redirection in its programming philosophy. Denying a connection with MTV's low Nielsen numbers, Les Garland said he desired new directions for the channel. He explained to *Billboard* that there would be a return to the network's "rock 'n' roll roots." "We've tried to be all things to all people," he explained. "Now we're having a terribly difficult time balancing the high numbers of video on the channel with all the various musical styles we're expected to play." MTV was averaging over a hundred clips in their rotation at the time. He added, "We can't confuse MTV fans with AC music" indicating that AC should be on VH-1. He further admitted, "MTV has made various compromises and widened itself to more types of music. Why? Part of it was playing the *ratings* game, part of it is appealing to advertisers."[25] Garland confessed that the original ethos had eroded. "Four years ago, we were balanced heavily toward new acts, because they were the only ones making videos. Then when the big acts started making them, we leaned more that way. We know we have to play hit songs, but we are now seeking a balance."[26]

In mid-December some changes were undertaken. They were not drastic. Martha Quinn would be let go under the usual "amicable" conditions. Two rotations were eliminated: "new" and "breakout." This, however, did not mean a return to the four employed in 1983. Six remained. Garland shifted so-called adult contemporary videos to VH-1. Sam Kaiser unveiled a weekly "hip clip" to be aired every three hours for seven days. The playlist was "simpler" but hardly a regression to past years. Some record executives applauded the move. Robin Sloane of Elektra said, "I really think they're heading in the right direction." "Hip clips," according to early sales reports, was a marketing success. Others, especially those with AC artists, weren't so enthused.

Changes were highly evident in the executive suites. Every week it seemed a new press release was issued announcing another episode of corporate musical chairs at 1775 Broadway.

Viacom continued to synergize. They did not escape the targeting of arbitrageurs beginning in 1985. A number of corporate raiders focused on the communications giant. Viacom was vulnerable, as it borrowed heavily to acquire MTVN. In May 1986 it thwarted raider Carl Icahn's takeover bid at a cost of $1 billion. The so-called corporate "greenmail" cost for the famous arbitrageur's 17 percent of Viacom's stock was estimated at $227 million, mostly in cash and some stock warrants. Icahn's meddling left Viacom showing a $28 million second quarter loss. To discourage other takeover attempts the management chose another game plan in which MTV was central accounting for nearly a quarter of the parent company's revenues. Internally the Viacom management was attempting a $2.9 billion buy out.[27] The success of MTV was imperative. In discussing a coventure in the European market with British Telecom and Mirror Group Newspapers Kenneth Gorman observed, "It will build on the enormous success of MTV, the most profitable basic cable network in the U.S., and of MTV Networks, which remains one of Viacom's most important assets." This proclamation underlined the need for MTV's continued profitability. MTVers were more than aware of their significance to the parent company. The ratings situation had to be reversed minus Nielsen. Viacom's synergizing philosophy depended greatly with the on-going status of MTV.

MTV's ratings dissatisfaction would spread in early 1987. The overground ABC-TV network nationally discontinued the Nielsen service. Aware of the discontent with the use of diaries, Nielsen promised to revert to a People Meter, as the old system stressed an older demographic and rural residents. As of January at least ten major Madison Avenue firms were using the AGB measure originally tested in the Boston area.

The Boston test of 440 homes was discouraging. MTV was in 165 households, mirroring its national market share of 38 percent. Marshall Cohen observed, as a good methodologist, "It's hard to know much from such a small sample." AGB promised a 2,000-household sample by September 1987.

Viacom continued to expand into new areas. MTVN collaborated with Warner Reprise Video to produce a forty-one-minute video cassette excerpt from the 1986 awards cablecast featuring six clips and other highlights from the September program. The "MTV Video Music Awards Collection" was yet another expansion into new territory. Viacom syndicated the awards program to 110 commercial stations throughout the country. They also produced "The MTV VMA 1986 Pre-Game Show," a two-hour special hosted by NBC sportscaster Bob Costas and rocker Huey Lewis. The awards show would be synergized during September while the pre-game program was scheduled from August 15 to September 4.

Carolyne Heldman, a native of Aspen, Colorado, was officially named the fourth full-time veejay on MTV in December 1986. Abandoning her acting ambitions at the University of California at Santa Barbara, she worked at the campus radio station. "It was a great place to discover new music," she says. After a year's sojourn in Australia she joined KSPN (Aspen) as a deejay. Lee Masters said: "Carolyne was one of several thousand people who sent in tapes during our nationwide veejay search last summer. Once we saw her on the screen there was no question that her natural freshness, combined with her enthusiasm for the music, made her the perfect addition to the channel.''

She was professional on the Nero's Eve annual ball and as hostess for the syndicated "MTV Video Countdown."

The 1986 New Year's event again featured a contest. The high point of the four-hour program would be, according to the network: "The announcement of the grand prize winner of 'MTV Town,' " advertised as the twenty-four-hour video music network's most ambitious contest to date. One viewer would begin 1987 with 100 acres of land, a house equipped with a satellite dish and wide screen television, stereo equipment, 1,000 compact discs, and a Jeep, courtesy of MTV and Nabisco Brands. "MTV Town" also included a general store stocked with "Lifesavers, Carefree sugarless gum, Baby Ruth and Butterfinger candy bars, and $100,000 in spending money." The contest was sponsored by Nabisco Brands.

During the telecast the hyped contest played a minor role. Alan Hunter, in one of his few appearances, read, "Loretta Lowary of Jackson, Alabama the new mayor of 'MTV Town!' " She had sent in fourteen entries to win. The entire process took less than a minute.

The 1987 Nero's Eve Rock and Roll Ball, held at the Manhattan Center, featured artist-producer Dave Edmunds, Lone Justice, the Beastie Boys, Duran Duran's Andy Taylor, and the Georgia Satellites enjoying their first CHR hit "Keep Your Hands To Yourself."

The sixth year gala differed considerably from previous shows. It featured a concept format, downplaying the role of the veejays and comedic personalities. "Nero Throws a Party" the opening read, segueing to a toga-clad rotund figure sawing away on a violin totally off key. Bacchus approaches the fake emperor repeating, "You gotta have rock music." Actor Joe Piscopo is the host or "emperor of the evening."

Andy Taylor began the rock segment with Bob Seger's "Roselie" and material from an up-coming solo album. Unlike other years, Taylor provided a spirited performance with songs like "When the Rain Comes Down," with MTV "pinch hit veejay" Dweezil Zappa, and "Don't Let Me Die Young."

Fifteen-year veteran Dave Edmunds was easily the highlight of the night, running through a series of rock-a-billy songs and other 1950s favorites such as Dion's "The Wanderer" and "Paralyzed." To heighten the nostalgia aspect Carl Perkins joined the Edmunds group for the set close with two songs, ending with the classic "Honey Don't." The inebriated Beastie Boys and Lone Justice did not fare as well.[28] The white-rap Beasties version of "You Gotta Fight for Your Right to Party" was an exercise in not falling off the stage. Lone Justice proved itself basically a studio band. Weird Al Yankovic and the Polkaolics did a poor parody of "Sledgehammer."

The Georgia Satellites, a southern rock band, performed some oldies such as Chuck Berry's "School Days" and material from their Elektra album. While lacking the vigor and energy of Taylor or Edmunds, they were for many viewers the discovery of the New Year's bash.

The veejays were barely seen. Mark Goodman did attempt an interview with two members of Twisted Sister, asking his usual "What do you have lined up for 1987? (Shades of 1986:) The question was ignored. Julie Brown and Goodman introduced acts from the sidelines between sips of champagne. Piscopo was more visible. From a critic's perspective this was the best New Year's show staged by MTV, due to the quality of three of the acts and the departure (almost) of overbearing veejays.

Rolling Stone's 1986 Yearbook summarized MTV's year. "MTV took its share of hard knocks this year," the writer opinioned. "Executives, including founder Bob Pittman, bailed out. Superbands and record-company honchos questioned the importance of videos. New veejays came: Julie Brown, for however long she lasts. Some veejays went *sayonara:* Nina Blackwood and J.J. Jackson. The annual awards show was a big-time snooze."[29] *Cablevision's* quarterly cable operators' poll indicated that MTVN was faring respectably with CATVs and households:

Basic Services	Affiliates	Subscribers
Hit Video USA	41	1,700,000
Music Television (MTV)	4,269	30,700,000
Video Hits One (VH-1)	1,189	14,100,000

Source: *Cablevision,* November 17, 1986

The subscriber growth was impressive although outstripped by specialty networks such as ESPN and CNN. However, as Kenneth Gorman of Viacom noted, MTV was the "most profitable basic channel in the U.S."

Hit Video USA continued as an irritant. Having signed with Group W, coowners of the Nashville Networks, the Wodlingers surpassed Ted Turner's abortive CMC subscriber base. They continued to make allegations against MTV in the media. Mark Wodlinger charged that MTV's agreements with cable operators demanded that VH-1 be added prior to taking another music service. The reference was obvious to his channel. He continued to allege that MTV was blacklisting the videos of artists who appeared on Hit Video USA in interview situations. Barry Kluger replied that the accusations were "totally without merit."[30]

The Wodlingers were a vexation as the only competing twenty-four-hour video cable service. They did not pose a realistic threat to MTV. Some locals in major markets were another matter. "Local channels were having a difficult time surviving. Why? They have little audience, and no advertising support. We have said in the past that, at this stage of the game, music cannot compete with music on TV," noted Les Garland. Garland was correct concerning a shakeout of the 100 musical imitations of MTV. By the closing months of 1986 the shakeout was over. The survivors broadcasting in prime time in major markets did challenge MTV. Many of these programs enjoyed specific connections with AOR stations. A video/marketing promotion person said, "Nationals are important, but exposure on thirty-five regionals in prime time is better than three times a week in off-hours of the morning on the nationals." There was a silver lining for MTV: even the most successful locals, such as Boston's V66, have been bumped for other programs such as Home Shopping. The Campus Network and RockWorld, aimed at institutions of higher learning, appear to be the most secure.

Martha Quinn best captured the ethos of MTV's fifth year in her departing remark, after her option was not renewed: it was "in keeping with the evolution of the channel."

The tinkering at MTVN continued. Beginning in January MTV would be showing thirty-nine vintage Beatles cartoons on Saturday and Sunday mornings at 10 A.M. EST. The series originally aired September 25, 1965 on NBC-TV to capitalize on *Help,* the Fab Four's blockbuster musical comedy film. Reportedly the MTV command hoped lightning would strike twice—"The Beatles as a follow-up to the Monkees" (a number of people would appear as a historical *camera obscura*). An interview show from Australia, "The Medrum Tapes," was added to the roster. Ian "Molly" Medrum was quite popular "down under."

VH-1 accumulated 200 hours of newsreel and "oldies" footage from Halcyon Days Productions to be interspersed during the twenty-four-hour rotations. The series was titled, "Blasts from the Past," a highly original title!

Cablevision reported on January 19 that MTV was considering moving to a large building with the veejays on display in a glassed-in studio allowing for paid tours to come through as at Universal Studios on the West Coast. (As of this writing this act of synergizing had not yet taken place.)

There exist two views of the future. One is that MTV is "still in its infancy" despite its status within the world of cablecasting. The other was expressed by Joan de Regt of the International Resource Development firm. She warned, "They appeal to the same fickle faddish, twelve to twenty-four year age group and eventually become very boring in their repetitiveness," making a comparison to video games of the early 1980s.

Comparing MTV to the video game craze is a bit extreme; however, the question does remain as to the channel's ability to rekindle the irreverent excitement of its early years. Few, if any, media have been able to accomplish that feat. One astute insider partially concurred: "One scenario is MTV fractionalizing to the point of irrelevance. Nick' and VH-1 could gain. VH-1 already has with AC/MOR artists. They appeal to the magic demographic [25–49 years-of-age] for Madison Avenue. Beatle cartoons could move to Nick' and carry the pre and early teens to the channel. What's left then, for MTV? Bob [Pittman] may have seen the handwriting on the printouts." The channel claims, "MTV is going where no Network has gone before."

MTV's vision of the future appeared in a December 15, 1986 ad in *Cablevision:*

December 15, 1986. What was to follow in the Summer of 1987 was scrambling by Viacom's three basic services following in the footsteps of pays Showtime and The Movie Channel. The number of TVRO's or satellite dish owners willing to pay extra for commercial programming remains a mystery. One-and-a-half million dish owners are too large a demographic to totally dismiss.

The "what's next" question was partially answered by mid-March of 1987. In *USA Today,* Tom Freston admitted, "We took the soul out of the channel . . . our staff had been aging a bit" (ergo the personnel changes). The strategy was *partially* back to basics. Chrysalis vice president Dan Glass said the channel was "happening again." Heavy metal groups were welcomed back. The playlist was trimmed to eighty clips per week. Urban contemporary (black) artists resumed their pre-1984 presence. Narrowcasting ascended to its original posture. "We're committed to playing rock 'n' roll of any color. We're color blind here," argued Sam Kaiser in familiar tones. *Billboard*'s Steven Dupler echoed BET's Robert Johnson's thesis of 1983: "They aren't the affirmative action station." One observer recited the French cliche, "All things change so they can remain the same." "It's a tremendous challenge to stay hip and cool and up to the minute without getting hokey" reiterated Freston.[31]

Only time will tell if this format tinkering will be successful.

Notes

1. *TV Guide,* March 3, 1986, p. 5. Cf. March 21, 1987, pp. 27–38.
2. *Rolling Stone,* July 3, 1986, p. 11.
3. *Cablevision,* January 19, 1987, p. 42.
4. *Inquirer,* November 3, 1982, p. D–1.
5. *USA Today,* April 29, 1986.
6. *Cablevision,* September 15, 1986, p. 26.
7. *USA Today,* April 19, 1986, p. B–1.
8. *Billboard,* April 19, 1986, pp. 1, 91.
9. *Billboard,* May 10, 1986, p. 1.
10. *Billboard,* April 26, 1986, p. 82.
11. *Cablevision,* February 17, 1986, p. 16.
12. *Rolling Stone,* September 15, 1986, p. 36.
13. *Newsweek,* November 17, 1986, p. 83.
14. *Billboard,* March 29, 1986, p. 54.
15. *Billboard,* April 26, 1986, p. 84.
16. *Billboard,* March 8, 1986, p. 91.
17. *Cablevision,* April 14, 1986, p. 22.
18. *New York Times,* June 12, 1986, p. C–21.
19. *Cablevision,* September 15, 1986, p. 32.
20. Plans were being formulated to withdraw from the Nielsen service. On January 9, 1987 ABC-TV dropped the Nielsens at the national level. The USA cable network subscribed to AGB at the same time.
21. *Billboard,* November 22, 1986, p. VM–3. General manager John Riordan indicated that the actual number was 452 households metered by Nielsen.
22. *Billboard,* April 12, 1986, p. 84.
23. *Billboard,* June 14, 1986, p. 58.
24. *USA Today,* May 12, 1986.
25. Garland's comments dealing with the Nielsen ratings at best can be characterized as ambiguous. A month after disavowing ratings as a causal factor for programming changes he told the same reporter, "How can you believe a 0.8 or 0.7 rating, when you run a contest and get 500,000 entries?" On January 9, 1987 Garland found an ally in Capital Cities (ABC-TV). They cancelled their national subscription to Nielsen.
26. *Billboard,* October 11, 1986, p. 90.
27. *Cablevision,* October 13, 1986, pp. 20, 22.
28. "Bein' bad news is what we're all about. . . . It's a real teen-oriented subculture music," observed Mike "D" Diamond (*Newsweek,* February 2, 1987, p. 70). The appearance helped the group, as their album sold 2.5 million units by March.
29. *Rolling Stone,* January 1, 1987, p. 73.
30. *USA Today,* June 18, 1986, p. 3D. By February 1987, according to Ms. Wodlinger, Hit Video USA was available in 6 million households.
31. *Billboard,* March 19, 1984, p. 4D.

Selected Bibliography

A complete bibliography concerning MTV would be a waste of space and reader's time. The channel did not penetrate the two major media markets, New York and Los Angeles, until January 1983. Resultantly, the news of the first sixteen months of MTV's existence was generally relegated to trade publications. Only the *Los Angeles Times'* Bob Hilburn covered the development of music television in the popular print medium.

The trade publications during that period reported the gospel according to MTV. Margaret Wade orchestrated a skillful media blitz to approach the industries MTV was courting.

Accounts in the rock, film, advertising, and television press usually stressed the specialty of the journalist. Compounding the problem was the geographical distribution of cable systems, many of which were serviced almost entirely by wire services mirroring the agenda setting of the *New York Times* and *Washington Post*. (As of this writing D.C. is still without cable.)

The result of this neglect in the press is a series of retrospective accounts by a very defensive and controlled MTV hierarchy. As one former executive acknowledged, the role of the MTV press relations people was to structure, not necessarily to inform.

Making researchers' tasks even more problemsome is the fact that most of the *key* players, such as John Lack, were unavailable for journalistic or scholarly probes as of 1983. Orwellian "double speak" became the ethos (see *Esquire,* December 1985). In addition, practically no decision makers at MTV were directly accessible. The use of "spokesperson" or "insider" throughout this volume is a testimony to the off-the-record nature of collecting data on MTV operations.

Of particular interest to those concerned with MTV or music videos in general are trade publications such as *Cablevision, On Cable, Variety, Billboard, Radio and Records,* and *Broadcasting.* In digesting the articles, the reader will find it useful to ask, "What are they trying to communicate and to whom?"

Rock Video, later retitled *Hard Rock Video,* hit the news stands in April 1984. Although the format was geared to an adolescent market, it contained some interesting, occasionally insightful material by Jim Bessman, Lisa Robinson, and Jonathan Gross. The publication also mirrored the original MTV mood and captured the mentality of a large segment of the music video audience. It ceased publication in October 1986.

It has become customary to cryptically annotate bibliographies; the literature concerning MTV, with one exception, does not justify such an endeavor. The exception is Mike Shore's *The Rolling Stone Book of Rock Video* (1984). It has an excellent review listing of music videos and the discussion of the filming of Cyndi Lauper's "Girls Just Wanna Have Fun" is enlightening. His historiography leaves much to be desired, however. John Lack, the "Father of MTV," receives one sentence. The journalistic "Five Ws" are violated repeatedly. This proved disheartening in that Shore's credibility in parts of the book which are verifiable comes into question. Otherwise, as the first published long-form effort on the subject it is quite helpful in the spheres mentioned.

Bibliography

Books

Chu, John, and Cafritz, Elliot. *The Music Video Guide*. New York: McGraw Hill, 1986.

Denisoff, R. Serge. *Tarnished Gold*. New Brunswick, N.J.: Transaction Books, 1986.

Latham, Caroline. *Miami Magic*. New York: Zebra Books, 1985.

Marsh, David. *Rock and Roll Confidential Report*. New York: Pantheon Books, 1985.

Roman, James W. *Cablemania*. Englewood Cliffs, N.J.: Spectrum Books, 1983.

Shore, Michael. *The Rolling Stone Book of Rock Video*. New York: Quill Press, 1984.

Shore, Michael with Dick Clark. *The History of American Bandstand*. New York: Ballentine Books, 1984.

Articles

"A Flood of 'X-Rated Music' Hits Airwaves, Concert Hall, Record Shops." *U.S. News and World Report,* October 31, 1977, p. 47.

Albin, Glenn. "Veejays Inject the Human Element into MTV." Unpublished manuscript.

Applebaum, Simon. "Cable Music Channel Launches with 2.5 Million Less Subs Than Hopes." *Cablevision*. October 29, 1984, p. 16.

———. "CMC's into Cable But Numbers Are Not What Execs Hoped For." *Cablevision,* November 19, 1984, p. 11.

———. "Discovery Music Postpones Launch to Make Marketing Push for Cable." *Cablevision,* December 24, 1984, p. 10.

———. "Music Video Stepping Out Soon?" *Cablevision,* April 30, 1984, p. 22.

———. "MTV Goes M.O.R. in Pre-emptive Strike at TBS Rock Video Strategy." *Cablevision,* September 3, 1984, pp. 13–14.

———. "Response to Launch of VH-1 Exceeds Initial Expectations." *Cablevision,* January 7, 1985, p. 10.

———. "TBS Shuts Down CMC, Plans to Lay Off Staffers." *Cablevision,* December 10, 1984, p. 12.

———. "Turner's CMC Battles MTV For Subs, Ad Dollars." *Cablevision,* November 5, 1984, p. 16.

———. "Turner Prepared to Rock the Industry and CMC Takes on the World of Video." *Cablevision,* September 24, 1984, p. 18.

"Arms of the Octopus." *Rock & Roll Confidential,* March 1984, p. 3.

Atkinson, Terry. "Rating the Rivals to the MTV Throne." *Los Angeles Times,* August 22, 1983, pp. 68–69.

Baird, Jock. "Narrowcasting Under Fire." *Musician,* May 1983, p. 10.

Balanzich-Rimassa, Milena. "Producer–Packagers and Cable Execs Strike Sparks." *Billboard,* December 19, 1981, p. 55.

"B.B. Gets Kingly Treatment." *Billboard,* March 2, 1985, p. 37.

Benedek, Emily. "Inside 'Miami Vice.' " *Rolling Stone,* March 28, 1985, pp. 56–62, 125.

Bernstein, Fred. "A Hard Day's Night with MTV's Video Jocks." *People,* October 17, 1983, pp. 100–01.

Bessman, Jim. "Black Cable Network Makes Heavy Commitment to Clips." *Billboard,* March 30, 1985, p. 30.

———. "Heavy Metal Video Sales Gain." *Billboard,* January 10, 1987, pp. 38–39.

———. "Kahan Explores Virgin Territory of VH-1." *Billboard,* March 23, 1985, p. 30.

———. "Label Executives: MTV's Hip Clip Boosts Sales." *Billboard,* January 17, 1987, p. 46.

———. "Video Lowdown." *Rock Video,* July 1985, p. 6.

———. "MTV's New Channel Gets a 'Unique' Logo." *Billboard,* January 12, 1985, p. 31.

"BET Launching 'Video Soul.' " *CV/CED,* June 13, 1983.

"BET Makes Video Waves." *TV-Cable Week,* July 24, 1983, p. 30.

"BET Plans Fall Debut of Video Music Show." *Multi Channel News,* June 20, 1983.

"BET to Launch 'Video Soul.' " *Cablevision,* June 27, 1983.

Bianculli, David. "Creativity Makes 'Night Flight' Soar." *Philadelphia Inquirer,* May 5, 1984, p. 8–D.

"*Billboard*'s Third International Video Entertainment/Music Conference." *Billboard,* October 10, 1981, pp. 51–59.

"*Billboard*'s Fourth International Video Entertainment/Music Conference." *Billboard,* December 18, 1982, pp. 42–49.

"*Billboard*'s First International Video Music Conference." *Billboard,* December 15, 1979, pp. 47–58.

"*Billboard*'s Seventh Annual Video Music Conference." *Billboard,* December 21, 1985, pp. 25–31.

"*Billboard*'s Sixth Annual Video Music Conference." *Billboard,* December 15, 1984, pp. 32–37.

Billingsley, L. "Rock Video: 24-Hour-a-Day Pacifier for TV Babies." *Christianity Today,* July 1984, p. 70.

"Black Music Making Cable Gains." *Billboard,* June 18, 1983, pp. 1, 72.

Brandt, P. "MTV/Music Television." *MS,* November 1983, pp. 42–43.

Bronson, Gail. "Music Video—TV's Newest Wrinkle." *U.S. News and World Report,* February 27, 1984, p. 72.

Brown, Andrew C. "Products of the Year." *Fortune,* December 28, 1981, p. 66.

Brown, Ben. "Ted Turner Kicks Off His Challenge on MTV." *USA Today,* October 31, 1984, 3–A.

Brubach, Holly. "Rock-and-Roll Vaudeville." *Atlantic,* July 1984, pp. 99–101.

Bruning, F. "The Perils of Rock on the Box." *Macleans,* November 1983, p. 21.

Bulter, Jeremy. " 'Miami Vice': The Legacy of Film Noir." *Journal of Popular Film and Television* 13 (Fall 1985):126–38.

"Cable TV: The Choice." *Vogue,* July 1983.

"Cable Viewers Rocked by MTV." *Wall Street Journal,* October 5, 1983.

"Cable's Rock Around the Clock." *Time,* November 29, 1982, p. 97.

Caplan, Richard E. "Violence Program Content in Music Video." *Journalism Quarterly,* 1985, pp. 144–47.

Capuzzi, Cecilia. "Ad Folks Want Their MTV." *Cablevision,* April 30, 1984, p. 24.

———. "MTV Connecting in Retail Market." *Cablevision,* November 14, 1983, p. 34.

———. "MTV Pushes Local Avails." *Cablevision,* February 4, 1985, p. 24.

"CBS Records Will Demand Video Payment." *Billboard,* April 21, 1984, pp. 1, 61.

Christgau, Robert. "Rock 'n' Roller Coaster." *Village Voice,* February 7, 1984, pp. 37–38, 40–45.

Christopher, Maurine. "Turner Considers Competition for MTV." *Ad Age,* August 13, 1984, p. 69.

Cieply, Michael. "Records May Soon Carry Warnings that Lyrics Are Morally Hazardous." *Wall Street Journal,* July 31, 1985, p. 19.

"Cincinnati PTA Wants Ratings of Sexual Lyrics of Records and Tapes." *Sentinel Tribune,* May 31, 1984, p. 6.

Cocciolone, Carole. "Music, Music, Music." *Satellite Orbit,* April 1985, pp. 26, 28.

"Competitors Play Down MTV's Premiere Deals." *Cablevision,* July 16, 1984, p. 26.

"Cool Cops, Hot Show." *Time,* September 16, 1985, pp. 60–63.

Cooney, John E. "Cable TV Will Get All Music Channel Running 24 Hours." *Wall Street Journal,* March 4, 1981, p. 56.

Crook, David. "TV's Ted Turner Facing the Music Now." *Los Angeles Times,* October 30, 1984, pp. 1, 100.

———. "Warner/Amex Plans 'Video Radio.' " *Los Angeles Times,* March 4, 1981.

Crook, David, and Patrick Goldstein. "MTV Sued Over Exclusivity Contracts." *Los Angeles Times,* September 9, 1984, pp. 1–2.

Dalton, Joseph. "The Televisionary." *Esquire,* December 1985, pp. 380–87.

Darling, Cary. "Label Execs Kick Video Around." *Billboard,* December 19, 1981, pp. 51, 57.

———. "MTV Viewership Growing in Los Angeles." *Billboard,* January 29, 1983, p. 3.

———. "R&B Denied?" *Billboard,* November 28, 1981, pp. 4, 62.

DeCurtis, Anthony. "CBS Cutting Back on Videos." *Rolling Stone,* April 24, 1986, p. 14.

———. "Clive Davis Blasts Radio." *Rolling Stone,* July 3, 1986, p. 11.

———. "Pittman Leaving MTV." *Rolling Stone,* September 25, 1986, p. 17.

———. "Stars Reject Videos." *Rolling Stone,* June 5, 1986, p. 11.

Demkowych, Christine. "Music on the Upswing in Advertising." *Ad Age* 3-38-36: S-5.

Denisoff, R. Serge. "Heavy Metal Music May Be Rusting." *Sentinel-Tribune,* April 29, 1985, p. 17.

———. "Music Videos and the Rock Press." *PMS* 10, no. 1 (1985): 59–61.

———. "Impact on Youth One Complaint About MTV." *Sentinel Tribune,* September 15, 1983, p. 5.

DeVoss, David. "Aural Sex: The Rise of Porn Rock." *Human Behavior,* July 1976, pp. 64–68.

Dimauro, Phil. "MTV Launches Ad Campaign with Network TV Time Buys." *Variety,* October 20, 1985.

Director, R. "Turning on Rock Video." N.A. April 1983, p. 104.

"Discovery Music Looks to B'Cast." *Cablevision,* December 3, 1984, p. 24.

Donlon, Brian. "A 2-Front Challenge to MTV." *USA Today,* June 18, 1986, 3D.

———. "Music TV Goes Beyond Hit Videos." *USA Today,* April 29, 1986, 1D–2D.

———. "MTV for Adults Grows Up." *USA Today,* May 12, 1986, 3D.

———. "TV Crime Is Paying for Liddy." *USA Today,* January 23, 1986, 3D.

Dudar, Helen. "Rock Video: The Most Exalted Junk on the Box." *Wall Street Journal,* September 26, 1983.

Dupler, Steven. "CBS May Pass on MTV 'Countdown.' " *Billboard,* March 8, 1986, pp. 1, 92.

———. "Impact of VH-1 Debated: Does Channel Sell Records." *Billboard,* April 12, 1986, pp. 1, 84.

———. " '120 Minutes': Right Idea, Wrong Time?" *Billboard,* March 29, 1986, p. 54.

———. "Lyrics: Video Outlets Seen Confident." *Rolling Stone,* September 21, 1985, pp. 3, 72.

———. "MTV: Changes at the Channel." *Billboard,* October 11, 1986, pp. 1, 90.

———. "MTV Chief Speaks Out." *Billboard,* May 17, 1986, p. 60.

———. "MTV Financial Data Revealed." *Billboard,* August 11, 1984, p. 8.

———. "MTV Looks into International Programming." *Billboard,* February 15, 1986, p. 42.

———. "MTV: Playlist Cuts Give Rock a Better Shot." *Billboard,* December 20, 1986, pp. 1, 71.

———. "MTV's VH-1 Opens on Optimistic Note." *Billboard,* January 12, 1985, pp. 1, 61.

———. "National PTA Asks Labels: Institute Ratings System." *Billboard,* October 27, 1984, p. 70.

———. "Nielsen Publishers Disputed MTV 4th-Quarter Ratings." *Billboard,* April 26, 1986, p. 84.

———. "See Pittman's Departure from MTV in Mid-'87." *Billboard,* August 23, 1986, p. 92.

———. "Seminar Probes Video Exclusivity." *Billboard,* August 18, 1984, pp. 3, 54.

———. "Settlement in Vidclip Exclusivity Suit." *Billboard,* May 3, 1986, pp. 1, 71.

———. "Targeting the Video." *Billboard,* September 28, 1985, pp. NT-3, 10.

———. "Turner Moves Up Music Bow." *Billboard,* September 6, 1984, pp. 1, 62.

———. "Vidclip Charges Create Program Casualties." *Billboard,* February 22, 1986, pp. 3, 76.

———. "Vidclip Output Faces Trim." *Billboard,* April 19, 1986, pp. 1, 91.

———. "Video Music." *Billboard,* December 27, 1986, pp. Y-52-3.

———. "VH-1 Prepares to Enter 'New Age.' " *Billboard,* December 14, 1985, p. 39.

———. "Warner Amex Listening to Buyout Offers." *Billboard,* May 25, 1985, p. 4.

Durkin, Mary Beth. "Fred and Alan: Cable's Newest Wunderkind." *Village Voice,* October 4, 1983, pp. 86, 88.

El Nasser, Haya. "Advertisers Want MTV." *USA Today,* July 17, 1986, 5B.

Evanow, Peter. "The New Gold Rush: Video Rock 'n' Roll." *Cablevision,* August 24, 1981, pp. 33, 36.

"Exclusives Extended." *Billboard,* October 11, 1986, p. 90.

Farley, Ellen. "Videos: New Kid in Town Rocks the Music Business." *Los Angeles Times,* August 21, 1983, pp. 30, 33.

———. "Videos Rock the Music Industry." *Los Angeles Times,* August 21, 1983, pp. 1, 33–34.

Fiske, John. "Video Clippings." *Australian Journal of Cultural Studies,* May 1984, pp. 110–14.

Ford, Tom. "Rock Music with Pictures: A New and Disturbing Art." *Toledo Blade,* June 3, 1984, G1.

Forkan, James P. "Things Up Beat at Music TV." *Ad Age,* September 14, 1981.

Foti, Laura. "Labels Mull Pay-for-Play." *Billboard,* July 30, 1983, pp. 1, 54.

———. "MTV Cable Channel Exposing New Acts." *Billboard,* August 15, 1981, pp. 3, 58.

———. "MTV, Labels Talk Payments." *Billboard,* February 11, 1984, pp. 1, 74.

———. "New Act Pacts Take Vidclip $ from Royalties." *Billboard,*

———. " 'Night Flight' Flying High: Kudos for Cultural Bravo." *Billboard,* April 3, 1982, pp. 10, 67.

———. "Programming a Good BET: Fine-Tuning Time at MTV." *Billboard,* March 6, 1982, pp. 12–13.

———. "Stereo Sound Prominent in Music TV Offerings." *Billboard,* May 1, 1982, p. 13.

———. "Study Profiles MTV's Audience." *Billboard,* February 12, 1983, p. 4.

———. "Vidclip $$ Issue Heats Up." *Billboard,* July 30, 1983, pp. 1, 54.

———. "Wide Variety of Music on Cable in August." *Billboard,* July 31, 1982, pp. 9, 45.

Freeman, Kim. "Radio Caught Up in New Controversy Over Lyrics." *Billboard,* June 8, 1985, pp. 1, 78.

Fricke, David. "TV: The Shape of Things to Come." *Melody Maker,* March 27, 1982, p. 31.

Frost, Deborah. "Heavy Metal Rears Its Ugly Head Again." *Rolling Stone,* September 27, 1984, pp. 82, 84.

Gardner, Fred. "MTV Rocks Cable." *Marketing and Media Decisions*, August 1983, pp. 66–69.

Gehr, Richard. "The MTV Aesthetic." *Film Comment*, August 19, 1983, pp. 37–40.

Gelman, Eric et al. "Rocking Video." *Newsweek*, April 18, 1983, pp. 96, 98.

George, Nelson. "MTV Row Flares Again at BMA Conference." *Billboard*, November 19, 1983, pp. 3, 70.

———. "Slick Rick Says MTV Is Sick." *Billboard*, February 19, 1983, p. 32.

George, Nelson, and Dupler, Steven. "BET Boycotts Profile Product." *Billboard*, August 23, 1986, pp. 3, 92.

Gergen, David. "X-Rated Records." *U.S. News and World Report*, May 20, 1985, p. 98.

Gett, Steve. "Pop Sound Tracks Caught in Updraft of Video Revolution's Impact on TV and Movies." *Billboard*, June 21, 1986, S–3, S–10, S–11.

Gladstone, Brooke. "MTV Sparks Sex, Violence Concern." *Cablevision*, April 30, 1984, p. 48.

Gold, Richard. "Labels Limit Videos on Black Artists." *Variety*, December 15, 1982, pp. 73–78.

———. "Black Video Production." *Variety*, March 14, 1984, pp. 127–28.

———. "Wamex Music Channel Acquires Library of 400 Promo Tapes; Requires Stereo Transmission." *Variety*, May 27, 1981, pp. 89, 91.

Goldberg, Michael. "MTV Snaps Up Video Rights." *Rolling Stone*, August 16, 1984, pp. 31–32.

———. "Record Companies Balk at Deals with MTV." *Rolling Stone*, August 30, 1984, p. 32.

———. "USA for Africa." *Rolling Stone*, March 14, 1985, pp. 11, 60–61.

Golden, Marcia. "Retailers See Music TV Boom as a Boost to Record Sales." *Billboard*, September 10, 1983, pp. 28, 31.

Goldstein, Patrick. "Fans Turned Off and On by MTV." *Los Angeles Times*, August 21, 1983, D–1, 5.

———. "In Rock, to Be or Not to Be May Depend on MTV." *Los Angeles Times*, August 22, 1983, D–1, D–4.

Goldstein, Toby. "Doing the Perpetual Bop at a Flick of the (Cable) Dial." *Creem*, April 1982, pp. 36–38.

Goodman, Fred. "Krasnow Says Elektra will Sign with MTV." *Billboard*, August 25, 1984, pp. 1, 70.

Graham, Jefferson. "Animation Is MTV's Newest Rising Star." *USA Today*, October 31, 1985, 3D.

———. "During the LP Lull, MTV Is in 'Rerun Season.' " *USA Today*, March 26, 1985.

———. "Heavy Metal on the Outs at MTV." *Rolling Stone*, April 11, 1985, p. 16.

———. "MTV Lightens Up on Its Heavy-Metal Menu." *USA Today*, February 14, 1985.

———. "Planning for MTV in the Long Run." *USA Today*, May 29, 1985, 3D.

———. "Turner's Music Video Venture Is in Trouble." *USA Today*, November 8, 1984, 1–A.

———. "Video's VH-1 Heads into Year 2 on the Upbeat." *USA Today*, December 30, 1985.

Graham, Jefferson, and Johnson, Harriot. "MTV Pays $1 Million for Ted Turner Rival." *USA Today,* November 29, 1984, p. 1.

Grein, Paul. "Turner Vid Channel Will Pay for Play." *Billboard,* October 27, 1984, pp. 1, 61.

———. "30 Years On, 'Bandstand' Still Targeting the Teens." *Billboard,* October 31, 1981, pp. 3, 16.

———. "TV Ads Focus of Labels' Yule Push; Cable Gets Big Test." *Billboard,* November 19, 1983, pp. 1, 67.

———. "VH-1 Aims to Fulfill Viewers' Fantasies." *Billboard,* July 20, 1985, pp. 6, 75.

Grossberger, Lewis. "Welcome to Our City—Blow Up What You Like." *TV Guide,* July 27, 1985, pp. 27–29.

Grubb, K. "Cinematic Terpsichore." *Dance Magazine,* May 1983, pp. 154–55.

Hall, Claude. "WNBC Switching to Rock." *Billboard,* August 13, 1977, pp. 4, 15.

Hall, Peter. "MTV Wants It All." *Village Voice,* February 21, 1984, pp. 48, 69.

Handler, David. "It's Rock 'n' (Bank) Roll." *TV Guide,* March 12, 1983, pp. 16–18.

Hartman, John K. "I Want My Ad-TV." *Popular Music & Society,* in press.

Hecht, Alan. "MTV: Searching for a Groove." *The Record,* December 1981, p. 15.

Hedegaard, Erik. "Discovery Network Sues MTV." *Rolling Stone,* November 8, 1984, p. 61.

———. "MTV's VH-1: Music Video for Housewives." *Rolling Stone,* January 17, 1985, p. 38.

———. "Ted Turner Takes on MTV." *Rolling Stone,* October 25, 1984.

Hilburn, Robert. "Flashrock—MTV's Brave New World." *Los Angeles Times,* August 21, 1983, pp. 60, 67–68.

———. "MTV: The Birth of a Rock Sensation." *Los Angeles Times,* August 21, 1983, pp. 80–83.

———. "Music TV: Hope Rocks Fort Lee." *Los Angeles Times,* August 4, 1981, pp. 1, 3 (Sec. VI).

———. "TV Goes FM." *Los Angeles Times,* May 17, 1981, pp. 6 (Sec. D).

Hodge, Robert. "Videoclips as a Revolutionary Form." *Australian Journal of Cultural Studies,* May 1984, pp. 115–21.

Holland, Bill. "NAB's Fritts Urges Labels: Supply Radio with Lyrics." *Billboard,* June 15, 1985, pp. 1, 73.

———. "NAB President Speaks Out on 'Porn Rock,' " *Billboard,* June 1, 1985, pp. 6, 77.

———. "National PTA Asks Record Rating System." *Billboard,* July 7, 1984, p. 4.

———. "PTA, PMRC Unite on Lyrics." *Billboard,* September 21, 1985, pp. 1, 72.

———. "Senators to Labels: Clean Up Your Act." *Billboard,* September 28, 1985, pp. 1, 82.

———. "Washington Mothers Blast 'Pornographic' Rock Lyrics." *Billboard,* May 11, 1985, p. 80.

Hornberger, Carole. "MTV Has Video Monopoly." *BG News,* December 14, 1984, p. 6.

Hughes, Scott. "Already Got My MTV." *American Film,* November 1984, p. 65.

Ingrassia, Michele. "MTV: Fashion to the Beat." *Cleveland Plain Dealer,* February 12, 1984, 1–C, 17–C.

Irwin, James. "Clones of MTV." *Forbes,* December 3, 1984, pp. 162–63.

Ivany, John Shelton. "Lowering the Boom on Heavy Metal." *Billboard,* July 6, 1985, p. 10.

Jaeger, Barbara. "Rock Shows Its Ugliest Face." *Cleveland Plain Dealer,* April 15, 1984, 1–D, 9–D.

Jordon, Nick. "The Making of the MTV Playlist." *Rock Video,* August 1985, pp. 48–49.

Kannar, Bernice. "Can't Stop the Music Channel." *New York,* October 11, 1982, pp. 18, 20–21.

Kaplan, P.W. "MTV: 21st Century-Box." *Esquire,* March 1983, p. 123.

Kerver, Tom. "Own a Piece of the 'Rock.' " *Cable TV Business,* July 15, 1984.

Kirby, Kip. "Discovery Network Unveils Five-Point Marketing Plan." *Billboard,* September 1, 1984, p. 1.

———. "Indie Label 'Risk Takers' Discuss the Search for Alternative Clip Outlets." *Billboard,* December 15, 1984, p. 35.

———. "It's Turner's Turn for Cable Rocker." *Billboard,* August 18, 1984, pp. 1, 60.

Kirby, Kip, and Seideman, Tony. "New 24-Hour Vidclip Net Due in December." *Billboard,* August 4, 1984, pp. 1, 62.

Kirkeby, Marc. "MTV, 'Night Flight' Lead Cable-TV Rock Invasion." *Rolling Stone,* December 10, 1981, pp. 64, 66–67.

Kitman, Marvin. "M-TV Torture." *New Leader,* January 9, 1984, pp. 20–21.

Kleinfield, N.R. "Warner Amex Head to Resign." *New York Times,* November 24, 1982, Sec. D, pp. 1, 6.

Kneale, Dennis. "Weinder Is Better in the Red-Hot Land of Rock Videos." *Wall Street Journal,* October 17, 1983, pp. 1, 14.

Knoedelseder, William, Jr. "MTV Turning Video Rock into Gold." *Los Angeles Times,* August 26, 1984, pp. 1, 4.

Kopp, George. "Cable, Pay TV, Satellite Distribution Loom Big." *Billboard,* January 10, 1981, p. 54.

———. "Labels Seen Lagging on Video Programming." *Billboard,* February 28, 1981, pp. 1, 42.

Kozak, Roman. "Caution: MTV May Be Hazardous to Your Mind." *Billboard,* September 11, 1982, pp. 10, 60.

———. "Take Off Nears for 'Night Flight' Films." *Billboard,* May 16, 1981, pp. 12, 85.

———. "Warner Amex MTV: Debuting New Music." *Billboard,* August 22, 1981, pp. 12, 52.

Kozak, Roman, and Sacks, Leo. "Meet Seeks to End New Music Doldrums." *Billboard,* July 25, 1981, p. 12.

Krupp, C. "The New Music TV Stars." *Glamour,* March 1983, p. 123.

Kunes, Ellen. "17-Second Interview: MTV's Martha Quinn." *Seventeen,* February 1984, p. 55.

La Pointe, Kirk. "MTV Deals Haunt Much Music." *Billboard,* September 8, 1984, p. 58.

Lazenby, Mark. "Emporia, Va., Teens Want Their MTV Back." *Sentinel Tribune,* May 15, 1984, p. 4.

Leonard, John. "Evil Under the Sun." *New York,* October 8, 1984, p. 80.

"Let's Talk About It." *Billboard,* June 30, 1984, p. 8.

Levine, Ed. "TV Rocks with Music." *New York Times Magazine,* May 8, 1983, pp. 42–45, 61–63.

Levy, Steven. "Ad Nauseam: How MTV Sells Out Rock and Roll." *Rolling Stone,* December 8, 1983, pp. 30–37, 73–79.

Lippert, Barbara. "Jagger Leads Way in Rock-Cable Ads." *New York Post,* August 2, 1982.

———. "Nielsen Numbers Show America Wants Its MTV." *Ad Week,* June 13, 1983, p. 17.

Livingston, Victor. "Battle of the Broadbands: Turner Takes on MTV." *Cablevision,* August 20, 1984, pp. 11–12.

———. "MTV Imitating the Clones." *Cablevision,* March 26, 1984, p. 61.

———. "Whole Lot of Shakin'." *Cablevision,* April 30, 1984, Plus 1–12.

Livingston, Victor, and Russell, Sally. "Turner, MTV Spar Over Idea of Another Music Video Service." *Cablevision,* August 27, 1984, p. 15.

Loftus, Jack. "Warner Amex Preps All-Music Cable Channel." *Variety,* March 4, 1981, pp. 1, 108.

London, Julia. "Images of Violence Against Women." *Victimology,* February 1977–78, pp. 510–24.

Love, Robert. "Furor Over Rock Lyrics Intensifies." *Rolling Stone,* September 12, 1985, pp. 13–15, 83.

Lyons, Donald. "Bopping on the Potomac." *Hard Rock Video,* January 1985, pp. 29–31.

Macias, Vicki. " 'Video Soul' to Feature Black Music." *The Houston Post,* June 14, 1983.

MacKenzie, Robert. " 'Miami Vice.' " *TV Guide,* November 10, 1984, p. 1.

Marbach, William et al. "MTV's Message." *Newsweek,* December 30, 1985, pp. 54–57.

Marks, Jill. "Laid Back Launch." *Cable TV Business,* February 15, 1985, p. 10.

McCullaugh, Jim. "Cable Channel Seen Helping Record Sales." *Billboard,* March 14, 1981, pp. 1, 80.

———. "Consistency Leads to Audience Growth." *Billboard,* April 19, 1986, p. 49.

———. "First National Cable Vidshow." *Billboard,* March 3, 1980, pp. 1, 38.

———. "MTV Cable Spurs Disk Sales of Artists Hired." *Billboard,* October 10, 1981, pp. 1, 68.

———. "MTV to Be in 4½–5 Million Homes: Lack." *Billboard,* October 10, 1981, pp. 68, 82.

———. "Nesmith's Pacific Arts Preps Video-Disk Market." *Billboard,* March 1, 1980, p. 33.

———. "Study Says MTV Is on Target with Audience." *Billboard,* May 1, 1982, p. 6.

McCullaugh, Jim, and Foti, Laura. "Music's Role Upbeat in Cable TV Future." *Billboard,* May 1, 1982, pp. 1, 13.

McKenna, Kristine. "Videos—Low in Art, High in Sex and Sell." *Los Angeles Times,* August 21, 1983, pp. 66–67.

McWhirter, Nickie. "Dreadful Music Videos Have Comic Book Appeal." *Detroit Free Press*, September 1984.

Melanson, Jim. "Cable TV—A Novel Disk Promo Vehicle." *Billboard*, April 12, 1975, pp. 1, 8.

Miller, Kenneth. "Video Giant Wants Its MTV." *Rolling Stone*, October 10, 1985, p. 12.

"Million Dollar Bash from MTV." *Billboard*, December 21, 1985, p. 24.

Mitchell, Elvis. " 'Miami Vice' Losing Its Virtue." *Rolling Stone*, March 27, 1986, pp. 45, 136.

———. "Video Valium: The VH-1 Experience." *Village Voice*, June 4, 1985, p. 39.

Morse, Margaret. "Rock Video Sychronizing Rock Music and Television." *Fabula* 5 (1985): 13–32.

Motavalli, John. "Change Ahead for VH-1 as Metheny Departs." *Cablevision*, April 21, 1986.

———. "Mid-way Into Year Two, VH-1 on Target But Still Evolving." *Cablevision*, May 5, 1986, pp. 20–22.

———. "MTV Battling for Channel Slots." *Cablevision*, December 1, 1986, p. 24.

———. "MTV Broadens Format with 'Monkees' Series." *Cablevision*, February 17, 1986, p. 16.

———. "MTV May Add Weekly Movie to Schedule." *Cablevision*, April 14, 1986, p. 22.

———. "MTV Sees Low-Cost Programming Ingenuity as Key to Sustaining High Profitability." *Cablevision*, September 15, 1986, pp. 26, 32, 34, 37–38.

———. "Robertson Lambasts MTV, Questions Advertiser Support." *Cablevision*, March 24, 1986, p. 12.

———. "MTV Series to Feature International Videos." *Cablevision*, February 10, 1986, p. 28.

———. "Pittman: Sell Basic Ads Like Magazine Ads." *Cablevision*, February 10, 1986, p. 39.

———. "The People Meter Quandary." *Cablevision*, January 19, 1987, pp. 42–44.

"MTV." *Billboard*, August 6, 1983, MTV-1-32 (special insert).

"MTV Ad Campaign." *Broadcasting*, November 11, 1985, p. 49.

"MTV Chief Speaks Out." *Billboard*, May 17, 1986, p. 60.

"MTV Co-founder to Be Network President." *Cleveland Plain Dealer*, December 20, 1985.

"MTV's Message." *Newsweek*, December 30, 1985, pp. 54–56.

"MTV Nets Alters Public Offering." *Cablevision*, August 6, 1984, p. 11.

"MTV Networks Signs Agreement with Warner Record Companies." *Cablevision*, May 20, 1985, p. 60.

"MTV's New Logo." *USA Today*, February 6, 1986.

"MTV's New Service Offers an Integrated Musical Mix." *Billboard*, January 19, 1985, pp. 51, 54.

"MTV, Nickelodeon Profits Revealed in Stock Offering." *Billboard*, June 30, 1984, p. 3.

"MTV: 1981–1986." *Billboard* (supplement), August 2, 1986, MTV1–18.

"MTV Readers Beefed-Up News Coverage." *Billboard*, December 15, 1984, pp. 40, 48.

"MTV Rocks America." *Teen Beat Video Rock Stars*, Fall 1983, pp. 70–73.

"MTV Scores Higher on Nielsens." *Cablevision*, July 21, 1986, p. 11.

"MTV Seeks Exclusives with Record Cost." *Cablevision*, February 27, 1984, p. 22.

"MTV Sets Anniversary Promo." *Billboard*, July 31, 1982, p. 9.

"Music Programming Lags Within Cable TV Industry." *Billboard*, June 13, 1981, pp. 5, 76.

"Music's Role Upbeat in Cable TV Future," *Billboard*, May 1, 1982, pp. 1, 13.

"Music Videos—Going the Way of Videogames?" *Cable Communications Magazine*, November 1983, p. 92.

"New Era Starting with Video Jockeys." *Billboard*, August 8, 1981, p. 29.

"Now It's Labels On 'Porn Rock' to Protect Kids." *U.S. News and World Report*, August 26, 1985, p. 52.

Occhiogrosso, Peter. "Music Video Comes of Age." *On Cable*, January 1985, pp. 19–21.

———. "Video Dreams: MTV Goes to the Movies." *Village Voice*, July 31, 1984, p. 36.

O'Connor, John J. "MTV—A Success Story with a Curious Shortcoming." *New York Times*, July 24, 1983, sec. H.23.

———. "Music Video Is Here, with a Vengeance." *New York Times*, July 1, 1984, H–19.

$1 million 'Rock It' Is Shooting in Canada." *Variety*, April 11, 1979, p. 52.

Ostrow, Joanne. "Cable Music Channels—Now There Are Three." *Denver Post*, March 10, 1985.

"Other Clip Outlets Blast MTV Pacts." *Billboard*, June 23, 1984, p. 67.

Paige, Earl. "PTA Meet Looks at Ratings." *Billboard*, March 2, 1985, pp. 27, 33.

Palmer, Robert. "Noisy Rock Returns." *New York Times*, April 21, 1985, H–29.

Pareles, Jon. "MTV Makes Changes to Stop Ratings Slump." *New York Times*, June 12, 1986, C–21.

"Parents vs. Rock." *People*, September 16, 1985, pp. 46–51.

Paton, Richard. "Charity Concerts: A Safe Form of Commitment." *Toledo Blade*, September 28, 1986, E–1, 3.

———. "The Furor Over Rock Lyrics." *Toledo Blade*, September 15, 1985, pp. 1–50.

Patterson, Rob. "Clips Sell—But How Much?" *Billboard*, October 29, 1983, pp. 48, 51.

Pettigrew, Jim. " 'Art and Industry' Examined." *Billboard*, May 14, 1983, pp. 53, 56.

"Pittman Successor Unnamed." *Cablevision*, August 18, 1986, p. 11.

Polskin, Howard. "MTV Rocks and Rolls Over Its Rivals." *TV Guide*, September 22, 1984, pp. 41–44.

———. "There's a Flip Side to Its Success." *TV Guide*, August 23, 1986, pp. 38–40.

Ponce, John. "No Surprise but Turner Folds CMC Because of MTV's Strong Pat Hand." *Satellite TV Week*, December 16, 1984, F–9.

Potts, Mark. "Pacts of MTV, Record Firms Probed." *Washington Post*, October 10, 1984, C1, C4.

"Problems at Warner Amex." *Business Week*, December 20, 1982, pp. 76–77.

"PTA Wants Full Disclosure of Music Lyrics on Records." *Sentinel Tribune*, September 14, 1985, p. 3.

"Ranking Rock." *Toledo Blade*, November 13, 1985, p. 16.

Rapping, Elayne. "Empty v: Mindless, Sure But Vicious Too." *The Guardian*, February 8, 1984.

"Rick James Blasts Vanity 6, Charges MTV with Racism." *Rolling Stone*, April 14, 1983, p. 47.

Ridgeway, Leslie. "Music Video Grows Grayer." *Satellite TV Week*, January 20, 1985, F–9.

———. "Video Violence, Cruisin' for a Bruisin'." *Satellite TV Week*, February 3, 1985, F–4.

Roblin, Andrew. "Antichrist Cooled Down for MTV Debut." *Billboard*, May 4, 1985, p. 37.

———. "Study on Violence Endorsed." *Billboard*, January 12, 1985, p. 32.

"Rock and Video." *Film Comment*, August 1983, p. 43.

"Rock Music Warning 'Zapped.' " *Sentinel Tribune*, September 19, 1985, p. 1.

"Rocking Video." *Newsweek*, April 18, 1983, pp. 96–98.

Romanowski, William, and Denisoff, R. Serge. "Soundtrack Fever." American Culture meetings, March 1987.

Rosen, Jay. "The President Who Wasn't There." *Channels of Communications*, January-February 1986, p. 13.

Ross, Andrew. "Rock Video—How Long Will People Watch?" *Cleveland Plain Dealer*, January 22, 1984, 1–D, 9–D.

Russell, Sally. "CMC Flop Could Be a Mixed Blessing for TBS." *Cablevision*, December 10, 1984, p. 12.

———. "Record Companies Greet Possibility of a Third Music-Video Service." *Cablevision*, September 3, 1984, p. 18.

———. "Major Shifts at Warner; New Chief for MTV, Nick." *Cablevision*, July 30, 1984, p. 16.

———. "MTV Network Sells Over 5 Million Shares." *Cablevision*, August 27, 1984, pp. 39–40.

———. "MTV Nick Go Public—By One-Third." *Cablevision*, July 2, 1984, pp. 20–21.

———. "Turner Broadcasting Inters Public Offering to Repay Debut." *Cablevision*, November 5, 1984, p. 11.

Sacks, Leo. "Madison Ave. Warming to MTV." *Billboard*, July 2, 1983, pp. 1, 64.

———. "MTV's Impact at Retail and Radio." *Billboard*, April 16, 1983, pp. 63,80.

———. "MTV Seen Aiding AOR Stations." *Billboard*, May 28, 1983, pp. 1, 60.

———. "Promo Clips: Who Should Pay?" *Billboard*, July 16, 1983.

———. "Turner Vid Clip Show Bowing." *Billboard*, June 4, 1983, pp. 1, 64.

Schlosberg, Karen. "Media Eyes." *Trouser Press*, Dec. 8–10, 1984, p. 56.

"School Is Out," *Rock 'n Roll Confidential*, March 1985, p. 2.

Schruers, Fred. "Facing the Music." *Home Video*, February 1983, pp. 30–33.

Seideman, Tony. "Changes in MTV Playlist." *Billboard*, November 3, 1984, p. 42.

———. "Exclusivity Key to MTV Deals Says Pittman." *Billboard*, April 14, 1984, pp. 3, 61.

————. "Four Labels Ink Vidclip Deals with MTV." *Billboard,* June 23, 1984, pp. 1, 67.

————. "Labels Split on Video Service." *Billboard,* July 14, 1984, pp. 4, 68.

————. "Labels Weigh Vidclip Economics." *Billboard,* September 22, 1984, pp. 3, 71.

————. "MTV Aging Via Second Net." *Billboard,* September 1, 1984, pp. 1, 58.

————. "MTV Asks FCC to Block Competing Vidclip Outlet." *Billboard,* July 13, 1985, p. 78.

————. "MTV Cuts Back on Airtime for Heavy Metal Vidclips." *Billboard,* February 23, 1985, p. 3.

————. "MTV Pacts Stir Reaction." *Billboard,* July 21, 1984, pp. 1, 69.

————. "MTV Plan Shakes Label Executive Suites." *Billboard,* March 31, 1984, pp. 1, 60.

————. "New York's Ritz Teams with MTV." *Billboard,* April 20, 1985, p. 39.

————. "Producers Hike Vidclip Costs." *Billboard,* June 2, 1984, pp. 1, 61.

————. "Rockamerica Panel Take Close Look at TV." *Billboard,* August 17, 1985, p. 31.

————. "Rough Start for Turner's Music Channel." *Billboard,* November 17, 1984, pp. 1, 78.

————. "Turner Clip Net Calls It Quits." *Billboard,* December 15, 1984, pp. 1, 72.

————. "VH-1 Off to Fast Start Says MTV." *Billboard,* March 30, 1985, p. 30.

————. "VH-1 Sending Sales Signals." *Billboard,* February 16, 1985, pp. 1, 84.

Shales, Tom. "Is MTV Too Violent for the Younger Set?" *Cleveland Plain Dealer,* January 29, 1984, 1-D, 9-D.

————. "MTV Monster Meal or Mind Mush?" *Washington Post,* reprinted in *Satellite TV Week,* August 25, 1985, p. 36.

————. "The Re-Decade." *Esquire,* March 1986, pp. 67–72.

Shalett, Mike. "On Target." *Billboard,* December 21, 1985, p. 15.

————. "Studying MTV's Impact on Consumers." *Billboard,* September 8, 1984, p. 21.

Shepherd, Stephanie. "Exposing the Role of MTV." *Billboard,* June 30, 1984, p. 8.

Shore, Michael. "Rock Video Forecast, Hot But Cloudy." *Village Voice,* October 16, 1984, p. 82.

————. "The Tube Goes Clip Crazy." *Record,* October 1984, pp. 39–40.

Simon, Ellis. "Why Wall Street Is Saying 'I Want My MTV (Networks).' " *Cable Marketing,* May 1985.

Simpkins, Ray. "Cables Rock 'Round Clock.' " *Time,* 22 (1982): 97.

Sippel, John. "Inside Track." *Billboard,* May 25, 1985, p. 86.

Sloane, Leonard. "A Network Man Moves to Cable." *New York Times,* November 13, 1979, D-2.

Small, Michael. "Who Tells Martha Quinn What To Do?" *People,* May 21, 1983, pp. 52, 55.

Smith, Sally Bedell. "Rock Video: A Cultural Shock Wave." *Cleveland Plain Dealer,* April 21, 1985, 1-P, 3-P.

Sperling, Dan. "Explicit Hits Have Some Folks All Shook Up." *USA Today,* March 14, 1985, 3D.

————. "Mixed Feelings on Video Violence." *USA Today,* December 17, 1984.

Spillman, Susan. "Contracts Prompt MTV Suit." *Ad Age,* September 24, 1984.

————. "TV Advertisers All Want Their MTV." *On Cable,* May 1985.

————. "Feds Probe MTV's Video License Deals." *Ad Age,* September 27, 1984, pp. 1, 63.

————. "MTV's New Music Network May Prove Tougher Ad Sell." *Ad Age,* August 27, 1984.

————. "Turner/MTV Face 'Cut Throat War.' " *Ad Age,* September 3, 1984, pp. 2, 68.

Spotnitz, Frank. "Record Firms Divided Over Rating Labels." *Sentinel Tribune,* October 16, 1985, p. 21.

Stein, M.L. "The MTV Generation." *USA Today,* May 10, 1986, p. 16.

Stroud, Kandy. "Stop Pornographic Rock." *Newsweek,* May 6, 1985, p. 14.

"Survey Finds MTV Strongly Affecting Record Sales." *Billboard,* September 11, 1982, pp. 3, 60.

Sutherland, Sam. "Clive Davis Blasts Radio Conservatism." *Billboard,* May 17, 1986, p. 3.

————. "Copyright Body Debates MTV." *Billboard,* January 29, 1983, p. 43.

————. "Extensive Research Behind New Stereo Music Channel." *Billboard,* June 13, 1981, pp. 6, 15.

————. "Videos Termed Effective." *Billboard,* May 10, 1986, pp. 1, 91.

Swartz, Herb. "MTV: Facing the Music." *Continental Cablevision Magazine,* November 1983, pp. 14–15.

Tannenbaum, Rob. " 'Miami Vice' Goes On Research." *Rolling Stone,* October 24, 1986, p. 16.

Taub, Eric. "DMN Rock the Boat of MTV's Exclusive Video Agreements." *Cablevision,* October 1, 1984, p. 19.

————. "Purveyors of a Phenomenon." *Cablevision,* December 12, 1983, pp. 30–32, 34, 36–37, 44, 46.

————. "Turner to Launch Music Video Service, Expects 5 Million Subs." *Cablevision,* September 10, 1984, pp. 13–14.

Taylor, Clarke. " 'TV Generation' Key to Cable Success." *Los Angeles Times,* April 18, 1981, sec. B, p. 8.

"TBS Fashions New Music Video Angle." *Ad Age,* September 17, 1984.

Terry, Ken. "Exclusivity May Be a Double-Edged Sword." *Variety,* June 20, 1984, p. 57.

"That Smell . . ." *Rock & Roll Confidential,* August 1984, pp. 4–5.

"The Copy Cats That Are Chasing Music Television." *Business Week,* September 3, 1984, pp. 57–58.

"Timing Seen Critical in Vidclip Strategies." *Billboard,* 1986, p. 3.

Titsch, Robert. "Music for the Eyes." *Cablevision,* August 17, 1981, p. 6.

Tiven, Jon and Sally. "MTV Music Television: Music Comes to Cable." *Audio,* May 1982, pp. 36–38.

Torgoff, Martin. "Oh Say Can You See." *ASCAP in Action,* Fall 1983, pp. 32–35.

Trachtenberg, Jeff. "MTV: Banking on Irreverence." *View,* June 1984, pp. 80–81.

Turan, Kenneth. "How To Tell TV's Good Videos from the Bad Ones." *TV Guide,* August 10, 1985, pp. 10–14.

Turner, Grame. "The Musical Roots of Video Clips." *Australian Journal of Cultural Studies,* May 1984, pp. 122–26.

"Turner to Sell Music Channel to Competing MTV Networks." *Washington Post,* November 29, 1984, C-3.

Vagnomi, Anthony. "Madison Avenue Rocks." *Back Stage,* July 29, 1983.

Vare, Ethlie Ann. "Beyond Video: Media Flips for Clips." *Billboard,* September 28, 1985, NT–3, 10.

———. "MTV Retreat Threatens to Cast Metal Back into Dark Age—With Gold Lining." *Billboard,* April 27, 1985, HM 4, 17.

———. "Music Video an Oldie to Clark." *Billboard,* August 27, 1983, p. 6.

"Viacom, Warner Complete Merger Deal." *Broadcasting,* September 12, 1983, p. 64.

"Video Music Conference Coverage." *Billboard,* October 10, 1981, pp. 49, 52, 54, 56, 58–62.

"Video: Music's Worst Best New Thing." *Campus Life,* March 1984, p. 61.

"Video Sells the Radio Stars." *Broadcasting,* September 5, 1983, pp. 38–39.

"Videodrone: MTV's Never-Ending Story." *Rolling Stone,* October 24, 1985, p. 9.

"W-A Receives Bid for MTV Equity." *Cablevision,* May 20, 1985, p. 20.

Wadsley, Pat. "Rock Around the Clock." *Video,* April 1982, pp. 48–51.

———. "Video That Rocks." *Video,* January 1983, pp. 82–83, 108.

"Wamex Vidmusic Channel Finds Potential Homes Now at 2.1 Million." *Variety,* June 10, 1981, p. 48.

Ware, Jeffery. "Audacious Comparisons." *Billboard,* June 4, 1983, p. 10.

"Warner Hires Lack to Manage and Expand Programs, Markets." *Variety,* January 10, 1979, p. 74.

Warren, Jan, and Lamp [sic], Rob. "MTV: Video Rocks Around the Clock." *U.S. Press,* August 7, 1984, p. 9.

" 'Washington Wives' Set Their Sights on Video." *Rolling Stone,* October 10, 1985, p. 18.

"We Want Our Own MTV: Black Music Video." *Backstage,* 14B ff.

Weinger, Harry. "Fade to Black." *Videofile,* June 1984, p. 6.

Weiss, George. "Porn-Rock: A Script for Censorship." *Billboard,* June 29, 1985, p. 10.

"What Entertainers Are Doing to Your Kids." *U.S. News and World Report,* October 28, 1985, pp. 46–49.

"What Made Amex Buy 50% of Warner Cable." *Business Week,* October 1, 1979, pp. 42–43.

Whatley,. "Rick James Cleans Up." *Record,* October 1985, p. 10.

White, Adam. "A Day In the Life of MTV: 164 Clips." *Billboard,* November 17, 1984, pp. 31, 33.

———. "Acts Get VH-1 Exposure." *Billboard,* January 12, 1985, pp. 1, 61.

———. "Study Says Music Video Is Boon to Labels." *Billboard,* January 11, 1984, pp. 1, 64.

Whitney, Dwight. "The Great Revolt of '67." *TV Guide,* September 23, 1967, pp. 4–9.

Williams, Christian. "MTV Is Rock Around the Clock." *Philadelphia Inquirer,* November 3, 1982, D-1, D-4.

Williams, Wendy. "Top of the Pops." *Satellite TV Week,* November 4, 1984, F/ 4-5.

———. "Teens Talk Back to TV." *Satellite TV Week,* August 2, 1986, p. 6.

Winslow, Ken. "Music Videos: Hollywood Hand-maiden in a Hit Movie Business." *Billboard,* November 14, 1981, pp. 58, 74, 75, 76.

Wisehart, Bob. "MTV: Rock Around the Clock." *Baltimore Sun,* August 23, 1982, B-6.

Wolf, Ron. "Ad Slogan, 'I Want My MTV,' Becoming a Popular Demand." *Philadelphia Inquirer,* July 1982.

Wolfe, Arnold. "Rock on Cable: On MTV—Music Television, The First Music Channel." *Popular Music & Society,* 1983, pp. 25–40.

Wolmuth, Roger. "Rock 'n' Roll 'n' Video: MTV's Music Revolution." *People,* October 17, 1983, pp. 96, 99.

Zeichner, Arlene. "Rock 'n' Video." *Film Comment,* May 1982, pp. 39–41.

Ziegler, Peggy. *Music Channel News,* September 17, 1984, p. 1.

Zorn, Eric. "Memories Aren't Made of This." *Newsweek,* February 13, 1984, p. 16.

Zucchino, David. "Big Brother Meets Twisted Sister." *Rolling Stone,* November 7, 1985, pp. 9–10, 15–17, 62, 64–67, 69.

Zuckerman, Faye. "Coalition Blasts Violence in Clips." *Billboard,* December 22, 1984, pp. 35–36.

———. "Filmmakers Explore Music Clips." *Billboard,* October 8, 1983, p. 41.

———. "MTV Outlines Plans for About-To Debut VH-1." *Billboard,* December 22, 1984, p. 86.

Zuckerman, Faye, and Kirby, Kip. "Lawsuit Challenges MTV Deals." *Billboard,* September 29, 1984, pp. 1, 68.

Transcripts

Porn Rock, "Donahue," July 17, 1985.

Porn Rock, "Nightline," September 13, 1985.

Record Labeling Hearing before the Committee on Commerce, Science and Transportation, United States Senate (September 19, 1985) Washington: U. S. Government Printing Office, 1985.

The Money Making Merger of Music and Video, "Money World," August 4, 1985.

Robert W. Pittman
(courtesy of Wasec)

John Sykes
(courtesy of MTV)

John A. Lack
"The Father and Architect of MTV"
(courtesy of Pacific Vending Tech. Ltd.)

Marshall Cohen
"Survivor and Chief Number Cruncher"
(courtesy of MTVN)

Index